Sources for Studying the Holocaust

Sources for Studying the Holocaust provides a pathway for readers to engage with questions about what sources can be used to study the Holocaust.

For many historians, the challenge has been how to rescue the story from oblivion when oft-used sources for other periods of history introduce even more issues around authenticity and reliability. What can be learned of what transpired in villages and towns numbering several thousand people, when all its Jewish inhabitants were totally obliterated through Nazi action? Who can furnish eyewitness testimony, if all the eyewitnesses were killed? How does one examine written records preserving knowledge of facts or events, where none were kept or survived the onslaught? And what weight do we put upon such resources which did manage to endure the destruction wrought by the Holocaust? Each chapter looks at one of a diverse range of source materials from which scholars have rescued the history, including survivor testimony, diaries, letters, newspaper accounts, photographs, trial documents, artefacts, digital resources, memorials, films, literature, and art. Each chapter shows how different types of records can be utilised as accurate sources for the writing of Holocaust history. Collectively, they highlight the ways in which all material, even the most fragmentary, can be employed to recreate a reliable record of what happened during the Holocaust and show how all sources considered can be employed to find meaning and understanding by exploring a range of sources deeply.

This book is a unique analysis of the types of sources that can be used to access the history of the Holocaust. It will be of invaluable interest to readers, students, and researchers of the Holocaust.

Paul R. Bartrop is a Professor Emeritus of History at Florida Gulf Coast University, Fort Myers, Florida, and a Principal Fellow in History at the University of Melbourne. He is the author or editor of over 30 books, including the Routledge titles *The Routledge History of the Second World War* (2022), *The Holocaust: The Basics* (2019), *Genocide: The Basics* (2015), *Fifty Key Thinkers on the Holocaust and Genocide* (2011), and *The Genocide Studies Reader* (2009).

Routledge Guides to Using Historical Sources

How does the historian approach primary sources? How do interpretations differ? How can such sources be used to write history?

The *Routledge Guides to Using Historical Sources* series introduces students to different sources and illustrates how historians use them. Titles in the series offer a broad spectrum of primary sources and, using specific examples, examine the historical context of these sources and the different approaches that can be used to interpret them.

History and Economic Life
A Student's Guide to approaching Economic and Social History sources
Edited by Georg Christ and Philipp R. Roessner

Approaching Historical Sources in their Contexts
Space, Time and Performance
Edited by Sarah Barber and Corinna M. Peniston-Bird

Reading Primary Sources
The Interpretation of Texts from Nineteenth and Twentieth Century History, 2nd edition
Edited by Miriam Dobson and Benjamin Ziemann

Sources for the History of Emotions
A Guide
Edited by Katie Barclay, Sharon Crozier-De Rosa, and Peter N. Stearns

Games of History
Games and Gaming as Historical Sources
Apostolos Spanos

Doing Spatial History
Edited by Riccardo Bavaj, Konrad Lawson and Bernhard Struck

Sources in the History of Psychiatry, from 1800 to the Present
Edited by Chris Millard and Jennifer Wallis

Sources for Studying the Holocaust
A Guide
Edited by Paul R. Bartrop

For more information about this series, please visit: https://www.routledge.com/Routledge-Guides-to-Using-Historical-Sources/book-series/RGHS

Sources for Studying the Holocaust
A Guide

Edited by Paul R. Bartrop

LONDON AND NEW YORK

Cover image: © DeymosHR

First published 2023
by Routledge
4 Park Square, Milton Park, Abingdon, Oxon OX14 4RN

and by Routledge
605 Third Avenue, New York, NY 10158

Routledge is an imprint of the Taylor & Francis Group, an informa business

© 2023 selection and editorial matter, Paul R. Bartrop; individual chapters, the contributors

The right of Paul R. Bartrop to be identified as the author of the editorial material, and of the authors for their individual chapters, has been asserted in accordance with sections 77 and 78 of the Copyright, Designs and Patents Act 1988.

All rights reserved. No part of this book may be reprinted or reproduced or utilised in any form or by any electronic, mechanical, or other means, now known or hereafter invented, including photocopying and recording, or in any information storage or retrieval system, without permission in writing from the publishers.

Trademark notice: Product or corporate names may be trademarks or registered trademarks, and are used only for identification and explanation without intent to infringe.

British Library Cataloguing-in-Publication Data
A catalogue record for this book is available from the British Library

Library of Congress Cataloguing-in-Publication Data
Names: Bartrop, Paul R. (Paul Robert), 1955- editor.
Title: Sources for studying the Holocaust : a guide / edited by Paul R. Bartrop.
Description: Abingdon, Oxon ; New York, NY : Routledge, 2023. | Series: Routledge guides to using historical sources | Includes bibliographical references and index.
Identifiers: LCCN 2022053961 (print) | LCCN 2022053962 (ebook) | ISBN 9781032164519 (hardback) | ISBN 9781032164502 (paperback) | ISBN 9781003248620 (ebook)
Subjects: LCSH: Holocaust, Jewish (1939-1945)--Historiography. | Holocaust, Jewish (1939-1945)--Study and teaching. | Holocaust, Jewish (1939-1945)--Sources.
Classification: LCC D804.348 .S68 2023 (print) | LCC D804.348 (ebook) | DDC 940.53/18072--dc23/eng/20221115
LC record available at https://lccn.loc.gov/2022053961
LC ebook record available at https://lccn.loc.gov/2022053962

ISBN: 978-1-032-16451-9 (hbk)
ISBN: 978-1-032-16450-2 (pbk)
ISBN: 978-1-003-24862-0 (ebk)

DOI: 10.4324/9781003248620

Typeset in Times New Roman
by MPS Limited, Dehradun

Contents

List of Illustrations vii
List of Contributors viii

Introduction 1

PART I
The Personal Domain 7

1 Oral History: Hearing the Voice of the Survivors 9
  JOANNA SALAPSKA-GELLERI AND PAUL R. BARTROP

2 Letters: An Intimate and Innocent Window into History 21
  TYLER HALLATT

3 Written Remnants of Catastrophe: Holocaust Diaries as Historical Sources 33
  AMY SIMON

4 Analysing Memoirs: Gone but Not Forgotten 45
  KAYLA M. STANTON

5 A Thousand Unspoken Words: Reading Photographs of the Holocaust 58
  JOSHUA FORTIN

PART II
The Public Domain 75

6 Considering Nazi Propaganda as a Source for Studying the Holocaust 77
  PAUL R. BARTROP

7 Using Trial Documents for Holocaust Study 90
  MICHAEL DICKERMAN

Contents

8 Understanding Holocaust Memory Through Museums and Memorials 103
   ABIGAIL WINSLOW

9 Using Church Documents for Holocaust Study 117
   MICHAEL DICKERMAN

10 Contemporary Newspapers as Sources for Approaching Holocaust Study 130
   EVE E. GRIMM

11 Using Yiddish Sources in Studying the Holocaust 142
   FREDA HODGE

12 Researching the Holocaust in a Digital World 154
   RACHEL TAIT-RIPPERDAN

13 Persistence of Memory Through Artefacts 166
   MELISSA MINDS VANDEBURGT AND BAILEY RODGERS

PART III
The Popular Domain 179

14 Learning About the Holocaust Through Movies 181
   PAUL R. BARTROP

15 How Holocaust Documentaries Defined Documentary Cinema 194
   YVONNE KOZLOVSKY GOLAN

16 Humanising the Holocaust: Literature as a Source for Studying the Holocaust 208
   KINSEY BROWN

17 Art as a Source for Studying the Holocaust 222
   LAURA MOROWITZ

PART IV
Epilogue 243

18 Thinking About and Using Documents From the Perpetrators 245
   BETH GRIECH-POLELLE

   Chronology of the Holocaust 257
   PAUL R. BARTROP

   Index 264

Illustrations

5.1	Executions of Jews by German army mobile killing units (Einsatzgruppen) near Ivangorod Ukraine	59
5.2	Stroop report—Warsaw Ghetto Uprising 08	62
5.3	Nazi officers and female auxiliaries (Helferinnen) pose on a wooden bridge in Solahütte. The man on the right carries an accordion	63
5.4	Polish Jews captured by Germans during the suppression of the Warsaw Ghetto Uprising (Poland)	67
17.1	David Olère, *Selections for the Gas Chamber*	224
17.2	Felix Nussbaum, Self Portrait in the Camp, 1940	229
17.3	Helga Weissova, *Transport Leaving Terezin*, 1943	231
17.4	Esther Lurie, portrait of Chaim Nachman Shapiro, Kovno. Ghetto, 1942	232
17.5	Hirsch Sylis, landscape in the Lodz Ghetto after Aktion 1942	233
17.6	Karl Scheswig, 4 Mock stamps from Gurs camp, 1940	234
17.7	Manci Anis, portrait of Susan Weiss, 1944	236
17.8	Edith Birkin, *The Death Cart in Lodz Ghetto*	237
17.9	Zoran Music, *We Are Not the Last*, 1970	238

Contributors

Paul R. Bartrop, FRHistS, is a multi-award-winning scholar of the Holocaust and genocide. He is a graduate of La Trobe University (BA Hons, MA) and Monash University (PhD). Until December 2020 he was Professor of History and Director of the Center for Holocaust and Genocide Research at Florida Gulf Coast University, Fort Myers, Florida, and is now Professor Emeritus of History there and Principal Fellow in History at the University of Melbourne. He has also held numerous other positions including as Visiting Professorial Fellow at the University of New South Wales, Canberra, and Stockton University, New Jersey. He is the author, co-author, and editor of 30 books, the most recent of which are: *The Holocaust and Australia: Refugees, Rejection, and Memory* (2022); *The Holocaust: The Essential Reference Guide* (2022); *The Routledge History of the Second World War* (2022); *Children of the Holocaust* (2020); and *The Holocaust: An Encyclopedia and Document Collection* (co-editor, which won the Society for Military History Distinguished Book Award, 2017). He is currently editing *The Routledge History of the First World War*, among many other projects. He is a former Vice-President of the Midwest Jewish Studies Association and is a Past President of the Australian Association of Jewish Studies.

Kinsey Brown holds an MA in English from Florida Gulf Coast University (FGCU). Her research focuses on modern European literature. Her research has examined the Swedish Red Cross White Bus Rescue Action of 1945; in her role as an Archival Assistant for FGCU, she travelled to Germany to perform in-depth research at the Ravensbrück concentration camp site. She is now pursuing additional studies at the University of Illinois' iSchool in Library and Information Science.

Michael Dickerman is a member of the adjunct faculty at Stockton University, New Jersey, teaching a range of undergraduate courses in Holocaust and Genocide Studies. He also teaches graduate courses in Holocaust and Genocide Studies at Gratz College, Pennsylvania. He is the co-editor of *The Holocaust: An Encyclopedia and Document Collection* (4 volumes, ABC-CLIO, 2017), winner of the 2018 Distinguished Book Award by the Society of Military History, and the 2018 Judaica Reference Award by the Association of Jewish Libraries.

Joshua Fortin is an Adjunct Professor of History and Integrated Studies at Florida Gulf Coast University, Fort Myers, Florida. Since 2015, he has taught courses that explore systems theory as it relates to memory and public history in the fields of public health and housing. His chapter "Western Europe under Occupation" has been published in *The Routledge History of the Second World War*. He has also engaged in advanced research on genocide during the Middle Ages, as well as human rights abuses during nineteenth-century colonialism in Africa and the United States.

Beth Griech-Polelle holds the Kurt Mayer Chair of Holocaust Studies at Pacific Lutheran University in Tacoma, Washington. She earned her bachelor's degree at Chestnut Hill College, Philadelphia, Pennsylvania, and her MA and PhD at Rutgers, the State University of New Jersey. Her books include *Trajectories of Memory: Intergenerational Representations of the Holocaust in History and the Arts* (co-editor, 2008); *Bishop von Galen: German Catholicism and National Socialism* (2002); (ed.) *The Nuremberg War Crimes Trial and Its Policy Consequences Today* (2nd ed., 2020); and *Antisemitism and the Holocaust: Language, Rhetoric, and the Traditions of Hatred* (second revised and expanded edition, 2023).

Eve E. Grimm is a former Senior Advisor to the Center for Holocaust and Genocide Research at Florida Gulf Coast University, Fort Myers, Florida. Her published work has appeared in the journal *Without Prejudice*, and she was a key contributor to *The Holocaust: An Encyclopedia and Document Collection* (2017). She is the co-author of three books: *Perpetrating the Holocaust: Leaders, Enablers, and Collaborators*, *Children of the Holocaust* (both 2019), and *The Holocaust: The Essential Reference Guide* (2022).

Tyler Hallatt is an independent scholar based in Florida. He received his BA and MA from Florida Gulf Coast University. His primary area of study encompasses Western American history during the nineteenth century. His research led him to present at the Western Historical Association conference in 2020, as a result of which his research will be published in the journal *California History*, through the University of California.

Yvonne Kozlovsky-Golan is the Head and founder of the MA Interdisciplinary Program for Culture and Film Studies at the University of Haifa. Her interdisciplinary research addresses the encounter between history, legal history, and their representation in film and media. Her research focuses on the audio–visual representation of memories from the period of World War II and the Holocaust and their impact on the construction of the historical consciousness of societies throughout the twentieth and twenty-first centuries. Her research follows the expression of these memories in film and media and analyses artistic and historical aspects of the cinematic corpus, according to the spirit of the time and place in which they were created. She is the author of five books on film and history.

Laura Morowitz is a Professor of Art History at Wagner College, New York. She is a recipient of a National Endowment for the Humanities grant for her book in progress, *Art, Exhibition and Erasure in Nazi Vienna*, and a co-editor, with Megan Brandow-Faller, of *Erasures and Eradication: Modern Viennese Art, Architecture and Design* (2022). She was co-organiser, with Lori Weintrob, of the 2021 international symposium *Heroines of the Holocaust: New Frameworks of Resistance*.

Bailey Rodgers, a graduate in Anthropology from Florida Gulf Coast University with a focus on archaeology, cultural history, and social justice, is currently pursuing an MS in Library and Information Science at Florida State University. She is the

Archives Specialist I at Florida Gulf Coast University's Bradshaw Library University Archives and Special Collections. She has curated exhibitions for students and the broader community and was a key participant in Florida Gulf Coast University's celebrated exhibition *To Life: The Liberation of Ravensbrück.*

Joanna Salapska-Gelleri is an Associate Professor of Cognitive Psychology and the head of the Department of Psychology at Florida Gulf Coast University. She holds her PhD in Cognitive Experimental Psychology from the University of Nevada, Reno. Her primary research studies the fallibility of memories, the processes and factors that distort and enhance recall, and how language affects the consolidation of autobiographical information. She is the co-Principal Investigator of the "Childhood Narratives of World War II on the Home Front" project, a collection of oral histories of individuals who were children during World War II, and has authored several publications on childhood recollections of World War II. Her broader research interests include the nature of the multilingual brain and the relationship between human cognition and artificially intelligent technology.

Amy Simon holds the William and Audrey Farber Family Chair in Holocaust Studies and European Jewish History at Michigan State University. She teaches at James Madison College, the Department of History, and the Michael and Elaine Serling Institute for Jewish Studies and Modern Israel. She has worked as a researcher at the United States Holocaust Memorial Museum in Washington, DC, and she held a Leon Milman Memorial Fellowship for research there. Her work on Holocaust fiction, memoir, diaries, and pedagogy has appeared in *Holocaust Studies: A Journal of Culture and History, Jewish Historical Studies,* the *Journal of Jewish Identities,* and several edited volumes.

Kayla M. Stanton is a graduate of Florida Gulf Coast University. She interned at the Center for Holocaust and Genocide Research at FGCU and is currently researching themes of gender politics and power dynamics in Early Modern England while pursuing her Master of Liberal Arts in History Extension Studies from Harvard University Extension School.

Rachel Tait-Ripperdan holds a Master of Library and Information Science degree as well as a Master of Arts degree in History. She is a liaison librarian at Florida Gulf Coast University, specialising in teaching information literacy skills to students within history, language and literature, communication, and philosophy. She has co-authored an article in *Pedagogy: Critical Approaches to Teaching Literature.*

Melissa Minds VandeBurgt holds a Master of Library and Information Science from the University of Illinois, Urbana-Champaign, with additional certifications in rare books and special collections. Throughout her many years in academic libraries, she has sought to integrate the work of archives, special collections, museums, and digital services in an effort to share the human experience. As an Associate Director of University Archives and Special Collections at Florida Gulf Coast University, she has built a department with a unified mission to collect and preserve both the material culture and oral history of the region. Her passion for cultural heritage and storytelling drives her desire to push special collections and rare books out of the vault and make them globally accessible to a broader audience through exhibitions and digital repositories. Between 2021 and 2022, she served as an Interim Director of FGCU's Center for Holocaust and Genocide Research.

Abigail Winslow is a curator at London's Museum of the Home, where she has worked since 2021. She obtained her first MA in History from Florida Gulf Coast University in 2020, focusing on themes relating to Public History. She then undertook a second MA at Durham University in Museum and Artefact Studies and worked with fellow students and the Museum of Archaeology to create an online exhibition about the largest archaeological collection of late- and post-medieval artefacts discovered in the North of England. She also interned at The Bowes Museum in Barnard Castle, County Durham, and has previous experience working in museums and archives.

Introduction

Paul R. Bartrop

Silvano Arieti was a world-renowned Italian American psychiatrist, a pioneer in the field of schizophrenia. In 1939, as a young man aged 24, he left Italy following the antisemitic race laws introduced by the fascist government of Benito Mussolini the year before. In 1979, he published a book based on the life of the head of the Jewish community in his hometown of Pisa, Giuseppe Pardo Roques, who had been brutally murdered by the Nazis on 1 August 1944. Reflecting on the volcanic explosion of hatred that consumed Roques and millions of others and characterised the entire period, Arieti wrote:

> The epidemic of evil that seized Europe in the 1930s and 1940s was the most ferocious of its kind ever to appear on earth. Since this illness swept over the Western world in our lifetime, it is incumbent upon us to expose it in the most minute detail. Each of us who survived has the obligation to reveal what he came to know. Sometimes one moment, fully understood, can shed light on the whole.[1]

Arieti's statement was not a cry for understanding; it was, rather, a challenge to find ways to remember, using whatever tools were available, in the hope that by doing so, all approaches could coalesce as an aid to comprehending the "epidemic of evil" to which he referred. The task he put to his readers was a steep one, possibly Sisyphean, as no single discipline or line of attack could accomplish the task alone.

Indeed, the Holocaust was a time that saw an immense amount of history taking place throughout Europe. In 1966, the Israeli historian Jacob Robinson observed that the challenge for the Holocaust scholar was one of "rescuing from oblivion a history as eventful and rich as that of a thousand years."[2] Given the event-laden historical richness which Robinson described, it might seem as though such rescue would be a relatively easy (if time-consuming) process, but this is not the case. Yes, there was an enormous amount of activity taking place in many areas, but the destruction was so widespread, so all-consuming, that dozens of major cities, together with many hundreds of small towns and villages, were completely devastated and sometimes even expunged from the face of the earth. What happened there? How did the Holocaust manifest itself in these communities? How do we arrive at an appreciation of the fears, miseries, and other attributes of life for those living through the agony of the concentration, labour, and death camps? We might never have a full grasp of such things, but the process of rescuing that history from oblivion, having started, must remain ongoing and tackled from every possible angle.

This book seeks to provide a pathway for those seeking further understanding of this devastating event. It is divided into three parts: the first examining what might be

DOI: 10.4324/9781003248620-1

termed personal sources (oral interviews with survivors, letters, diaries, memoirs, and photographs); the second looking at available public sources (propaganda, trial documents, museums and memorials, church documents, newspapers, Yiddish-language sources, digital repositories, and artefacts); and the third considering sources that can be accessed through popular culture (movies, documentaries, literature, and visual art). It ends with an epilogue in the form of a personal reflection from a scholar who has used sources generated by Holocaust perpetrators, detailing the difficulties involved in reading this material and employing it for the purposes of teaching. The overall intention is that this volume will provide an accessible thematic analysis of the many ways in which the study of the Holocaust can be approached. The chapters here are indeed diverse, in both theme and style; this serves to reinforce how varied are the topics being covered and demonstrates clearly why there is no "right" or "only" way to study the Holocaust phenomenon.

If we consider the many ways in which the study of the Holocaust can be approached, it will be obvious that doing so can only serve to enhance how we might consider the individuals, ideas, movements, and events which it comprised. In the first quarter of the twenty-first century, examination of the personal, social, and cultural dimensions of the Holocaust, both then and since, serves as a definite aid to remembrance. With this in mind, we can see how the many and varied considerations of how to approach the Holocaust can be utilised as pathways for further research as younger scholars search for additional ways to add to the wide body of familiarity and expertise we already possess about Arieti's "epidemic of evil."

By way of illustration, the nature of survivor testimony can have both positive and negative dimensions. A court of law would look at a piece of testimony from the point of view of whether that evidence would convict or acquit an accused, and for this reason might reject much of what a survivor could relate about what happened to them. But the kind of questions asked by court officials would not look for the textures, smells, sights, and contours of a person's experience; they would not, moreover, explore the wider contextual backdrop against which things occurred. The historian of the Shoah not only uses all these devices to reach an understanding of the past; he or she also permits the survivor to discuss what made a special impression on them at the time, often devoid of *ex post facto* reflections. Survivor testimony, in this sense, is thus based on a vastly different attitude to what happened than that found in a courtroom, and even if it cannot always pass for the truth as a court would require it, it is nonetheless often more valuable for the historian than the kind of response a judge or jury might elicit.

These varied sources provide us, in the words of American historian Donald C. Swain, with a sense of "emphasis" and "atmosphere" which "may open the door to the subjective 'feel' of a person or a period." The conversation, he writes, will be revealing:

> The emphasis on certain words, the suppressed chuckle when a seemingly humorless phrase comes up, are intangibles not found in documents. The excitement, frustration, boredom, or humor of a particular situation are often not discernible in the written record. Oral history techniques offer the possibility, without guaranteeing success, of recapturing the mood and the spirit of men and their times.[3]

The authors in this volume show how different approaches can be employed as sources for the writing of Holocaust history. Collectively, they highlight the ways in which *all* material, even the most fragmentary, can be employed to recreate a reliable record of what happened during the Holocaust.

A broad range of different disciplines feed into an overall analysis of the Holocaust, and while no single individual can gain command over all areas of scholarly activity, he or she can nevertheless employ a range of source types to enhance their work. The chapters here display how researchers can work with the materials across a broad span. Quite clearly, no discipline is of itself the only means by which understanding can be achieved, but this volume outlines how different types of material can be shared across disciplines, and what scholars can find through this diversity of sources. The aim is to enhance the ways in which students of the Holocaust—at whatever level—can arrive at that most crucial of destinations, understanding.

Deciphering the hidden language of sources in Holocaust history is vitally important in this quest. These embrace style and form, the kind of information they elicit (in both what they say and what they do not say), and how accurate the material itself is—that is, its reliability. This level of understanding should be expected from experienced scholars, but often (especially among some younger researchers or students) the subtleties to be found in the language of Holocaust sources are not so apparent. Nor, for that matter, are the multifaceted uses to which they can be put. A specific source can have several different applications; the chapters in this volume not only show how *all* sources can be employed but also how *a single* source can be utilised for different purposes. The chapters show how students and researchers can find meaning and understanding by exploring sources much more deeply than if they were simply to take them at face value.

In 2001, one of the great pioneers of Holocaust Studies, Raul Hilberg, produced *Sources of Holocaust Research: An Analysis*, which demonstrated his commitment to the use of documents in historical writing. Here, he looked at the varied types of source material scholars have available from which to rescue the history of the Holocaust, attempting to develop an accessible means whereby scholars can amalgamate data and draw conclusions about the nature of the Third Reich. He analysed survivor testimony, contemporary government memoranda, diary entries, letters of all kinds, newspaper accounts, and many other sources of Holocaust history with the intention both of alerting readers to their diversity, and of showing some of the ways in which the material can be employed. Looking at his own work, he asked:

> what is the nature of my sources? They are not identical to the subject matter. They have their own history and qualities, which are different from the actions they depict and which require a separate approach.[4]

As he showed, engaging in such work is not always easy. Moreover, he insisted documents could be as significant for what they do not say, as for what they describe explicitly. Overall, he demonstrated that different types of documents can be utilised as accurate sources for the writing of history. He showed the ways in which *all* material, even the most fragmentary, can be employed to create a reliable record of what happened during the Holocaust. Since Hilberg wrote, we have seen the emergence of film, digital resources, and the ability to review sources and identify dispassionately what the upsides and downsides are to the use of particular sources. Depending on the questions being asked, not all sources are equal when it comes to providing answers.

Massive human evil such as the Holocaust does not appear out of nowhere, and both its context and its development need to be examined in the minutest detail if a full appreciation is to be derived from it. This book demonstrates to researchers studying the Holocaust that even the most insignificant of source material can possess value, and that nothing should be dismissed, or devalued, or taken for granted in the quest for precision and awareness.

While the academic study of history-as-historiography has a long and honoured record, there is one work which has proven to be of lasting value and an inspiration for countless students and many research scholars. In 1970, George Kitson Clark, late Fellow of Trinity College, Cambridge wrote *The Critical Historian*, which was dedicated to all those who "have the great responsibility of teaching history." Had he known it, the themes he explored are of direct relevance to the current work. Among his chapters are History and the Law Courts; the Framework of Fact; Observation and Inference; Documents Genuine and Spurious; developing a Scholarly Attitude; Generic Statements; Myths, Impressions, and Quantification; and others which, though not apparent by their titles, are nevertheless germane to studying the Holocaust as represented by the chapters in this volume.[5] As such, it might be said that studying the Holocaust provides a paradigm for the kind of techniques Kitson Clark was highlighting over half a century ago, within a single generation removed from the Second World War and the Holocaust.

In 1945, with the end of the war, Vivette Hermann, a Jewish aid worker and rescuer of Jewish children in France during the Holocaust, threw herself into the work of repatriating and resettling the children who had been saved because of her and others' efforts. Later, reflecting on her work as a rescuer during the German occupation, she made the conscious decision to move on with her life and not dwell on the past or turn it into the focus of her future. She did not want to define herself by what she had lived through, at the same time never forgetting the experience of the war years. As she wrote, "I've decided to turn the page, not to forget but to learn from the past and to struggle against today's evils, which are the same as those of yesterday—exclusion, rejection, and intolerance." She then decided to commit her recollections to paper as "an inheritance" and "a history to transmit." She wanted "to bring its actors to life, to testify about the response necessary in the depths of the night, and to affirm—for all times and all places—the absolute primacy of life over death."[6] This volume, it might be said, adds to that inheritance.

As editor I find it necessary to express my thanks to the "two Eves" who have been instrumental in ensuring that this volume reached fruition, and without whom it could not have been completed. In the first place, my publisher, Dr. Eve Setch at Routledge, who first proposed the idea of such a volume to me, having confidence in my ability to conceptualise it and recruit the outstanding authors who have contributed to it. Second, full acknowledgement and thanks are due to Eve Grimm, who performed sterling service as Project Manager, keeping a tight rein throughout and aiding the chapter authors from the very beginning.

I would also like to acknowledge the ongoing encouragement of my home institution throughout the duration of the project, Florida Gulf Coast University. The Library staff at FGCU, in particular the History subject librarian, Rachel Tait, assisted in numerous ways throughout the project and deserve my deep respect and gratitude.

Of course, my thanks must also go to the exceptional scholars who have contributed to this volume, some of whom composed their chapters in situations of personal difficulty, tight timelines, or crushing work demands during the period of the

Coronavirus pandemic. Then, towards the very end of the project, the lives of several contributors were thrown into disarray as a result of the devastating Hurricane Ian, which hit the state of Florida with unparalleled ferocity.

To one and all, my sincere thanks.

Notes

1 S. Arieti, *The Parnas: A Scene from the Holocaust*, Philadelphia: Paul Dry Books, 2000 (first published, 1979), p. 4.
2 J. Robinson, "Research on the Jewish Catastrophe," *Jewish Journal of Sociology*, 8:2, 1966, p. 192.
3 D.C. Swain, "Problems for Practitioners of Oral History," *The American Archivist*, 28:1, January 1965, p. 68.
4 R. Hilberg, *Sources of Holocaust History: An Analysis*, Chicago: Ivan R. Dee, 2001, pp. 7–8.
5 G. Kitson Clark, *The Critical Historian*, London: Heinemann, 1970.
6 V. Samuel, *Rescuing the Children: A Holocaust Memoir*, Madison: University of Wisconsin Press, 2002, p. 147.

Part I
The Personal Domain

1 Oral History: Hearing the Voice of the Survivors

Joanna Salapska-Gelleri and Paul R. Bartrop

Introduction: Listening to Survivors

As history deals with people who lived during the twentieth century, scholars aiming to study the Holocaust must consider the words of those who lived through it. It was a different experience to that of people living through other cataclysmic events in earlier times, such as the Crusades or the Thirty Years' War. Historian Joan Ringelheim, one of the pioneers of oral history technique relative to the Holocaust, has written about the need to acknowledge difference when studying the destruction of the European Jews:

> We need to be able to listen to those who experienced the Holocaust, to understand the differences in those experiences and to hear the silences ... the silences of the survivors who have not been allowed to speak or haven't had a place to speak to those of us who have had questions. It is important for us to share, to listen to each other, to realize the extent to which we don't know about each other's lives.[1]

Writing in 1983, Ringelblum's focus expanded beyond how the Holocaust should be interpreted; she extended her ideas by considering the nature of survivorship, at that time a burgeoning topic within the broader field of Holocaust interpretation.[2] Further, she noted that as we address the issue of survivorship and discuss it with those who lived through the experience, we must take cognisance of the differences within that experience:

> What men, women and children experienced was not one event, but a myriad of events which we've tied into an analytical knot so we can speak about it with ease and with single breaths. The Holocaust is made up of individual experiences. They may have been momentous experiences for some, but it seems to me that the momentousness often occurs after we've identified what the event is. There was no such language for those experiences when people were going through them. It also seems to me important to say that not everyone experienced this event in the same way.[3]

David Boder and the Early Oral Histories

In July 1946, David Boder, an American psychologist, decided to go to Europe and interview Holocaust survivors with a view to preserving their stories while at the same time studying the psychological impact of the war on its victims. After arriving in Paris, he spent the next nine weeks recording 109 interviews in 16 locations across France, Germany, Switzerland, and Italy, mainly with Jews who originally had come from Eastern Europe. A linguist fluent in several languages, he conducted his interviews without need of an interpreter. Returning to the United States in October 1946, Boder began transcribing his conversations; by 1949, some of his work had been published in a ground-breaking book entitled *I Did Not Interview the Dead*.[4] The book showcased eight of the testimonies he had collected, but it did not receive public recognition and was dropped quickly by the book-buying public. Five decades later, however, in 1998, American historian Donald L. Niewyk edited a collection of some 36 of Boder's original interviews and published them for a new generation of readers and scholars. As Niewyk wrote in a highly acute introduction, Boder's work recording the Holocaust interviews was "the first oral history of its kind and the only one done before Yad Vashem began its work in Israel a decade later."[5]

The significance of Boder's efforts is not to be downplayed: as Niewyk identifies:

> Accounts by Holocaust survivors are most readily available as published memoirs and recorded interviews. Each has its virtues. Written memoirs impose style and structure on the chaos of memory. Oral recollections ... put a premium on spontaneity and raw directness. Both have this in common, however: most of the accounts available to us were set down long after the events they describe. ... Only a handful came into being in the immediate postwar years.[6]

This is why Boder's work was so vitally important. His method was simple: "unbound by an interview questionnaire, Boder asked his subjects where they were when the war began and let them take over as much as they were willing to do." As he recounted later,

> I would sit behind the person, so that he would not be influenced by the facial expression of the interviewer. No other persons were permitted in the room where the interview was taking place, and never was the person interviewed permitted to resort to the use of prepared notes.

Sometimes his interviewees needed little prompting; on other occasions, the task was much more difficult and "he had to drag information out of his subjects."[7]

Around the same immediate post-war period as Boder worked in, others also attempted to record and collect first-person testimonies, though many of these were in written rather than oral form. Foremost among these were a series of accounts first published in Yiddish, in the journal *Fun Letzten Khurben* (*From the Last Destruction*), which was produced between 1946 and 1948 in post-war Germany. As with Boder's oral testimonies, those offering up their accounts were then in Displaced Persons' camps awaiting transfer to new lives. The purpose of the testimonies was, in many cases, to serve as a lasting, published memorial to those who had been killed—a headstone, so to speak, for those who had no known grave. It was only in 2018 that several of these very early Yiddish testimonies were collected into a single volume, translated into English, and published.[8]

The Value of Oral History

Since David Boder's pioneering efforts, oral history has come into its own as a legitimate, accepted, and important element of Holocaust research. It plays a crucial role in addressing how we perceive those who survived, primarily because the written record only tells part of the story. Contemporaneous survivor accounts from the Holocaust often need to be treated differently from other oral sources: they are the reminiscences of European men and women who circumstances decreed were persecuted under inhuman conditions with no guarantee of enduring. Survivors came from all walks of life, and from all corners of Europe. Historians have spoken to them from the perspective of a few months or after the reflection of many years.

How can such subjectively true accounts be assessed as reliable historical sources? They deal with events which the survivors attempt to impart to their listeners, often aiming to tell their stories in as clear a manner as possible to convey the essence of what they went through—though sometimes the clarity is lost in view of the emotional content of the topic being examined. What is the historian, coming on the scene much later, to do with such material?

Questions might elicit factual knowledge, but also (perhaps more importantly) the textures, smells, sights, and contours of a person's experience. Historians can therefore permit survivors to discuss what made a special impression at the time. Even if it would not always pass for "the truth," it is nonetheless invaluable for more than this when trying to recreate the past beyond the dry data of what, when, and how.

Survivor testimony should not, however, be taken at face value and without putting it through any tests. Fifty years ago, in an acclaimed debate, Israeli historians Kurt Ball-Kaduri, Zvi Bar-On, and Dov Levin undertook to address the "best" way to conduct oral history interviews and what one should do with the material thereby obtained.[9] Ball-Kaduri's important essay concluded that "it is impossible to set down theoretical rules for such a selective process"[10] when assessing or collecting survivor testimony. As an example, if a survivor mentions an incident to which he or she says they were witness, the historian can accept or reject their account of the facts based on known context and a broader understanding of the incident being recounted, but they cannot dismiss the survivor's *impressions* of the incident once it is firmly established that the survivor saw it take place. Ball-Kaduri wrote that

> testimony given by five to ten witnesses in regard to the same incident, is valid evidence. But it is not true to say that only one testimony, not supported by other evidence is valueless. Especially in the field of active Jewish life [during the Holocaust] there are cases where only one witness has survived, and nevertheless, or even because of this fact, his evidence is of value.[11]

By contrast, Ball-Kaduri's colleagues Zvi Bar-On and Dov Levin, in the same issue of *Yad Vashem Studies*,[12] considered the necessity of adopting a much more scientific approach to the collection of oral evidence, given that:

> When the collection of verbal evidence is involved ... the investigator finds himself in virgin territory. The facts that will constitute the subject matter of the evidence have not yet been recorded and though they form the conscious or unconscious content of the mind of living persons, they do not yet amount to evidence proper.

To what extent this warped complex of personal and impersonal memories, experiences, emotions and reflections will be converted into inter-subjective terms and committed to writing, depend on the manner in which the evidence is elicited and assembled.[13]

The result requires "meticulous planning of the method in which evidence is to be taken down,"[14] meaning, as they saw it, that "methodical rules" must apply in the collection of evidence: "One of the most important distinguishing features of systematic interviewing consists in the fact that it is based on a detailed questionnaire which has been prepared in advance."[15] The essential difference between Ball-Kaduri's approach and that of Bar-On and Levin was that the former allowed for a more fluid approach to data collecting, and the latter relied on a highly developed questionnaire. Each approach has its merits, and each will, even today, have its partisan supporters who will view the other view with scepticism.

It is quite true that every account should be verified where possible, but often, it simply is *not* possible. The challenge for the Holocaust scholar is great: given the event-laden historical richness of the period under discussion, it is far from the case that rescuing history is easy. Yes, there was an enormous amount of activity taking place in many areas, but what may we know of such things where no-one survived to tell the tale? How, indeed, do we come to appreciate the fears, miseries, and other aspects of life under such duress that characterised the Nazi period *without* recourse to survivor accounts? Where some smaller ghettos were concerned, we simply do not have anything else to go on. The same is true of resistance activities in the forests. Again, we are drawn to the conclusion that even one survivor account places us in a better position to understand, and we are thus reliant upon whatever we can find to begin the long process of comprehending the overall ordeal.

It is thus necessary to consider every piece of survivor testimony individually, and to assess each on its merits. If all we must go on are the accounts of survivors, then we must treat these accounts seriously. Above all, we must be aware of just what it is the survivors are trying to convey: in the main, they are interested in conveying a sense of what happened to *them*, as *they* remember it. Do they wish to be seen in a particular light? Perhaps. Is their intention to tell the "truth," as they understand it? Certainly. Do they hope to convey a particular set of images concerning their persecutors, or whether they fought back against them? In many cases, yes. Taken overall, the reflections and reminiscences of survivors are intimate accounts of individual experiences which hopefully they wish to share with others.

The issue of representativeness is also important. In asking how representative oral testimony might be of a given situation, does it tell the full—or only—story? Perhaps not, but it nonetheless can provide insight; its value depends on what questions are asked and how much work the historian is prepared to do to address the responses provided. As wide a range of testimonial accounts, embracing both the superlative and the inarticulate (and everything in between), should be employed.

Indeed, it is far from appropriate to take one or two (or even half a dozen) testimonies as the last word on the subject, unless we have nothing else to go on. We must look at a survivor's testimony alongside those of as many others as we can find: a piece of testimony can no more be dismissed because of its paucity of detail than it can for a lack of sensitivity, or, as psychiatrist Dori Laub has noted in relation to his interviewing of a female survivor, "my attempt as interviewer and as listener was precisely to respect—not to upset, not to trespass—the subtle balance between what the woman *knew* and what she *did not*, or *could not, know*."[16]

Quite clearly, neither history nor psychology is the only correct path to understanding. For most survivors, the experiences they describe have become embedded in their souls, and the descriptions they provide almost always recount an atmosphere which is true for them, if not always necessarily believable for us. Many provide dates, for example, which we know are incorrect, and in some cases even a full chronological sequence of events is dubious. But we need to bear in mind that a great many of those caught up in the maelstrom of the Holocaust lived according to a timescale that was not dictated by a calendar in the same sense that we understand it. As Ball-Kaduri has shown, however, dates that were intrinsic to a person—the date on which they left for the forest, or engaged in their first combat action, or the date of liberation—are usually remembered accurately.[17]

Survivors do not ask us to try to imagine the Holocaust; for the most part, that is not what they are attempting to achieve. For many, it is sufficient simply to tell their story, to record, to bear witness, to show that the world through which they lived was in fact all too real. The challenge is not one of asking us to imagine the Holocaust. Rather, it is of conveying to the world an understanding of what the survivor went through, as seen from the perspective of one who was there as a participant-observer. They do not attempt to make magic, nor do they attempt to imagine the unimaginable. They simply try to tell the story from their own individual perspectives.

Oral testimony is far from being a "top up" for history and has as much (and arguably more) validity than a contemporary government memorandum, a diary entry, a letter, or a newspaper account. Its applicability should of course be weighed prior to its use and employed or rejected on that basis rather than according to some more subjective standard—but over this issue specifically, very little rejecting should occur, as all accounts have their place. It is just a matter of finding where and how to use them.

Assessing Oral Testimony

Survivor testimonies play the most crucial role in forming our understanding of what life was like during the Holocaust. Testimonial accounts, by virtue of their special status as first-hand narratives written by people who lived through the barbarities of the Nazi system, are our primary link to the SS state as viewed from the victims' perspective. As such, they are vitally important pieces of evidence which must be considered and respected as historical data. There is merit in every survivor account, even those which at first glance would seem to be of little use to the historian.

We therefore need to examine how oral testimonies may be assessed as reliable sources. They relate events either directly witnessed by the survivors or told to them by others at the time. It is this truth, and these events, which the survivors attempt to impart to their interviewers. What is the historian, coming on the scene much later, to do with such material?

Implanted within this need to tell the story as they know it is a particular consciousness of what surviving is all about. Of course, the reasons for survival varied from one inmate to another, but for many who have recounted their experiences a motivation is the urge to bear witness to the evils of the Holocaust. It is, perhaps, also a form of revenge against the Nazis, but this need to bear witness has often been part and parcel of the reason for survival itself. As recounted be Terrence Des Pres, "The testimony of survivors is rooted in a strong need to make the truth known, and ... is evidence of a profoundly human process. Survival is a specific kind of experience, and 'to survive as a witness' is one of its forms."[18] Doing so permits the survivor to allow the dead their voice[19]; it serves as a call to humanity, a signal to everyone of the power of radical evil, a warning for the generations of the future.

Survivor accounts do not readily permit themselves to be so easily classified. There is no right or wrong way for a survivor to remember their experience. As every survivor's story is unique and intimate to themselves, we must look at the totality of that experience alongside those of as many of their fellows as we can find and ask broad questions which might be capable of being narrowed down later. Many survivors identify a powerful duty to get their story down as accurately as possible. As Shoshana Felman has put it, for survivors to bear witness "is to take responsibility for the truth." Consequently, the process of testifying

> is thus not merely to narrate but to commit oneself, and to commit narrative, to others: to *take responsibility*—in speech—for history or for the truth of an occurrence, for something which, by definition, goes beyond the personal, in having general (nonpersonal) validity and consequences.[20]

For most survivors, the experiences they describe have become embedded in their souls,[21] and the descriptions they provide almost always recount an atmosphere which is true for them, if not always in accord with established facts.

Further, we need to bear in mind that those who survived the Holocaust—particularly those in the concentration and extermination camps—lived under an oppressive regime, and that certain details slipped by them: Nazi institutions and ranks, for example, or activities undertaken by prisoners in other parts of the same ghetto or camp. It must be borne in mind that Jews during the Holocaust were subjected to a gigantic administrative apparatus; trying to make sense of the whole from ground level was for most an impossibility, exacerbated by the deliberate obfuscation of the Nazis in telling the Jews they were being "deported to the East" rather than to their deaths in extermination camps. Felman, writing of such things in the present tense, observes that the prisoners "see, but they do not understand the purpose and the destruction of what they see: overwhelmed by loss and by deception, they are blind to the significance of what they witness."[22] And all this, of course, was compounded if the prisoner did not speak or understand German. All a prisoner could "know" was the reality of which he or she formed a part. The rest inevitably had to be filled in later.[23]

Oral History Techniques and the Holocaust

In 1998, the United States Holocaust Memorial Museum, situated in Washington, DC, produced its *Oral History Interview Guidelines*, a comprehensive manual for Museum staff fulfilling the mandate of collecting and producing video and audio-taped testimonies from a wide range of people who had lived during the Holocaust and period of the Third Reich—survivors, rescuers, liberators, resistance fighters, prosecutors, perpetrators, and bystanders. The *Guidelines* volume was revised in 2007, with the Museum by then justifiably proud of its record of having produced an oral history archive of over 9,000 testimonies. As identified by the Museum's website, the

Jeff and Toby Herr Oral History Archive is now "one of the largest and most diverse collections of Holocaust testimonies in the world."[24]

The *Guidelines* volume is an ideal resource for anyone looking to conduct oral history interviews with survivors, providing insight covering every possible strategy and pitfall faced by interviewers. As a manual designed specifically for Holocaust researchers, it is probably the most comprehensive and user-friendly handbook of its kind.

No oral history of the Holocaust can take place without meticulous preparation on the part of the interviewer—not only regarding the subject and the period under discussion, but also concerning the method by which the interview takes place. Unquestionably, personal stories put a human face on the raw data of the Holocaust but obtaining such stories can present problems unless the interviewer has given deep thought to the task beforehand. In some respects, this recalls the debate involving Kurt Ball-Kaduri, Zvi Bar-On, and Dov Levin over six decades ago. Should the interviewer allow for a free-ranging and open-ended conversation (in the style of David Boder), or proceed from a highly structured questionnaire? Should it be taped, or should the interviewer take notes? What would be the optimal language in which the interview should take place? Where should it be held—the interviewee's home, the interviewer's office, or a neutral venue? And of what duration should the interview be? Such questions as these are but the tip of a very large logistical iceberg. For some, therefore, oral history technique is a science, while for others it is more of an art.

Above all, interviewers should never lose sight of the fact that those to whom they are speaking are human beings, often traumatised, aged, and sometimes frail, rather than bland subjects simply to be studied. As renowned American scholar of the Holocaust Harry James Cargas wrote in 1989, "too many interviewers may rush into a taping session before being adequately prepared to do so," a result being that "the meetings become less useful than they might, even become counterproductive on occasion because a survivor might get 'turned off' by the incident and refuse to be very cooperative on the first or even subsequent interviews." Cargas emphasised that "the seriousness of such an encounter cannot be overstressed, and neither can the preparation for it."[25]

While there is undeniably a massive benefit for both historians and survivors where oral history is concerned—the one scholarly, the other therapeutically—there can, nonetheless, be limits to how effective the gathering of data from oral sources can be. As historian Donald C. Swain wrote as early as 1965,

> Human beings have an extraordinary facility for forgetting unpleasant things. Moreover, many men whose memories may once have been faultless will have lost track of important details by the time oral historians reach them. Most persons interviewed will be apologetic and even defensive; many will embellish their own role in the events under discussion.[26]

As a primary source, therefore, oral history can have its advantages, but are also disadvantages. One of these is where an individual recalls an event incompletely or through what some have termed "false memory." Another is the recollection being only one person's point of view. Although Swain considers that "oral history is worth doing," he argues that as a research tool "oral interviews have definite limitations."[27]

The notion of false memory is a concern for historians. Where the Holocaust is concerned, the events being recalled took place decades ago, possibly resulting in the individual having trouble remembering the exact details of their experience (making it difficult to corroborate the events they describe), or their memory having been influenced by later understandings that have become internalised over the years and are now part of the interviewee's remembered experience. A further problem sees a merging of time periods, leading to confusion regarding dates and events.

Many survivors have elected not to look back at the evil that was, preferring to go forward and make the best of their future. Yet when faced with their advancing years, others have chosen to tell of their own fate, and that of their families, under the Nazis. They feel personally motivated not to die before relating what happened to them. Such accounts, of course, can be subject to memory loss due to the passage of time, selective refining of their memories and the distance—physical as well as chronological—from the horrible events they endured.

When considering the value of oral history, it is crucial to recall that while the person being interviewed is capable, to a greater or lesser degree, of telling their own story, they were usually not able to see the big picture beyond what was happening to them. Thus, for example, while someone who was in Auschwitz in 1944 might recall hoping or praying for Allied aircraft to bomb the camp, their testimony is likely to be unreliable if they use that opportunity to say something about American or British or Soviet strategic policies regarding the bombing of Auschwitz. This is not something they could have known as a prisoner at ground level: but researchers must, however, be very careful not to call out an interviewee as "wrong" when making statements that go beyond their own personal recollections, even though being wrong is always a possibility.

Oral Testimonies and Memory

The oral testimonies of survivors and witnesses of the Holocaust stand as a most personal and visceral record of the strength of the Jewish people; they also tell of those who helped, and those who murdered. Oral accounts bring to life the seemingly impossible circumstances of the persecuted and the hunted, who lived and were slaughtered through the most horrible of circumstances. It should never be forgotten that these acts were committed against human beings by other human beings—men and women who did not see anything wrong with what they were doing. Oral histories can help us learn about the victims' hopes and dreams and tell us something not only about those recounting them, but also about the generation from which they came. The survivors to whom we speak help us see and sense what was experienced during the Shoah and allow the briefest glimpse into the lives of those whose existences were cut short only because, as one author has written, of "the crime of their very existence,"[28] or, as another author has it, that "our crime was being Jewish."[29]

Oral histories are personal accounts, relayed to an interviewer, by the individuals who experienced them. Although there are many other types of testimonies that have survived and been recovered, including diaries, artistic depictions, and other forms of recorded and written narratives, oral histories are a special class of evidence that provide us with the details of the lives and experiences of survivors and, through them, of those who died before their stories came to public light. Through the efforts of many organisations, large collections of witness and survivor accounts began to be collected and archived even before the end of the war.[30]

Of what, then, do oral histories comprise? Taken generally, it might be said that they are a reconstruction of autobiographical events, sometimes recent, sometimes decades old. Time and life experiences are the filters through which these testimonies are passed, as the recollection is rebuilt from components of what is stored in long-memory.[31] From a cognitive science perspective, memory can be described as a set of components that influence one another when activated. *Sensory memory* is the immediate experience of the sensations around us: it lasts between 1 and 2 seconds and then, unless it is very meaningful or rehearsed, is lost. Next is *short-term memory*, the system that allows us to "work" with information to which we are currently paying attention or retrieving from long-term storage. It lasts about 18–20 seconds and (again) is lost unless it is highly salient or rehearsed on a deep level. The memories that we traditionally associate with ourselves, our lives, and the events that we recall are stored in a seemingly limitless neural network that can last our entire lives, but can be highly malleable, referred to as *long-term memory*.[32]

Saying it can last a lifetime is significant, as it does not always remain in the same state as when it was encoded or retrieved. Thus, memory is at once the sum total of who we are—our experiences and knowledge, as well as an amalgam of our current states and the practice and influences of retrieval together with our willingness to activate it. Seen in this sense, oral histories are thus reconstructions of the events that individuals experience and offer a powerful context for both the individual and collective events shared by a group present at those events. This powerful aspect of autobiographical memories can at once be considered a challenge and a benefit for those studying the Holocaust, but recognising that the experiences and knowledge gained by the narrators during their lifetime is a component of these memories and often helps to elucidate critical aspects of the daily life and culture so terribly disrupted (and often wiped out) by the SS state.[33]

Although autobiographical memories as recounted in oral histories are a vital part of the Holocaust record, they are also reconstructed memories. Cognitive science helps shed light on this aspect of human memory by demonstrating that what is encoded in our long-term memory stores are fragments and components of events that are then reassembled to connect the timeline and details of a to-be recalled event. Human memory is a critical component of what makes us individuals and what helps us survive and adapt to our environments, but it is also pliable and subject to change over time. The changeable nature of our schemas and what we know about the world and ourselves is, in the usual run of events, one of their strengths. If not for this malleable aspect of memory, we would not be able to evolve intellectually or learn anything about the world we live in. As children, we rely on our memories to help us encode and absorb what we are exposed to for the first time and what consequently becomes a norm or often encountered situation, object, or experience. For example, as we learn to differentiate between the types of animals we encounter, our perception of those animals changes as does our ability to infer where they fit into the schema of our knowledge of the natural world.

Thus, the contents of our memories need to (and do) adapt to our current beliefs and intellectual capabilities. They are also influenced by our existing knowledge about the world, both material and historical. Beyond that, time and information can play a key role in the way we reconstruct the events we witness and in which we participate. Emotions and sensorial cues also tend to contribute to the vividness and visceral strength of recollections, whereas events that activate our deep emotions, positive as well as negative, tend to be more strongly encoded, providing us access to them over longer periods of time than mundane everyday occurrences. However, the relative likelihood of retrieval of those memories, given that they are a significant part of our lives, also tends to increase with the strength of the emotions elicited by the events we are trying to recall. For example, when asked to speak about events that survivors witnessed, the narrative of those memories may be a blend of the memory as well as the small and subtle changes that may have crept into the recollection as a specific memory is retrieved and relayed to others over the course of many discussions. Thus, as powerful as oral histories may be to helping us learn about the experiences of Holocaust survivors, they tend to be recollections that also draw on the narrator's intellectual maturity and understanding about the world at the time of the recollection.

An Ending?

As the mortality of the Holocaust generation approaches swiftly, a new term—"survivor scarcity"—has entered the jargon of some researchers conscious of how limited their options remain to interview those few remaining. The passage of time has meant that an experience taking place between 80 and 90 years ago has reduced considerably the chance of conducting interviews, which is, in effect, no longer a viable option for researchers.

The legacy of all the good work done since the 1980s, however, as the survivors themselves began to see the necessity of getting their story told while they were still able, has meant that what remains is already an outstandingly rich resource for future generations. Accessing oral histories of survivors, defenders, supporters, aggressors, and murderers involved in the Shoah has been made easier by organisations and historical societies that have made it their charge to collect, catalogue, and make accessible these critical sources of first-hand experiences. The United States Holocaust Memorial Museum and Yad Vashem in Israel are foremost among these, but others, such as the YIVO Institute for Jewish research in New York and the Zydowski Instytut Historyczny (Jewish Historical Institute, also known as the Emanuel Ringelblum Jewish Historical Institute) in Warsaw contain tens of thousands of oral history interviews collected over several decades.

In 1994, renowned Hollywood director Steven Spielberg established the Survivors of the Shoah Visual History Foundation, dedicated to producing audio-visual interviews with survivors and witnesses of the Holocaust. In January 2006, the Foundation partnered with and relocated to the University of Southern California (USC) and was renamed the USC Shoah Foundation—The Institute for Visual History and Education. Acknowledging that Holocaust survivors are becoming fewer and fewer, the USC Shoah Foundation's Visual History Archive Online now provides access to all the metadata of the 55,000 testimonies in the Archive as well as a subset of more than 4,000 testimonies for immediate viewing online and has extended its mandate from covering only the Holocaust, and has collected personal testimonies from Cambodia, Rwanda, Armenia, Guatemala, Myanmar, Bosnia, and Nanjing.[34] The early work done in relation to the Holocaust is now of immense benefit to those studying the other genocides that have taken place since 1945. Indeed, with so few Holocaust survivors left to interview, the torch is being passed increasingly to oral historians dealing with more recent genocides. And it takes place, moreover, automatically as a strategy of first record, not, as it was with the Holocaust, as an afterthought or adjunct to written sources.

With the end of the war, Holocaust survivors were forced to face the most uncertain of futures. While this leads us into new realms of investigation, it is nonetheless worthwhile to pause on how survivors contemplated the challenge of survival in a newly liberated world. Could life go on? There is perhaps no more appropriate a note on which to end than the words of Micheline Maurel, a French political prisoner arrested and incarcerated in Ravensbrück in August 1943. Evacuated at the end of the war via a death march, she was liberated by Soviet troops in 1945. Her reflections emphasise just how far the process of surviving was ongoing even though the war was over, and the Nazis defeated:

> I feel that there is a staggering sum of suffering to be made up. I am torn by that suffering. I feel the camp around me. There is someone who walks in Geneva, who goes by my name: it is a phantom, a dream of the other me, the real me, who remains seated back there because she can no longer walk, holding out her empty bowl. My poor, my dear companions, all alike, all wretched, you the survivors and you the dead, I know it well: the camps have not been liberated. Each survivor has brought his camp back with him; he tries to obliterate it; he tries to stifle in the barbed wire and under the straw mattresses all those despairing *schmustics* [that is, the empty chatter people were using to fill up the silence], but suddenly a date or a photograph brings back the entire camp around him. He would like to run away, shielding his eyes with his arm in order to see, howling in the corner not to hear. But the entire camp rises again slowly, for it has not been destroyed and nothing has made up for a single day of suffering.[35]

Her words here, though written and published, would probably have been echoed by most survivors in their oral interviews. Repeatedly, we hear their voice as an affirmation of life despite their experience, even though that experience will never, and can never, go away.

Notes

1 J. Ringelheim, opening address, in J. Ringelheim and E. Katz (ed.), *Proceedings of the Conference on Women Surviving the Holocaust*, New York: Institute for Research in History, 1983, p. 24.
2 See, for example, Terrence Des Pres, *The Survivor: An Anatomy of Life in the Death Camps*, New York: Oxford University Press, 1976; and the counter-position articulated by Bruno Bettelheim in his *Surviving and Other Essays*, New York: Random House, 1980. A full articulation of the debate between these two scholars is to be found in P.R. Bartrop, *Surviving the Camps: Unity in Adversity during the Holocaust*, Lanham (MD): University Press of America, 2000.
3 Ringelheim, opening address, pp. 23–4.
4 D.P. Boder, *I Did Not Interview the Dead*, Urbana: University of Illinois Press, 1949; see also A. Rosen, *The Wonder of Their Voices: The 1946 Holocaust Interviews of David Boder*, New York: Oxford University Press, 2010.
5 D.L. Niewyk (ed.), *Fresh Wounds: Early Narratives of Holocaust Survival*, Chapel Hill: University of North Carolina Press, 1998, p. 3.
6 Ibid., p. 1
7 Ibid., pp. 4–5.
8 F. Hodge (ed.), *Tragedy and Triumph: Early Testimonies of Jewish Survivors of World War II*, Clayton (Victoria): Monash University Publishing, 2018.

9 K.Y. Ball-Kaduri, "Evidence of Witnesses, Its Value and Limitations," *Yad Vashem Studies*, III, 1959, pp. 79–90.
10 Ibid., p. 89.
11 Ibid.
12 Z. Bar-On and D. Levin, "Problems Relating to a Questionnaire on the Holocaust," *Yad Vashem Studies*, III, 1959, pp. 91–117.
13 Ibid., p. 92.
14 Ibid.
15 Ibid., p. 117.
16 S. Felman and D. Laub, *Testimony: Crises of Witnessing in Literature, Psychoanalysis, and History*, New York: Routledge, 1992, p. 61 (emphasis in text).
17 Ball-Kaduri, "Evidence of Witnesses," p. 82.
18 Des Pres, *The Survivor*, p. 30.
19 Ibid., p. 36.
20 Felman and Laub, *Testimony*, p. 204 (emphasis in text).
21 Ball-Kaduri, "Evidence of Witnesses," p. 82.
22 Felman and Laub, *Testimony*, p. 208.
23 In this regard, see especially H. Greenspan, *On Listening to Holocaust Survivors: Recounting and Life History*, Westport: Praeger, 1998.
24 See the Archive's website at https://www.ushmm.org/collections/the-museums-collections/about/oral-history. This also contains a link to the 2007 Guidelines.
25 H.J. Cargas, *Reflections of a Post-Auschwitz Christian*, Detroit: Wayne State University, 1989, p. 140.
26 D.C. Swain, "Problems for Practitioners of Oral History," *American Archivist*, 28:1, January 1965, p. 68.
27 Ibid.
28 M. Berkowitz, *The Crime of Our Very Existence: Nazism and the Myth of Jewish Criminality*, Berkeley: University of California Press, 2007.
29 A.S. Pitch, *Our Crime Was Being Jewish: Hundreds of Holocaust Survivors Tell Their Stories*, New York: Skyhorse, 2015.
30 In this regard, see D.A. Ritchie (ed.), *The Oxford Handbook of Oral History*, Oxford: Oxford University Press, 2012.
31 D.C. Rubin, S.E. Wetzler, and R.D. Nebes, "Autobiographical Memory across the Lifespan," in D.C. Rubin (ed.), *Autobiographical Memory*, Cambridge: Cambridge University Press, 1981, pp. 202–21; F. Davey and J. Salapska-Gelleri, "'We Hung around the Radio with Great Interest:' Accessing Childhood Recollections of World War II through Interdisciplinarity," *Oral History Review*, 47:1, 2020, pp. 52–72.
32 N.C. Waugh and D.A. Norman, "Primary Memory," *Psychological Review*, 72, 1965, pp. 89–104; R.C. Atkinson and R.M. Shiffrin, "Human Memory: A Proposed System and Its Control Processes," in K.W. Spence and J.T. Spence (ed.), *The Psychology of Learning and Motivation* (2nd ed.), New York: Academic Press, 1968, pp. 89–195.
33 On autobiographical memory specifically, see Daniel Schacter, who writes that research into autobiographical memories demonstrates that "the act of remembering sad episodes can bring people to tears in moments, and remembering happy incidents can induce an almost immediate sense of elation." D. Schacter, *Searching for Memory: The Brain, The Mind, and the Past*, New York: Basic Books, 1996, p. 4. See also M. Viorica and U. Neisser, "Language-Dependent Recall of Autobiographical Memories," *Journal of Experimental Psychology*, 129:3, 2000, pp. 361–68; and G. Cohen and D. Faulkner, "Life Span Changes in Autobiographical Memory," in M.M. Gruneberg, P.E. Morris, and R.N. Sykes (ed.), *Practical Aspects of Memory: Current Research and Issues, Vol. 1, Memory in Everyday Life*, New York: Wiley, 1988, pp. 277–82.
34 As a starting point in any exploration, see the Foundation's website at https://sfi.usc.edu/what-we-do.
35 M. Maurel, *Ravensbrück*, London: Anthony Blond, 1959, p. 141.

2 Letters: An Intimate and Innocent Window into History

Tyler Hallatt

When discussing the Holocaust from a pedagogical perspective, a wide range of source material is available to enable scholars to undertake thorough research. The Holocaust stands as a unique moment that is not only depicted and understood as historically significant but as an emotionally connected memory. Understanding this critical component is essential when detailing the event's history and utilising sources from Holocaust victims to explain it. Although many primary sources help expand and contextualise the Holocaust, letters from Holocaust victims stand out as a vital resource that, when employed appropriately, can elevate understanding of the tragedy, give voice to the victims, extend an emotional connection to readers, and give insight into the events, unlike any other sources.

When used in historical writing, the most significant aspect of letters is the empathetic impact it causes on the readers. It is one thing to learn about the actions taken against Jews and methods of destruction through factual evidence; however, reading first-hand accounts from the victims presents the history with the legitimate fear and existential dread accompanying each day through which they lived. One such letter personifying this existential dread is a final letter from Pinchas Eisner, a Jewish teenager from Budapest who had been taken to a concentration camp following the Nazi invasion of Hungary and forced to work until his death. This letter, written to his "Dear Brother" Mordechai, serves as the last conversation from Pinchas to his family:

> Goodbye! Think of the talk that night. I felt as one with you. I knew that, if it were you whose life would end, I would go on living as if I had lost half of my body and soul. You said that, if I die, you will kill yourself. Think of what I told you, that if you stay alive I will live on within you, I would have liked to continue my life, with you and with your family. Plans, desires, hopes were before me. I longed for the unknown. I would have liked to know, to live, to see, to do, to love ... But now it is all over. In the city, Jews were exterminated from entire streets. There is no escape. Tonight or at the latest tomorrow it will be our turn. At seventeen I have to face certain death. There is no escape. We thought that we would be exceptions, but fate made no exceptions.[1]

This tragic letter represents the final conversation between two brothers: one home with his family, another isolated. With his last days ahead of him, 17-year-old Pinchas wanted to share his last thoughts so his brother could live the life he wished for him. The hope and aspirations that resonated in this young man channelled through to his final letter. Although his circumstance caused extreme mental, physical, and spiritual

DOI: 10.4324/9781003248620-4

devastation, his most raw and genuine thoughts carried through to his pen. It brings readers into the eyes and mind of the victim, providing a dynamic perception of the individual, encapsulating a remarkable amount of his own humanity, discussing his aspirations and unachievable futures, and then demanding his brother to live a fulfilling life, if not for himself, then for his lost counterpart. One can feel the emotions radiating from the page. The sensations displayed in the letters help fill in parts of Holocaust history that are left absent in standard texts. Readers can connect with the victim's humanity, recognising their perspective and better understanding the overall historical topic. Letters provide insight that other historical instruments are not able to encapsulate.

When discussing letters from the Holocaust, it is essential to note that they can contain a large tranche of direct benefit to historians. Letters can help expand on broader narratives of the Holocaust and provide a far more personal perspective. Scholarly writing requires the subject material to be comprehensive and not told from an individual perspective: if historians only took a single viewpoint, it would not be an accurate reflection of the historical event and could severely damage the study of the subject. Historians need to leverage the abundant resources surrounding their topic.

When discussing the Holocaust, various mediums and types of sources are utilised to expand the general understanding of the event. Seemingly, letters from historical actors during this period showcase unique perspectives allowing scholars to understand more clearly the thoughts of the Jewish victims and reflections on their current circumstances. Letters act as great resources to contextualise the events as they took place and provide first-hand answers to questions posed by scholars in ways that other narratives can only infer. A major example is "why did Germans so deride European Jewry, and did all Germans feel the same way?" Acting as windows into the thoughts and minds of historical players, they can provide clear answers to the questions posed. In the case of "did all Germans feel the same way?" historians can investigate letters written by Nazi Germans to appreciate both general sentiments and specific opinions.

As one example, Wilhelm Kube can be considered. During the war, Kube—a vehement antisemite—became a senior official in the occupied territories of the Soviet Union, where he participated in numerous war crimes, penned a letter to his superior regarding the Jewish slaughters in Lithuania, saying,

> I am certainly a hard [man] and willing to help solve the Jewish question, but people who come from our own cultural sphere just are not the same as the brutish hordes in this place ... I couldn't do it. I beg you to give clear directives [in this matter] with due consideration for the good name of our Reich and our Party, in order that the necessary action can be taken in the most humane manner.[2]

In this letter, we see that Kube, though still supportive of solving the Jewish question, did not want to commit inhumane atrocities against specific factions of Jews in Lithuania. This letter helps give context to the thoughts of this single Nazi, providing a perspective that outlines the realities of the Holocaust. However, this line of reasoning in understanding the inner machinations of Nazi sentiment cannot be taken solely as fact but as one segment of Nazi belief. When discussing material gained from letters, historians cannot extrapolate from one person's opinion and attempt to infer that all persons of a similar capacity feel the same. When utilised in academic writing, letters are primarily used in a manner that contextualises and supports fact, not standing alone as the absolute fact alone. However, there are unique cases where indisputable facts are gained from a letter based on its internal evidence. Typically, this is seen when dates, locations, specific historical actors, or actions committed against persons are confirmed within the text.

Letters offer great benefits when leveraged appropriately but can also hurt the legitimacy of a researcher's writing if misused. If a historian took Wilhelm Kube's letter and attempted to state that none of the German Nazis really wanted to commit inhumane acts against Europe's Jews, then that would be stunningly inaccurate. For the same reason that letters are employed as windows into the authors of the period, they can also reveal information that may seem supportive of the researcher's argument but is only a sentiment carried by a minority of the people. So although Kube argues against the inhumane treatment of the Jews, that does not mean that all others felt the same. Moreover, it would be vitally important that in this instance questions are asked as to why Kube adopted the line he did.[3]

One example of an opposing view is German soldier Hugo Behncke. In the summer of 1944, the SS was recruiting older men to serve as sentries in the concentration camps, and the 56-year-old Behncke was one of them. Posted to a satellite camp of Neuengamme, he was far from enthusiastic about his posting but in writing to his wife concerning the Jewish prisoners, he stated:

> The prisoners were all sick, dirty and thin as skeletons. All they were good for was to be burned in the Neuengamme crematorium. And a lot of them thought they were being brought to Neuengamme to be burned. Of course, many of them are stupid, primitive people.[4]

The letters from Kube and Behncke are excellent examples of how letters can help support a historical conversation. Separately, these letters provide isolated views of Germans serving in the Holocaust and can be utilised to argue different sides of the discussion of how Jewish prisoners were treated. Together, they can show the complex nature of the Holocaust and how every person held their own individual beliefs. Much like today, everyone has differing opinions, and although some may find themselves agreeing on specific topics, they do not necessarily agree on everything. The very same can be said about historical figures. This insight helps build a web or multi-dimensional conversation, not a two-sided argument. Although letters can be, and at times are, employed only to support a historian's viewpoint, they hold even more intrinsic value that helps amplify the quality of research and analysis.

Another professional omission that can be generated from the utilisation of letters, although unintentional, is the dichotomy between oppressors and oppressed. When scholars read final letters that draw emotion, a narrative can emerge that the authors were helpless and somehow complicit in their own death. This false juxtaposition between oppressor and oppressed can occur because the letters that are primarily utilised are those from Jewish victims and families or German officials and soldiers. Discussing Jewish letters solely from victims, if not approached with proper care, can establish the false narrative that Jewish victims were passive during the Holocaust.

Although this misrepresentation may be unintentional, it is a reality that can take away the agency of Jewish resistance during the Holocaust. As shown by historian Jeffrey Blutinger, "Our bias towards historical actors leads us into a false dichotomy between oppression and resistance, implicitly disparaging those who, for whatever reason, did not resist but who suffered and died nonetheless."[5] It must be emphasised that letters being utilised from the Jewish victims, although emotionally raw and heart-breaking, do not suggest they simply lied down against the Germans. This unintentional effect of using letters can undermine and even deny the actions taken by Jews who resisted, whether physically, spiritually, or passively. This effect is avoidable when understood, centring the conversation on the emotional toll and allowing the letters to provoke psychological impacts due to the extreme situations, but scholars should not utilise personal letters to generalise across the entirety of the Holocaust.

Using any sort of victim or survivor narrative comes with a responsibility to handle the material appropriately, to elevate the conversation, and share the writer's experiences. Letters from the Holocaust differ markedly from other primary sources because they continue to possess a spiritual weight and connection to the Jewish community. The generational trauma and memory instilled within the community are severe and must be handled with care and respect. Without solely understanding the responsibility for the generations that are alive now, the letters hold more than just a physical connection to the families but a spiritual one as well. The Holocaust is an emotionally charged event that has blurred the lines for using primary sources in entirely unique ways. When utilising them, historians must consider how the sources are effectively explained within their writing and the impacts they could have for Jewish—indeed, for all—readers.

Letters from Holocaust victims show the writers as human beings with emotions and importance, providing a clear separation between their first-hand experiences and becoming just another number situated within their historical context. Although discussing history from a quantitative perspective is critical, it detracts from the importance of each distinct and unique situation. Every single one of the six million lives lost during the Holocaust has its own story. Letters can convey a large and varied amount of factual information. This can range from the evidence of atrocities committed against the victims, their general attitude and disposition, and the names and actions of the perpetrators. Letters mirror survivor stories in that they can offer a first-hand perspective detailing the victim's actions. They describe and provide context, discussing Holocaust atrocities from a first-person perspective, allowing historians and scholars to feel like they are in the victims' shoes.

Historian Donald Bloxham explains that survivor accounts "provide a poignant, intimate enhancement of the main historical narrative,"[6] and his depiction of the survivor stories mirrors that of letters from the victims. However, as the survivors grow older, survivor stories can unintentionally change over time (whether due to age or accidental hyperbole), whereas letters written during the Holocaust cannot be altered similarly.[7] The historical insight provided through letters treads a line between the intimate introspection of the victims and factual evidence. This is not to say that letters stand as absolute fact and evidence but are, instead, a summary of emotions proceeding from the most wrenching of real events.

Letters offer a similar avenue for understanding the Holocaust as do photographs, audio recordings, documentary movies, and survivor testimonies. All these approaches provide an exclusive dive into this history and allow the reader to understand the severity of the atrocities committed. However, letters offer a unique means to understanding the Holocaust due to the level of intimacy and familiarity they convey. Historians can enter the victims' hearts and minds, allowing a bridge to form beyond the other evidence-based approaches. Employing letters allows the authors to balance narrative-based history with in-depth primary sources. This juxtaposition enables historians to balance their writing with microhistorical perspectives. Using such analysis in academic writing can prove helpful in building an intimate connection with those being studied, clarifying the reasoning behind documented events, and revealing unexamined aspects of larger historical periods. Microhistorical writing can encompass a large section of Holocaust history, whether basing the examination within a specific region, a particular Jewish resistance faction or body of prisoners in specific camps, or in some cases, compositions of general sentiments of certain subsets of people.

Microhistorical writing, when crafted correctly, uses perspectivism to detail more commonly discussed historical events. German philosopher Friedrich Nietzsche discussed perspectivism as an essential and core method for understanding life (and history), showing how differing perspectives between people can alter or add to an understanding of specific events. It leans towards studying history through the eyes and minds of those who endured experiences through the eyes of those who were there as the most beneficial way to foster understanding. Nietzsche's philosophy is that absolute truth is layered when discussed through various perspectives and that overarching truth can never be unconditional. Nietzsche believes all truth is crooked, hidden by appearance, making it elusive.[8]

Nietzsche's support of perspectivism leads directly to the importance of microhistory when discussing historical events. Employment of letters in academic writing provides a strong foundation of perspectivism and, in turn, an unravelling of historical truth. The Holocaust, being such an encompassing world event that touched the lives of so many people, possesses countless perspectives. However, it must be noted that just because differing views help shed light on the historical event, it does not mean that each perspective is necessarily wholly correct. In fact, there are many times when perspective history, specifically contemporary letters, is blatantly wrong and contradicts factual evidence uncovered through other forms of historical analysis. But this leads directly to the importance of the mistaken author's perspective. Why did the letter's author believe his or her facts were correct, despite evidence contradicting them? Does it have to do with the author's opinion on current events? Does their physical location or surroundings during the events affect their viewpoints and subsequent statements within their letter? Perhaps, indeed, they could only view things through their own, intimate lens, often unable to see the bigger picture.

Letters written during the Holocaust are essential, however, to processing a much larger amount of information. Whether a letter was written by a Holocaust victim, a family member, a collaborator, or a front-line soldier, they hold an essential and intrinsic value for historians. Holocaust victims wrote letters to express their feelings about current events and how those events impacted upon them. Letters from Holocaust victims are, at times, the most descriptive evidence of the atrocities against European Jewry and how the Nazis carried out their actions. Letters written from families and friends elsewhere, who often did not feel the physical effects of the Holocaust, can provide a more global perspective, adding another layer to the complexity of how letters can contextualise aspects of this history. Letters written by Nazis or collaborators are sometimes composed with disdain and antipathy, though these, too, can hold as much value as those they were persecuting. Historians seeking to understand the atrocities committed against the Holocaust victims search for reasons behind these acts. Why did the Nazis believe in Jewish extermination? How did Nazi sentiment against Jews get to that point? Understanding the thought process and motivations of the Germans is integral to Holocaust history. Historian Michaela Kipp explains, "These letters are a valuable source for the study of the motivations of German Wehrmacht soldiers, including perpetrators of war crimes and genocide actions."[9]

Holocaust victims did not expect their letters to become public and, in most cases, included conversations intended to be private and intimate. This level of intimacy is what makes these personal windows essential to understanding the Holocaust. Prominent historical works depicting the Holocaust are challenged to encompass all aspects of this history, giving genuine respect to each component. Many authors juggle with the notion of writing all-inclusive histories that attempt to detail as many aspects of the event as possible. Historian Richard Evans, the author of *The Third Reich* Trilogy, attempts to craft an all-encompassing history of the rise and fall of the Third Reich.[10] Evans explains that his work "is written to be read from start to finish, as a single, if complex, narrative, interspersed with description and analysis."[11] The trilogy is an expertly crafted staple of the history of Nazi Germany, providing factual evidence that accurately represents this history—part of which, inevitably, must include the Holocaust.

Although comprehensive pieces in Holocaust history are essential for providing readers with description and analysis, understanding the empathetic and emotional perspective of the victims is just as crucial. These victims dealt with unimaginable situations and catalogued them in their most personal notes. Historians must understand that the letters were written by men and women, mothers and fathers, adolescents and children, members of political parties and youth movements, each with their own individual story.[12] Holocaust historians discuss the death of millions of victims, explaining the processes and the tainted reasoning behind them, but nothing can depict the hardships in quite as detailed a fashion as letters from the victims. They are often hard to read and can cause emotional distress when attempting to understand the writer's situation. One of the more challenging letters to read is from Zlata Brizitz, a Jewish resistance fighter who helped aid fleeing victims and those yet to be captured. The letter follows Zlata after her attempted suicide at the sight of her husband's capture and subsequent murder. After being resuscitated by her captors, she was ordered to reveal information about the Jewish underground but refused. Her refusal to provide information led to her execution. Before her death, she wrote her last letter depicting the horrors of her final days and her thoughts on the matter.

> I write you today for the last time. How strange life is. So much time has gone by since our Yozek is not with us any longer. They took him away from me. He died like a true hero. He calmed me down, he kissed me on my mouth ... The day they took him, I slit my throat. The Germans took me to the hospital and treated me until I recuperated. Despite this, I am going today to my Yozek. My dear, I want you not to forget who our executioners are. Think of this in the name of Katanko. Even if I see him again one day, remember everything that happened to him. I taught Yozek to die with dignity. From you, on the other hand, I request my whole heart: you must continue to live! I bless you. I kiss you.[13]

Zlata explained the trials and tribulations she experienced from the loss of her husband, thinking only suicide could offer an escape from a similar fate. But even that incredibly personal and intense decision was denied her by her tormentors. She felt that her only escape was to kill herself, ending her misery. Despite the preferences of the Nazis, however, Zlata did not reveal any information that could be detrimental to those who had still eluded them. Through Zlata's letter, readers today can build a thoroughly empathetic connection with her. They are invited to look into a window that Zlata creates. By way of contrast, any other pathway would pale by comparison.

In Zlata's case, historical analysis can help establish factual evidence of the events, such as the personal details of her age, her height, activities within the Jewish underground, and even the date and time of her death—if these details can be found. However, nothing builds her up as the headstrong resistance heroine she became nearly as much as her intimate letters. Zlata's words carry an emotional depth that defines her in a way that no factual analysis could. Much like Zlata's letter to her family, letters from Holocaust victims often carry such energy and tone that they can sound like spoken words. Historian Dalia Ofer recognised this same aspect when studying Jewish refugees fleeing to Yugoslavia, noting that the written letters carried "a 'tone' and oftentimes bordered on the audible."[14]

Despite these letters being unique and complimentary instances within the history of the Holocaust, they can also possess certain drawbacks. As mentioned, letters depict the author's situation as seen through their eyes. This means that material within the letters may not contain complete factual evidence but, rather, a version of it. These accounts do not ensure that everything they discuss is accurate: moreover, they can certainly display personal bias. Historians understand that these accounts, although of immense benefit, cannot be consumed as absolute truth. Letters in all fields of history are often discussed with metaphorical asterisks alongside because of the bias they contain able to alter the events being reported, as shown by scholar of history education, Keith C. Barton.[15]

Barton questions whether letters can genuinely and accurately portray historical events through specific criteria. He explains that testimonial sources in history can contain bias based on their situation during the historical events, such as whether they completely understood the circumstances surrounding them to explain the events or the time in which they authored the testimonial and how it could affect their perspective.[16] Some historians, he argues, often discuss whether letters can genuinely be trusted due to an inherent prejudice that may exist. This discussion of validity possesses some merit when talking about letters in general; however, Barton refutes this dismantling of letters as practical depictions of history. Although the criteria may infer that letters and testimonial histories can be flawed in that they do not present a complete version of the history, they do, however, offer a window into the period from which they originate. Barton's view is that due to their underlying bias, letters cannot be utilised as sole sources for understanding Holocaust history. They are best applied when using them as supplementary materials and to fill in the gaps of broader historical evidence.

When letters are mentioned within that context, they are often explained as written documents from one historical actor to another. Although this circumstance is the most common and often-used aspect of letters, it does not represent the only type of letter historians can use. Holocaust letters usually needed to be vetted and reviewed at some point before they touched the hands of the targeted recipient. At times, for example, third-party organisations such as the International Committee of the Red Cross (ICRC) would play a hand in transmitting mail. Where possible, the ICRC would assist with the passing of letters from victims to recipients residing in the rest of the free world outside Nazi control and vice versa. The ICRC did mandate that any letters they helped send out would have to be limited to just 25 words and only serve as a "Proof of Life" statement, that is, expressing nothing more than evidence that the writing party was alive. Although this limitation is immediately seen as a hindrance as it restricts the victims and family members from conveying their thoughts and messages, the ICRC's regulation allows for another benefit. The restriction of only 25 words ensured that the letters can fit onto a single piece of paper, leaving room for necessary information such as full names, dates, and exact addresses. The advantage of this is that it allows historians to pinpoint the victims and their families at specific locations during the war. These letters provide multiple layers of historical analysis that assists Holocaust historians in their research, as seen in one such letter written by Szmul Frydman in the Warsaw Ghetto to his relatives living in Palestine:

The Sender (*First and Family Name*): Szmul Wolf Frydman

Detailed Address: 47 Muranowska St., Apt. 38

Requests to transit to the Addressee: (*First and Family Name*): Mendel Frydman

Detailed Address: Palestine, Tel-Aviv, 10 Fajerberg St.

(Maximum 25 words)

Dear Parents. We are all well. Heniek is moving from his apartment. How are Benek and family, Reginka and family? Here without changes. The Hamers are alive the Cukiers [message cut off here]

(DATE) *16.VI.1942.*[17]

The letter is remarkably short, only allowing Szmul to write minimal information and restricting the historical perspective within the text. Despite this letter containing less "tone" as mentioned by Ofer, it holds importance equivalent to that of both Zlata and Pinchas Eisner. The difference is that the significance of Szmul's letter sits within the ICRC requirements. Although factual evidence within the content of a letter can hold a bias and cannot be fully trusted, evidence within a single note, as presented by organisations like ICRC, can. The organisation required all letters to follow a similar style so they could track and monitor the communications. Therefore, historians can understand with some accuracy where people were located when they penned their letters. This style of communication, in short, can help scholars depict the historical setting with some degree of certainty.

Letters also offer an opportunity for individual accounts and lives to be shared in ways they could not have been in the aftermath of the war. Most of those who died during the Holocaust are not mentioned or spoken about outside of those whose lives were affected directly. Whether they were a lover or a spouse, son or a daughter, father or mother, they touched and affected the lives of others, and their tragic stories ended with their death. Sharing and writing about their letters offers both victims and their families the chance to tell the story of their loved ones. Unfortunately, not all those writing their last letters knew it would be their last, signifying that most of the final communications between loved ones were ordinary conversations, with neither party knowing it would be the last time they would be in touch with each other.

By way of illustration of how any single missive could be the last, we can consider a non-Holocaust related letter from a British airman, Royal Air Force Flying Officer James (Hamish) Bell to his sweetheart, June Mary Bennett. James met June at a friend's wedding, where she had been a bridesmaid. James said he fell in love with June the night he met her: he began writing to her shortly after and continued to write throughout his different military postings. Over the next year, they wrote often and continued to meet during his moments of leave. They were deeply in love and planning their future following James's time in the RAF. They often left their signature with remarks like "all my loves and kisses" or "I will write you again in a few days." Much like their regular communications, filled with details of their recent days' work and life, James wrote his last letter to June, leaving as his final words:

> The memories of our last night together are very fresh in my mind. Now about this leave question. I am due for some time next month but there is no definite date laid down as yet. However, I shall do my very best so that some part of my leave will coincide with yours and we can spend a weekend together.[18]

Shortly after James wrote this letter, his plane was shot down, and he perished. June would not receive another letter from her love and only knew something was wrong when her last letter was returned "missing." June grieved. Upset that she had more time while he did not, she explained that she spent the rest of her life unmarried, sleeping with his letters in her nightstand every evening.

This example is not intended to lessen the importance or representation of Jewish victims of the Holocaust but rather to act as an additional component to an appreciation of how letters may be employed in Holocaust history. This style of emotional last letters between lovers, family members, or friends existed in all forms during the Holocaust. Unlike Zlata, most of those who lost their lives did not know ahead of time, unaware of when or whether a letter would be their last. Not knowing as we do what the future held, these letters evoke such emotion, often leading the readers to place themselves in the shoes of the author or recipient, allowing them to feel a connection to the history. Employing the letters to tell the story keeps the memory alive of those who were lost.

When discussing letters in Holocaust history, it is difficult not to mention the significant impact certain historians and books have made. A few of the most notable books employing Holocaust letters have already been cited and used in this chapter due to their overwhelming influence on Holocaust history. One of the most prominent, *Final Letters from Victims of the Holocaust*, has made a substantial impact due to its heavily researched material originating from the Yad Vashem Archives in Jerusalem. This collection of letters has been relied upon heavily by Holocaust historians due to its deeply emotional contents, which include the last letters of many of the victims. Focusing on their victims' final thoughts, this compilation uncovered a clear connection between the fate of the victims and their surviving friends and family.

Additionally, many writers in *Final Letters* discussed the future of the Jewish people as a whole and the importance of retaining a Jewish existence. Chaim Herzog, the former President of the State of Israel, provided the book's Foreword, expressing the absolute importance of the publication and its role in Holocaust memory. Herzog discussed how important it is to show these letters to the world as almost a form of generational resistance against the Nazis, as he explained:

> It may be said that every one of these messages not only survived the Holocaust, but actually reached their destination. This may be thought to be some measure of consolation for the victims—if indeed, consolation can exist in the face of the terrible experiences they all underwent.[19]

Herzog, much like the broader Jewish community, believes that uplifting the stories of Holocaust victims and telling them helps to continue their memory. Specifically, sharing Holocaust letters aids in spreading their experiences, sharing them with each generation and expanding the connected memory.

Another ground-breaking publication centring around Holocaust victims' final communications is *Last Letters from the Shoah*, edited by Walter Zvi Bacharach. Bacharach expands on the earlier work by exploring the varied mindsets of the victims and making a stronger connection between them and collective memory. He discusses how each letter holds vital importance because it provides distance from the mindset of "the six million" dying in the Holocaust as though the immensity of the crime formed them into a singular collective casualty.[20] He continues to expand on the notion that each letter acts almost as a *Yizkor* (memorial prayer) because many writers requested that their names be remembered for future generations, with whom they could build a connection. Bacharach also collaborated with the Yad Vashem Archives to compile his collection and expanded the scope of the earlier *Final Letters* set by showing how Holocaust letters can be studied and dissected to enhance our understanding.

Letters contain the innate ability to tell a story of the Holocaust that is unique to itself, helping to contextualise broader conversations. Readers can feel the victim's pain, both physical or emotional, and gain a tiny insight into how the Holocaust was experienced at the most intimate level.

Pinchas Eisner's letter, with which this chapter began, focused on the life he was going to miss due to his current situation, revealing his most intimate and vulnerable thoughts. This young man was missing out on most of his life because it was stolen from him. This chapter also looked at the final acts of defiance from Zlata, who was prepared to take her own life rather than aid or be a captive of the Nazi oppressors. Her fearlessness in her final days matched her wish for her name to carry on, far surpassing her death. In this way, the weight of her legacy—and that of all the victims of the Holocaust—was placed on the shoulders of those reading her letters. The raw emotions in Zlata's letter were conveyed through her voice and tone. Her letter displayed several layers of Holocaust history: Jewish resistance, Holocaust memory, and the request for memorial prayer and remembrance.

When discussing the letter between James and June, readers get a peek into the soft love of two young adults and the affection they share. This innocence was penned only for the eyes of each other and gave insight into the love they were building, unaware of the misfortune that lay ahead. It is an excellent example of how their lives can live in a beautiful microcosm while the world is aflame.

Each of these letters offers various perspectives, showcasing how letters can effectively expand on existing narratives, contextualising and expanding more formal scholarly writing. However, regardless of how beneficial letters can be as sources for understanding Holocaust history, the humanity that exists within them must always remain paramount. Not only for understanding the history surrounding them but recognising that each letter, though unique by itself, exists as a singular person within the six million deaths of the Holocaust.

As discussed throughout this chapter, historians of the Holocaust bear an awesome responsibility, not only to those who remain but also to those who lost their lives. This responsibility comes with the obligation to respect the intimacy and innocence that lay within their letters.

Despite the desperation shown by Pinchas Eisner, he still retained a semblance of optimism and hope. His purity shines through the letter to his brother, exemplifying the power letters hold and how they can explain the extremes of the Holocaust in a way that no other medium can. Pinchas's final sentences express hope. Although he knows his remaining days are few, he looks past his awaiting death and into whatever awaits him afterward. Much like other letters from victims that extend a generational and familial memory of those lost, Pinchas is no different:

> Farewell, dear, sweet Brother. Farewell! Remember me. I hope that I, too, will be able to think of you even from over there. I would like to hug and kiss you once more. But who knows to whom I write these lines? Are you alive?! Farewell, my dear brother, my sweet Mordachele, live happily. Kissing you for the last time—till we meet again,
>
> Your loving Brother.[21]

Letters have the innate ability to contextualise and humanise moments in history. For those researching the Holocaust, it is essential to help understand the weight and gravity of the events. The emotional evocation within letters from Holocaust victims provides an unparalleled frame of reference to the suffering of the victims. When discussing Holocaust history, quantitative evidence is often produced to explain death tolls and massacres in ways that usually remove the empathetic aspect of history. Although large numbers can show the gravity of the situation and explain the sizeable impact of the Holocaust, they cannot show the human dimension. Letters from Holocaust victims offer an in-depth perspective, providing a realistic dimension to the tragedy and elaborating on the quantitative aspects of its history, as is seen throughout the entirety of Pinchas's letter.

When used appropriately in historical writing, Holocaust letters provide necessary descriptions of the hearts and minds of the victims to explain the wide range of emotions that occurred. Outside of the emotional and empathetic aspect of letters, they can also serve as great resources to examine the geographical and social constructions of the period, as seen with the letter sent through the ICRC, which regulated mail and communications. Letters contain the ability to aid in historical writing and education through many avenues. They are essential to grasping the full scope of the Holocaust and without them, the work of scholars would be incomplete as they attempt to explain the impact of the atrocities on the victims.

Notes

1 R. Dafni and Y. Klaiman (ed.), *Final Letters: From Victims of the Holocaust*, New York: Paragon House, 1991, p. 45.
2 Wilhelm Kube to Gauleiter Hinrich Lohse, Riga, 16 December 1941, in Y. Arad, Y. Gutman, and A. Margaloit (ed.), *Documents on the Holocaust*, Jerusalem: Yad Vashem, 1981, p. 409.
3 As it turned out, Kube was complaining about the lack of precise orders concerning the units under his command, and whether they should be responsible for killing the Jews in his

zone of control in Byelorussia. His preference was that the task should be undertaken by Lithuanian militias than by Germans, owing to the prevalence of epidemic disease among Jews in the area. On Kube, see R. Rhodes, *Masters of Death: The SS Einsatzgruppen and the Invention of the Holocaust*, New York: Alfred A. Knopf, 2002, pp. 244–7.
4 Hugo Behncke to his wife, 28 January 1945, available online at http://www.camps.bbk.ac.uk/search.html?q=hugo+behncke.
5 J.C. Blutinger, "Bearing Witness: Teaching the Holocaust from a Victim-Centered Perspective," *The History Teacher*, 42:3, 2009, pp. 269–79.
6 D. Bloxham and T. Kushner, *The Holocaust: Critical Historical Approaches*, Manchester: Manchester University Press, 2008, p. 44.
7 The altering of Holocaust survivor stories is noted in A.M. Wyatt-Brown, "Holocaust Survival Stories: Change Over Time," *Journal of Aging and Identity*, 5, 2000, pp. 91–108. Although the stories never drastically change, their details and complexities can alter over time.
8 L. Lampert, *Nietzsche's Teaching: An Interpretation of Thus Spoke Zarathustra*, New Haven: Yale University Press, 1986, p. 165.
9 M. Kipp, "The Holocaust in the Letters of German Soldiers on the Eastern Front (1939–44)," *Journal of Genocide Research*, 9:4, 2007, p. 601.
10 R.J. Evans, *The Coming of the Third Reich*, London: Penguin Books, 2003; R.J. Evans, *The Third Reich in Power*, London: Penguin Books, 2005; R.J. Evans, *The Third Reich at War: How the Nazis Led Germany from Conquest to Disaster*, London: Penguin Books, 2009.
11 Evans, *The Third Reich at War*, p. xvi.
12 D. Ofer, "Personal Letters in Research and Education on the Holocaust," *Holocaust and Genocide Studies*, 4:3, 1989, p. 341.
13 W.Z. Bacharach (ed.), *Last Letters from the Shoah*, Jerusalem: Yad Vashem, 2013, p. 345.
14 D. Ofer, "Personal Letters in Research and Education on the Holocaust," p. 341.
15 K.C. Barton, "Primary Sources in History: Breaking through the Myths," *The Phi Delta Kappan*, 86:10, 2005.
16 Ibid., p. 748.
17 Dafni and Klaiman (ed.), *Final Letters*, p. 64.
18 T. Day-Lewis (ed.), *Last Letters Home*, London: Macmillan, 1995, p. 139.
19 Dafni and Klaiman (ed.), *Final Letters*, p. 8.
20 Bacharach (ed.), *Last Letters from the Shoah*, p. 11.
21 Dafni and Klaiman (ed.), *Final Letters*, p. 45.

3 Written Remnants of Catastrophe: Holocaust Diaries as Historical Sources

Amy Simon

One of the most famous documents of the twentieth century is a Holocaust diary. The author was Anne Frank, whose face and words have become ubiquitous the world over. Her diary, written in hiding in Amsterdam from 1942 to 1944, was published in the original Dutch in 1947, in English in 1952, and since then into over 70 other languages. The story and likeness of the young Anne, who was 13 years old when she began writing in her diary, have captured the hearts of millions—her story appears in Holocaust museums and exhibits around the world, her writing has inspired numerous theatrical and filmic interpretations, scholars have published serious research on her writings and popularity, and she is a regular subject of social media. Almost 80 years after her death, Anne Frank is a veritable pop icon because of her diary. Despite the "Phenomenon of Anne Frank" that has made her writing so well-recognised, most people have no idea about the huge corpus of other Holocaust diaries that were written and preserved and can serve as important sources for understanding the Holocaust.[1] This chapter will discuss diary writing and reading in historical context, consider questions of methodology and genre, address the diary's place within Holocaust studies in particular, and suggest the enormous benefits and significant challenges in using Holocaust diaries as a source for writing history.

Diary Writing in Context

Diaries are one of the oldest known traditions of writing; examples have been discovered in places from ancient Mesopotamia to stories related in the Hebrew Bible.[2] Broadly defined as a "book of days," diaries have helped people keep both public and private records, provided outlets for thoughts and feelings, and served as companions in dark times. Since the seventeenth century in particular, diary writing became a popular genre within Europe's middle and upper classes, as exemplified by the diary of British naval administrator Samuel Pepys. Written in the seventeenth century, it was published in 1825 and became a best seller, going through multiple editions in the first few decades after its initial publication. Simultaneously in France, diary writing was seen as a popular activity, especially for girls. From the nineteenth century on, reading published diaries and keeping one's own was seen as important to a girl's education.[3] Farther east, elite women in Poland began taking part in society's culture, also learning to express their emotions through diary writing.[4] The genre became part of the mainstream, including the publication of both male and female diaries for general consumption. By the twentieth century and World War II, diary writing had undergone yet another renaissance, as many

DOI: 10.4324/9781003248620-5

people, especially soldiers, had composed and published diaries about their experiences in World War I.[5] Diaries written in extremis, they set the stage for the Holocaust diaries that would be written less than a generation later.

Holocaust Diaries

Individual Holocaust diaries like Anne Frank's and converted German-Jewish intellectual Victor Klemperer's have received much scholarly and popular attention for many years.[6] Their descriptions of everyday life under Nazi rule, their candid reactions to the people and situations around them, and in these cases, their exemplary literary style, have inspired interest in the Holocaust more generally. Frank and Klemperer, like many other Holocaust diarists, were responding to a long tradition of diary writing and reading prevalent in Europe from the eighteenth century, as discussed earlier.[7] For example, we know that Anne Frank received the diary as a birthday gift and was encouraged by her family to write in it. Klemperer was an even more direct descendant of famous historical and literary diary writers such as Samuel Pepys and Walter Scott;[8] as an intellectual, he would have been well acquainted with works like these and may have used them as models for his own diary.

Many Holocaust diaries written by Jews also followed specifically Jewish literary traditions. The long history of writing in response to Jewish catastrophes was well known to many diarists, who were often religiously as well as secularly educated. David Roskies's book, *The Literature of Destruction: Jewish Responses to Catastrophe*, specifically places diarists writing from within Holocaust ghettos in the long line of authors responding to Jewish tragedy from Biblical times, to the destruction of Herod's Temple, the Spanish Expulsion, the pogroms of Kishinev, and World War I.[9] More particularly, many diarists themselves wrote about the works of previous Jewish authors who had responded to suffering through literature.[10] They saw their texts as part of a clear Jewish tradition of writing about the tragedies that befell the Jewish people throughout the ages. Not surprisingly, then, thousands of known individuals, and likely many more whom we will never know, wrote diaries during the Holocaust. Jews undergoing Nazi persecution kept diaries no matter what part of the Holocaust they experienced. People such as Klemperer wrote in Germany in relative freedom; his diary recounts the gradual suffocation of anti-Jewish laws from within the Nazi regime. People like Anne Frank wrote in hiding, describing the fear and difficulty of everyday life with little access to the outside world. Others wrote from within the ghettos in occupied Eastern Europe and documented detailed experiences of daily life in the forced communities created by the Nazis but largely administered by Jewish functionaries.[11] Finally, people wrote even from within the concentration camps. Facing the ultimate in surveillance and struggling to find time and materials to write, these diarists demonstrated an enormous will to record their experiences.[12]

Though some famous diaries of non-Jewish victims also exist, this chapter focuses on Jewish victim diaries.[13] It should be noted that many gentiles who were not victims wrote during the war as well, and some even addressed the Holocaust. Non-Jews in Poland witnessed the persecution of Jews around them including ghettoisation, forced labour, deportation, and concentration camps.[14] Even perpetrators sometimes wrote about their crimes against the Jews in diaries kept during and after the war.[15] The remainder of this chapter revolves around a series of questions researchers must ask themselves when reading diaries as primary sources. Though many of the theoretical considerations apply to all diaries, the relevant questions refer specifically to reading victim diaries and the ways in which those diaries can, and cannot, inform our historical understanding of the Holocaust.

Issues of Genre

Robert A. Fothergill, in his foundational work on English diaries, explained the form of diary he found most fitting of the genre: "the 'personal' diary, that is to say the diary whose prime subject is the life of the writer, valued for its own sake."[16] In such a diary, the author seeks to create or confirm an identity through writing him- or herself into the text. The diary does not simply record the events of the day but serves as a place for the author to determine his or her own character in written thoughts about the world. As diary scholar Batsheva Ben-Amos has written,

> The diary is a private literature. When it is published, the diarist's private thoughts, emotions, and actions expose his or her intimate self to the public eye. When real, imagined, or vague future readers are in the writer's mind's eye, the diary is still conveying the private self. The diaristic impulse is writing of the self for the self.[17]

The majority of Holocaust diaries, however, do not fit squarely into this traditional definition of diary, but rather to another of Fothergill's classes of diary writing, the "public diary." These are diaries that

> resort more and more to the recording of public material as being more various and interesting than [the diarist's] own immediate experience. A frequent cause of the latter process is the onset of Historic Events, especially a war, which confer on the diarist the self-important role of eye-witness.[18]

Not surprisingly, even if they begin as more traditional personal diaries, diaries written by Jews during the Holocaust often detail a broader story than simply their own. The example of Etty Hillesum's diary, written by a young Jewish woman in Amsterdam, proves instructive. Hillesum started her diary in 1941 purely as part of a therapeutic exercise, and while her focus remained on an exploration of her inner world throughout, it also noted more and more the persecution faced by Jews in the Netherlands. By the time she was sent to the Westerbork transit camp in 1943, "Historical Events" had taken over.[19]

Another set of important questions relate to those of motivation and audience. Especially in these diaries, created amid such disaster, authors often wrote for more than one reason and for multiple audiences. Sometimes the impetus was clear: many Holocaust diarists only began writing with the advent of war and for the express purpose of chronicling events. As Herman Kruk, living in Vilna, wrote on 23 June 1941, the day after the German invasion of the Soviet Union:

> I make a firm decision: I leave myself to the mercy of God; I'm staying. And right away, I make another decision: if I'm staying anyway and if I'm going to be a victim of Fascism, I shall take pen in hand and write a chronicle of a city. Clearly, Vilna may also be captured. The Germans will turn the city Fascist. Jews will go

into the ghetto—I shall record it all. My chronicle must see, must hear, and must become the mirror and the conscience of the great catastrophe and of the hard times. I have decided to write a chronicle of the events of Vilna.[20]

Kruk saw his daily entries not as a way of contemplating his inner life, but rather as a way to keep a record of the terrible events happening to and around him. Likewise, his audience was not himself, but his future readers. Thus, the suggestion that diary writing is inherently private does not hold for these texts.

Anne Frank and Etty Hillesum similarly wrote with an eye towards future publication and discussed the possibility openly in writing, but their writings also remained private, or at least personal. As historian Alexandra Garbarini has argued,

> historical diaries or war diaries should be considered forms of selfwriting. War diaries have generally been construed as having little in common with private diaries because they tend to point to the external world rather than to 'the internal world of a single ego' ... Though not classical journaux intimes, however, they do reveal aspects of their author's thoughts and feelings.[21]

Complicating this interpretation, Amos Goldberg has posited that Holocaust diaries may, by definition, be *unable* to function as typical self-writing. He argues that Holocaust diarists were undergoing such trauma at the time of writing that they cannot be read as "full, autonomous, conscious, [authors] whose sense of identity always prevails."[22] In this way, Holocaust diarists are different from those writing from a non-threatened position, thereby making the nature of their writing different as well. Goldberg calls into question diarists' very authorial voices, making us doubt the reliability of their texts as historical documents.[23] If the diaries do not present traditional forms of life-writing, then what *do* they present?

Form is also essential to defining the diary genre. The most basic definition of the term is an etymological one: "The word itself tells us that it is day-to-day writing: a series of dated written records."[24] However, with Holocaust diaries, this is not always the case. Because of physical and psychological upheavals, writing was not always a straightforward endeavour. Many diarists who discussed the creation of the ghettos, for example, could not write amidst the chaos of the event; instead, they often had to look back to the past week, for example, in constructing their entries.[25] Some texts described as diaries were written after the war based on diaries written during it. Others are presented as diaries written during the war, but actually were edited and published later, only sometimes retaining the original text.[26] As suggested by Garbarini, it seems that the most important element of diary writing is that it demonstrates the slow uncovering of knowledge and the contemporary lived experience that laid bare the changes in perception that came with it.[27] A focus on writings that demonstrate this kind of ethos allows us most closely to examine the mindset of those living during the Holocaust—the major benefit, I would argue, of using Holocaust diaries as historical sources.

Representation

While diaries are a singular source for understanding the inner worlds and everyday lives of Holocaust victims, how to interpret these texts has been debated and theorised for decades. The earliest and most comprehensive body of work on Holocaust diaries rests within the realm of literary studies.[28] One of the literary scholars to first address Holocaust diaries, Lawrence Langer, suggested that a sensitive reading of these as well as fictional representations of the Holocaust can help us to understand something of the "reality" of the offenses committed against the Jews during World War II. As he remarks in *Admitting the Holocaust,* we need to use victim sources (here diaries) to better understand the two planes on which the Holocaust takes place in human memory, the historical and the rhetorical.[29] In other words, diaries can help us both to understand the history of the Holocaust and also the ways that the history has been interpreted, spoken about, used, and abused in the post-war period. James E. Young similarly demonstrated the value of diaries for historical study in a 1987 article.[30] In it, he suggests that it is impossible to use diaries as purely literal representations of historical events. Diaries give much more than a straightforward accounting of events, as they contain so much of the author's own personality, personal biases, and points of view. They, like all written discourse, indicate the ways that "time and place combine with other structurally mediating factors like language and political orientation, for example, to shape the representations of these experiences by different writers."[31]

Holocaust diaries also call up questions of historical interpretation. Because these diarists lived amid the persecution, they could not always understand the historical importance of daily events. As suggested by Goldberg, the trauma they faced on a regular basis also affected the types of events they chose to describe and the ways they were able to describe them. Similarly, because of their lack of good information and the prevalence of rumours, due to their situation as victims kept purposely in the dark, they could not always contextualise their experiences. Finally, because diaries are personal documents written by individuals, the biases they reveal sometimes obscure the overall story of the place and time in which they lived. Because these texts are naturally subjective, it is difficult to assess the objective reality of their claims. Often, reading multiple accounts of the same situation in different diaries will reveal quite distinct interpretations. In recognising these hurdles to using diaries as historical sources, Young therefore proposes a model that recommends historians read and use diaries and memoirs to comprehend not necessarily the facts of the Holocaust, but rather the *ways* in which the events of the Holocaust were understood and represented by its writers.

Historical Understanding

Historians, however, have not always favoured this method of reading sources; likewise, using diaries in historical research on the Holocaust has undergone several major shifts. In 1944, the Central Jewish Historical Commission was founded by Holocaust survivors in Lublin and operated to "chronicle the cataclysm of Polish Jewry for future generations and to help rebuild Jewish life in Poland."[32] The Commission administered questionnaires and collected diaries and testimonies about Jewish experiences in Nazi-occupied Europe. It emphasised that every element of Jewish persecution was worth recording, as survivors tried to put their lives back together, and Soviet Poland began ignoring the recent mass murder of the Jews.

Almost concurrently, the Central Committee of Liberated Jews in Germany began its own document collection project in Munich. Like the organisation in Poland, this group consisted of Holocaust survivors whose focus was to collect documents and testimonies on all aspects the Holocaust experience, including diaries.[33] In fact, Philip Friedman, founding member of the Polish Historical Commission, became head of the Education Department in the Jewish Displaced Persons camps in the American Zone in Germany for the Joint Distribution Committee, also working as an advisor to the Central Historical Commission affiliated with Munich's Central Committee.

Although the Historical Commissions' tasks were to document and record, not to analyse, from them developed the first post-war Holocaust researchers. Survivor-scholars Philip Friedman, Rachel Auerbach, Nachman Blumental, Isaiah Trunk, Israel Kaplan, Bernard Mark, and Artur Eisenbach began using the wealth of materials made available through the commissions, as well as private and official documents, to construct the earliest histories of the Holocaust.[34] Their reliance on personal Jewish sources helped them answer their most pressing question—what happened to Jews during the Holocaust? However, outside of Jewish circles, the Jewish perspective was rarely examined, and was often ignored entirely. In Western Europe and the United States, early historical inquiries into World War II often left out the Jewish experience altogether, asking not what happened to the Jews, but how could/did a "civilised" society like Germany's cause so much destruction? Similarly, the earliest Holocaust historians, such as Raul Hilberg, argued for the necessity of examining official sources over personal ones to reveal the "objective" truth of how the Holocaust occurred. To do this, scholars in the West favoured an explanatory narrative that focused on the perpetrators rather than the victims. This was different in Israel, where scholars relied on Jewish sources to describe primarily Jewish experiences, especially those of resistance. In fact, the Israeli school of Holocaust research developed a narrative focused on the idea of "*amidah*," a term meant to encapsulate and emphasise quite a broad definition of Jewish resistance during the Holocaust which could mean anything from armed resistance to diary writing.[35] An entire scholarship has thus arisen which treats diary writing primarily as a form of resistance.[36]

With historical shifts towards *alltagsgeschichte,* microhistory, and the history of emotions in the 1980s, Holocaust scholars began re-examining diaries as primary sources. They took cues from literary studies in how to interpret these often private, personal, and certainly biased and limited sources as responsible historians. The pinnacle of this kind of work appeared in Alexandra Garbarini's 2006 study, *Numbered Days*. In it, Garbarini sought to understand how Jews made sense of the Holocaust through an in-depth examination of their diaries—the only historical monograph to do so. She provided descriptions of diarists' major concerns and motivations for writing during the Holocaust that address some of the most salient historical questions at stake—why did people write diaries, what purpose did the diaries serve, who did they write for, what do their diaries reveal about their thoughts and feelings at the time, and what are the limitations of reading these diaries as sources for history writing? These questions move past previous debates on whether diaries are legitimate historical sources by proposing a useful set of parameters for interpreting them on their own terms.

Holocaust Diaries in Historical Research: Benefits

Following Garbarini's focus on diaries as an important historical source, this chapter suggests a number of significant benefits of using these texts to understand the Holocaust and write its history. First, these diaries were written during the persecution, while perceptions were still fresh. Written in response to the vagaries of daily experience, these diaries follow the fluctuations of daily life and rest on the uncertainty of outcomes, as opposed to post-war memoirs, which were written at the distance of some months and sometimes many years and had the benefit of hindsight. Compared with memoirs, then, these diaries have the ability to reveal truths about everyday life seldom found in post-war testimonies. These can be in the form of information about everyday experiences that would otherwise be lost. For example, after the war, it did not seem as pertinent to survivors to recount the daily weather, the exact quantity of rations, or the casual interaction with a German that are exactly the types of accounts that would appear in a diary. Diaries are perhaps the only source to capture the mundane experiences of life during the Holocaust. These truths can also take the form of emotional expressions described at the time but later forgotten or eclipsed by further traumatic experiences.

Furthermore, diaries are not affected by problems of memory or post-war cultural and national influences as memoirs can often be. Instead of responding to life as a Displaced Person, questions of loyalty to a new country, or issues of fitting in to a new society, they rely on their past and Holocaust-era social, religious, and political worlds to make sense of their experiences. As such, they are excellent historical sources for understanding Jewish perspectives at the start of the war and charting their changes over time. Some scholars emphasise the continuity of ideas and values that infuse the diaries, while others argue for a focus on rupture and discontinuity. For example, the "constructivist" approach to reading ghetto diaries, championed by David Roskies, requires that "those who study these writings must ... be able to situate each eye-witness account or diary ... at the precise intersection of Jewish tradition and European culture."[37] However, pre-war society no longer seemed to apply to many undergoing the worst of Nazi atrocities. The language used within diaries written especially in the ghettos and camps changes and morphs into something created out of the confrontation between the old world, informed by religion, enlightenment, and modern scholarship, and the new world, which saw all of this destroyed.[38]

Finally, as James E. Young suggested, diaries are excellent sources for studying perceptions, reactions, thoughts, and feelings. This is especially useful for scholars approaching Holocaust study through the lenses of empathic history or the history of emotions. Some limitations in accurately assessing these will be addressed later, but the fact remains that diaries, as individual self-narratives, are better suited than any other source for examining this kind of subjective history. Furthermore, examining multiple diaries of the same place and time can provide different perspectives on similar events, leading to new and innovating historical conclusions.

Holocaust Diaries in Historical Research: Limitations

Despite their many advantages for writing history, diaries also offer significant limitations. Aside from the questions of genre discussed earlier, there are other theoretical and practical issues at stake. The decision to use diaries as sources necessitates a familiarisation with the large corpus of scholarly work extant on the subject. This chapter has laid out some of the major debates, but the literature itself is significant. An encounter with that literature alerts one to the serious questions of representation and witnessing that must come into any assessment of Holocaust diaries. Unlike the traditional evaluations historians must make regarding author, context, audience, dates, etc. when using official documents, one must also consider the narrative quality of diary writing. While these texts are authentically historical, their construction is largely literary. As in writing an autobiography, diarists choose what, from an enormous amount of possible material, they will write about and how they will do so. Some diaries consist of vague notes meant to trigger reminders for a later date, some give a straightforward accounting of events the authors find important, and some consciously use literary devices to tell a story about their experiences. How scholars read these diaries depends as much on the form as the content.

For example, one of the most substantial issues that academics and diarists alike must consider is that of the difficulty of language for describing a "limit" event like the Holocaust. Holocaust survivor and author Primo Levi best described the problem of language and the Holocaust in his comment on the inability of language to bridge the divide between survivors and others and to express the reality of what happened. He wrote of language as perceived by Holocaust victims, "Just as our hunger is not that feeling of missing a meal, so our way of being cold has need of a new word. We say 'hunger,' we say 'tiredness,' 'fear,' 'pain,' we say 'winter' and they are different things."[39] At the most basic level, then, if language is unable to describe the events of the Holocaust, how can we read or understand diarists' representations of those events? The diarists themselves recognised these questions and tried to provide answers within their works.

Herman Kruk, for example, used a variety of genres to attempt to capture the mood of ghetto life. Besides his diary, he also wrote short stories and collected historical documents, which he appended to his diary. Some diarists themselves, such as Josef Zelkowicz in the Lodz ghetto, expressed the inability of people to understand and believe, and thus to capably represent, the atrocities going on around them. On 6 September 1942, he wrote:

> But won't truth remain "true?" This truth will cry out: Not only is everything that has been written absolute truth, but no pen and no human force has the ability and the talent to describe all of these events as they really occurred ... No pen, no tongue has a vocabulary capable of conveying even a small fraction of the emotions and sensitivities that overtake anyone who has observed and heard everything that has occurred in recent days.[40]

It seems clear from these examples and more that though diarists felt the frustrations of the limitations of human language to explain the depth of horror they experienced, they nonetheless sought to overcome those boundaries through persistence, creative approaches, and an ultimate faith that people in the post-war world would be able to understand at least something of the "truth" of their experiences, despite the inadequacy of language to describe them.

Other limitations to using diaries as historical sources are more practical. A major problem is that of survival. Most Holocaust diaries which survived were written by people in privileged positions to write and with some agency to hide or otherwise preserve their texts. This means that diaries are not necessarily representative of the Jewish population at large, omitting especially the apolitical, the lower classes, the religious, and women. For example, though women were culturally encouraged to write diaries, once the Nazi persecution began, many found themselves too busy to write as they took on new roles with new responsibilities, including advocating for their families and forced labour.[41] Aside from the fact that not everyone wrote a diary during the Holocaust, and that those who did often fit into a particular intellectual, middle-class milieu, those diaries that survived made up quite a small proportion of the diaries that were most likely written. Some authors, such as Anne Frank and Etty Hillesum, were able to hand off their diaries to friends or family for rescue after their own deportation. Most diaries recovered after the war from the ghettos were saved through organised underground archival projects which had the resources and manpower necessary to preserve texts in the midst of destruction.[42] A number of famous diaries have been and continue to be found as former persecution sites are excavated, people investigate the vestiges of old attics or crawlspaces, or safety deposit boxes are emptied to reveal Holocaust-era texts.[43] The vast majority of Holocaust diaries, however, remain unpublished. This means that research using them necessarily sends scholars to multiple archives around the world. Many copies of diaries saved through organised efforts exist at the United States Holocaust Memorial Museum in Washington DC, YIVO in New York, Yad Vashem and Ghetto Fighters' House in Israel, and the Jewish Historical Institute in Warsaw. Local archives in Poland, Germany, France, Lithuania, Czech Republic, and other countries occupied by the Nazis contain their own collections of diaries deposited there.

A related problem is that of language. Because the Holocaust was a world event, the diaries kept by victims, perpetrators, and bystanders are written in many different languages. The majority of Jewish diaries appear in Yiddish, Polish, and Hebrew. Large numbers also exist in German, French, Dutch, and Russian. Some have been published and translated into various languages, including English, but most have not. Many of these diaries, then, are left inaccessible to those who do not read the languages. Of those that have not been published, other difficulties lay in deciphering the original documents, many of which have undergone extensive damage. Because they were often buried or otherwise hidden, diaries were subject to the elements, sometimes for many years, before being found and preserved.

A last note about the difficulty of using Holocaust diaries as historical sources is: as rich as these texts are, much of that value derives from the fact that these were documents written every day for years on end. As such, they are lengthy. Reading them, especially unpublished diaries stored in various archives around the world, takes an enormous amount of time, commitment, and patience. Some diaries only include fragments of what was clearly a longer original text (another place in which interpretation needs to be handled carefully—what is missing can be as important as what remains), but others are more complete and comprise many hundreds of pages. In other words, reading diaries is a task that cannot be taken on lightly, as they require much time and attention. As Phillipe Lejeune has written,

> this is an astonishing feature of the diary that makes it unlike almost any other type of text: no outside reader can read it in the same way as the author, even though the very purpose of reading it is to discover its private contents. ... To get close to the truth of another person's diary, then, one must read a lot of it for a long time.[44]

Conclusion

Using Holocaust diaries in historical research can be a rewarding, even revelatory experience. Becoming intimately acquainted with an historical actor's inner world allows one deep insight into their experiences and perceptions. Following them day by day through their life-writing can make the researcher feel a close connection with the author. Especially with Holocaust diaries, this is both a benefit and a drawback. Reading Holocaust diaries empathically provides access to insights about the authors' historical experiences not available to scholars through any other source. However, the kind of long-term engagement one must have with a Holocaust diary can also be emotionally draining. Reading the personal perceptions and emotions around the radically traumatic situations people had to endure requires the researcher to face the horror directly. Human nature prefers to turn away from such pain, but Holocaust diaries do not allow such turning away. Considering the academic issues of genre, context, language, representation, subjectivity, and perception discussed here, to think through the types of "truth" presented by Holocaust diaries, is one way to step back and analyse these texts from a more objective position. It seems to me that the best kind of history is one that achieves this balance—engaging victims on their own terms, listening closely to what they have to say, while periodically grounding oneself in the familiar world of academic analysis. A sensitive approach to Holocaust diaries can help us understand the strengths and limits of the "human" during an event that tested the very concept.

Notes

1 D. Barnouw, *The Phenomenon of Anne Frank*, Bloomington: Indiana University Press, 2018.
2 B. Ben-Amos and D. Ben-Amos (ed.), *The Diary: The Epic of Everyday Life*, Bloomington: Indiana University Press, 2020, pp. 5–6.
3 Philippe Lejeune outlines this history for girls in France in "The 'Journal de Jeune Fille' in Nineteenth-Century France," in S.L. Bunkers and C.A. Huff (ed.), *Inscribing the Daily: Critical Essays on Women's Diaries*, Amherst: University of Massachusetts Press, 1996, pp. 107–22.
4 M. Bogucka, "Women and Culture in Poland in Early Modern Times," *Acta Poloniae Historica*, 80, July 1999, pp. 61–97.
5 L.V. Smith, "Diary and Narrative: French Soldier and World War I," in Ben-Amos and Ben-Amos (ed.), *The Diary: The Epic of Everyday Life*, Bloomington: Indiana University Press, pp. 333–47.
6 *Anne Frank: The Diary of a Young Girl* was first published in English in 1952, and Victor Klemperer's *Tagebücher* first appeared in Germany in 1995.
7 Lejeune, "The 'Journal de Jeune Fille' in Nineteenth-Century France," pp. 107–22.
8 S. Pepys, *Memoirs of Samuel Pepys … Comprising His Diary, from 1659 to 1669. And a Selection from His Private Correspondence*, ed. Richard Lord Braybrooke, London: F. Warne and Co., 1870; Sir Walter Scott, *The Journal of Sir Walter Scott*, New York: Harper, 1891.
9 D. Roskies, *The Literature of Destruction: Jewish Responses to Catastrophe*, Philadelphia: Jewish Publication Society, 1988.
10 See, for example, H. Kruk, *The Last Days of the Jerusalem of Lithuania*, ed. Benjamin Harshav, New Haven: Yale University Press, 2002, pp. 116–17, in which he mentions Hayim Nachman Bialik's *In the City of Slaughter*, written as a response to the Kishinev Pogrom of 1903.
11 R.M. Shapiro (ed.), *Holocaust Chronicles: Individualizing the Holocaust Through Diaries and Other Contemporaneous Personal Accounts*, Hoboken (NJ): Ktav, 1999.
12 D. Schroeder, *"Niemand ist fähig das alles in Worten auszudrücken": Tagebuchschreiben In Nationalsozialistischen Konzentrationslagern 1939–1945*, Göttingen: Wallstein Verlag, 2020.
13 Of the former, see, for example, O. Nansen, *From Day to Day: One Man's Diary of Survival in Nazi Concentration Camps*, Nashville: Vanderbilt University Press, 2016.
14 R. Feldhay Brenner, *The Ethics of Witnessing the Holocaust in Polish Writers' Diaries from Warsaw, 1939–1945*, Evanston: Illinois University Press, 2014.

15 E. Klee, W. Dressen, and V. Riess (ed.), *The Good Old Days: The Holocaust as Seen by Its Perpetrators and Bystanders*, Old Saybrook (CT): Konecky & Konecky, 1991.
16 R.A. Fothergill, *Private Chronicles: A Study of English Diaries*, Oxford: Oxford University Press, 1974, p. 3.
17 Ben-Amos and Ben-Amos (ed.), *The Diary*, p. 14.
18 Fothergill, *Private Chronicles*, p. 16.
19 E. Hillesum, *An Interrupted Life: The Diaries of Etty Hillesum, 1941–1943*, New York: Pantheon Books, 1984.
20 Kruk, *The Last Days*, p. 47.
21 A. Garbarini, *Numbered Days: Diaries and the Holocaust*, New Haven: Yale University Press, 2006, p. 18.
22 A. Goldberg, "Holocaust Diaries as 'Life Stories,'" *Search and Research: Lectures and Papers*, 5, 2004, p. 18.
23 A. Goldberg, *Trauma in First Person: Diary Writing During the Holocaust*, Bloomington: Indiana University Press, 2017.
24 Ben-Amos and Ben-Amos (ed.), *The Diary*, p. 2.
25 Y. Rudashevski, *The Diary of the Vilna Ghetto, June 1941-April 1943*, Tel Aviv: Ghetto Fighters' House, 1973, pp. 28–40.
26 A famous example of this kind of writing is the diary of Masha Rolnikaite, published under the title *I Must Tell*. According to Alexandra Zapruder's research for *Salvaged Pages: Young Writers' Diaries of the Holocaust*, New Haven: Yale University Press, 2002, pp. 468–9, Rolnikaite apparently wrote the diary while in the Vilna ghetto but reconstructed it from memory after the war. There was also a long publication history of the diary in Lithuanian, Russian, and Yiddish, with post-war political issues leading to various changes in the text.
27 Garbarini, *Numbered Days*, p. 17.
28 Feldhay Brenner, *The Ethics of Witnessing the Holocaust*.
29 L.L. Langer, *Admitting the Holocaust*, New York: Oxford University Press, 1995.
30 J.E. Young, "Interpreting Literary Testimony: A Preface to Rereading Holocaust Diaries and Memoirs," *New Literary History*, 18:2, Winter, 1987, pp. 403–23.
31 Ibid., p. 416.
32 L. Jockusch, *Collect and Record! Jewish Holocaust Documentation in Early Postwar Europe*, Oxford: Oxford University Press, 2012, p. 84.
33 Ibid., p. 4.
34 Selected bibliography from these authors: many of Philip Friedman's early works are collected in *Roads to Extinction: Essays on the Holocaust*, New York: Conference on Jewish Social Studies: Jewish Publication Society of America, 1980; R. Auerbach, *Der Yidisher Oyfshtand: Varshe 1943*, Warsaw: Central Committee of the Jews in Poland, 1948; R. Auerbach, *Oyf di Felder fun Ṭreblinḳe: Reporṭazsh*, Warsaw and Lodz: Central Jewish Historical Commission, 1947; N. Blumental, "The Yiddish Language and the Fight Against the Nazi-Regime," *Bleter far Geshikhte* 1:3–4, 1948, pp. 106–24; B. Mark, *Di Umgekumene Shrayber fun di Getos un Lagern in Zayere Verk*, Warsaw: Yiddish Book, 1954; I. Trunk, *Judenrat: The Jewish Councils in Eastern Europe under Nazi Occupation*, New York: Macmillan, 1972; I. Trunk, "Jewish Labor-Camps in the Wartheland," *Bleter far Geshikhte*, 1:1, 1948, pp. 114–69; I. Kaplan, *Dos Folḳs-moyl in Natsi-ḳlem: Reydenishn in Geṭo un Katseṭ*, Munich: Central Historical Commission of the Liberated Jews in Germany, 1949; A. Eisenbach, "Scholarly Research in the Warsaw Ghetto (According to the Materials from the Ringelblum-Archive)," *Bleter far Geshikhte* 1:1, 1948, pp. 55–113; A. Eisenbach, "Scholarly Research in the Warsaw Ghetto (According to the Materials from the Ringelblum-Archive)," *Bleter far Geshikhte* 1:2, 1948, pp. 69–84.
35 Yehuda Bauer is a leader of this school of thought. See Y. Bauer, *They Chose Life: Jewish Resistance in the Holocaust*, New York: American Jewish Committee, 1973; Y. Bauer, *Rethinking the Holocaust*, New Haven: Yale University Press, 2001.
36 R. Feldhay Brenner, *Writing as Resistance: Four Women Confronting the Holocaust: Edith Stein, Simone Weil, Anne Frank, Etty Hillesum*, University Park (PA).: Pennsylvania State University, 1997; Z. Waxman, *Writing the Holocaust: Identity, Testimony, Representation*, Oxford: Oxford University Press, 2006; A. Payne, *My Life, My Friend, and Ally: Diaries as a Form of Resistance in the Warsaw Ghetto*, Saarbrücken: VDM Verlag Dr. Müller, 2008.

44 *Amy Simon*

37 D. Roskies, "Landkentenish: Yiddish Belles Lettres in the Warsaw Ghetto," in R.M. Shapiro (ed.), *Holocaust Chronicles: Individualizing the Holocaust through Diaries and Other Contemporaneous Personal Accounts*, Hoboken (NJ): KTAV, 1999, p. 13.
38 For interesting collections of terminology coined in Yiddish during the Holocaust, see USHMM RG 15.083M, Der Aelteste der Juden vom Litzmannstadt Getto, "Ghetto Encyclopedia," Reel 256, file 1103; Y. Kaplan, *Dos Folks-moyl in Natsi-klem: reydenishn in geto un katset*, Munich: Tsentraler historisher komisye baym ts. k. fun di bafrayte Yidn in der Amerikaner zone in Daytshland, 1949.
39 P. Levi, *Survival in Auschwitz*, New York: Simon and Schuster, 1996, p. 123.
40 J. Zelkowicz, *In Those Terrible Days: Writings from the Łódź Ghetto,* ed. M. Unger, Jerusalem: Yad Vashem, 2003, p. 355.
41 M. Kaplan, *Between Dignity and Despair: Jewish Life in Nazi Germany*, Oxford: Oxford University Press, 1999.
42 For a discussion of the most famous of these, the *Oyneg Shabes* archive, see S. Kassow, *Who Will Write Our History? Rediscovering a Hidden Archive from the Warsaw Ghetto*, Bloomington: Indiana University Press, 2007.
43 For published diaries with particularly dramatic survival stories, see B. Mark, *The Scrolls of Auschwitz*, ed. Isaiah Avrech, Tel Aviv: Am `Oved, 1985; R. Laskier, *Rutka's Notebook: January-April 1943*, Jerusalem: Yad Vashem, 2007; R. Spiegel, *Renia's Diary: A Holocaust Journal*, New York: St. Martin's Press, 2019.
44 Ben-Amos and Ben-Amos (ed.), *The Diary*, pp. 3–4.

4 Analysing Memoirs: Gone but Not Forgotten

Kayla M. Stanton

Introduction

A memoir is a creative non-fiction work that focuses on the author's interpretation of events, thoughts, and memories. Written accounts told from a first-person perspective typically concentrate on a single aspect or period of the person's life, unlike biographies and autobiographies, which cover the entirety of the subject's lifetime and are more rooted in chronological, researched facts. The recreated event through storytelling offers a more intimate insight into the author's feelings.[1]

For those studying the Holocaust, navigating the vast sea of information is daunting. However, of the millions of documents, artefacts, pictures, and testimonies available for analysis, published memoirs prove to be among the most invaluable and powerful sources available. The written testimonies of those who witnessed the Holocaust first hand provide devastatingly emotional and thought-provoking perspectives with the power to convey the memories of the forgotten; however, their use as historical source material has split scholarly opinion regarding their reliability. This chapter seeks to explain their values, caution their limitations, and clarify how this source impacts our understanding of the Holocaust.

Benefits

Frequently viewed by scholarly critics as problematic, memoir literature's narrative writing style is also an asset. Although fact-based, authors' primary objective is to depict their views of events and sensations felt through storytelling. Many writers have more flexibility with narration because they focus on producing an engaging story rather than proving (or disproving) their views. The style of the memoir can read more like a fictional novel because the author is recording events and how they remember them with the freedom of creative expression, rather than reciting exact events. The emotional statements and detailed descriptions of people, places, and events enable readers vicariously to experience the history and gain a deeper insight on the subject that fact-listing history texts lack. Collectively, the stylistic approach gives depth to the author's experience and makes them more relatable.

Memoirs elicit a more primal and empathetic response that makes history *feel* real in a way that sterile, academic texts cannot. According to Keith Oatley, director of the Cognitive Science Program at the University of Toronto, reading stories is a "simulation that runs on minds of readers just as computer simulations run on computers." He contends that in our brain's simulations of written narratives, "personal truths can be explored that allow readers to experience emotions—their own emotions—and understand aspects of them that are obscure, in relation to contexts in which the emotions arise."[2] In other words, human brains react similarly to real-life events and reading about experiences.[3] As a result, narratives stand out because the reader experiences the unfolding events in their imaginations.

First-hand accounts induce each reader to experience the horrors recounted empathetically. Shoshana Felman and Dori Laub claim in their 1992 examination of memory, *Testimony*, that the division of eyewitnesses created "an event ... cognitively and perceptually without a witness both because it precludes seeing and because it precludes the possibility of a community of seeing."[4] The Holocaust was not only a "scheme of the literal erasure of its witnesses" but "the unprecedented, inconceivable historical advent of an event without a witness."[5] The depth of emotion present in survivor testimony realises the Holocaust and is the only way that the crimes perpetrated against humanity can successfully be understood.[6]

The Holocaust's imagined "vicarious witnessing" has a noteworthy and valuable quality. For example, prisoners arriving at Auschwitz were notoriously sorted by gender and age, with the young, old, sick, and unlucky sent to their deaths without a second glance. This information is sad and powerful, but the narrative account elicits an emotional response:

> Our turn came. My mother, my sons, and I stepped before the "selectors." Then I committed my second terrible error. The selector waved my mother and myself to the adult group. He classed my younger son Thomas with the children and aged, which was to mean immediate extermination. He hesitated before Arvad, my older son.
>
> My heart thumped violently. This officer, a large dark man who wore glasses, seemed to be trying to act fairly. Later I learned that he was Dr. Fritz Klein, the "Chief Selector." "This boy must be more than twelve," he remarked to me.
>
> "No," I protested.
>
> The truth was that Arvad was not quite twelve, and I could have said so. He was big for his age, but I wanted to spare him from labors that might prove too arduous for him.
>
> "Very well," Klein agreed amiably. "To the left!"
>
> I had persuaded my mother that she should follow the children and take care of them. At her age she had a right to the treatment accorded to the elderly and there would be someone to look after Arvad and Thomas.
>
> "My mother would like to remain with the children," I said.
>
> "Very well," he agreed again. "You'll all be in the same camp."
>
> "And in several weeks you'll all be reunited," another officer added, with a smile. "Next!"
>
> How could I have known? I had spared them from hard work, but I had condemned Arvad and my mother to death in the gas chambers.[7]

Olga Lengyel's devastating account of her family's last moments together resonates with readers and increases the reality of events. The suffering of an individual is relatable, whereas factual evidence comes across as cold. Memoirs enable readers to "experience" events and effectively humanise history.

Memoirs give insightful knowledge that enhances the historical record, and together with other autobiographical survivor recollections sometimes serve as the only information source of people or events. Human life was not the only significant loss of the Holocaust. During "the detention and murder of academics, teachers, writers, [and] journalists," knowledge and history were simultaneously devastated by "the plunder of libraries, universities, churches and private collections."[8] Historical connections to the Jewish community and learning—records, books, art—were lost. However, pieces of that lost knowledge survive in memory and can be found written in Holocaust testimony. For example, 85 percent of Poland's Jewish population was brutally murdered during the Holocaust, and with them, their knowledge and culture, but fragments of information about pre-war Jewish society in accounts such as Mielnicki's, Szpilman's, and Gold's help bridge gaps in knowledge.[9] Their memories of conversation, tradition, and daily rituals are critical pieces in reconstructing our understanding of pre-war Jewish society.

Memoirs also serve as integral sources of information in the ghettos and camps. Autobiographical narratives detail the evolving social relationships that produced avenues of resistance and survival. Nearly all female memoirists credit friendship and collaboration in the camps to their survival.[10] Women report forming alliances and close emotional bonds with their fellow prisoners and sometimes creating surrogate families. For example, Ruth Klüger's mother adopted a girl in Birkenau and cared for the child until after the war. Lucille Eichengreen formed a surrogate family with three sisters in the Lodz ghetto after both their remaining families were deported. Relationships gave companionship and protection, but other bonds served in the camps as well.

In addition to illuminating aspects of the Holocaust, another asset of autobiographical narratives is their capacity to challenge commonly accepted beliefs and counter popular history. The victors write history, but the reality of events does not always line up with what is taught. For example, the liberating allied troops are often portrayed as sympathetic heroes—patient and kind—but some memoirs paint the liberation of the concentration camps in a more realistic light. Written recollections from memoirists such as Jorge Semprún, Ruth Klüger, and Primo Levi all testify to the psychological or physical suffering they endured at the hands of their liberators. Survivor testimony serves both to affirm and deny the validity of popular history.

Memoirs drastically improve Holocaust study through the variety of perspectives recorded. Individual interpretations of events mean there is "no singular Holocaust experience."[11] Experiences vary based on gender, age, location, culture, religion, and socioeconomic status. For example, the information available to a Jew hiding by passing as Aryan was different than what a person hidden in an attic or imprisoned in the camps experienced: a man lived a different experience of the Holocaust from a woman, an adult from a child, and a Jew from a Nazi. Each factor shaped the author's account of the Holocaust and resulted in a unique testimony with exclusive knowledge.

Pitfalls

History has a vexed relationship with memory, for memory is fragile and predisposed to error. A significant limitation to memoirs as source material is that they do not give evidence of an event but instead reveal the author's interpretation of events as they remember them.[12] Many who have published Holocaust memoirs experienced the Holocaust in their youth and wrote about their life experiences decades after the events. Thomas Buergenthal's preface to *A Lucky Child* freely discloses the limitations of his memory:

> These recollections, I am sure, are coloured by the tricks that the passage of time and old age play on memory: forgotten or inaccurate names of people; muddled facts and dates of events that took place either earlier or later than recounted; and references to events that did not happen quite as I describe them or that I believe I witnessed but may have only heard about.[13]

This passage of time creates a natural degradation that may leave memories unclear.

Holocaust memoirs may contain another fault: that of communal memory versus individual memory. Scientists argue that members of communities often unintentionally develop similar patterns of thought through extended periods of close social interaction that include repetitively shared similar experiences. Individuals are effectively "socialized to accept certain views of the past and to incorporate these views into their own lives via collective memory."[14] This "social contagion" and other acts of "collective memory" occur when those experiences inadvertently shape how the community remembers the past.[15]

Conversations among individuals of these susceptible groups enable the spread of shared memory. Brown, Kouri, and Hirst claim that interactions of social remembering make individuals "vulnerable to incorporating" unexperienced details into memory and unconsciously misappropriate them as their own.[16] Stefan Mächler contends that suggestive questions may also influence the generation of false memories.[17] Thus, the line between real memory and historical memory may be blurred. Thomas Buergenthal wrote that he

> found it difficult, if not impossible ... to distinguish clearly between some events I actually remember witnessing and those I was told about by my parents or overheard them discuss. All I can say is that as I wrote about them, I seemed to remember them clearly as first-hand experiences.[18]

Similarly, Nobel Prize winner François Mauriac expressed his experience with the phenomenon in his Foreword to Elie Wiesel's *Night*, noting:

> nothing I had witnessed during that dark period had marked me as deeply as the image of cattle cars filled with Jewish children at the Auschwitz train station ... Yet I did not even see them with my own eyes. It was my wife who described them to me, still under the shock of the horror she had felt.[19]

Statements such as these give evidence to those who doubt memoirs' reliability as source material.

The fallacy of memory is only one constraint. A significant challenge and limitation of memoir literature relates to its inherently subjective and selective bias. Personal and cultural opinions and prejudices inadvertently shape the processes by which a person remembers life experiences. In the case of memoirs, the written memories are refined over time. Knowledge of the outcome of events permits authors to consider carefully which information to include and what to omit. Furthermore, the "processed" memories may be reassessed and reconstructed to protect self-interest, conform to societal expectations, or appeal to a particular audience demographic. In other words, memoirs are simple individualised arrangements of interpreted memories and experiences an author deems relevant at the time of composition.

Bias often manifests within memoirs through personal, social, and commercial censorship. Aspects are consciously (and sometimes subconsciously) omitted from testimony to prevent embarrassment or pain. Elie Wiesel confessed that "certain events will be omitted, especially those episodes that might embarrass friends and, of course, those that might damage the Jewish people."[20] Omission poses a challenge for the historian as it is difficult to ascertain to what degree excluded content may influence the reader's perception of the text's meaning. For instance, the published memoirs written by former Nazis frequently use a combination of censorship tactics. Adolf Eichmann and Albert Speer both strategically excluded incriminating information about their participation in the Final Solution. At the same time, SS commandant Rudolf Höss attempted to change the narrative by playing the victim with strategic information gaps and self-professed "secret doubts."[21] Voids in information require the same textual analysis as the content presented, and censorship, through selective language or content alterations, whether deliberate or unintentional, mars their dependability as source material as there is no way to gauge omitted information.

Writing for a target audience did not always occur before printing. Sometimes author censorship manifests after successful publication. Thematic significance and audience demographic shape how memoirs are written and published. Elie Wiesel's memoirs were self-edited and censored to suit culturally different audiences. Between the Yiddish version, *Un di velt hot geshvign* (*And the World Remained Silent*), and the later French translation, *La Nuit* (*Night*), the information and tone of writing changed based upon which demographic was being addressed. The Yiddish version includes information specifically significant to the book's intended audience by introducing Sighet as "the most important city [*shtot*] and the one with the largest Jewish population in the province of Marmarosh,"[22] whereas the French version gives the brief note: "that little town in Transylvania where I spent my childhood."[23]

La Nuit eliminated much of the indignant language prevalent in *Un di velt hot geshvign*. For example, in French, the first acts of freedom are innocently depicted as follows: "The next day, some *young men* ran into Weimar to *pick up* potatoes and clothes—and to *sleep with girls*. But of revenge, no trace."[24] Comparably, the Yiddish version describes a dystopian world of crime and retribution. "Early the next day *Jewish* boys ran off to Weimar to *steal* clothing and potatoes. And to *rape German girls* [*un tsu fargvaldikn daytshe shikses*]. The historical commandment of revenge was not fulfilled."[25] The language of each text plays to their respective audience. *Un di velt hot geshvign* states the Jewish boys intended to rape German girls, while *La Nuit* leaves the description as young men and girls. It stands to reason that the exclusion of violent acts and discriminatory language from the French version resulted from anticipated adverse reactions among the targeted readerships.

Correspondingly, social and cultural taboos affect what information is deemed unacceptable for public consumption and further limits the full extent of events. Written testimonies in the years following the Holocaust are more direct in their accounts of the conditions and experiences in the ghettos and camps than the later accounts, which had testimony sanitised by the authors. Accounts admitting to sexual abuse and more extreme forms of violence are rare. Many female memoirists stated that they did not want their families to know the extent of sexual abuse endured in the camps.[26] Survivor Judith Isaacson wrote, "The Anne Franks who survived rape don't write their stories."[27] Men exclude incidences of their rape or prostitution even more frequently than women out of shame and fear of societal stigma.[28] However, omissions of more personal aspects, such as sexual abuse, do not detract from the memoir's use as a source. Each story has relevancy because each recollection gives unique information from a distinct perspective. However, those seeking to utilise memoirs should be aware that aspects will always be missing from this type of literature.

The consequences of textual alterations in memoir literature are apt to compound with translation. The use of language is deliberate. The significance of a word or phrase may be lost during linguistic revisions. The vernacular in one language may not have a direct translation in another. Many published accounts, particularly those authored by first-generation witnesses, have unique terminology that makes it difficult to interpret accurately and convey to readers of another language in a different time. In his notes, Andrew Pollinger wrote of the limitations encountered during memoir translations:

> Translating from one language to another is not easy. People of a different culture and language use words, sentence structures, and idioms in a way that when they are translated literally would be meaningless. Differences in historic times with their accompanying differences in thinking further add to the difficulty.[29]

For Holocaust memoirs written in more than a dozen languages and published in dozens more, this is a marked impediment to their use as sources. However, it does not mean they do not have a place in scholarly literature.

Sometimes translations are helpful to modern understandings because language and thought are both subtle and ever evolving. For example, Caroline Schaumann has found that "the Holocaust acquires different meanings at different times for different people and needs to be translated linguistically as well as culturally."[30] The implication for translated texts is that rather than a literal word-for-word exchange from one language to another, translation is instead an act of "rewriting." Ruth Klüger adopted this view by openly acknowledging changes between her 1992 German memoir, *Weiter leben: eine Jugend*, and the 2001 English version, *Still Alive,* as "neither a translation nor a new book: it's another version, a parallel book, if you will."[31]

Publisher censorship is an often-unobserved drawback to using published memoirs for Holocaust analysis. Once in the hands of publishers, the narrative becomes a commodity, and the manuscripts undergo a series of processes before their final form takes shape for printing. Editors may abridge the text to meet publisher needs. For example, according to Misha Defonseca's ghost-writer Vera Lee, the publisher, Jane Daniel of Mount Ivy Press, "wanted the book longer and wanted more sentimental and emotional content." Both Defonseca and Lee refused. Consequently, Lee was fired while "Daniel took over the writing and rewriting and published the book with only Defonseca's name on the cover."[32] Defonseca's issues highlight the publishing troubles faced by many memoirists. Pages may be cut or added to accommodate the desired length, content edited to appeal to different demographics, or the language altered for readability. Any issues arising due to copyright, fair use, right of privacy, right of publicity, and defamation vetted in publishing legal processes may also result in changes to or the exclusion of information. However, all changes may influence the original tone or message the author intended.

Publishing houses do not check the accuracy of their memoirist's claims, further denying memoirs a position as trustworthy source material in the eyes of some academic scholars. According to Paul Antze and Michael Lambek, "memory has entered public discourse to an unprecedented degree,"[33] providing Holocaust survivors with significant respect and the status of moral authority in public culture.[34] The "mantle of a survivor" is what frequently causes publishing houses and their editors to accept manuscripts classified as "memoir" without verifying the story's authenticity. Random House's publicity director, Sally Martin, has stated that "it is not possible to have or describe any 'standard' pre-publication review procedure for nonfiction titles."[35] Through acts of weak or non-existent fact-checking combined with blind trust, publishers' carelessness has led to disastrous media and academic controversies surrounding memoir literature's suitability as a source of Holocaust study.

Controversy

Disputes have plagued Holocaust memoir literature as historians and journalists have discredited several published personal histories. Some popular published pieces of literature claiming the genre "memoir" have been proven significantly embellished or completely false. Exaggerated stories include Martin Gray's ghost-written composition, *For Those I Loved*,[36] and Herman Rosenblat's *Angel at the Fence*,[37] while Benjamin Wilkomirski's award-winning *Fragments: Memories of a Wartime Childhood*[38] and Misha Defonseca's *Misha: A Mémoire of the Holocaust Years*[39] were proven complete fabrications. Each false "memoir" damages the credible reputation of the nonfiction genre.[40]

Martin Gray's 1971 ghost-written memoir *For Those I Loved* was an international bestseller. At the time of Gray's death in 2016, the book had been translated into 26 languages and sold 30 million copies in addition to various other published format options such as a multivolume graphic novel and an abridged young adult edition in French. Concerns were raised regarding the story's validity in the 1970s by historian and investigative journalist Gitta Sereny. Sereny interviewed Gray's ghost-writer, Max Gallo, who admitted to fabricating aspects of the story in an interview, claiming that while the majority of Gray's story was true, it needed "a long chapter on Treblinka because the book required something strong for pulling in readers." Sereny pressed that Gray had "never been to, nor escaped from Treblinka," to which Gray "despairingly" responded, "But does it matter? Wasn't the only thing that Treblinka did happen, that it should be written about, and that some Jews should be shown to have been heroic?"[41] The answer is yes, it does, particularly where historians are concerned.

Benjamin Wilkomirski's completely fabricated memoir *Fragments: Memories of a Wartime Childhood* received worldwide acclaim and multiple awards, including the US National Jewish Book Award, the *Jewish Quarterly* Literary Prize in the UK, and France's *Prix de Mémoire de la Shoah*, all before it was proven to be false. As an apparent survivor, Wilkomirski participated in academic conferences, lectured on Holocaust testimony, and contributed the book's popularity for a fundraising tour to benefit the US Holocaust Memorial Museum.[42] However, journalist Daniel Ganzfried discovered that contrary to claims stated in the story, Wilkomirski was not a Jewish concentration camp survivor from Latvia, but a Christian, Swiss citizen named Bruno Dössekker who spent the war in relative comfort in his adoptive parents' home.

The most farfetched of the published false memoirs noted here is Misha Defonseca's 1997 ghost-written book *Misha: A Mémoire of the Holocaust Years*. The outlandish story describes a seven-year-old Belgian girl's search for deported family members across a 3,000-mile journey from Brussels to Ukraine and back. Along the way, Misha claimed to stab a Nazi to death, enter and escape the Warsaw Ghetto, travel on the underside of a moving train, and be cared for by a pack of wolves. The book was translated into 18 languages and became a European bestseller, but date discrepancies and dubious claims prompted an investigation. The documentation proved that Defonseca, whose real name was Monique DeWael, was not a Holocaust survivor or even Jewish, but, like Wilkomirski, a baptised Christian cared for by family.

Distorted truths are more damaging and wider reaching in the present due to widespread media access to television and the Internet. Oprah Winfrey hailed Herman Rosenblat's story as "the single greatest love story," in the show's history.[43] After the story's initial printing in a *New York Post* love story contest, it was featured in *Reader's Digest* and *Chicken Soup for the Couple's Soul*, before the couple appeared on *The Oprah Winfrey Show* twice. Hundreds of news articles followed, precipitating the publication contract and a movie deal. However, Rosenblat's *Angel at the Fence* was proven exaggerated after the former director of Jewish Studies at Michigan State University, Kenneth Waltzer, gave evidence of the chronicle's embellishment. Considering the deception, the publisher, Berkley Books, cancelled the release of *Angel at the Fence* before its 2009 debut. Even though Rosenblat did survive a Nazi concentration camp during World War II, the crux of the story was rooted in fiction. Rosenblat's media popularity in print and television brought false testimony in memoir literature to the foreground of popular debate.[44]

Each instance of falsified testimony evoked outrage. Jewish and Holocaust specialists agree that fictitious accounts, whether partial lies or complete fabrications, skew data and call into question the veracity and reliability of other survivors' remembrances. Emory University's Deborah E. Lipstadt emphatically declared that survivor memoirs

> do not need to be aggrandized or exaggerated to be made to sound any worse than they were. They also do not need to be rendered as joyful love stories that make us feel good about what happened. Both are insults to the survivors and inimical to the pursuit of historical truth.[45]

It is necessary to recognise these frauds as the exception to an exceedingly honest and trustworthy source of Holocaust information.

In the classroom, memoirs as a teaching medium make a highly effective resource. They are engaging, accessible, and compelling tools that authenticate the past; however, one US public school district has recently taken a stand regarding one of the iconic pieces of autobiographical Holocaust literature. Art Spiegelman's Pulitzer Prize-winning graphic memoir *Maus*[46] has come under fire as an inappropriate study source and was banned from a Tennessee school district's curriculum by a unanimous vote. The reason? The book was "too adult-oriented"—not for its depictions of ethnic violence but for foul language and inappropriate imagery. Discussions regarding images of hangings and the murder of children led board member Tony Allman to make the stand: "We don't need to enable or somewhat promote this stuff." In Allman's view, "it is not wise or healthy" to promote the imagery. History teacher Julie Goodin countered that "there is nothing pretty about the Holocaust ... and [Maus is] a great way to depict a horrific time in history" to the younger generations who were not even born to see the violence of 9/11.[47] The McMinn School Board fails to recognise that graphic imagery bombards children everywhere. Movies, television, novels, the news (the list is endless)—yet this particular use of "objectionable language" and imagery was targeted. The unanimous vote to remove the graphic memoir has sparked a nationwide debate in the news and social media about Critical Race Theory, censorship in schools, and Holocaust education in the classroom.[48]

Iconic Literature

There are several thousand published survivor accounts written by Jews, and many more written by others who experienced one of a multitude of aspects surrounding the events. All Holocaust memoirs improve the historical record with their publication, but there are a handful that are deemed "iconic" for their outstanding remembrances and contributions to the understanding of the Holocaust. Some have attained cult-like status, most are prize-winning works, and all are recognised for their merit in and out of academic spheres.

Among the quintessential memoirs, no list would be complete without the inclusion of perhaps the best known and widely read account of the Holocaust, *The Diary of a Young Girl*, by Anne Frank.[49] Frank's final published product has sold more than 30 million copies, in 70 languages, and is consistently used in high school curricula across the world. The personal story of a young girl in hiding with her family translates the Holocaust into more tangible insights into the Jewish experience, allowing readers to understand and connect with the information in a way that facts and statistics cannot. It has numerous versions in various literary formats, including five different editions of the diary, two graphic biographies, and five children's books. It has also been adapted into a Pulitzer Prize-winning play as well as numerous cinematic expressions, including seven documentaries, one BBC television series, and three films, one of which won multiple Academy Awards. *Time* named the memoir "One Hundred Best Young Adult Books of all Time" and bestowed the Honorary Award of the World's Children's Prize.

Critics widely consider Nobel Prize laureate Elie Wiesel's autobiographical text *Night* to be one of the most powerful written expressions of the Holocaust. The autobiography has sold an estimated ten million copies, translated into 30 languages, and become a standard text for Holocaust curricula in high schools and colleges worldwide.[50] *Night* is often paired as a "companion" or "antidote" to *The Diary of a Young Girl*. Oprah Winfrey added it to her book club list, asserting that *Night* "should be required reading for all humanity."[51]

Maus by Art Spiegelman is another of the memoirs with a cult-like following. The graphic memoir, which depicts Jews as mice and Nazis as cats, was released in 1986 and has been one of the most widely taught accounts of its type worldwide since then. It won a Pulitzer Prize in 1992 and was chosen by the *New York Times Book Review* as one of the top ten in the 100 most significant books of the last century. The US Holocaust Memorial Museum stated that *Maus* had, and continues to play, a "vital role" in the public's education about the Holocaust. Readers describe *Maus* as "the most compelling of any [Holocaust] depiction ... only the caricatured quality of comic art is equal to the seeming unreality of an experience beyond all reason."[52] In addition, it has been translated into 25 languages, sold millions of copies, and is credited with changing readers' perception of graphic novels from a child's entertainment to more adult, appreciable literature.

Widely praised as a literary masterpiece and the most powerful description of the Holocaust ever written, Primo Levi's 1948 memoir, *Survival in Auschwitz (If This Is a Man)*,[53] rose to international acclaim a decade after it was first released. Levi's biographer, Ian Thomson, eloquently stated: "No other work interrogates our recent moral history so incisively. For its quiet testimony of man's inhumanity to man, it remains one of the essential books of our age."[54] Like Wiesel's *Night*, Levi's work is one of the "classic" Holocaust texts that resonates through time, remaining a pertinent and powerful testimony of survival.

The last iconic memoir was named "one of the ten most influential books" in a 1991 survey by the Library of Congress and Book of the Month Club. Viktor E. Frankl's psychological memoir *Man's Search for Meaning*[55] has been recognised as "an enduring work of survival literature" by the *New York Times* and "one of the great books of our time" by Harold Kushner. Upon Frankl's death in 1997, *Man's Search for Meaning* had 73 reprintings, had been translated into more than 50 languages, and sold over 16 million copies. Like *Night, Maus,* and *Diary of a Young Girl*, Frankl's text is used in classrooms in high schools and universities to teach and understand the Holocaust.

Although memoirs are often classified as a narrative source with their fluidity of parameters, memoirists' observations provide powerful insights into the atrocities inflicted during the Holocaust. Nevertheless, as with all source material, memoirs must be approached critically. Understanding the benefits and pitfalls of such a valuable source is imperative to the literature's utilisation. The saying, "the death of one man is a tragedy, but the death of millions is a statistic," resonates in considering memoirs for Holocaust study—data points and statistics are words and numbers on a page. However, a first-hand chronicle of events provides the necessary context to understand the immensity of the Holocaust. Written testimony enhances the historical record with details unavailable in other documentation sources and corroborates or disproves other material. They can be selective and perhaps compromised by age, limiting their academic applications, but history would be massively impoverished without them.

Notes

1 The memoirs focused on in this chapter are stand-alone published narratives written or translated into English. This does not limit the historical significance of memoirs in anthologies, edited volumes, or those housed in unpublished, un-transcribed, or untranslated archives worldwide. This chapter focuses on first-generation memoirs almost exclusively, with the one exceptional example of *Maus* by Art Spiegelman. Second-generation memoirs are also important sources; however, most academics favor direct testimony to obtain the most accurate information.
2 K. Oatley, "Why Fiction May Be Twice as True as Fact: Fiction as Cognitive and Emotional Simulation," *Review of General Psychology*, 3:2, June 1999, pp. 101–17.
3 For scientific studies on brain activity during story consumption, see G.J. Stephens, L.J. Silbert, and U. Hasson, "Speaker-Listener Neural Coupling Underlies Successful Communication," *Proceedings of the National Academy of Science USA*, 107:32, 10 August 2010, pp. 1425–30; J. González et al., "Reading Cinnamon Activates Olfactory Brain Regions," *NeuroImage*, 32:2, 2006, pp. 906–12.

4 S. Felman and D. Laub, *Testimony: Crises of Witnessing in Literature, Psychoanalysis, and History*, New York: Routledge, 2013, p. 211.
5 Ibid.
6 Giorgio Agamben touches more on witnessing in *Remnants of Auschwitz: The Witness and the Archive*, Cambridge (MA): MIT Press, 1999.
7 O. Lengyel, *Five Chimneys*, Chicago: Academy Chicago, 1995 (first published, 1947), p. 27.
8 A. Rydell and H. Koch, *The Book Thieves: The Nazi Looting of Europe's Libraries and the Race to Return a Literary Inheritance*, New York: Viking, 2017, p. 196.
9 M. Mielnicki, *Bialystok to Birkenau: The Holocaust Journey of Michel Mielnicki*, Vancouver: Ronsdale Press, 2000; W. Szpilman and W. Hosenfeld, *The Pianist: The Extraordinary Story of One Man's Survival in Warsaw, 1939–1945*, New York: Picador, 1999; B. Gold, *The Life of Jews in Poland before the Holocaust: A Memoir*, Lincoln: University of Nebraska Press, 2007.
10 M. Goldenberg, "Lessons Learned from Gentle Heroism: Women's Holocaust Narratives," *The Annals of the American Academy of Political and Social Science*, 548:1, November 1996, pp. 78–93.
11 D. Magilow and L. Silverman, *Holocaust Representations in History: An Introduction*, New York: Bloomsbury Academic, 2015, p. 105.
12 M. Bernard-Donals, "Beyond the Question of Authenticity: Witness and Testimony in the Fragments Controversy," PMLA: Publications of the Modern Language Association of America, 116:5, October 2001, p. 1308. One of the more outspoken historians against the use of memoirs and other autobiographical sources is the French Holocaust historian Annette Wievorka. In her book *The Era of the Witness*, Ithaca: Cornell University Press, 2006, she vehemently protests the use of emotional first-hand accounts because it retards historians' efforts of analysing and giving contextual meaning to facts based on physical evidence.
13 T. Buergenthal, *A Lucky Child: A Memoir of Surviving Auschwitz as a Young Boy*, New York: Back Bay Books, 2015, p. 10.
14 K. Douglas, *Contesting Childhood: Autobiography, Trauma, and Memory*, New Brunswick: Rutgers University Press, 2010, p. 23.
15 For more information on collective memory, see F.C. Bartlett and W. Kintsch, *Remembering: A Study in Experimental and Social Psychology*, Cambridge: Cambridge University Press, 1995; N. Gedi and Y. Elam, "Collective Memory—What Is It?" *History and Memory*, 8:1, 1996, pp. 30–50; M. Halbwachs and L.A. Coser, *On Collective Memory*, Chicago: University of Chicago Press, 1992; J.V. Wertsch, "The Narrative Organization of Collective Memory," *Ethos*, 36:1, 2008, pp. 120–35; A. Confino, "Collective Memory and Cultural History: Problems of Method," *American Historical Review*, 102:5, 1997, pp. 1386–403.
16 A.D. Brown, N. Kouri, and W. Hirst, "Memory's Malleability: Its Role in Shaping Collective Memory and Social Identity," *Frontiers in Psychology*, 3, 2012, p. 257.
17 S. Mächler, *The Wilkomirski Affair: A Study in Biographical Truth*, New York: Schocken Books, 2001, p. 68.
18 Buergenthal, *A Lucky Child*, p. 10
19 F. Mauriac, Foreword, in E. Wiesel, *Night*, New York: Hill and Wang, p. i.
20 Wiesel, *Night*, p. 17.
21 Examples of Nazi memoirists with texts translated into English include those by Alfred Rosenberg, Rudolf Höss, Ernst von Weizsäcker, Adolf Eichmann, Melita Maschmann, and Albert Speer. It is important to note that while researchers do not learn much about the victims, those sources do give glimpses into how and why such atrocities were planned and executed. These sources also validate and verify limited archival documentation found elsewhere. See A. Rosenberg, *Memoirs of Alfred Rosenberg*, New York: Ziff-Davis, 1949; R. Höss and S. Paskuly, *Death Dealer: The Memoirs of the SS Kommandant at Auschwitz*, New York: Da Capo Press, 1996; E. von Weizsäcker, *Memoirs of Ernst Weizsäcker*, Chicago: Henry Regnery, 1951; M. Maschmann, *Account Rendered*, New York: Abelard-Schuman, 1965; A. Speer, *Inside the Third Reich*, London: Weidenfeld & Nicolson, 1995.
22 N. Seidman, "Elie Wiesel and the Scandal of Jewish Rage," *Jewish Social Studies*, 3:1, 1996, p. 6; E. Wiesel, *Un di velṭ hoṭ geshvign*, Buenos Aires: Tsenṭral-farband fun Poulishe Yidn in Argenṭina, 1956, p. 7.

23 E. Wiesel, *La Nuit*. Paris: Les Éditions de Minuit, 2007 p. 31 (original: "cette petite ville de Transylvanie où j'ai passé mon enfance").
24 Ibid., p. 199.
25 Cited in Seidman, "Elie Wiesel and the Scandal of Jewish Rage," p. 6 (emphasis mine).
26 For a more complete analysis on female sexual violence, see B. Chalmers, *Birth, Sex and Abuse: Women's Voices Under Nazi Rule*, Guildford (UK): Grosvenor House Publishing 2015; N. Ephgrave, "On Women's Bodies: Experiences of Dehumanization During the Holocaust," *Journal of Women's History*, 28:2, 2016, pp. 12–32; S.M. Hedgepeth and R.G. Saidel (ed.), *Sexual Violence against Jewish Women during the Holocaust*, Waltham (MA): Brandeis University Press, 2010; D.L. Bergen, "Sexual Violence in the Holocaust: Unique and Typical?" in D. Herzog (ed.), *Lessons and Legacies VII: The Holocaust in International Context*, Evanston (IL): Northwestern University Press, 2006, pp. 179–200; N. Shik, "Sexual Abuse of Jewish Women in Auschwitz-Birkenau," in D. Herzog (ed.), *Brutality and Desire: War and Sexuality in Europe's Twentieth Century*. Basingstoke: Palgrave Macmillan, 2009, pp. 221–47; and H.J. Sinnreich, "'And It Was Something We Didn't Talk about:' Rape of Jewish Women during the Holocaust," *Holocaust Studies: A Journal of Culture and History* 14:2, 2008, pp. 1–22.
27 J. Isaacson, *Seed of Sarah* (2nd ed.), Carbondale: University of Illinois Press, 1991, pp. 144–5.
28 For more on the silence of rape victims, see M. Nutkiewicz, "Shame, Guilt and Anguish in Holocaust Survivor Testimony," *Oral History Review*, 30:1, 2003, pp. 1–22. For an analysis of male sexual violence during war see, T.J. Curry, "Thinking Through the Silence: Theorizing the Rape of Jewish Males during the Holocaust Through Survivor Testimonies," *Holocaust Studies*, 27:4, 2021, pp. 447–72. For one of the few male memoirs with admissions to sexual abuses, see N. Leipciger, *The Weight of Freedom*. Toronto: Azrieli Foundation, 2015, pp. 91–4.
29 Höss and Paskuly, *Death Dealer*, p. 17.
30 C. Schaumann, "From weiter leben (1992) to Still Alive (2001): Ruth Klüger's Cultural Translation of Her 'German Book' for an American Audience," *German Quarterly*, 77:3, 2004, p. 336.
31 Klüger, *Still Alive: A Holocaust Girlhood Remembered*. New York: Feminist Press at the City University of New York, 2001, p. 210.
32 D. Mehegan, "Incredible Journey," *Boston Globe*, 31 October 2001.
33 P. Antze and M. Lambek (ed.), *Tense Past: Cultural Essays in Trauma and Memory*, New York: Routledge, 1996, p. vii.
34 See also Magilow and Silverman, *Holocaust Representations in History*.
35 K. Newman, "Book Publishing, Not Fact-Checking," *The Atlantic*, 3 September 2014, available online at https://www.theatlantic.com/entertainment/archive/2014/09/why-books-still-arent-fact-checked/378789/.
36 M. Gray and M. Gallo, *For Those I Loved*, Boston: Little, Brown, 1972.
37 H. Rosenblat, *Angel at the Fence*, New York: Berkley, 2009.
38 B. Wilkomirski and C.B. Janeway, *Fragments: Memories of a Wartime Childhood*, New York: Schocken Books, 1996.
39 M. Defonseca, *Misha: A Mémoire of the Holocaust Years*, Boston: Mt. Ivy Press, 1997.
40 For a more complete analysis of false memoirs, see J. Geller, "The Wilkomirski Case: 'Fragments' or Figments?" *American Imago*, 59:3, 2002, pp. 343–65; S. Mächler, *The Wilkomirski Affair: A Study in Biographical Truth*, New York: Schocken Books, 2001; S.R. Suleiman, "Problems of Memory and Factuality in Recent Holocaust Memoirs: Wilkomirski/Wiesel," *Poetics Today*, 21:3, 2000, pp. 543–59; and S. Vice, "Translating the Self: False Holocaust Testimony," *Translation and Literature* 23:2, 2014, pp. 197–209.
41 G. Sereny, "The Deceit of Those Who Whitewash Nazism," *New Statesman*, 2 November 1979, p. 673.
42 Magilow and Silverman, *Holocaust Representations in History*, p. 135.
43 Oprah, "Love Lessons," *Oprah*, 1 January 2006, available online at https://www.oprah.com/relationships/love-lessons-from-amazing-couples/all.
44 G. Sherman, "Ken Waltzer on Canceled Memoir: 'Where Were The Culture Makers'?" *New Republic*, 27 December 2008; G. Sherman, "The Greatest Love Story Ever Sold," *New Republic*, 25 December 2008; Newman, "Book Publishing, Not Fact-Checking."

45 D. Lipstadt, "Commentary: Holocaust Love Story an Insult to the Survivors," *CNN*, 31 December 2008, available online at http://www.cnn.com/2008/SHOWBIZ/books/12/31/lipstadt.holocaust/index.html.
46 I include *Maus* by Art Spiegelman as a memoir because it is a written factual record of memories told in two first person perspectives, Vladek (the father and Holocaust survivor) and Art (the son and second-generation survivor) Vladek's memories were recounted directly to Spiegelman. It has been declared a memoir by some historians and numerous literary institutions including the *Washington Post*, *The Times*, and Pantheon Publishing.
47 McMinn County Board of Education, "Board Statement," 2022, available online at https://www.mcminn.k12.tn.us/article/639918.
48 CNN, "'Maus'" author reacts to his book being pulled from curriculum, 27 January 2022, available online at https://www.cnn.com/videos/us/2022/01/27/maus-tennessee-school-board-art-spiegelman-newday-vpx.cnn; S. Kasakove, "The Fight Over 'Maus' Is Part of a Bigger Cultural Battle in Tennessee," *New York Times*, 4 March 2022; L. Clawson, "Tennessee School Board Tries to Defend Banning 'Maus.' It's Not a Success," *Daily Kos*, 28 January 2022.
49 I have included *The Diary of a Young Girl* by Anne Frank in my list of memoirs even though its original format was a diary. However, due to specific circumstances surrounding its composition, I have included it here as well. Diaries are written with the intention that they are a private recording of thoughts, and as such are unencumbered by edits or self-censorship. The published compilation that began as Anne Frank's diary went through multiple edits. She herself copied an edited version of her diary with the intention of its ultimate publication. After her death, Anne's father compiled a third version of the diary from her two originals, and it is this edited amalgamation that was published. For further information, see *The Complete Works of Anne Frank*, Anne Frank House, available online at https://www.annefrank.org/en/anne-frank/diary/complete-works-anne-frank/.
50 A. Lifson, "Elie Wiesel," *National Endowment for the Humanities*, n.d., available online at https://www.neh.gov/about/awards/national-humanities-medals/elie-wiesel.
51 E. Wyatt, "Oprah's Book Club Turns to Elie Wiesel," *New York Times*, 16 January 2006.
52 P. Buhle, "Of Mice and Menschen: Jewish Comics Come of Age," *Tikkun* 7:2, 1992, p. 6, available online at https://www.documentcloud.org/documents/2893148-7-2-9-16-Buhle.html.
53 P. Levi, *If This Is a Man*, New York: Orion Press, 1959.
54 I. Thomson, *Primo Levi: A Life*, New York: Metropolitan Books/Henry Holt, 2003, p. xii.
55 V.E. Frankl, *Man's Search for Meaning: An Introduction to Logotherapy* (4th ed.), Boston: Beacon Press, 1992.

5 A Thousand Unspoken Words: Reading Photographs of the Holocaust

Joshua Fortin

The Holocaust was the first genocide to be documented photographically on a large scale. The German answer to the so-called "Jewish Question" was documented in photographing nearly two million times from the perspective of perpetrators, victims, bystanders, and collaborators.[1] Many images, taken as evidence (though for different reasons) by both perpetrators and resisters, were destroyed or lost to history through accident or to cover up Nazi crimes. The photographs that survived were often hidden away by those who sought to preserve the truth in the face of atrocities otherwise designed to erase it. The Nazi obsession with documenting and cataloguing their racial superiority created a culture where collections like the Karl Höcker album, a collection of photographs believed to have been collected by SS officer Karl-Friedrich Höcker containing 116 images of the lives and living conditions of the officers and administrators at Auschwitz-Birkenau, and SS General Jürgen Stroop's report of the liquidation of the Warsaw ghetto, were normalised. Many of the images commonly associated with the Holocaust became publicised during the International Military Tribunal and the subsequent Nuremberg trials conducted by the US military. More have emerged in recent years as they are rediscovered or published before the memory and their owners have died.

In an era where truth is debated, denied, or vindicated as a matter of perspective, the fidelity of Holocaust media must continue to remain critically examined and researched while also being maintained and protected from misuse or misinformation. Holocaust denial is nothing new, even involving images which might otherwise be unquestioned.

One example of this relates to what became known as the Ivanhorod *Einsatzgruppen* photograph, an image showing a German soldier aiming a rifle at a woman who is trying to shield a child with her body in Ivanhorod, Ukraine, in 1942. In addition to the woman and her child, there are six other Jews also in the image, huddling from German soldiers. Despite being published 60 years before the era of Deep Fakes or Fake News, on 26 January 1962 a far-right German newspaper, the *Deutsche Soldaten Zeitung*, declared the photograph to be a fake created by Polish communists. Over the next three years, debates took place over the photo's veracity, before the claims of fabrication were finally debunked.[2] In 2018, a documentary from New Zealand filmmaker Peter Jackson, *They Shall Not Grow Old*, brought footage of the First World War to modern audiences by colourising and transforming images into vibrant moving video. Within four years, the technology used by Jackson's team to animate still images and provide voiceover and special effects could be located on mobile app stores. Currently, anyone with a smartphone can attempt to manipulate Holocaust

DOI: 10.4324/9781003248620-7

Reading Photographs of the Holocaust 59

Figure 5.1 Executions of Jews by German army mobile killing units (Einsatzgruppen) near Ivangorod Ukraine.

Source: https://commons.wikimedia.org/wiki/File:Einsatzgruppen_murder_Jews_in_Ivanhorod,_Ukraine,_1942.jpg.

images as they see fit. The security of Holocaust photography is therefore not in the originality of an image, but rather in discerning its sourcing and intent.

Defining Holocaust Photography

The need to define Holocaust photography may seem unnecessary, but an ever-expanding access to photographs, and the ease with which they can be used or mishandled, requires it. Put simply, Holocaust photography is just that, photographs of or on the topic of the Holocaust. They may be primary sources surreptitiously captured and secreted away for future use; alternatively, they can be secondary or even tertiary sources like Anton Kusters's *One Thousand and Seventy-Eight Blue Skies*, which captures the skies of the location of concentration camps. Taken between 2012 and 2017, they are not "photos of the Holocaust" but are Holocaust photography.[3]

Rather than being two separate categories, Holocaust photography encompasses the smaller, "photographs of the Holocaust." Therefore, to determine what Holocaust photography is, it might be easiest to explain what it is not. Much like determining whether a source is primary or secondary, historians determine how an image is understood from its context, construction, use, and intent. A photograph of the Holocaust is any photo taken that involves or relates directly to people, places, objects, or events of the Holocaust as one would with a documentary. The wider field of Holocaust photography includes these but is removed from the period and the events to which they are related to evoke the context or history of that moment.

Evidence of Collaboration

Most Holocaust photographs were created by and for the Nazis, most often under their direct supervision or on their orders. Not only are these images evidence of a culture of systematic dehumanisation and cruelty, but they also serve as moments of reality stolen by anyone and for anyone. In fact, many of the images of the Holocaust were created as keepsakes for those who perpetrated the crimes. These early records, whether official or informal (though authorised) were made to illustrate not only how Jews were dehumanised but also why. By capturing what was considered bizarre or lesser on film, the Nazis sought to create a visual guide and documentation to the genocide—a documentation that was never to be made public owing to the secrecy with which the Holocaust was perpetrated.

The most common of these images were collected systematically in the ghettos and concentration camps by Nazi officials, military propaganda companies, or those in their service. Regardless of the utility or aesthetic of each photograph, they served to reinforce the deluded notions of racial superiority which underpinned all Nazi ideology. Vulnerability, subjection, and complicity are continually juxtaposed alongside of violence and domination, either directly in the image or indirectly from the position of the photographer.

The Warsaw Ghetto was established by German decree on 12 October 1940. Prior to its creation, the Jewish quarter of Warsaw bustled with people and shops.[4] Within a month, the quarter was sealed behind ten-foot walls.[5] Among the earliest images from within the ghetto were those photographed by former hotel owner, and now a sergeant in the German army, Heinrich Jöst. On 19 September 1941—his birthday—he had a day off and decided to spend the day in the ghetto with his camera. He took 140 photographs of the Jews he encountered there. Walking in uniform with camera in hand, Jöst was greeted with a bow or hat removed by those he passed. His sightseeing led him to photograph the bodies of children dead or starving in the street, soldiers buying black market goods, and people pulling carts like beasts of burden.[6] His captions convey a postcard-like atmosphere but lament the "ragged' figures in the foreground. Jöst walked, unmolested, through a ghetto of nearly half a million Polish Jews confined to 2.4 square miles and took pictures like a man on safari. Shocked by what he had witnessed, he later locked the rolls of film away for the next several decades: his photos remained unpublished until the he neared his death in the 1980s.

His justification for taking and keeping the photographs was that prior to entering the ghetto, he had no idea what transpired there and that he entered the ghetto out of curiosity. He did not share his experience for fear of upsetting others.[7] Despite sharing his photographs with a journalist from *Stern* magazine, Günther Schwarberg, in 1982, the majority were not published until they were turned over to Yad Vashem in Jerusalem five years later. For researchers, the choice of a soldier to spend his birthday photographing the fragility of life and absoluteness of death inflicted upon those he was "sightseeing" must be considered. Cameras did not have automated features as do modern digital cameras. Colour, composition, focus, lighting all had to be carefully considered along with the cost of purchasing, storing, and developing film.[8] Not only did Jöst decide to photograph the horrors of the ghetto, but he also developed and saved his photos for decades afterwards. As none of his explanations point to the unusual nature of his actions, Jöst's photographs provide insight into how photographers were able to compartmentalise the impact of their actions on those being photographed. Though he might have been upset by what he saw, nonetheless his actions give insight into the unthinking, ruthless behaviour that supported the viewpoints of Aryan righteousness. The lack of empathy in the photos shows a collection not for evidence of crime, but to collect snippets of what, in his mind, would soon cease to exist.

Another German soldier who took photographs in the Warsaw Ghetto was Joe Heydecker, who, at the beginning of 1941, was transferred to Warsaw as a photo laboratory technician while in the German army. He twice entered the ghetto and began to take photographs of what he saw there. An anti-Nazi, the composition of Heydecker's photographs was more deliberate than that of Jöst and focused on the ghetto's desolation. He stated later that at no time did he take photographs as part of his official duties, and his empathy with the Jewish people was displayed through the images he captured. He was aware of the risk he was taking by taking unauthorised photographs in the ghetto—an activity which was forbidden—but he was determined to bear witness to what he saw.

Heydecker's wife and friends helped to conceal the photographs until the war was over, when they were used in evidence at Nuremberg. After this, he vowed to keep his photographs hidden until they could be shown to the world—but it took him 40 years before he could bring himself to publish the photographs, when he exhibited them in São Paulo, Brazil, in 1981. Seeing the Jews as individuals, for Heydecker there were no stereotypes: he was haunted by the knowledge that those he had met in Warsaw before the war were now being murdered in conditions of the most abject degradation. He was, in short, chronicling nothing less than the perpetration of the Holocaust, carried out before his very eyes.[9] Were these photographs a means of capturing evidence by a man who felt helplessness over his inability to stop the events around him? Were they a way of refusing his participation?[10] As one looks at these images, it is difficult to be certain as to whether Heydecker's photos were taken to record acts of evil or serve as acts of penance. It is apparent that he was torn by a sense of shame and helplessness, unable to do anything to help the unfortunate Jews living in the ghetto other than take photographs of them.

The Stroop Report is perhaps the most infamous collection of photographs of the Holocaust outside of camp liberation photos taken by the Allies in 1945. Intended to be a gift for Heinrich Himmler by SS General Jürgen Stroop, the report documents the Warsaw Ghetto Uprising and its subsequent liquidation after his arrival in 1943.[11] The original title, "The Jewish Quarter of Warsaw Is No More!" evokes a celebratory air reinforced by the painstaking craftsmanship accompanying the report as a presentation volume.[12] The intentions of the photographers are subject to the same estimation and conjecture as the those who took them, though it is clear that all were taken as a record of Nazi triumph over the Jewish resisters in the ghetto. The report was created to demonstrate Stroop's prowess as a commanding officer confronting the Jewish resisters—men, women, and children who were labelled (in German cursive writing) as "bandits."

62 Joshua Fortin

Figure 5.2 Stroop Report—Warsaw Ghetto Uprising 08.
Source: https://commons.wikimedia.org/wiki/File:Stroop_Report_-Warsaw_Ghetto_Uprising_08.jpg.

The image of one of the women resisters, Hasia Szylgold-Szpiro standing defiantly amid raised arms on Nowolipie Street, has been used ever since the report was made public as a symbol of defiance and resistance. It is essential to remember that each image was created during the Nazi process of ghetto obliteration. Why then, would Stroop (or his assistants) include an image with such wilful defiance in the report, especially when other photos exist of Hasia with her arms raised in surrender? The appearance of this "bandit," defiant yet detained, served Stroop's delusional message of superiority. Like many images captured by perpetrators of the Holocaust, the Stroop Report was designed to demonstrate the achievement of Nazi military objectives, namely, the ruthless suppression of the ghetto. Instead, the report was used as the evidence that secured Stroop's conviction and execution by the Warsaw Criminal District Court in 1951. The report's legacy was that it showed him at the very centre of the murderous action which condemned him.

One year later, Karl-Friedrich Höcker, adjutant to the commandant of Auschwitz, created his aforementioned album of 116 photos capturing the life of German soldiers at the SS resort Solahütte, located around 30-km south of Auschwitz. The album shows senior officers and SS *Helferinnen* (female administrative auxiliaries) engaging in relaxation and festivities in a holiday like atmosphere that completely omits any reference to the jobs from which they were resting. In one of the images, identification of the nearly 70 people singing along with an accordion is difficult but those at the foreground were also those responsible for the murder of nearly 420,000 Hungarian Jews: they include Otto Moll, head of the crematoria and burn pits; Rudolf Höss, the former commandant of Auschwitz who tested and formalised the use of gas chambers;

Figure 5.3 Nazi officers and female auxiliaries (Helferinnen) pose on a wooden bridge in Solahütte. The man on the right carries an accordion.

Source: https://commons.wikimedia.org/wiki/File:Photographie_prise_%C3%A0_Solah%C3%BCtte_en_juillet_1944_-_collections_USHMM_-_34585A.jpg].

Richard Baer, the commandant of Auschwitz at the time of the photo; Josef Kramer, who led the selection parades of new arrivals at Auschwitz II-Birkenau and was later commandant at Bergen-Belsen; Franz Hössler, who managed the camp kitchens and helped construct Solahütte; and Dr. Josef Mengele, the infamous "Angel of Death" who carried out hideous human medical experiments on Jewish women and children.[13] Despite these photos being taken as the German army was surrendering *en masse* to Allied forces, Höcker attempted to preserve the delusion that when not working the gas chambers, these men and women enjoyed themselves feasting on blueberries and singing camp songs.

Created simultaneously with Höcker's recreational album, the *Auschwitz Album* was not published until 1980. Instead of SS officers reclining in the company of women, these photos, captured by Ernst Hofmann and Bernhard Walter, showed the arrival of Hungarian Jews as they awaited the selection process for destruction or slave labour. Containing 193 photos over 56 pages, the album collates, without context, the nature of Jewish life and death under the SS.[14]

Much like Höcker's album, it avoids photos of the gas chambers or direct violence, preferring an antiseptic appearance of efficiency and superiority. It leaves the viewer with little doubt that this was the place where the Final Solution took place, and much like Stroop's report, the photographs serve as clear evidence which, while initially serving their desire to aggrandise their murderous aims, eventually consumed them as evidence for convictions.

The photos of Wilhelm Brasse provide an interesting look into the opportunity to use photos of the Holocaust against its perpetrators and the capacity for photography to aid in resistance activities. Brasse, of mixed Austrian-Polish background, was a professional photographer imprisoned at Auschwitz. Viewing himself as Polish rather than German, he refused to be drafted into the German army as an "ethnic German" (*Volksdeutsche*) and attempted to escape to Hungary from where he could move to France to join the Free Polish Army. Instead, he was captured and deported to Auschwitz.[15] During his five-year stay, he was assigned to the camp's *Erkennungdienst*, the identification department. Here, he photographed events in the camp and was ordered to take identity portraits for the inmates' files, totalling around 50,000 prisoners between 1940 and his liberation in 1945.

These photos were formulaic and designed by the SS to dehumanise prisoners by reducing their identity to the contents of the mugshots. Each series contained three signature shots: profile, direct portrait, and finally an angled shot with hat or shawl. Like a police line-up, each individual is made to look unremarkable. Those that were remarkable through physical ailment or perceived deformity garnered the attention of SS guards or Dr. Mengele. Most disturbing to Brasse were the photos of grisly experiments he was forced to document and develop in colour. During his time in the camp, Brasse maintained his morale by helping to reassure those he photographed, putting them at ease despite their intense vulnerability.[16] In his position as a non-Jewish prisoner who photographed the Holocaust on direct orders of the Nazis, he was also a resister by illicitly photographing people as they entered the gas chamber. In this way, he was responsible for preserving their memory in the face of certain destruction. As the Red Army approached, he and his assistant secreted photographs around the laboratory and sabotaged efforts to destroy negatives and proofs. By the time the survivors were marched out of Auschwitz, Brasse and his associates had managed to save a staggering 38,916 photographs.[17]

For scholars employing Holocaust photography, it is important to recognise that the overwhelming majority of images were created with the intent to emphasise Nazi superiority and domination as inevitable, justifiable, and replicable if followed meticulously. As such, photographs require the utmost care and critical assessment before being used. The fondness among some people for photos to appear as "moments in time" undercuts how many of these were staged, shaped, or even doctored to present a specific, often nefarious, message. Underlying messages of Jewish passivity, or overwhelming German superiority, can easily be transmitted if researchers do not take steps to question the photographer and his or her intentions in composing the photo. Many were taken deliberately for propaganda purposes to illustrate and reinforce Nazi law and ideology.

Evidence of Resistance

Photographs attesting to Holocaust resistance are far fewer in number, owing largely to the fact that Jews under German control or occupation were prohibited from owing cameras as early as 1936.[18] Such photos as do survive are different in their composition, often candid, and lacking the staging, structure, and clarity of other types. Instead, they offer much needed perspective to events otherwise dominated by a photographic record created by the perpetrators.

Reading Photographs of the Holocaust 65

Prior to the German invasion of Poland, the American Jewish Joint Distribution Committee (JDC) hired a Russian-born American photographer, Roman Vishniac, to travel through Eastern Europe and document Jewish poverty and relief efforts, thereby assisting JDC fundraising campaigns. From 1935 to 1939, he posed as a travelling fabric salesman, photographing some of the large Jewish communities which would soon be among the first places to face Nazi persecution. In addition to growing political antisemitism within Poland, Vishniac also had to carry over a hundred pounds of camera and developing equipment along his journey. Religious and social difficulties also limited his photos, as he faced difficulty from Orthodox Jews resistant to photography as it made "graven images" in contravention of religious law. Using a hidden camera and working under difficult circumstances that included evading local police—and, later, the Nazis—he took thousands of photographs. Before he finished the tour, he had been jailed 11 times and placed in an internment camp in Vichy France.[19] Only 2,000 of his 16,000 photos made it back to the United States with Vishniac in 1940. Most were hidden by sewing negatives into his clothing or secreting them with his family in France.[20] The candid nature of his photographs, coupled with the difficulty of record keeping under increasingly antisemitic scrutiny, mean that Vishniac's photos are often the only record of what he referred to as a "vanished world."

As a photographer tasked with capturing photos to raise financial support for the JDC, Vishniac focused predominantly on poor or pious Jews (frequently the same) living in squalid conditions. A major critique of his work is the possible staging or exaggeration of accounts to better to solicit donations for the JDC.[21] When compared to the meticulousness of the documentation of perpetrator photographs, it can be easy for critics to write off Roman Vishniac's work. Despite this, his actions show him as one who did his best with a resistance mission in mind. His photos capture the progression of antisemitism into genocide chronologically, geographically, and above all, graphically.

In like manner, photographs of the Lodz ghetto by Mendel Grosman and Arie Ben Menachem bear similarities to those of both Brasse and Vishniac. Employed by the ghetto's statistics department to make identification documents of the inhabitants, Grosman's task was to record those who believed their work ethic could stave off destruction. It is not these official photos that are the focus of Grosman's resistance, but rather the nearly 10,000 pictures taken from 1940 to 1944 that he and Arie Ben Menachem took illegally using their work camera hidden in the pockets of a long coat. In the four years he photographed, Grosman garnered support from those in the ghetto by making prints for the people he photographed. The industry of the Lodz ghetto meant greater access to materials and one workshop made him a lens to photograph from afar.[22] Despite this, he kept no prints for himself and hid his negatives in cans which were discovered by his sister, who found them after his death. Perhaps the most tragic of Grosman's photos is their loss during and after the Israeli War of Independence in 1948. What survives comes from the prints he distributed during his lifetime. Understandably, these are difficult to authenticate, source, and preserve. The composition of Grosman's photos are similar to those of Vishniac's later snapshots that show gritty, violent reality without time for lighting, focus, or angles. Despite, or perhaps because of this, Grosman's photos of Lodz show the progression of ghetto life under heavy Nazi repression.

The only known photos of the liquidation of the Warsaw Ghetto other than the Stroop Report were taken by Polish firefighter Leszek Grzywaczewski. In total, there are around a dozen or so, most taken from an upstairs window and showing rows of

66 *Joshua Fortin*

people being herded by soldiers.[23] Unlike Stroop's carefully curated photos, Grzywaczewski's capture unfocused images of crowds of deportees on Nowolipie and Zelasna Streets. The images are often blurred through movement, with oversaturated backgrounds making the scale of the dark huddled figures stand out in number rather than fine detail. Few details surround the decision of Grzywacczewski to take these photos. The method, means, and eventual publication to online sources are as undefined as the fate of the resistance member who took them.

Another notable resistance member, Faigel "Faye" Schulman, captured photographs during her time as a partisan fighting the Nazis in eastern Poland. When the Germans killed 1,850 Jews in the ghetto at Lenin, in the Pinsk region of Byelorussia, she was spared for her skills in photography learned from working in her brother's studio. Schulman was tasked with taking portraits and developing photos for Nazis as souvenirs. After learning of her parents' death when developing a photo of their mass grave, Schulman fled to the forest during a partisan raid. Joining a group of former Red Army POWs was risky, and Schulman was forced to conceal that she was Jewish due to the violent antisemitism of the men around her.[24] For two years, she served as a nurse for her partisan unit, despite her lack of training. During this time, she used the cover of a raid on the Lenin ghetto to recover her photographic equipment. When not performing battlefield first aid or wielding her rifle, she dug makeshift darkrooms in the forest floors to develop her photos. After each mission she would bury, and then recover, her camera equipment for preservation and recovery.[25] The endurance of Shulman's photography speaks to several points. First, she is the only known Jewish partisan photographer who served on active duty in Eastern Europe during the war. Second, her shots are composed to capture acts of resistance in a way few such photographs are capable. There is no trace of the perpetrator's myth of victimhood or the victims' acceptance of their destruction.[26] Instead, Schulman preserves the bravery and camaraderie of her fellow partisans while documenting the atrocities of those they fought.

Finally, mention must be made of the group known as the *Sonderkommando* photographs, a group of four blurred and indistinct photo taken clandestinely by prisoners at Auschwitz in August 1944. They were taken as a collective act of resistance involving the person smuggling the camera into the camp, the prisoner taking the pictures, those guarding him, and those who smuggled them out of the camp and into the hands of the Polish resistance. The singular purpose behind taking the photographs was to show the world what was happening at Auschwitz, bearing witness to the extermination of the Jews. These four photographs, taken under immense duress and fear of being found out, are the only photos depicting the process of mass killing at the gas chambers, and as a result they are immense importance as a record of the undeniable veracity of the Holocaust. They could not be properly framed or posed; the photographer had no time to aim the camera effectively, pressing the shutter and hoping to capture something. Two of the photos were taken from inside one of the gas chambers, and two from outside.[27]

Reading Photographs

When studying (or "reading") Holocaust photographs, the approach developed by the US Library of Congress (LOC) is instructive. The Library's five step program is as follows: Read the Photograph; Get to Know the Photographer; Consider how the Photos Were Made; Explore the Photographer's Era; and Interpret the Story.[28]

Reading Photographs of the Holocaust 67

Another approach, by Yad Vashem in Jerusalem, does not delineate steps, but rather offers a framework to consider how researchers can use Holocaust photography to teach, whether as propaganda or as documentation.[29] Here, we can model these practices for researching and utilising Holocaust photography through examination of a single case study.

Figure 5.4 Polish Jews captured by Germans during the suppression of the Warsaw Ghetto Uprising (Poland).

Source: https://commons.wikimedia.org/wiki/File:Stroop_Report_-_Warsaw_Ghetto_Uprising_06b.jpg#cite_note-6.

"A Jewish Boy Surrenders in Warsaw," or as it is more commonly referred to, "The Boy," is an iconic image produced in the Stroop Report embodying the elusiveness of photographs of the Holocaust. It is well documented, consisting of several verifiable individuals and the figure of a small boy whose identity is still openly debated among historians.[30]

The first step to reading a photograph effectively is determining how it has been encountered: did the researcher deliberately choose it, or was it stumbled across in an archive or database? Once this has been determined, a close examination of the photo, using magnification where possible, allows the viewer to observe and catalogue points of evidence. Commonly referred to as image tagging, the researcher should list or catalogue every identifiable person, object, and activity visible. This process should be done without assumption, and unidentified figures can be noted by physical attribution as in: "boy with arms raised in askew eight-panel cap."

Where physical copies are being examined, observation of framing or mounting should be considered as separate processes, as mounting and developing are not always simultaneous events. In the case of "The Boy," the black and white photo is adhered to a plan manilla sheet with the words "*Mit Gewalt aus Bunkern hervorgeholt*" ("forced out of bunkers"), written in German script. In pencil, the numbers 91 and 16 are written on the top.

In the picture, around two dozen faces can be seen with another three or four people being obscured behind others, visible by their feet or hands. The subjects of the photo are Polish Jews captured during the Warsaw Ghetto Uprising. Each is dressed in layered clothing with armbands and bags indicating the possibility of travel outside of the ghetto.[31] The soldiers in the photo are armed and in full uniform with a relaxed, almost methodical, demeanour. Each person is clearly aware of the photographer as their deportation is documented.

Identifying civilians and soldiers forms most historical inquiry for this photo. For example, in the lower left of the photo are two female figures, Matylda Lamet Goldfinger and her eight-year-old daughter Hania Lamet, who Yad Vashem was able to confirm were murdered at Majdanek around the same month this image was taken.[32] Following identification, sources regarding these individuals, or alternative photos from the Stroop Report showing rows of people bearing their possessions, can be used to build context surrounding the liquidation process in the ghetto.

The second step when reading a photograph requires the researcher to build context by getting to know the photographer. The existence of bias can be assessed through in-depth research using primary and secondary sources. For images that stand alone—where there are no alternative photos or context surrounding the people, date, or location—this second step can prove the most trying. While Stroop is credited as the author of the report, the photos are typically the work of *Propaganda Kompanie nr 689*, a unit of German military photographers who photographed the suppression of the uprising. In his trial Franz Konrad, a subordinate of Stroop, admitted that he took several of the photos in the report but did not confirm that he was the photographer of "The Boy."[33]

The increasing consumption of digital Holocaust media means that facial recognition and cross-referencing are becoming easier as technology improves. Within the Stroop Report there are certain individuals who reappear with sufficient frequency to determine some associations and context. In the surviving copies of the Stroop Report the Warsaw copy is published with an image of Stroop and his staff just below a picture of Askaris (local militia), whereas the copy in the US National Archives is only of Stroop and his staff.[34] Despite these differences, a researcher can use photos within the report to build some context using definitive information, in this case, by using the image of the Nazi officer Josef Bloch, facing the camera in the picture of "The Boy." When comparing all five images of Bloch found in the report, the research reveals new connections and new questions. In some pictures, he wears goggles on his helmet; in some, his boots are new; in others they are creased, worn, or covered in mud and ash.[35] One's first instinct might be to attribute these as evidence of chronology or staging. Did Bloch put on fresh boots for staged photos with other Nazis and then change into his "work boots" during the ghetto liquidation process? Questions like these cannot and should not be answered with certainty. Instead, the information should be acknowledged, though without speculation. If cross-referenced with testimonies and service records, a researcher could attempt to construct a chronology surrounding the events of the image and develop an understanding of why the events occurred and more importantly, why they were captured by the photographer.

The third step identified by the LOC for reading a photograph is to consider the process by which the photos were made. This includes identifying the camera, film, and developing medium used, as each indicates aspects and requirements of composition that went into producing the photo. The development process for many Holocaust photographs, however, is (and remains) unknown. More notable images are often kept by the US National Archives and Records Administration (NARA) or Poland's Institute of National Remembrance. As researchers are increasingly utilising digital archives, special care should be taken to determine the authenticity of the digitised artefact. For the most part, researchers will actually be examining a digital image of the original photo, which, nonetheless, should be subject to the same technical protocols as the original source (colour correction, filters, cropping, and so forth). In addition to these technical concerns, the context of the photographer's environment is essential. What were the time or income restrictions of the photographer? Was there a monetary incentive behind the photo? Or was it captured simply for art's sake?

In the case of "The Boy," the body of research surrounding it means not only is it catalogued in the United States and Poland, but there are details surrounding the materials used in its construction that are not found in digital archives. The Stroop report lists it as being printed on albumen paper but provides no reference for that information requiring the researcher to corroborate the information through their own research. The photo itself is not described meaning that the type of camera, film, and development are also unknown from the catalogue description. *Propaganda Kompanie nr 689* could have used any of Leica, Kodak, Ermanox, or even a personal camera to capture this image.[36] Consideration of the photographer's need to take the photo is also essential. The Warsaw Ghetto Uprising bloodied the nose of the SS in Warsaw and Stroop needed to demonstrate that rather than being caught by surprise, he was at the head of a successful and orderly liquidation process. To accomplish this, he utilised *Propagandakompanie nr 689*, which was not restricted by the ban on capturing images of atrocities issued by Otto Wöhler, Chief of Staff of the 11th Army, which clearly forbade such photographs.[37]

This to one side, having identified the surroundings and the person behind the lens, the researcher can move on to developing an understanding of the photographer and their relationship to the photo's audience. There is no certain reason why "The Boy" was taken and then reproduced in Stroop's report: within its own context, it could have been to highlight the people, their possessions, or to act as beacon of Nazi culture.

The LOC's fourth step of reading a photograph seeks to place the photographer's era into perspective. The world of Holocaust photographs often seems to exist in parallel, where everyday life clashes or merges with violent evil that polarise viewers and researchers into compassion for victims and anger at the perpetrators' inhumanity. This empathic reaction is a potential pitfall regarding the study of atrocity photographs. Explaining perpetrator actions to evil or madness limits the understanding of how these people perceived the world and were positioned or shaped into making their choices.[38]

A focused approach to how the period influenced the photographer, their audience, and the decision to capture the photo is crucial for developing the context of the events. "The Boy" doesn't seem to be staged as it lacks the linear organisation of people so favoured in German compositions. It is unclear under what pretence the photo was taken: if the photographer knew it was for Stroop's personal album or to serve as the cover for antisemitic propaganda magazines like *Der Stürmer*, which had previously used photos of the harassment of Jews by German soldiers for its cover.[39] The figures emerging from the shadows of their bunker display confusion and uncertainty rather than what would be anticipated if the photographer had staged or posed the subjects.

As developed by the LOC, the fifth step to reading a photograph is to interpret carefully the story uncovered throughout the process. The understanding developed over each step builds the narrative of families, drawn out of a bunker in the ghetto and bound for an unknown destination. Looking at the Stroop Report photos, the identification of individuals within families leads to possible bonds and understanding of lingering looks or furtive glances. The victims and survivors within "The Boy" do not appear anywhere else in the Stroop Report. Insight and connections must be gleaned from what information exists on the victims or survivors, or by studying the perpetrators in the photo. The prevalence of "The Boy" in Holocaust research means that there is a wealth of written information through photo collections (both organised and unorganised) that can be coaxed, often with the assistance of reference librarians or archivists, to provide enough context to create a final interpretation.

It is possible for a researcher to follow each step with fidelity and find little to no success in establishing a greater context for a photo being examined. Many Holocaust photographs are condemned to remain in the twilight of contextualisation. The very nature of the Nazi actions sought not only to eliminate the people they saw as inferior, but also those things that defined these people as nothing other than *Untermensch*, "subhuman."

Commemoration

The Holocaust was photographed by perpetrators, victims, and bystanders. All, essentially, did so to serve as proof—dreadful or evincing—of the events through which they lived. As most of the photography was performed by or for perpetrators, special care must be taken when using images for Holocaust commemoration. Despite the abundance of Holocaust photos, many did not garner public attention until they were used in trials or became part of the scholarly culture of Holocaust research. Further, as much primary source material and testimony requires translation from Yiddish, German, or Polish, early experiences with Holocaust photography in many Western countries can be through secondary or tertiary sources.

Acts of national remembrance often focus on the specific role of their respective citizens as much if not more than the events themselves.[40] Certain photos have ebbed and flowed with use or changing cultural perceptions of appropriateness. These same perceptions are also responsible for what is deemed iconic. Many American researchers, if asked to identify a photograph of the Holocaust, would point to images of prisoners in striped clothing before considering a Jewish child with his arms raised in uncertain surrender.[41]

Commemoration requires mindfulness to prevent voyeurism, misinformation, or the vindication of perpetrators. Most often, photographs are tasked to assist in transmitting the scope and scale of these atrocities, or to humanise the abstract acts into a self-reflective awareness. The underlying message of commemoration is the hope that by using photos to communicate the testimonies of victims and survivors, they will serve as pathways to further research and inquiry that will help prevent humanity from replicating these events. To accomplish this, several considerations must be addressed to ensure the intended and appropriate message is communicated.

The first such consideration should be the intended use of the photograph. Does it relate directly to the event in question, or is it simply to realise the abstract through shock—something to be avoided when possible—but if graphic images are to be used, they should be appropriately explained and consider the distress of the audience and presenters so as to not dehumanise the individual being photographed.[42] Overly repeated images can inure the audience to one's intention, but care should be taken to draw only from trusted sources utilising unaltered photos to maintain the entirety of the events when possible.[43] Finally, the desire to rewrite or personalise history in a new way should be avoided. Holocaust photos should never be recreated or altered except to enhance their collection and understanding—and the alteration should also be explained.

Conclusion: The Values and Limitations of Holocaust Photographs

The adage "a picture is worth a thousand words" is a popular example of the mythos that photographs capture. Like the fleeting dregs of a dream upon waking, they demand explanation or meaning. The use of Holocaust photography in the twenty-first century is largely for the purposes of education and inspiration. Each of these requires the user to understand the context of the photo, the intent with which it is being used, and the impact of their use on culture surrounding the Holocaust.

What is the purpose of looking at or studying Holocaust photography? Decades of study has organised nearly a dozen motives as to why Holocaust photographs were taken.[44] Do we rely on iconic images to shape our idea of the past, revealing or distorting, while allowing the unidentified or ineffable photos to gather dust in archives? Do we allow the mystery of an image to drive our curiosity into years of research, as with Holocaust scholar Wendy Lower's dive into *The Ravine* or Dan Porat's *The Boy*?[45] Can a single image unlock a truer understanding of the Holocaust eight decades after it began?

Cameras are not neutral, and the risks of using photographs without assessing the biases in their construction, as one would a monograph or diary, risk not only misinformation but the degradation of both the character of the individuals pictured and the belief in the reliability of the image. Photographs of perpetration can also end up glorifying the very perpetrators by furthering perceptions of acceptance, passivity, or simply otherisation of the victims.[46]

Historians are the guardians of collective memory. Memories are not static, each recollection risking altering the events or even recollections of the memory rather than the event itself.[47] Because memories of the Holocaust should not and cannot stop, we must accept that those memories, and histories, will continue to alter.[48] By continuing to bear witness, the world agrees to stop the atrocities from returning.[49] The ethics of historians, archivists, and librarians must then take responsibility for that which we have seen, that which we show, and that which we read to understand. When reading photos of the Holocaust, there can be no looking back.

Notes

1 M. Hirsch, "Surviving Images: Holocaust Photographs and the Work of Postmemory," *Yale Journal of Criticism*, 14:1, 2001, p. 8.
2 C. Liebowicz, "Preparing for a World of Holocaust Deepfakes," *Tablet*, 4 May 2021, available online at https://www.tabletmag.com/sections/news/articles/holocaust-denial-deepfakes-misinformation-claire-leibowicz.

3 A. Kusters, *One Thousand and Seventy-Eight Blue Skies*, Zürich, Lars Mueller, 2018.
4 In an otherwise huge literature, a good overview of Warsaw as a Jewish hub can be found in G. Dynner and F. Guesnet (ed.), *Warsaw, the Jewish Metropolis: Essays in Honor of the 75th Birthday of Professor Antony Polonsky*, Leiden: Brill, 2015; and W. Bartoszewski and A. Polonsky, *The Jews in Warsaw: A History*, Oxford: Blackwell, 1991.
5 On the Warsaw Ghetto generally, see I. Gutman, *The Jews of Warsaw, 1939–1943: Ghetto, Underground, Revolt*, Bloomington: Indiana University Press, 1982; and B. Engelking and J. Leociak, *The Warsaw Ghetto: A Guide to the Perished City*, New Haven: Yale University Press, 2009.
6 Przemysław Batorski, "A Walk in Hell. Photos by Heinrich Jost from the Warsaw Ghetto," Jewish Historical Institute, available online at https://www.jhi.pl/en/articles/a-walk-in-hell-photos-by-heinrich-jost-from-the-warsaw-ghetto,4296. See also G. Schwarberg, *In the Ghetto of Warsaw: Photographs by Heinrich Jost*, Göttingen: Steidl, 2001.
7 M. Killian, "A German Soldier Captures the Horror of the Warsaw Ghetto," *Chicago Tribune*, 11 September 1990, available online at https://www.chicagotribune.com/news/ct-xpm-1990-09-11-9003160157-story.html.
8 A suitable comparison of Jost's photos as compared to others taken in the ghetto around the same time demonstrate the skill and precision he applied to his photographs. A range of other photographs from the Warsaw Ghetto can be seen at https://encyclopedia.ushmm.org/content/en/gallery/warsaw-photographs.
9 See Heydecker's own account in J.J. Heydecker, *Where is Thy Brother Abel? Documentary Photographs of the Warsaw Ghetto*, São Paulo: Atlantis Livros, 1981.
10 S. Sontag, *On Photography*, New York: Farrar, Straus and Giroux, 1977, p. 177.
11 On Stroop, see K. Moczarski, *Conversations with an Executioner*, Englewood Cliffs (NJ): Prentice-Hall, 1981. The report itself has been published: see J. Stroop, *The Stroop Report: The Jewish Quarter of Warsaw Is No More!* New York: Pantheon Books, 1979.
12 Indeed, it was described by historian Robert E. Conot as "the finest example of ornate German craftsmanship, leather bound, profusely illustrated, typed on heavy bond paper." See R.E. Conot, *Justice at Nuremberg*, New York: Carroll & Graf, 1984, pp. 269–70.
13 https://auschwitz.net/en/the-hocker-album/.
14 This vital source has been published as *The Auschwitz Album: A Book Based upon an Album Discovered by a Concentration Camp Survivor, Lili Meier*, New York: Random House, 1981. The introductory text was written by New York journalist and author Peter Hellman. See also the treatment given the album by Yad Vashem, where the album now resides, available online at https://www.yadvashem.org/yv/en/exhibitions/album_auschwitz/index.asp.
15 An interesting account is an interview between British writer and photographer Janina Struk with Wilhelm Brasse in 2004. See J. Struk, "I Will Never Forget These Scenes" (interview with Wilhelm Brasse), *The Guardian*, 20 January 2005. A more detailed analysis of Holocaust photographs can be found in her *Photographing the Holocaust: Interpretations of the Evidence*, London: I.B. Tauris, 2004.
16 G.B. Griffin, "The Auschwitz Photographer," *Fourth Genre*, 10:1, 2008, pp. 67–8.
17 See "The Man who Captured Hell on Camera: He Was Spared Death at Auschwitz to Photograph Its Doomed Inmates and Risked His Life so the Nazis Couldn't Hide Their Atrocities," *Daily Mail*, 10 March 2021, available online at https://www.dailymail.co.uk/news/article-9344309/Wilhelm-Brasse-risked-life-Nazis-hide-atrocities.html. See also L. Crippa and M. Onnis, *The Auschwitz Photographer*, New York: Doubleday, 2021.
18 https://www.bl.uk/learning/histcitizen/voices/info/decrees/decrees.html.
19 See Roman Vishniac's own record of his efforts in R. Vishniac, *Polish Jews: A Pictorial Record*, New York: Schocken, 1976 (first published, 1947); and R. Vishniac, *A Vanished World*, New York: Farrar, Straus and Giroux, 1983.
20 https://magnes.berkeley.edu/news/vanished-no-more-giant-photography-roman-vishniac-finds-home-magnes/.
21 A. Newhouse, "A Closer Reading of Roman Vishniac," *New York Times Magazine*, 2 March 2010, available online at https://www.nytimes.com/2010/04/04/magazine/04shtetl-t.html.

22 M. Grossman, *With a Camera in the Ghetto*, New York: Schocken Books, 1977; L. Dobroszycki (ed.), *The Chronicle of the Lodz Ghetto 1941–44*, New Haven: Yale University Press, 1984.
23 J. Radzilowski, "Remembering the Ghetto Uprising at the U.S. Holocaust Museum," *The Historian*, 55:4, 1993, pp. 635–40.
24 F. Schulman, *A Partisan's Memoir: Woman of the Holocaust*, Toronto: Second Story Press, 1995, p. 104.
25 https://www.jewishpartisans.org/partisans/faye-schulman.
26 https://web.archive.org/web/20151208050945/http://www.ojmche.org/experience/pictures-of-resistance-the-wartime-photographs-of-jewish-partisan-faye-schulman.
27 G. Didi-Huberman, *Images in Spite of All: Four Photographs from Auschwitz*, Chicago: University of Chicago Press, 2008.
28 United States Library of Congress, *Every Photo Is a Story. Researching Photographs—Video Series and Exercises*, 8 July 2015, available online at https://www.loc.gov/rr/print/coll/fbj/Every_Photo_home.html.
29 F. Reiniger, *Teaching the Holocaust Using Photographs*, Yad Vashem, 19 April 2015, available online at https://www.yadvashem.org/education/educational-videos/video-toolbox/hevt-photographs.html.
30 D. Porat, *The Boy: A Holocaust Story*, New York: Hill and Wang, 2010.
31 D. Margolick, "Rockland Physician Thinks He Is the Boy in Holocaust Photo Taken in Warsaw," *New York Times*, 28 May 1982, p. 1.
32 The State Museum at Majdanek, *Kinderaktion, The Fate of the Jewish Children at Majdanek*, available online at https://www.majdanek.eu/en/news/kinderaktionen_the_fate_of_the_jewish_children_at_majdanek/1275.
33 K. Person, "The Adventures of a Stamp Collector in the Warsaw Ghetto: Franz Konrad's Story," *Holocaust Studies and Materials*, 3, 2013, pp. 293–309.
34 Office of the U.S. Chief of Counsel for the Prosecution of Axis Criminality. 5/2/1945-10/24/1946 File Unit: USA Exhibit 275, 1943–1946 R238: National Archives Collection of World War II War Crimes Records, 1933–1949, p. 121; Stroop, *The Stroop Report*, p. 228.
35 Compare images 89823, 89829, 89835b, and 89859, available online at https://catalog.archives.gov/id/6003996.
36 S. Linfield, *The Cruel Radiance: Photography and Political Violence*, Chicago: University of Chicago Press, 2012, p. 67.
37 C. Busch, "Bonding Images: Photography and Film as Acts of Perpetration," *Genocide Studies and Prevention*, 12:2, 2018, p. 72.
38 Ibid., pp. 54–83.
39 On *Der Stürmer*, see especially R.L. Bytwerk, *Julius Streicher*, New York: Cooper Square, 2001; and D.E. Showalter, *Little Man, What Now? Der Stürmer in the Weimar Republic*, Hamden (CT): Archon Books, 1982.
40 As an example, see the statement from United States Secretary of State Antony J. Blinken on the occasion of Yom Hashoah in 2022: A.J. Blinken, *Commemorating the Day of Holocaust Remembrance*. Press Statement, April 28, 2022, available online at https://www.state.gov/commemorating-the-day-of-holocaust-remembrance/.
41 P. Carrier, E. Fuchs, and T. Messinger, *The International Status of Education about the Holocaust, A Global Mapping of Textbooks and Curricula*, Paris: UNESCO, 2015, p. 153.
42 Historian Sybil Milton provides four clear questions to ask about every photo; S. Milton, "The Camera as a Weapon: Documentary Photography in the Holocaust," *Simon Wiesenthal Center Annual*, 1, 1984, pp. 45–68.
43 Holocaust Memorial Day Trust, *Guidance on How to Use Images*, available online at https://www.hmd.org.uk/resource/guidance-on-how-to-use-images/.
44 Busch, "Bonding Images: Photography and Film as Acts of Perpetration," pp. 72–4.
45 "Wendy Lower and Paul Salmons Discuss 'The Ravine,'" Museum of Jewish Heritage, 28 April 2021, available online at https://mjhnyc.org/blog/the-ravine-book-talk-with-wendy-lower-and-paul-salmons/; Dan Porat, *"The Boy,"* Lecture at the University of Illinois, 28 October 2010, available online at https://www.c-span.org/video/?296933-1/the-boy-holocaust-story. See also Porat, *The Boy: A Holocaust Story*, and W. Lower, *The Ravine: A Family, a Photograph, a Holocaust Massacre Revealed*, London: Head of Zeus, 2021.

46 Busch, "Bonding Images: Photography and Film as Acts of Perpetration," p. 79.
47 M. Paul, "Your Memory Is Like the Telephone Game," *Northwestern Now*, 19 September 2012.
48 S.A. Crane, "Choosing Not to Look: Representation, Repatriation, and Holocaust Atrocity Photography," *History and Theory*, 47, October 2008, pp. 309–30.
49 B. Zelizer, *Remembering to Forget: Holocaust Memory through the Camera's Eye*, Chicago: University of Chicago Press, 1998, p. 212.

Part II
The Public Domain

6 Considering Nazi Propaganda as a Source for Studying the Holocaust

Paul R. Bartrop

Defining Propaganda

Propaganda is an organised or deliberate action or set of actions undertaken for the purpose of disseminating a doctrine and ensuring its acceptance. Where the Holocaust was concerned, what can be termed "hate propaganda" played an important role in alienating the target population (the Jews) from those who were its persecutors (the Nazis); in providing reasons to the general population for the "necessary" persecution of the Jewish target population; in suggesting the means such persecution should employ; and in serving as a reinforcement to the Nazi government as it was undertaking and directing the persecution. For the most part, this propaganda was disseminated through the major media arms, particularly radio, the print media (of all kinds), posters, and films—as well as through word of mouth and public speeches.[1]

The central ambition of a propagandist is to persuade others to share his or her view about the target group; as a result, simplified messages shorn of any possibility of debate or further discussion are the preferred device for convincing the greatest number of people as to the veracity of the propagandist's claims. In Nazi Germany, the entire SS state apparatus was employed against all of Nazism's enemies, but most importantly—and incessantly—the Jews.

When studying the Holocaust, how can propaganda be identified? This is a crucial question for anyone seeking to understand how the Nazi state communicated its policies and dominated society, for without the necessary tools it might be difficult to discern truth from ideological dogma.

A variety of instruments have been identified to describe propaganda techniques, and an extensive literature describing and discussing propaganda exists.[2] In the Nazi case, identifying propaganda can be reduced to five key elements: (1) name calling, in which a negative epithet is connected to a living person or group, weakening their legitimacy and reducing them to something of lesser value; (2) generalisations that superficially sound impressive but have little real meaning; (3) simple, short messages, directed towards an audience that will identify with the source of origin regardless of its class or educational origin; (4) generating a cause that seems so attractive that those standing outside of it will be alienated and rendered as "other"; (5) the creation of a clear choice between two absolutes, so that those choosing the "wrong" alternative will be transformed into an "enemy."

These and other propaganda techniques were employed by the Nazis when trying to manipulate society's values and belief systems. They have been employed as control devices, albeit in different ways, since time immemorial by many regimes, and

DOI: 10.4324/9781003248620-9

although the Nazis were by no means the first to use propaganda to attain their objectives, it was the way they went about it that was new, indeed, revolutionary.

The Place of Propaganda in the Third Reich

Propaganda saw the use of various means of communication to promote the Nazis' ideological agenda. This included the use of books, newspapers, art, cultural events, theatre, films, radio, and even television, then in its earliest stages of development.[3] In this context, the government was the primary purveyor of propaganda, though business, industry, education, and the military also provided necessary elements of the active process of indoctrination.

These devices and agencies were almost always manipulative and deceitful. Even before the beginning of the Nazi period in 1933, propaganda was employed to present the so-called "evils" of Jewry to the German public, and this later extended to anyone else exposed to Nazism in the occupied, neutral, and Allied countries. Seen in this light, propaganda was far from independent of the violence it encouraged. Indeed, it was an instrumental element of Nazism's destructive anti-Jewish violence.

That said, it is important to note that Third Reich propaganda was not only confined to antisemitism, though this was usually its most powerful manifestation. Nazi propaganda predated Hitler's ascent to office in several ways: through denouncing the 1919 Treaty of Versailles; through getting Hitler elected freely (which never happened); through establishing the Nazi state by taking over every aspect of social, economic, and cultural life; and then, during the years from 1939, through justifying and prosecuting war and destruction of those deemed to be "the other."[4]

These messages were in a vast number of cases also subliminal attacks on Jews. Hence, the deceitful lie that Germany's surrender in November 1918 was brought about by a "stab-in-the-back" (*Dolchstoss*) by left-wing politicians (read, Jewish) at home, who betrayed the army; the subsequent Treaty of Versailles (28 June 1919) was orchestrated by Britain, France, and the United States, behind which was the hidden force of "world Jewry"; the Russian Revolution and communism were part of a larger "Judeo-Bolshevik" conspiracy to take over the world; the war of 1939 was being prosecuted by Jewish interests in the Allied countries seeking to crush Germany and enslave the German people; and so on. Even where Jews did not feature in Nazi propaganda, they were ever-present.

Propaganda played a huge role in conditioning the German people to accept Nazi ideology and submit to the regime's dictates. It was insidious and ubiquitous: while emphasising the wonders of the Nazi regime and reinforcing Germany's greatness at every turn, it did so through contrasting these with dark and destructive forces. Often without direct reference, the Jews were at the core of such contrasts.

Managing Propaganda

Knowing something about propaganda is one thing, but it is also necessary to understand something about those who oversee and direct it. The Nazi regime possessed an army of writers, artists, directors, actors, and announcers—but it was really the managers of the propaganda edifice who charted its course, gave it inspiration, and ensured that the needs of the dictatorship were met. In this regard, two names stood out: Joseph Goebbels, Reich Minister of Public Enlightenment and Propaganda[5]; and Otto Dietrich, Reich Press Chief, and State Secretary within Goebbels's department.[6]

Serving the Nazi government across its full duration from 1933 to 1945, Goebbels ran all aspects of the regime's propaganda efforts. His ministry used modern media, including film, radio, and the press, to create a cult around Hitler and spread the Nazi message abroad. Goebbels organized the notorious Nuremberg party rallies that began in 1929 and was also the impetus behind the *Kristallnacht* pogrom of 9–10 November 1938, during which Jewish businesses and synagogues were destroyed and thousands of Jews were sent to concentration camps. He was known for his deep, virulent antisemitism, and remained dedicated to Hitler even after the war turned against Germany.

His sharp intelligence, gift of oratory, flair for theatrical effects, reckless pragmatism, and revolutionary dogma flourished in service to the party, his ministry using all forms of modern media to create a cult around Hitler and spread Nazi ideas widely outside Germany.[7]

On 1 May 1933, Goebbels organised a massive parade on what was designated the Day of National Labour, an event that marked the end of the German trade union movement. After that, on 10 May 1933, he supervised the burning of 20,000 books by Jewish and anti-Nazi authors. He then started a program of controlling all cultural aspects of German life, including art, music, literature, and mass media. Before long, the content of all of Germany's newspapers, books, novels, plays, and films was subjected to the ministry's control. Its large budget enabled Goebbels to bribe artists to cooperate with Nazi Party policies and threaten with violence those who did not. Strategically he envisaged that by controlling all forms of German culture he could bring about a spiritual mobilisation of the German people.

Goebbels used modern marketing ideas within the political realm, bringing eye-catching slogans and psychology into political advertising. His propaganda posters included bright red ink and a large typeface for attention grabbing headlines, and his innumerable rallies generated immense support for the regime as well as instilling fear among the Jewish population.

Adapting modern media for propaganda purposes, he made sure that every German should hear Hitler's words: as a result, he organised the production and sale of a cheap radio set known as a *Volksempfänger* ("People's Receiver") which cost only 76 marks. A smaller version was also made costing just 35 marks.[8] Loudspeakers were also put up in streets so that people could not avoid the Führer's words. Cafes and bars were ordered to broadcast Hitler's public speeches.

Otto Dietrich, who served as Nazi Press Chief and was an intimate of Adolf Hitler, became a member of the Nazi Party in 1929. On 1 August 1931, he was appointed Press Chief of the National Socialist Party, and on 1 November 1933 was named Vice President of the Reich Press Chamber (*Reichspressekammer*) until, on 28 February 1934, Hitler appointed him Reich Press Chief within the Nazi Party. In March 1936, he was elected to the Reichstag, becoming government Press Chief and a State Secretary in the Reich Ministry of Public Enlightenment and Propaganda on 26 November 1937.

Dietrich's relationship with Hitler resulted in him directing all the editorial work of the party and ensuring that every press publication issued in Hitler's name was cleared by Dietrich first. In this sense, Dietrich controlled all news—not only the newspaper press but also Nazi party publications relating to, and disseminated from, party agencies such as the SS and the Hitler Youth.

Dietrich's responsibilities as Press Chief often overlapped—and competed—with Goebbels's role as Propaganda Minister. Accounts of their demarcation disputes are many, with each appealing to the ultimate authority—Hitler—when one or the other was deemed to have overstepped their brief. Here, Dietrich was frequently supported, much to Goebbels's chagrin, by Hitler himself. As the main conduit between Hitler and the press, Dietrich not only summarised all press items that came to the Führer, but drafted and redrafted Hitler's speeches for publication. Through this close contact, Dietrich was one of Hitler's chief confidants almost to the end of the war in 1945.

Between them, Goebbels and Dietrich constructed and oversaw an imposing propaganda edifice that not only crushed all opposition but also deprived oxygen to any but approved media outlets. Can a researcher glean any understanding of the Holocaust through the lives of these two men? Considering how they were able to put their specific principles into action, the answer is yes, much. Both were early members of the Nazi Party (Goebbels joined in 1924 and Dietrich in 1929), and both attained an increasing measure of influence and authority within the party both before and after the Nazi accession to office. Moreover, each was a committed antisemite whose Jew-hatred intensified with each passing year. By looking at the motivations of the men in their respective high positions, we can ascertain something of where they thought their ideas should be taken, and how their goals were to be achieved. These ambitions would not only lead to the Holocaust but also play a crucial role in shaping it.

Film and Radio: Managing What Germans Saw and Heard

Nazism's use of modern technology saw Hitler and Goebbels embrace cinema, seeing it as an ideal vehicle for spreading propaganda. This intensified after the introduction of sound and spoken dialogue in the late 1920s so that by the time Hitler took office in 1933 a dynamic German film industry fed the ambitions of the nascent SS state.[9]

Goebbels held that cinema emphasising positive messages about the government and the nation was both entertaining and made for effective propaganda. Thus, at a time of economic distress and uncertainty about the future, he considered that the main goal of films under the Nazis should be to promote a happy, smiling population untroubled by the world outside. Nevertheless, the sugar-coated messages they saw should always ensure that there could be no doubt as to who the protagonists and antagonists were. Thus, much of the tightly controlled national film industry consisted of films based around light entertainment, with veiled propaganda messages included throughout.[10]

In this highly controlled environment, there were some films whose messages were more obvious than others. *Hitlerjunge Quex*, made as early as 1933, told the story of a German boy brought up in a communist family, who broke away from his background, joined the Hitler Youth, and was murdered by communists for doing so. Its clear message, particularly for young viewers, showed an older generation at odds with the vibrancy and progressive outlook promised by Nazism.

Arguably the most famous Nazi movie to employ antisemitic images was *Jud Süss*, directed by Veit Harlan in 1940.[11] Based on a novel written in Germany by Jewish author Lion Feuchtwanger in 1925, it chronicled the story of a powerful ghetto businessman, Oppenheimer, who believes himself to be a Jew. His ruthless business practices result in the betrayal of an innocent girl; for this, he is arrested and sentenced to death, the victim of anti-Jewish laws. Rather than turn against the Jews of the ghetto by declaring his non-Jewish identity, which he discovers through a set of letters given to him by his mother revealing that his father was in fact a Christian nobleman, he dies on the gallows with dignity and honour. Feuchtwanger intended the book to be an attack against antisemitism, an allegory on German society for his own day.[12]

In the Nazi film version, however, the story was transformed into a viciously antisemitic movie starring Ferdinand Marian in the title role. The plot was twisted to show Oppenheimer as a real (not imagined) Jew, and portrayed according to Nazi stereotypes: greasy hair, hooked nose, unscrupulous, bearded, cowardly, and a rapist. At his arrest and execution, he is seen as screaming and "unmanly"; by contrast, his executioners appear to be upright, solid citizens. After Oppenheimer's execution, the Jews of the city are driven into exile.

As a piece of propaganda cinema, the movie had a powerful effect on its audiences, conditioning the German public for further atrocities against Jews. Many viewed it as though it was a documentary and were driven to acts of violence against Jews in the street after having seen it. Heinrich Himmler, the head of the SS, ordered all members of the various organisations under his command to see the movie; this extended to local police and concentration camp guards. In this way, its effectiveness as a propaganda tool was thus limited to the public, as the film was used to motivate the police and guards to achieve specific dehumanising goals regarding the perceived racial enemy, encouraging violence against that enemy.

Other Nazi films, frequently under the control of well-known director Fritz Hippler, portrayed Jews as "subhuman" creatures infiltrating Aryan society. Hippler ran the film department within the Propaganda Ministry, with responsibility for deciding which foreign films would be allowed on German screens, and what parts would be cut. In addition, he also produced and directed movies. In 1940, he directed *Der Feldzug in Poland* (*The Campaign in Poland*), a propaganda film demonstrating the superiority of German arms in the first phase of the Second World War.

His most famous—indeed, infamous—creative work was undoubtedly another feature-length film from 1940, *Der Ewige Jude* (*The Eternal Jew*), arguably one of the most offensive antisemitic propaganda movies ever made.[13] The film consisted of documentary material combined with footage taken shortly after the Nazi occupation of Poland. Hippler filmed in the Jewish ghettos of Lodz, Warsaw, Krakow, and Lublin, the only such footage shot specifically for the movie. The rest consisted of stills and archival footage from other feature films—footage that was presented as if it was additional documentary film. *Der Ewige Jude* itself covered four essential tropes: "degenerate" Jewish life as seen in the Polish ghettos; the nature of Jewish political, cultural, and social values; Jewish religious ceremonies, teachings, worship, and ritual slaughter; and Adolf Hitler as the saviour of Germany. Jews were portrayed as wandering cultural parasites, the film comparing them to rats spreading disease, or subhumans consumed by sex and money.

While the intention of the film was to prepare the German population for the cleansing of Jews from the German population (though the Nazis had not themselves yet decided on mass annihilation as the means to destroy Europe's Jews), the movie failed to have the desired impact on the German public because *Jud Süss* had already appeared to rapturous acclaim employing top box office stars and building on captivating period drama. By contrast, *Der Ewige Jude* was a documentary based on limited original footage, still images, and archival film clips. Unlike *Jud Süss*, therefore, which was a great commercial success, *Der Ewige Jude* was a failure at the box office. As a propaganda film, it was shown more for training purposes to troops on the

Eastern Front and SS members, though a few foreign language voiceovers were made, and the film was exported to countries occupied by Germany.

Under the Nazi regime, Leni Riefenstahl, an accomplished dancer, actress, and photographer, became an innovator in the art of cinematography with the powerful and technically cutting-edge propaganda films she directed serving as her greatest professional and artistic achievements.[14] The film for which she is best known, *Triumph des Willens* (*Triumph of the Will*), released in 1935, chronicled the Nazi Party Congress held at Nuremberg in 1934. The film focused on Germany's seemingly invincible military strength, the almost reverential devotion of the German people to their Führer, and what was shown as the compelling nature of Hitler's charismatic leadership. Riefenstahl's unique use of cameras, including aerial photography, together with her overall directing skills, gave the film such power that it is considered today to be one of the most effective propaganda films ever made.

Riefenstahl directed another propaganda film also regarded as one of the best of its kind. Released in 1938, *Olympia* is a documentary of the 1936 Olympics in Germany. The cinematographic innovations it included—for example, slow motion footage—were ground-breaking at the time, and *Olympia*, like *Triumph of the Will,* was greeted with acclaim.

Contrasting the mass appeal of cinema, radio was a major disseminator of Nazi propaganda, reaching into German homes throughout the Reich. Indeed, radio, together with newspapers, provided most solid news and information to the German people, even though what they heard was biased, tightly controlled, and always delivered with a specific agenda. The radio network, in turn, relied on the information it received from its various sources (both in and outside Germany), which were, of course, under the control of Dietrich's Press Office. In this way, the German people heard only what the regime wanted them to hear—while at the same time believing that what they were hearing was true and accurate. The lack of any alternatives, moreover, only served to stifle the possibility of alternative views or information.

This played out most clearly during the war years after 1939, though by now the anti-Jewish message was so ingrained after incessant broadcasts about the Jews that radio messages dealing with Jewish perfidy and the like were to a large degree unnecessary other than for purposes of reinforcement. Where antisemitic radio broadcasting during the war was concerned, however, it found its best expression in messages directed towards Allied troops.[15]

William Joyce, American-born but raised in Ireland, was the most prominent non-German Nazi propaganda broadcaster during the Second World War, filing stories beamed into the United Kingdom and British troops serving in Europe and North Africa. Nicknamed "Lord Haw-Haw" throughout the English-speaking world because of his fake upper-class English accent, his main interest was in spreading defeatist messages that could sap Allied morale.[16]

Joyce and other dissatisfied British men were not the only non-German broadcasters spewing propaganda through the airwaves during the war. Famously, an American, Mildred Gillars, was also employed in Germany to disseminate Axis propaganda.[17] Nicknamed "Axis Sally," she was known for her addresses to US troops especially, working to weaken morale with stories of their wives and sweethearts back home. Joyce and Gillars, and many others less well known, used the radio to spread messages intended to undermine the Allied war effort, and their words were often punctuated with antisemitic tropes. Their effectiveness could be measured, however, by the virulence of the derision they faced from troops and civilians alike in Britain and the United States.

What Did Germans Read?

Germans were confronted by the written word wherever they went, no more so than when they were expected to show awareness of Hitler's philosophy and vision for Germany as laid out in his book *Mein Kampf* (*My Struggle*). While antisemitic rhetoric proliferated throughout Germany, it was the spread of this book that made it a major propaganda vehicle. By the end of 1933, more than 1.5 million copies had been sold, and after 1934 it was required reading in schools. From 1936, every couple married in accordance with Nazi state requirements received a copy to place in a prominent position in their home. Millions were sold by 1945, rendering Hitler a wealthy author. Hitler's messages about the universal centrality of race, of a hierarchy of superior and inferior races, and of the need to preserve Aryan purity, were central to his vision. Throughout *Mein Kampf*, he emphasised that it was the primary responsibility of the German people and state to ensure racial continuity. Put simply, *Mein Kampf* was a major racist and antisemitic propaganda piece, distributed widely for this purpose (and, along the way, making Hitler very wealthy).

It was reinforced, moreover, in the daily newspapers, especially, the *Völkischer Beobachter* (*People's Observer*).[18] Originally known as the *Münchener Beobachter*, a paper with antisemitic roots, in August 1919 it was renamed *Völkischer Beobachter*, and by 1920 it had been acquired by the German Workers' Party, the forerunner of the Nazi Party. It became the party's primary official organ reporting not only news but also Nazi Party activities. As such, it was one of Nazism's key propaganda instruments, with frequent articles from Joseph Goebbels decrying Jews within Germany and in other parts of the world.

Goebbels's own creation, *Der Angriff* (*The Attack*), was founded in 1927 in Berlin. It was conceived as a mass circulation paper opposed to the democratic Weimar government and the Jews who were alleged to support it. Its pugnacious and aggressive language was filled with party propaganda, and the paper did much to attract support for the party prior to elections. Goebbels wrote much of the copy in its early days, but others followed his lead. Projecting itself as a paper for the workers, its banner sported the slogan "For the oppressed against the exploiters" (*Für die Unterdrückten gegen die Ausbeuter*). Circulation began to decline after Hitler was appointed Chancellor, though it was propped up by party members in certain districts where it was a compulsory purchase.

By far the most rabidly antisemitic newspaper, published weekly between 1923 and 1945, was the tabloid *Der Stürmer* (*The Stormer*). Under the direction of Julius Streicher, *Der Stürmer* was aimed chiefly at Germany's lower and working classes.[19] Its content was invariably simplistic, one-sided, and overtly antisemitic. The paper took as its motto *"Die Juden Sind unser Unglück!"* ("The Jews are Our Misfortune!"). Some senior members of the Nazi Party were clearly embarrassed by the tabloid's content and appeal and tried to distance themselves from it, but others, including Heinrich Himmler, head of the SS, endorsed it completely. Adolf Hitler acknowledged the primitive nature of the publication but nevertheless saw it as an effective propaganda tool aimed especially at the lower and uneducated classes.

Der Stürmer emphasised the worst caricatures and stereotypes of Jews, alleging Jewish sexual depravity, purported Jewish aims to make a fortune at others' expense, and a Jewish propensity to be pro-communist. More damaging still were repeated charges that Jews had been responsible for the death of Jesus and were engaged in rituals that sacrificed the lives of non-Jewish children for the expiation of Jewish sins.

A major feature of *Der Stürmer* involved viciously grotesque cartoons and caricatures of Jews. Streicher's stated aim was to "educate" Germans on how to spot a Jew, with cartoons featuring hideous figures of Jews showing unkempt, overweight characters with prominent noses and thick lips. He also supplied plenty of details to "substantiate" his lurid and wildly inaccurate stories, printing the names of Jews who had supposedly committed various crimes, including rape, incest, and child abuse. *Der Stürmer*'s circulation grew enormously after Hitler came to power, from 25,000 copies per week in 1933 to nearly 500,000 copies per week by 1938.

As sources for studying the Holocaust, both *Der Stürmer* and Julius Streicher himself provide rich material. Immediately after his military service in the First World War, he became involved in radical, right-wing politics, soon founding the Nuremberg chapter of what was then known as the German Socialist Party, an entity that was not socialist but instead fiercely antisemitic, anti-Catholic, and nationalistic. Streicher arranged a merger of his party with Adolf Hitler's National Socialist German Workers' Party in 1922, making him one of Hitler's oldest political associates. One year later, Streicher began publishing *Der Stürmer*. As the founder, editor, owner, writer, and publisher, he excelled in producing graphically violent, obscene, and pornographic stories about "Jewish perfidy."

After Hitler came to power, Streicher organised the 1 April 1933 boycott of Jewish-owned businesses throughout Germany, and in 1935 he helped formulate the Nuremberg Laws on Race. However, internal party politics saw to it that by 1940 his star had fallen—though *Der Stürmer* persisted, ceasing publication just before the war ended in 1945. Streicher was arrested by Allied forces, tried and convicted by the International Military Tribunal at Nuremberg, and hanged on 16 October 1946.

There was one additional avenue by which readers were exposed to Nazi antisemitic propaganda—in this case, very small readers. Fairy tales were appropriated by the Nazis to socialise children into an instinctive Jew-hatred that would permit no opportunity for allowing exceptions or sentimentality.[20] The best-known case of such a corruption of childhood innocence, a children's book called *The Poisonous Mushroom* (*Der Giftpilz*), was published and spread widely by Streicher. Intended as antisemitic propaganda, it was a collection of 17 short stories written by Ernst Hiemer accompanied by brightly coloured illustrations from Philipp Rupprecht (known professionally as *Fips*).

The book's core purpose was to show children how Jews were the most detestable enemy of every German and that children should always be on their guard against them. As such, the aim of the stories was nothing less than the indoctrination of German children. Further, as suggested in the book's title, Jews often camouflaged themselves as Germans, making it difficult to tell them apart from regular society—just as poisonous mushrooms are frequently difficult to discern from those that are edible. The first of the stories recounts a German mother explaining to her son how, just as there are good and bad people, there are edible and poisonous mushrooms: "Just as it is often hard to tell a toadstool from an edible mushroom, so too it is often very hard to recognise the Jew as a swindler and criminal." The Jews, she says, are a "poison" inside Germany, and "Just as a single poisonous mushroom can kill a whole family, so a solitary Jew can destroy a whole village, a whole city, even an entire folk."[21]

The book's seductive approach did not stop there. The stories do not simply portray the Jews as evil and dangerous; children learn that they can themselves be heroic in identifying Jews, supporting their parents, and thereby saving Germany. As children learn the "truth" about the Jews, they demonstrate that they are trustworthy boys and girls who will grow up to become good Germans.

The depictions of Jews in all the stories are intended both to frighten and alert children to the dangers Jews pose. Jews are depicted as being abusive towards their German servants, while Jewish dietary laws cause extreme suffering to innocent animals. Young readers are warned of Jews concentrated in various occupations, such as business, the law, or certain trades, where they cheat honest Germans. Throughout the book, Jews are reviled as people who enjoy it when good Germans suffer.

Jewish men are presented as paedophiles and sexual predators, and Jewish doctors are child molesters, particularly of German girls. Jews also kidnap Christian children to use their blood in Passover matzah, in a restatement of the age-old blood libel accusation. One of the book's final chapters blames the Jews for the death of Jesus.

Focusing on any disquiet children might have as to where the Jews derive their malevolence, the book addresses the foundations of Jewish belief in the Talmud. A chapter relates numerous false claims, such as that the Talmud forbids Jews to do manual labour, that Jews are only permitted to engage in trade, that non-Jews ("Goys") are meant to be slaves, and that Jews are permitted to cheat non-Jews.

The book was viewed by the Nazi hierarchy as a boon for teachers, who were encouraged to utilise *Der Giftpilz* in the classroom when indoctrinating their students about racial hierarchy. In one story, after appropriate instruction from the teacher, a boy in the class describes Jewish features:

> One usually recognizes a Jew by his nose. The Jewish nose is crooked at the end. It looks like the figure 6. Therefore, it is called the 'Jewish Six.' Many non-Jews have crooked noses, too. But their noses are bent, not at the end but further up. Such a nose is called a hook nose or eagle's beak. It has nothing to do with a Jewish nose.

In the text accompanying this picture, the young German boy is portrayed as crying out to his brother in horror: "Those sinister Jewish noses! Those lousy beards! Those dirty, standing out ears! Those bent legs! Those flat feet! Those stained, fatty clothes! Look how they move their hands about! How they haggle! And those are supposed to be men!"[22]

Illustrated carefully for maximum effect, the accompanying captions leave their young readers with no illusions as to what should be concluded. Overall, the stories in *The Poisoned Mushroom* present the broad notion that Jews are inescapably evil, and that all good German children should hate them.

Summing Up: Conditioning the Population for Genocide

To implement its policies easily, the Nazi regime required a cooperative, compliant population. Propaganda was one of the most important tools by which this was achieved. The deeply held belief that Jews controlled the governments of the Soviet Union, Great Britain, and the United States, coupled with Nazi representations of the Jews as parasitic organisms—as leeches, lice, rats, bacteria, and carriers of disease—dehumanised Jews in such a way as to exclude them from the system of moral obligations that bind humankind together.

The aim of the Reich Ministry of Public Enlightenment and Propaganda was to ensure that the Nazi message was successfully communicated through art, music, theatre, films, books, radio, educational materials, and the press. The various forms of propaganda overseen by Goebbels presented divergent messages which served both to publicise the Nazis and to turn the German people against the Jews. This, combined with antisemitic attitudes already prevailing in many parts of Europe, resulted in violence, humiliation, and widespread anti-Jewish persecution.

Goebbels, Streicher, and others began shaping the beliefs of school children through the reading of assigned texts in which the use of stereotyped conceptions of Jews as lecherous old men seducing young Aryan women and girls, unscrupulous lawyers, hard-hearted landlords, rich businessmen and their wives ignoring the poverty around them, all combined to create thoroughly hate-filled images. Streicher sought through the pages of *Der Stürmer* to spread antisemitic propaganda to the public by creating and reinforcing a perception of Jews as subhumans threatening Germany. The total indoctrination of these beliefs to such an extent was to ensure that the population became convinced about Jewish inferiority and unworthiness, the resultant needed to eliminate the menace they posed to the purity of the Aryan race.

As we have seen, since not every German could travel to hear Hitler speak in person, Goebbels arranged a means where every citizen could have access to a cheap radio. Citizens (but not Jews) were expected to use these receivers, to take advantage of Hitler's regular broadcasts to the German people.

Books became the object of propaganda, and not only through Hitler's own *Mein Kampf*. Goebbels's ministry identified "degenerate literature" which included anti-Nazi or communist works, were written by Jews, or written by those sympathetic to Jews. These were removed from university and public libraries and subject to highly organised book burnings commissioned by the ministry.[23]

As the Final Solution was being carried out, SS officials at killing centres misled their victims to such an extent that the SS could maintain the deception needed to deport Jews from Germany and occupied Europe without resistance. These prisoners, many of whom would soon die in the gas chambers, were compelled to send postcards home saying they were well and living in good conditions. The authorities used this misinformation as propaganda to cover up the atrocities and mass murder which they were, even then, committing.

The Nazi regime used propaganda effectively to mobilise the German population to support its wars of conquest until the very end of the regime. Nazi propaganda was likewise essential for motivating those who implemented the mass murder of the European Jews. It also served to secure the acquiescence of millions of others—as bystanders—to racially targeted persecution.

Propaganda and Studying the Holocaust

What does any of this tell us when seeking to study the Holocaust? Do insights into that horrible event appear when examining propaganda? Any conclusion must be an unequivocal yes. Nazi propaganda translated into action, as it was intended: in acceptance of the regime in 1933[24]; in wilful ignorance of anti-Jewish measures in

Germany before the war; in denunciations of Jews during it; in the dehumanisation of Jews caught in the occupied countries; and in the murderous actions of SS, military, and police on the front lines of murder. In all these senses, Nazi propaganda served as a crucial socialising agent, conditioning the German people to an acceptance of exclusion, brutality, and, ultimately, a total disregard for the fate of those whom Nazi ideology had destined for death.

Could it be argued, therefore, that propaganda was a direct source of the Holocaust? Without hesitation, the answer must be in the affirmative. Historians should always avoid the trap of looking at the past from the perspective of the present: while we know where things led, those at the time did not. That said, there were certainly enough portents along the road giving more than a glimpse of where segregation and dehumanisation of an entire targeted population might lead. Without a many-years-long diet of unceasing Nazi propaganda, the Holocaust could not have happened.

Was Nazi propaganda representative of the regime itself? Yes, but this must be looked at more deeply. In a chicken-and-egg equation, which came first: acceptance of the Nazi government's antisemitism, or the conditioning that could allow for such acceptance? Possibly, in the long run, it might not matter too much, as the two—the regime and its expressions—were so inextricably intertwined that no amount of parsing could untangle them.

Are there, then, any limitations in examining Nazi propaganda when studying the Holocaust? For all that has been discussed earlier, perhaps the most striking is in looking for antisemitism where there was none. It must be remembered that although antisemitism lurked beneath everything the Nazis said and wrote, often the message was directed more overtly and deliberately towards other ends—labour, gender, politics, and so on—rather than race.

Another concern relates to our sensitivities towards the horrific realities expressed through such material. Images, whether written, spoken, projected, or otherwise articulated, can be so shocking to us today that we might well prefer not to engage with them as, indeed, with any of the visual evidence of the Holocaust we see through newsreel and other film footage. It was, however, extremely effective in its time, and students of the Holocaust must realise that history is not what we wish it to be, no matter how brutal the reality. It is what it is.

Finally, it should be borne in mind that Nazi antisemitic propaganda is a unique source for studying the Holocaust, unable to be measured the same way as others. It was not based on evidence; it proceeded from lies; and it asserted claims that no amount of logical argument to the contrary could be mounted successfully given the nature of the regime. The claims of the propagandist are based on belief rather than reason, and no compelling argument can be put to discredit a belief sincerely held devoid of thought.

The Holocaust can be studied without consideration of Nazi propaganda but doing so robs it of that most vital of all justifications for the study of history—understanding. And as a victim of the Holocaust, Marc Bloch wrote in *The Historian's Craft*, his famous primer for young historians, "we are never sufficiently understanding."[25]

Notes

1 Several key works examining Nazi propaganda have been produced. See, for example, J. Herf, *The Jewish Enemy: Nazi Propaganda during World War II and the Holocaust*, Cambridge (MA): Harvard University Press, 2006; D. Welch, *The Third Reich: Politics and*

Propaganda, London: Routledge, 1993; A.A. Kallis, *Nazi Propaganda and the Second World War*, London: Palgrave Macmillan, 2005; and R.L. Bytwerk, *Bending Spines: The Propaganda of Nazi Germany and the German Democratic Republic*, East Lansing: Michigan State University Press, 2004. An outstanding collection of illustrations can be found in S. Bachrach and S. Luckett, *State of Deception: The Power of Nazi Propaganda*, Washington (DC): United States Holocaust Memorial Museum, 2009.

2 See, for example, the essays in P. Baines, N. O'Shaughnessy, and N. Snow (ed.), *The SAGE Handbook of Propaganda*, London: Sage, 2019; and J. Auerbach and R. Castronovo (ed.), *The Oxford Handbook of Propaganda Studies*, Oxford: Oxford University Press, 2013. See also J. Stanley, *How Propaganda Works*, Princeton: Princeton University Press, 2015.

3 On television in the Third Reich, see N. Morley, *Radio Hitler: Nazi Airwaves in the Second World War*, Stroud (UK): Amberley, 2021, chapter 7.

4 See the excellent treatments of R.J. Evans's trilogy: *The Coming of the Third Reich*, New York: Penguin Books, 2003; *The Third Reich in Power*, New York: Penguin Books, 2005; and *The Third Reich at War*, New York: Penguin Books, 2008.

5 On Goebbels, see E. Bramsted, *Goebbels and National Socialist Propaganda, 1925–1945*, East Lansing: Michigan State University Press, 1965; F. Moeller, *The Film Minister: Goebbels and the Cinema in the Third Reich*, Stuttgart and London: Edition Axel Menges, 2000; and P. Longerich, *Goebbels: A Biography*, New York: Random House, 2015.

6 On Dietrich, see his autobiography, *The Hitler I Knew: Memoirs of the Third Reich's Press Chief*, New York: Skyhorse, 2010. See also A.G. Hardy, *Hitler's Secret Weapon: The "Managed" Press and Propaganda Machine of Nazi Germany*, New York: Vantage Press, 1967.

7 I. Kershaw, *The "Hitler Myth:" Image and Reality in the Third Reich*, Oxford: Oxford University Press, 1987.

8 Morley, *Radio Hitler*, pp. 25–7.

9 An argument asserting that Nazi cinema was broad-based and covered a wide range of themes can be found in E. Rentschler, *Ministry of Illusion: Nazi Cinema and Its Afterlife*, Cambridge (MA): Harvard University Press, 1996. See also D. Welch, *Propaganda and the German Cinema, 1933–1945*, London: I.B. Tauris, 1983.

10 See also H. Hoffmann, *The Triumph of Propaganda: Film and National Socialism 1933–1945*, New York: Berghahn Books, 1995.

11 A thorough treatment of the novel and the film versions—one German, the other British—can be found in S. Tegel, *Jew Süss: Life, Legend, Fiction, Film*, London: Continuum, 2011.

12 F. Noack, *Veit Harlan: The Life and Work of a Nazi Filmmaker*, Lexington: University Press of Kentucky, 2016.

13 T. Charman, "Fritz Hippler's *The Eternal Jew*," in T. Haggith and J. Newman (ed.), *Holocaust and the Moving Image: Representations in Film and Television Since 1933*, London: Wallflower Press, 2005, pp. 85–92.

14 There are several treatments of the life and work of Leni Riefenstahl. See, for example, D. Hinton, *The Films of Leni Riefenstahl*, Lanham (MD): Scarecrow Press, 2000; G.B. Infield, *Leni Riefenstahl: The Fallen Film Goddess*, New York: Crowell, 1976; and J. Trimborn, *Leni Riefenstahl: A Life*, New York: Faber and Faber, 2007.

15 Morley shows the considerable extent to which Nazi Germany went to broadcast its message to the world, with great expense underwriting a network of radio towers with a reach across Europe, North Africa, the Middle East, and even the United States. See Morley, *Radio Hitler*, especially pp. 261–3, where he provides a listing of German shortwave schedules as of 1943.

16 See, for example, F. Selwyn, *Hitler's Englishman: The Crime of Lord Haw-Haw*, London: Routledge and Kegan Paul, 1987. For other who similarly broadcast (often standing in for Joyce as Lord Haw-Haw), see A. Weale, *Renegades: Hitler's Englishmen*, London: Weidenfeld and Nicolson, 1994.

17 R. Lucas, *Axis Sally: The American Voice of Nazi Germany*, Philadelphia: Casemate, 2010.

18 On the newspaper press generally as well as the *Völkischer Beobachter*, see O.J. Hale, *The Captive Press in the Third Reich*, Princeton: Princeton University Press, 1964.

19 R.L. Bytwerk, *Julius Streicher: Nazi Editor of the Notorious Anti-Semitic Paper Der Stürmer*, New York: Cooper Square Press, 2001.
20 For a description of how children's fairy tales can be sullied for antisemitic ends, see S.K. Baum, *When Fairy Tales Kill: The Origins and Transmission of Antisemitic Beliefs*, Bloomington: iUniverse, 2008.
21 For extracts from *The Poisonous Mushroom*, see P.R. Bartrop and M. Dickerman (ed.), *The Holocaust: An Encyclopedia and Document Collection, Vol. 4, Documents on the Holocaust*, Santa Barbara: ABC-CLIO, 2017, pp. 1130–1. This volume also contains several other examples of Nazi antisemitic propaganda as well as documents relating to origin, implementation, and aftermath of the Final Solution.
22 P.R. Bartrop and E.E. Grimm, *Children of the Holocaust*, Santa Barbara: ABC-CLIO, 2020, p. 268.
23 In this regard, see M. Glickman, *Stolen Words: The Plunder of Jewish Books*, Philadelphia: Jewish Publication Society of America, 2016; R. Knuth, *Burning Books and Leveling Libraries: Extremist Violence and Cultural Destruction*, Westport: Praeger, 2006; and J. Rose, *The Holocaust and the Book: Destruction and Preservation*, Boston: University of Massachusetts Press, 2001.
24 P. Fritzsche, *Hitler's First Hundred Days: When Germans Embraced the Third Reich*, New York: Basic Books, 2020.
25 M. Bloch, *The Historian's Craft*, Manchester: Manchester University Press, 1954, p. 143.

7 Using Trial Documents for Holocaust Study

Michael Dickerman

A criminal trial's significance attaches to the documents it generates. Generally, the more significant the crime at issue, the more important its related documents. Thus, the documents generated by a homicide trial are inherently more important than those in a dispute over a parking ticket. From this perspective it is hard to imagine any set of trial documents of greater significance than those associated with the Holocaust.

There are two related problems with using post-Holocaust trial documents as a source of historical understanding and research. The first is that there are millions of pages of such documents. The second is that accessing the documents can be difficult—and perhaps feel impossible—for students, teachers, and historians alike. One of the reasons for the huge volume of documents is the very large number of post-Holocaust trials that were held.

Despite this, there are ways of navigating through this source. Websites provide access to the greatest number of documents. Some books provide the background of a trial and a discussion of its key issues, while other books primarily—and some entirely—consist of document collections in themselves. Journal articles offer in-depth examinations of well-defined issues. Further, these print sources almost always contain extensive footnotes or endnotes, many of which are replete with references to other document sources.

The purpose of this chapter is to introduce post-Holocaust[1] trial documents as a source for understanding and researching the Holocaust. To do that, the chapter provides an overview of selected post-Holocaust trials;[2] an examination of the related trial document sources; and a discussion of issues relating to using trial documents.

The Trials

The International Military Tribunal Trial, Nuremberg[3]

From 20 November 1945 to 1 October 1946, a trial before the International Military Tribunal (IMT) at Nuremberg (formally, the "Trial of Major War Criminals before the International Military Tribunal") was held for 24 Nazi war criminals.[4] In addition, seven organisations were charged with being criminal in character.[5] The intention to hold Germany and its allies responsible for atrocities was first set forth in the Moscow Declaration of 1943 by US President Franklin Roosevelt, British Prime Minister Winston Churchill, and Soviet Premier Joseph Stalin. It was then confirmed in August 1945 in the London Agreement and its implementation codified by an appended Charter (the "Nuremberg Charter") by the governments of Britain, the United States, the Soviet Union, and the French Republic. Judges from each of these countries presided together at the trial. The involvement of four countries in this military tribunal accounts for the reference to "international" in its name. This is an important point because it distinguishes this trial from others held separately by each of the four signatory countries. Defendants were charged with some combination of Crimes against Peace, War Crimes, and Crimes against Humanity.

This is the trial that most think of when examining post-Holocaust trials.[6] It is the subject of an almost endless number of books, studies, conferences, documentaries, and several feature films.[7] There are several reasons for this.

First, the defendants were major Nazi war criminals, some of the most senior surviving political, military, diplomatic, and economic leaders of the Nazi regime.[8]

Second is the primacy of the trial related to its *sui generis* nature. Robert H. Jackson, US Chief of Counsel, began his opening statement to the IMT by referring to the trial as "the first trial in history for crimes against the peace of the world." He made clear the moral basis on which the trial was conceived:

> That four great nations, flushed with victory and stung with injury stay the hand of vengeance and voluntarily submit their captive enemies to the judgment of the law is one of the most significant tributes that Power has ever paid to Reason.[9]

Third is the role that the trial played in the evolution of international law. Among many of the IMT's significant contributions is what is known as the Nuremberg Principles, a set of seven principles setting forth terms and standards for the prosecution of crimes under international law.[10] Of these, Principle VI defines crimes against peace, war crimes, and crimes against humanity—the three general categories of crimes on which the prosecution was based—as being "punishable as crimes under international law."[11]

Fourth, and most important to the topic of this chapter, the IMT was the source of millions of pages of Holocaust-related documents. The value of these documents cannot be overstated. It has been described as "the raw material of history in wonderful profusion."[12]

The Nuremberg Military Tribunals (NMT) Trials

Formally named "Trials of War Criminals before the Nuremberg Military Tribunals," the plural in this title refers to a series of trials that were held in Nuremberg after the IMT was completed. Note the absence of the word "International" in the title. Both changes from the name "International Military Tribunal" can be explained as follows:

> in Germany the four occupying powers (England, France, the United States and Soviet Russia) by quadripartite agreement authorized the establishment of war crimes courts in each of the four occupation zones. Twelve major trials have been held under the authority of this quadripartite enactment in the United States zone of occupation.[13]

Thus, the NMT trials were conducted by the United States alone. From October 1946 to April 1949, 177 defendants were tried in 12 trials, also held at Nuremberg. Since the NMT trials took place after the completion of the IMT trial, they are often referred to as the "Subsequent Trials." The documentary value of the trials is great:

92 *Michael Dickerman*

In view of the weight of the accusations and the far-flung activities of the defendants, and the extraordinary amount of official contemporaneous German documents introduced in evidence, the records of these trials constitute a major source of historical material covering many events of the fateful years 1933 (and even earlier) to 1945, in Germany and elsewhere in Europe.[14]

The following descriptions of the 12 Subsequent Trials of the NMT will make clear the focus of each trial[15]

- Case No. 1: United States v. Karl Brandt, et al., "Doctors' Trial" (also referred to as "The Medical Case"). This was a case against 23 leading Nazi physicians and scientists.
- Case No. 2: United States v. Erhard Milch, "The Milch Case." Erhard Milch, former German Air Force Field Marshal, was the only defendant.
- Case No. 3: United States v. Josef Altstötter, et al., "Judges' Trial" or "The Justice Case." The defendants were 16 German lawyers, judges, and officials in the Ministry of Justice and high-ranking court administrators.
- Case No. 4: United States v. Oswald Pohl, et al., "The Pohl Case." This was the first of three trials brought against high-ranking SS officials involved in the operation of concentration and labour camps and factories.
- Case No. 5: United States v. Friedrich Flick, et al., "The Flick Case." This was the first of three trials involving leading industrialists.
- Case No. 6: United States v. Carl Krauch, et al., or "The IG Farben Case." This was an indictment against 24 directors of the IG Farben industrial concern.
- Case No. 7: United States v. Wilhelm List, et al., or "The Hostage Case." This dealt with 12 generals involved in Germany's conquest and occupation of Greece, Albania, and Yugoslavia.
- Case No. 8: United States v. Ulrich Griefelt, et al., "The RuSHA Case." This was brought against 14 leading officials of organisations implementing the racial programmes of the Third Reich.
- Case No. 9: United States v. Otto Ohlendorf, et al., "The Einsatzgruppen Case."
- *Einsatzgruppen* were special mobile killing units of the SS which murdered more than one million Jews and many thousands of others.
- Case No. 10: United States v. Alfred Krupp, et al., "The Krupp Case." Prosecuted were Alfred Krupp, Head of Krupp Industries, and 11 of his associates.
- Case No. 11: United States v. Ernst von Weizsäcker, et al., "The Ministries Case." This was brought against 21 members of the German diplomatic corps and others involved in international affairs during the Nazi era.
- Case No. 12: United States v. Wilhelm von Leeb, et al., "The High Command Case." This was brought against 14 defendants, generals, field marshals and an admiral.

Dachau Trials

Not as well-known as the IMT or the subsequent 12 Nuremberg trials, the trials at Dachau were conducted by the US Army from November 1945 through December 1947. The defendants were not major war criminals as in the IMT, or the cohorts tried by the NMT. Instead, the primary focus of the Dachau trials was on low-ranking war criminals, namely, concentration camp personnel, including guards, medical personnel, and some SS units.

The scope of these trials was not limited to individuals only at the Dachau camp. Similar personnel in the Mauthausen, Flossenbürg, Buchenwald, and Nordhausen camps—and in the sub-camps of each of these—were tried in separate trials, all held at Dachau. The charges at the Dachau trials were focused primarily on war crimes, especially committed against Allied military prisoners.

To understand the focus of the Dachau trials, it is helpful to see the particulars of a charge sheet published on 14 May 1946, for the Flossenbürg trial component of the Dachau trials:

> In that [the defendants], German nationals or persons acting with German nationals, acting in pursuance of a common design to subject the persons hereinafter described to killings, beatings, tortures, starvation, abuses and indignities, did, at or near the vicinity of Flossenbürg Concentration Camp, near Flossenbürg, Germany and at or near the vicinity of the Flossenbürg out-camps ... and with transports of prisoners evacuating said camps, all in German or German-controlled territory at various and sundry times, between the 1st of January 1942 and the 8th of May 1945, wilfully, deliberately and wrongfully encourage, aid, abet and participate in the subjection of ... stateless persons ... [and] non-German nationals who were then and there in the custody of the then German Reich, and members of the armed forces of nations then at war with the then German Reich who were then and there surrendered and unarmed prisoners of war in the custody of the then Germany Reich ... the exact names and numbers of such persons being unknown, but aggregating many thousands.[16]

These trials have been described as representing "the most extensive prosecutions undertaken by the occupying American forces in post-World War II Germany. In two years of American military trials, 489 criminal cases and 1,672 defendants were tried at Dachau."[17]

Sources

This section will introduce and explain some of the sources for documents related to the trials already discussed. As with the trials themselves, this will not include all the available sources. Online document collections are by far the most accessible and comprehensive. The number of websites with Nuremberg Trials documents is extensive, with far fewer about the Dachau Trials. The most significant collections are the US government collections available through the Library of Congress (LOC), specifically *Library of Congress: Military Legal Resources: Nuremberg Trials, 1945–1949*.[18] The LOC Military Legal Resources contains an enormous number of relevant documents. There are three multi-volume sets of documents on the Nuremberg trials that are of particular importance. They are named the Blue Series, Red Series, and Green Series, named for the colour of the bound volumes in each of the sets.

- Library of Congress: Military Legal Resources: Trial of the Major War Criminals before the International Military Tribunal, *Nuremberg, 14 November 1945–1 October 1946* (the Blue Series).[19] The LOC has described this as "the official

94 *Michael Dickerman*

proceedings of the trial of the major war criminals." It is further described as "the official record of the trial of the major civilian and military leaders of Nazi Germany who were accused of war crimes." Volumes XXIII and XXIV of this 44-volume set constitute a two-volume Index to Volumes I through XXII.

- Library of Congress: Military Legal Resources: Nazi Conspiracy and Aggression: Office of the United States Chief of Counsel for Prosecution of Axis Criminality, Nuremberg, German (1945–1946) (the Red Series).[20] This is described by the LOC as the "documentary evidence and guide materials from that trial [the IMT]," formally called "'Nazi Conspiracy and Aggression.' ... Volumes I and II serve as an overarching guide for the Red Series."
- Library of Congress: Military Legal Resources: Trials of War Criminals Before the Nuernberg Military Tribunals Under Control Council Law No. 10, *October 1946–April 1949* (the Green Series).[21] According to the LOC, this contains the "official condensed record of the subsequent trials, formally called 'Trials of War Criminals Before the Nuremberg Military Tribunals Under Control Council Law No. 10.' ... The trials lasted two and a half years and produced more than 300,000 pages of testimony and evidence."

While these three LOC compilations represent an invaluable wealth of trial documents, it must be noted that the system of classifying and identifying these documents can be confusing, making it difficult to find documents on a specific subject or a chronological basis.[22] The classification method used in these volumes requires some explanation.

Each document is given a symbol—it can be thought of as a prefix—that precedes a number assigned to it. The prefixes consist of one to four letters that are based on different means of identification. Some symbols are based on subject matter. For example, "NG" stands for "Nuremberg, Government," meaning activities of the Reich ministries; "NO" stands for "Nuremberg, Organizations." Some are based on the name of a person on the IMT staff who selected them, and still other prefixes reflect the country that is the source of the documents (e.g., "UK" and "USSR").[23]

Other important LOC sources and links include:

- *NMT Indictments*, formally called "Nurnberg Military Tribunals: Indictments, Case No. 1–12."[24]
- *Final Report to the Secretary of the Army on the Nuremberg War Crimes Trials Under Control Counsel Law No. 10.*[25]
- *Report of Robert H. Jackson, US Representative, to the International Conference on Military Trials.*[26]
- *Military Legal Resources: Law Reports of Trials of War Criminals Selected and Prepared by the United Nations War Crimes Commission, 1947–1949.*[27] Trials covered in these volumes make clear the scope of Holocaust trials held other than by the IMT, the NMT and the Dachau Trials. These trials were adjudicated by, among others: the Supreme National Tribunal of Poland; the Permanent Military Tribunal at Lyon; the British Military Court, Brunswick; the Supreme Court of Norway; the US Military Commission, Augsburg, Germany; the Canadian Military Court, Aurich, Germany; the British Military Court, Rome; the British Military Court, Venice; and the Australian Military Court. This should serve as a reminder that post-Holocaust trials are not just those discussed in this chapter,

Using Trial Documents for Holocaust Study 95

and, further, that trial documents abound in multiple places regarding multiple charges, defendants, victims, and jurists.

It should be noted that the Foreword in each volume provides a brief overview of the trials that are included in the relevant work. The Foreword for each was written by Lord Wright, Chairman of the United Nations War Crimes Commission, and provide valuable insights in and of themselves for Holocaust research.

Issues

Concerns about Using Trial Documents

The trials at Nuremberg (the IMT, the NMT, and Dachau)[28] were, at the time and since, the subject of controversy. That does not mean that the process was anything less than monumental, unprecedented, and the source of many of today's most important concepts in international law. Nor does its controversial status suggest that it was not the most "orderly, accountable, legal procedure"[29] of several alternatives that were considered as the means of post-Holocaust justice, one of which called for summary trials (if trials at all) followed by the execution of the leading Nazi war criminals. That it is surrounded by controversy means that, like all undertakings, it took place at a specific time and in a specific environment fraught with forces that could not help but influence its structure, considerations, and outcomes. To think otherwise—that is, to see it as the perfect execution of justice against the Nazi regime—would be disingenuous. Further, ignoring the controversies surrounding the trials would diminish our understanding and use of the documents associated with the trials.

Many of the controversies are legal in nature. One of these involved the application of *ex post facto* law. In effect, the rule against *ex post facto* law means that a person cannot be charged with a crime that did not exist as a crime at the time of the action giving rise to the charge. In other words, a law cannot be broken if does not yet exist. As an example, although war crimes and crimes against humanity existed as well-founded legal concepts prior to the time of the Nazi regime, the law of crimes against peace did not exist when the Nazis took actions that would later be criminal under that concept.[30] Telford Taylor writes:

> More than anything else ... the defense counsel were interested in and critical of the *law* as applied to the trial by prosecution and Tribunal. Since crime against peace was a new criminal concept, of which all the defendants had been accused, of course they were violently opposed.[31]

The controversy surrounding the application of crimes against peace was intensified by the inclusion of the concept of "conspiracy" which appeared only regarding crimes against peace (that is, not crimes against humanity or war crimes). Article 6(a) of the Charter of the Nuremberg Trials includes this about crimes against peace: "planning, preparation, initiation or waging of a war of aggression ... or *participation in a common plan or conspiracy* for the accomplishment of any of the foregoing." Thus, crimes against peace did not exist as a legal concept when the Nazis "violated" it, and it included the charge of conspiracy to commit such crimes.[32] Conspiracy was to become central to the various prosecutions' understanding of criminality.

Another legal concern was the prohibition of the *tu quoque* defence, sometimes referred as the "you too" defence. This defence takes the form of a plea that the criminal actions of the defendants were no different than the actions of the forces represented by the prosecutors.

Lauding the NMT efforts but noting some of these legal concerns, legal historian Michael Bazyler writes:

> the American prosecutors and judges committed an exemplary job of providing due process to the defendants before the NMT. Heller concludes that, "with very few exceptions, the tribunals did everything they could do to provide the defendants with fair trials."[33] He does point out that (1) the prosecutors "enjoyed significant material and logistical advantages over the defense," and (2) the "prosecutors relied heavily on incriminating statements made by the defendants without the benefit of counsel."[34]

An important and problematic legal aspect of the Nuremberg Charter of the IMT related to determining charges for the treatment of the Jews by the Nazis. The Charter defined the charge of Crimes against Humanity to include "persecutions on political, racial, or religious grounds *in execution of or in connection with any crime within the jurisdiction of the Tribunal.*" Clearly, persecution of the Jews by the Nazi regime was on "racial or religious grounds," meaning all such persecution should be considered Crimes against Humanity. However, although persecution of the Jews was part of the Nazi regime from the very beginning in 1933, the Tribunal held that:

> the persecution of the Jews before 1939 [specifically, before September 1, 1939], although established beyond doubt, was in general not committed in execution of or in connection with any crime within its jurisdiction. [That is, it was not committed in execution of Crimes against Peace or War Crimes.] Such persecution after 1939 [after the war began] it found to be either a war crime or part of the aggressive warfare count.[35]

Other legal issues include, but are not limited to: the charge of victor's justice; the verdict and punishment of Julius Streicher who had no connection with the military or direct connection with the killing; the flawed Article 8 in the Charter that did not address the status of the defence that the defendant was obeying the command of a superior when a soldier did not know that the command was illegal; and the selection of defendants and the calibre of the Tribunal judges were controversial, where the former was considered to be flawed, and the latter was considered to be less than impressive. As to the selection of defendants, Priemel refers to it as a "haphazard, under-reflected process of choosing the defendants, which owed as much to public pressure for progress and diplomatic compromise as it did to inadequate research."[36]

Some of the controversies about the trial are historical and political in nature. For example, Taylor wrote that the biggest "political wart" on the trials "was the presence, necessary as it was, of the Soviet judges on the bench." This resulted in some of the actions by Stalin and the Russians sitting "uneasily beside the punishment of German crimes against peace."[37]

The trials took place at a time of great concern about Nazism arising again in Germany. The verdicts and punishments issued by the Tribunal were seen by some as being more than the rendering of judicial decisions, but also the sending of a message to all that rebuilding Nazism would be disastrous.[38]

Perhaps the most fundamental historical controversy had to do with the way in which the Nuremberg Trials would influence history's understanding of the 12-year period of the Third Reich. More specifically, would guilt and responsibility be seen as individual or collective, that is, was the broader role of Germany's support for Hitler and the Nazis to be ignored or woven into the prosecutors' narrative? Would the road taken by Nazi Germany be represented by the prosecution as the tragic influence of a single man's evil, thereby assuring Germans and the world that this was a unique confluence of personalities and events that could not be repeated, or would Nazi Germany's path be seen as a prototype for future authoritarian rulers?

Some of the controversies are not unique to the Nuremberg Trials but were perhaps amplified by the nature of the charges. One is the controversy about the bias that plaintiffs and defendants bring to their documents and verbal statements in any type of trial. Historian Lucy S. Dawidowicz has stated "every document slants the structure of historical events, reflecting its author's unconscious prejudices or deliberate intent."[39] More specifically, she argues that German documents "abound in attempts at self-vindication," while Jewish documents are subject to memory that "is often distorted by hate, sentimentality, and the passage of time."[40] To which we might add that the documents—regardless of their source—suffer from another bias. This is because they were chosen by the prosecution—not the court or the defense—to make its case that the defendants are guilty of the crimes with which they are charged. Dawidowicz makes this clear when she writes that the 40,000 documents chosen by the US prosecutorial team were screened "to search out the *most persuasive evidence* of war crimes and crimes against humanity by the Germans."[41] The result of that screening for "persuasive evidence" is the collection of 2,000 documents submitted as evidence.

Perhaps less of a controversy than a concern, the type of language used by the Nazis in various documents was often not standard German. Dawidowicz writes that it has been dubbed "*Nazi-Deutsch* ... [that] embodied the characteristics of totalitarian language ... [it] was designed not to extend, but to reduce the range of thought, to create a desirable mental attitude by the use of words constructed for political and ideological purposes."[42] Steven T. Katz takes up the same point, writing that the Nazis "regularly [used] language formulated to reveal only the barest outline of its real intentions ... This intentionally ambiguous linguistic usage was most notable where references to mass death were at issue."[43]

The controversies discussed here—by no means complete—must be considered when assessing the meaning and usefulness of documents from the Nuremberg Trials. The decisions made about the controversies in preparation for and presentation to these trials impacts their entire collection of documents. For the most part, the impact is in the documents that were *not* included in the 2,000 or so submitted as evidence. It must be remembered that these documents were the result of a selection process intended to create a specific narrative. British historian Geoffrey Cubitt has addressed this in the following way:

> historical narrative is based on selection—that in retaining some things, it represses others; that in focusing on the development or the interests of certain groups, it implicitly (if not explicitly) excludes or marginalizes other perspectives; that in promoting one kind of memory, it obstructs other ways of remembering.[44]

For example, the prohibition of the *tu quoque* defence would mean that any documents, no matter their value to the prosecution's case, that make clear or simply infer Allied actions akin in any way to the actions being charged against the defendants, would not be included.[45] Similarly, documents that included reference to actions by Russia during the period when it was Allied with the Axis powers would most likely not be chosen, lest it embarrass or inflame the Soviet judge, prosecutors, and staff. Further, documents that might be viewed as inconsistent with the message regarding the culpability of German citizens and the causes that led to Hitler's regime would most likely not be part of the chosen documents.

Care must be taken that German documents are not read and understood in a harsher light, nor Jewish documents in a softer light, than each document objectively requires. It must be remembered that the precise purpose of the Nuremberg Trials documents was to persuade, to win a trial of dramatic and unparalleled importance by showing beyond any question the commission by the defendants of crimes charged against them in the Indictment. That goal no doubt influenced the trial documents at Nuremberg that were chosen, as is the case regarding the documents chosen by the prosecution in any court case, meaning that no matter the breadth of the Nuremberg documents, they do not constitute the entire picture of the crimes of the Third Reich.

Copyright Concerns

Text and other media that are subject to copyright protection may not be used without permission of their creator.[46] Copyright law is complicated, in large part because there is no single rule that applies to all written text. Instead, whether text is protected by copyright is governed by a wide variety of factors. Further, there are exceptions that might allow text—or some part of it—to be used without permission even if it is properly copyrighted.

The copyright rule that is most germane to the documents we are discussing is that US government works generated by US government personnel are in the public domain.[47] However, there are exceptions to the rule, and exceptions to the exceptions.[48] As to the most important sources of documents made available by the US government on the Nuremberg Trials—the "Blue Series," "Red Series," and "Green Series," and others as noted earlier—there appear to be no restrictions on, nor permission needed for, the use of the documents contained in those volumes. As clear as this is, the LOC still suggests that its series of Nuremberg documents be subject to the user's discretion. Of course, proper citation to the documents in these volumes is always required.

Conclusion

Sir Norman Birkett, an alternate British Judge at the IMT, called the Tribunal "the greatest trial in history."[49] The validity of that statement depends, of course, on what is meant by "greatest." If it means the number of documents it has produced, or the amount of research that has been done about it, or its impact on international law, then it would seem Birkett cannot be faulted. If, however, "greatest" is based on absolute fairness, the credentials of judges, consistency of the punishment of defendants, application of laws in effect at the time the criminal act was committed, or even simply the ease of access of its documents for purposes of research, then Birkett's statement may be subject to legitimate dispute.

For all its faults, no matter the number of issues still in dispute, the Nuremberg Trials were and remain among the great achievements of the twentieth century. The trials were held but months after the greatest global conflagration since the prior recordholder—the Great War—established its dominance in infamy. Hardly recovered from the First, the Second World War demanded sacrifices once again of vast millions of people, some many thousands of miles removed from the source of the conflict. And this global conflict harboured an unprecedented genocide that itself was intended to be global. When all was over, action taken as an attempt to force evil to answer for its crimes was not taken in the shadows of the gallows or in front of a firing squad, but before a court in the Palace of Justice, in Nuremberg. As imperfect as it may have been,[50] it was, as Justice Jackson said in his opening address to the court, "one of the most significant tributes that Power has ever paid to Reason." Certainly, in that respect, Sir Norman Birkett was correct.

Trial documents hold a unique place among the almost limitless types of documents. They must meet the same standards of authenticity as any other historical documents, but they also must persuade while meeting the strict requirements of the law. All are not accurate, all are not comprehensible, but all sit within a particular context. When read without the context of a document—who wrote it, when was it written, why was it written, what was happening around the writer that might have influenced the content of the document, and so forth—it is reduced to a collection of words yielding only the lowest rung on the ladder of understanding. When read in context, however, it can bring truth to ignorance, and insight to confusion.

The Nuremberg Trial documents, when read and understood in their context, can achieve still more. They can force a mind to consider the unthinkable, to accept a reality that defies thought.[51] Nuremberg Trial documents have gravitas because they were assiduously vetted and then thoughtfully—even at times dramatically—presented as evidence in a trial focused on not only the life and death of the defendants but also nothing less than the survival of Western civilisation. Ideas and ideals were at risk during the Second World War. Principles of a free society were put to the test against authoritarianism, and it was these documents that drove the world's effort to vanquish the enemy, not on the battlefield—for that victory had already been won—but on the field of values, on the field of conflicting "isms" that determine what kind of world we live in. Documents that were brought to that battle are inherently worth our study and understanding, for through them comes the broader understanding of good and evil, and of freedom and totalitarianism. If used properly, documents from the Nuremberg Trials can give us insights that few if any other sources can.

Notes

1 Our focus rightly is on post-Holocaust trials, but notice should be taken that these were not the first trials involving the actions of Hitler or the Nazi Party. See D. King, *The Trial of Adolf Hitler: The Beer Hall Putsch and the Rise of Nazi Germany,* New York: Norton, 2017; B.C. Hett, *Crossing Hitler: The Man Who Put the Nazis on the Witness Stand,* Oxford: Oxford University Press, 2008; and G. Dawson, *Judgment before Auschwitz: The Holocaust in the Ukraine and the First Nazi War Crimes Trial,* New York: Pegasus, 2012.
2 The trials and related documents discussed in this chapter are limited to those regarding crimes committed only in Europe by the Nazis, their allies, and collaborators. Further, they are limited to those trials that immediately followed the end of the war, namely, those conducted at Nuremberg and Dachau. Thus, for example, they do not include documents related to the Eichmann Trial (1961) or the Frankfurt Auschwitz Trial (1963–65).

100 *Michael Dickerman*

3 For those not already familiar with this trial, a brief but excellent overview can be found in the booklet prepared in 2018 by the Registry of the International Court of Justice in recognition of a project to digitise the audio and film components of the trial's evidence. See *Nuremberg Trial Archives, The International Court of Justice: Custodian of the Archives of the International Military Tribunal at Nuremberg*, 2018 ICJ (2nd ed.), especially pp. 11–9, 76–81, at library-of-the-court-en.pdf (icj-cij.org). Other sections of this source contain additional valuable information on many aspects of the Nuremberg trials.

4 Only 21 defendants were in the dock at the Tribunal. One defendant (Robert Ley) committed suicide before the start of the trial, one (Martin Borman) was tried *in absentia,* and the physical and mental condition of a third (Gustav Krupp von Bohlen und Halbach) caused him not to be tried.

5 The Groups or Organisations were the Reich cabinet, the Leadership Corps of the Nazi Party, Nazi Party *Schutzstaffel* (SS), the Security Service (SD), the Secret State Police (Gestapo), the *Sturmabteilung* of the Nazi Party (SA), and the General Staff and High Command of the German Armed Forces.

6 Often overlooked is a trial that was held in Wiesbaden just days before the IMT opened. Referred to as the Hadamar Trial (*U.S v. Alfons Klein et al.*), it was conducted from 8–15 October 1945, by a United States military commission. The seven defendants were Germans involved in the Nazi "euthanasia" program (*Aktion T-4*) which sought to "purify" the Aryan race by killing non-Jewish individuals whose mental or physical disabilities threatened that purity. See M.S. Bryant, *Confronting the Good Death: Nazi Euthanasia on Trial 1945–1953*, Boulder: University of Colorado Press, 2005, especially pp. 76–90.

7 See https://www.ushmm.org/collections/bibliography/the-nuremberg-trials for an excellent list of IMT resources—including trial proceedings and related documents, personal accounts and memoirs, and films and videos—that are part of the collection of the United States Holocaust Memorial Museum.

8 For a list of the defendants, including a brief biography on each, see International Military Tribunal: The Defendants | Holocaust Encyclopedia (ushmm.org).

9 Among the many sources that provide the text of Jackson's opening statement, see the Robert H. Jackson Center at https://www.robertjackson.org/speech-and-writing/opening-statement-before-the-international-military-tribunal/#:~:text=Jackson%2C%20Chief%20of%20Counsel%20for,world%20imposes%20a%20grave%20responsibility.

10 The "Principles of International Law Recognized in the Charter of the Nürnberg Tribunal and in the Judgment of the Tribunal" can be found at https://legal.un.org/ilc/texts/instruments/english/draft_articles/7_1_1950.pdf. See also *Resource Collection on the Nuremberg Principles,* International Nuremberg Principles Academy, available online at https://www.nurembergacademy.org/resources/resource-collection-on-the-nuremberg-principles/. For an excellent discussion of the trial's contribution to international law see "The Influence of the Nuremberg Trial on International Criminal Law" in the Robert H. Jackson Center website at https://www.robertjackson.org/speech-and-writing/the-influence-of-the-nuremberg-trial-on-international-criminal-law/.

11 The Tribunal split the charge of Crimes against Peace into two separate charges: "the planning, preparing, initiation, or waging of aggression"; and "participation in a Common Plan or Conspiracy for the accomplishment ... of the foregoing." Thus, defendants were facing some combination of four charges. See *Trial of War Criminals before the International Military Tribunal, Nuremberg*, Washington, DC: US Government Printing Office, 1946, Blue Series, Vol. I, p. 224.

12 T. Taylor, "Forum Juridicum: An Outline of the Research and Publication Possibilities of the War Crimes Trials," *Louisiana Law Review*, 9:4, May 1949, p. 497.

13 Ibid.

14 *Trials of War Criminals before the Nuremberg Military Tribunals under Control Council No. 10*, Washington, DC: US Government Printing Office, 1946, Green Series, Vol. I, p. III.

15 These are excerpts from descriptions of the 12 NMT trials in *The International Court of Justice: custodian of the archives,* pp. 57–63.

16 D. Riedel, "The U.S. War Crimes Tribunals at the Former Dachau Concentration Camp: Lessons for Today?" *Berkeley Journal of International Law*, 24:4, 2006, pp. 587–8, n. 241.

Using Trial Documents for Holocaust Study 101

17 "A Witness to Barbarism: Horace R. Hansen and the Dachau War Crimes Trials," a University of Minnesota Law Library Digital Exhibit, available online at http://moses.law.umn.edu/hansenwitness. For further insight into the Dachau Trials, see J. M. Greene, *Justice at Dachau: The Trials of an American Prosecutor*, Chicago: Ankerwycke Publishing, 2017.

18 See Search results for Military Legal Resources, Nuremberg Trials.html, available online at Library of Congress (loc.gov).

19 See Search results for Military Legal Resources, Blue Series, available online at Library of Congress (loc.gov).

20 See Search results for Military Legal Resources, Red Series, available online at Library of Congress (loc.gov).

21 See Search results for Military Legal Resources, Green Series, available online at Library of Congress (loc.gov).

22 Raul Hilberg, a doyen of Holocaust scholars, explains one of the many reasons it is difficult to find documents on a particular subject: "The assembled records, taken from various collections in the custody of Allied powers, were given accession numbers, so that any two items in numerical succession did not necessarily indicate proximity of content." R. Hilberg, *Sources of Holocaust Research: An Analysis,* Chicago: Ivan R. Dee, 2001, p. 197.

23 Special note must be taken of J. Robinson and H. Sachs (ed.), *The Holocaust: The Nuremberg Evidence, Part 1: Documents; Digest, Index, and Chronological Tables*, Jerusalem: Yad Vashem, 1976. It is an excellent source to approach the Blue, Red and Green Series of the LOC. Its preface alone is valuable for its explanation of how trial documents are classified (including a full list of prefixes, not just those in the examples, above). It provides a subject matter index that is correlated with a digest of trial documents, listed by prefixes, that includes citations to the Blue, Red and Green Series. For additional information on document classifications, see J. Mendelsohn, *Trial by Document: The Use of Seized Records in the United States Proceedings at Nürnberg,* New York: Garland, 1988.

24 See Nurnberg [Nuremberg] Military Tribunal, Indictments (loc.gov).

25 See Search results for Military Legal Resources, Nuremberg Trials.html, available online at Library of Congress (loc.gov).

26 See Report of Robert H. Jackson, United States representative to the International Conference on Military Trials London, 1945. Library of Congress (loc.gov).

27 See Search results for Military Legal Resources, Law-Reports-Trials-War-Criminals.html, Available Online | Library of Congress (loc.gov).

28 Telford Taylor writes about "Nuremberg—a name which conjures up the moral and legal issues raised by applying judicial methods and decisions to challenged wartime acts." T. Taylor, *The Anatomy of the Nuremberg Trials,* New York: Skyhorse Publishing, 2013, p. 626.

29 K.C. Preimel, *The Betrayal: The Nuremberg Trials and German Divergence,* Oxford: Oxford University Press, 2016, p. 98.

30 For an in-depth discussion regarding the application of *ex post facto* law in the Nuremberg Trials, including its roots in the Hague Convention, see M.C. Bassiouni (ed.), *International Criminal Law: International Enforcement* (3rd ed.), Vol. III, Leiden: Martinus Nijhoff Publishers, 2008.

31 T. Taylor, *Anatomy,* pp. 627–9 (emphasis in original). Taylor also writes that if it were purely an objective matter the defence counsel's arguments would prevail. But the decision to include this new criminal concept was ultimately based on "political and emotional factors." He describes those factors as including: "People whose nations had been attacked and dismembered without warning wanted legal retribution, whether or not this was 'a first time.'"

32 Although Robert Jackson's arguments in favour of including both crimes against peace and conspiracy "were intellectually weak," they nonetheless prevailed. See Priemel, *The Betrayal*, p. 79.

33 K.J. Heller, quoted in M. Bazyler, *Holocaust, Genocide, and the Law: A Quest for Justice in a Post-Holocaust World,* Oxford: Oxford University Press, 2016, p. 92.

34 Ibid.

35 Review by Will Maslow of S. Krieger and H. Monsky, *Nazi Germany's War Against the Jews*, New York: American Jewish Conference, 1947, in *Columbia Law Review*, 47:6, September 1947, pp. 1085–7. Elsewhere, Telford Taylor has written: "The International Military Tribunal in the first Nurnberg trial treated Nazi atrocities against Germans [and Jews] as crimes under international law only if they had been committed after the outbreak of the war, on the theory that such crimes committed thereafter constituted a part of the entire process of waging an aggressive war." See Taylor, "Outline," pp. 496–509.
36 Priemel, *The Betrayal*, p. 99.
37 Taylor, *Anatomy*, pp. 639–40. Some of these actions would include Soviet occupation of the eastern half of Poland pursuant to the Russia-Germany nonaggression pact made one week before Hitler invaded Poland in September 1939. Of course, that pact was broken by Hitler's invasion of Russia in June 1941. In addition, responsibility for the Katyn massacres in March 1940 was, at the insistence of the Russians, included in the charges against the Nazi defendants, although a strong case could be made that the Russians were the perpetrators. This was resolved in 2010 when the Russian parliament finally admitted that "it was Stalin who had ordered the murder of … as many as 22,000 Poles." M.R. Marrus, *The Nuremberg War Crimes Trial, 1945–46: A Brief History with Documents* (2nd ed.), Boston: Bedford/St. Martin's, 2018, p. 77, n. 36. See also F. Hirsch, *Soviet Judgment at Nuremberg: A New History of the International Military Tribunal after World War II*, Oxford: Oxford University Press, 2020.
38 Marrus, *The Nuremberg War Crimes Trial*, p. 73.
39 L.S. Dawidowicz, *A Holocaust Reader*, Springfield (NJ): Behrman House, 1976, p. 10.
40 Ibid., p. 11.
41 Ibid., p. 3 (emphasis added). See also, Krieger and Monsky, *Nazi Germany's War against the Jews*.
42 Ibid., p. 14.
43 S.T. Katz, Introduction to Y. Arad, I. Gutman, and A Margaliot (ed.), *Documents on the Holocaust: Selected Sources on the Destruction of the Jews of Germany and Austria, Poland, and the Soviet Union* (8th ed.), Jerusalem: Yad Vashem, 1996, p. vi.
44 G. Cubitt, *History and Memory*, Manchester: Manchester University Press, 2007, p. 53.
45 Legal scholar William A. Schabas writes: "Obviously, certain aspects of Nazi behaviour during the Second World War were not explored at Nuremberg because of a perceived Allied vulnerability to such a plea." See W.A. Schabas, *Genocide in International Law: The Crime of Crimes* (2nd ed.), Cambridge: Cambridge University Press, 2009, p. 397.
46 An important alternative to copyright protection are various types of Creative Commons licenses. See https://creativecommons.org/about/.
47 The law can be found at 17 US Code § 105. Prior to going directly to the law, however, it may be helpful to see https://www.copyrightlaws.com/copyright-laws-in-u-s-governmentworks/#:~:text=U.S.%20government%20works%20are%20in,these%20government%20works%20without%20permission for a clear explanation of the general rule regarding US government works, as well as exceptions to that rule.
48 See *LibraryLaw Blog:* "When Is It in the Public Domain?" for a fascinating discussion about whether Nuremberg Trial transcripts are in the public domain, available online at https://blog.librarylaw.com/librarylaw/2009/08/when-is-it-in-the-public-domain.html.
49 Quoted in Marrus, *The Nuremberg War Crimes Trial*, p. v.
50 Even Raul Hilberg has written: "In all, the selections for the Nuremberg trials were not encompassing. Some important agencies, formations, and corporations were not represented in the defendants' docks. The regional level was not fully reflected, and local offices received little attention." See Hilberg, *Sources of Holocaust Research*, p. 197.
51 A.C. Cohen, *The Tremendum: A Theological Interpretation of the Holocaust*, New York: Crossroad, 1988.

8 Understanding Holocaust Memory Through Museums and Memorials

Abigail Winslow

Introduction

Memory is a unique and complicated element of society that not only informs us but also allows us to reconstruct and understand the past. Generically, it is a truism that museums and memorials are steeped in memory, but for Holocaust museums and memorials specifically, memory is the foundation of their narrative. Holocaust museums encourage their visitors to recognise the atrocities to prevent future genocides. Memorials honour an event or individuals as a constant and permanent means of remembrance. Both museums and memorials provide excellent resources for studying the Holocaust as a way to ascertain memory in a particular region and understand the public's perception of this memory.

This chapter will analyse museums and memorials based specifically in Britain for two reasons. First, countries around the world depict the Holocaust differently. Some countries experienced the Holocaust on their soil, some possess a prominent Jewish culture, and others became the homes of displaced Holocaust survivors after 1945. To provide a more concise analysis, focus is placed on one country instead of choosing case studies from several. Second, Britain provides a unique and interesting perspective on Holocaust study. It not only aided in the liberation and became home to Holocaust survivors but also participated in the *Kindertransport* which brought Jewish children from Nazi Germany to safety before the war. This participation impacts the perspective and education of the Holocaust in Britain. Understanding the influences behind narratives and symbolism in museum exhibitions and memorials is the first step to using them as sources. Every source has biases, and museums and memorials are not exempt.

Using museums and memorials as sources for Holocaust research can be advantageous for understanding the transmission of memory. Educational curricula can illuminate the national memory created, but museums and memorials influence beyond teenage years. Memorials and museum exhibitions possess unique narratives depending upon the location, design, and available funding. Regardless of a curatorial team's intentions, funding often restricts what they can achieve, and this should be considered when using exhibitions as case studies.

These media provide several uses as sources, but for this chapter are viewed from the perspective of memory. A leading authority on memory and memorials, James E. Young, argues that memorials often create competing memories for the public due to the different narratives presented,[1] while there are always motives behind the creation of memorials, political or otherwise.[2] Exhibitions are similar as they are influenced by curators and donors: as Young shows,

DOI: 10.4324/9781003248620-11

To the extent that all societies depend on the assumption of shared experience and memory for the very basis of their common relations, a society's institutions are automatically geared toward creating a shared memory—or at least the illusion of it.[3]

While numerous examples could be analysed, the case studies examined here will look at four Holocaust exhibitions and memorials. Each example will explain methods of memory employed by influencers to understand the intended perspective behind memorials and museums. New methods and techniques are continually being explored and are reflected in the sources examined below. The case studies will illustrate how to use these sources to understand Holocaust memory in the United Kingdom.

Museums

The National Holocaust Centre and Museum, Newark

The Journey: Children of the Holocaust is a family-friendly exhibition at the National Holocaust Centre and Museum (NHCM) in Newark (Newark-on-Trent), Nottinghamshire.[4] Awarded Best Exhibition of 2009, this is the only child-centred Holocaust exhibition in the United Kingdom. From the perspective of a fictional ten-year-old Jewish child named Leo, it follows his journey from Berlin, living in hiding, to joining the *Kindertransport* and arriving safely in England.[5] The exhibition is an excellent example of how museums use design methods to influence the experience and memories of their visitors.

Memories are stimulated by the senses, for instance, through songs, smells, and visuals. This is known as encoding specificity.[6] The senses allow one to better access these memories or to create new ones. For instance, prosthetic memory, a term coined by Alison Landsberg, is a memory of an experience that the individual did not witness themselves. Museums can form a prosthetic memory for their visitor, by creating a sense of empathy through their narrative's depiction.[7] Many museums use this technique to effectively immerse visitors in the intended time period. By creating the feeling of walking in someone else's shoes, the visitor forms a prosthetic memory of the historical event.

The Journey illustrates how an exhibition uses prosthetic memory method within exhibition design. The exhibition leads visitors through different rooms which illustrate Leo's life over a few years. When visitors enter Leo's living room, there is a table under the window with a meal laid out, as if the family had recently left in haste. There are also vintage toys that children can play with while they listen to Leo talking about his life at the beginning of the Nazi rise to power. This theme continues throughout the exhibition, with each room depicting another stage of Leo's life between 1933 and 1938. The horrors in concentration camps are not addressed, but rather a child's confusion by his friends treating him differently because of his religion. One room reconstructs a street depicting his parents' destroyed shop following *Kristallnacht*, the "Night of Broken Glass," on 9–10 November 1938. There is a feeling of fear in this room as the lights dim when Leo's audio diary plays.

When using an exhibition as a source for a design method, it is important to point out specific aspects of the design that can trigger prosthetic memory. Within this exhibition, for example, there is a secret room placed behind rolls of fabric where the family hid. The room is dark, tight, and dingy, complete with a makeshift toilet. One might miss this room entirely, which makes finding it more impactful. The experience fosters prosthetic memory, compelling viewers to empathise with Leo's experience of the effects of the Holocaust. Creating an immersive experience allows visitors to get involved and interact with the exhibition. Both children and adults feel a part of history, by touching the props and finding the hidden room. Everything is life-sized, adding to the immersive effect, further establishing an impactful visit.

In the late 1990s, Lynn Dierking and John H. Falk studied the memories of school children's field trips to museums. They asked eight-year olds about visits a year or two prior, 13-year olds about visits six to seven years earlier, and young adults about visits 12–20 years previously. Almost all of them held memories of their visits and could describe them in detail.[8] Museum visits have a way of lingering with people, lasting long after leaving the museum. In another study by Dierking and Falk, museum memories remained stable for 25 percent of the museum visitors interviewed. The rest of the interviewees' recollections evolved and changed over time. They learned from this study that the details fade over time, but a more overarching perspective of the experience took their place.[9] As a source, this exhibition is a wonderful example of how an experiential space might encourage memories to last longer through the fostering of prosthetic memory.

The Imperial War Museum, London

The Holocaust Galleries at the Imperial War Museum (IWM), London opened to the public in 2022, after the previous exhibition finished an impressive 21-year run. From the onset of the exhibition, the curatorial team set the stage for the theme of the new galleries. Blue walls welcome visitors into a minimalist introduction space. A large screen set at an angle displays short clips of seemingly random current-day places throughout Europe, with only the location as context. After walking past this, a single quote on the far wall says: "I want the coming generation to remember our times ... I don't know my fate. I don't know whether I will be able to tell you what happened later" (Nachum Grzywacz, July 1942).[10]

The narrative attempts to remove the inevitability of the Holocaust from the visitor's mind. The individuals affected by the Holocaust could not have foreseen what would come, nor could those who planned the atrocities. This exhibition does not hint at the events which would occur. Each section depicts a different stage of the Holocaust, from eugenics to ghettos and concentration camps, with present tense quotes from those who experienced the events. This case study focuses on the contemporaneous voice that the IWM's curatorial team chose to use throughout the exhibition's text.

James Bulgin, Head of Content for the IWM Holocaust Galleries, authored *The Holocaust*, a guide to the galleries providing further historical background for each section of the exhibition.[11] While this provides a resource for understanding the galleries, nothing is mentioned regarding the creative decisions behind constructing the exhibition. Gaining insight from curators is the best option for determining the design choices made in an exhibition. For this case study, a presentation given by Bulgin at Royal Holloway, University of London in early 2022 offers evidence.[12]

Bulgin explained that the curatorial team wanted to avoid the trajectory of the Holocaust's narrative seeming inevitable but rather something that evolved throughout the war. He conceded that removing the inevitability of the Holocaust from public consciousness is challenging considering that media and films largely shape Holocaust knowledge as opposed to exhibitions and memorial sites. One of the ways they attempted this was to add light instead of darkness and allow the objects to drive the narratives. The most interesting method is the use of contemporaneous voice throughout the exhibition. Bulgin explained that those commenting on the event could never have known the inevitability of the Holocaust. The exhibition detours from other Holocaust exhibitions by focusing not on the process of systematic annihilation but rather on the murder of innocent people.[13]

Visitors might not register that contemporaneous voice is used in the galleries, but the perspective achieved by this narrative decision is what visitors take from the experience. Many people go into the exhibition with some knowledge regarding the Holocaust, but the exhibition approaches the topic from a new perspective. The use of light, colour, and present tense aid in illustrating how people's choices led to the Holocaust, not just a master plan.

The Holocaust Galleries, as a source, illustrates the power of narrative within a Holocaust exhibition. Whether this exhibition is changing collective memory regarding the inevitability of the Holocaust is still undetermined and deserves more research, but as a foundation, the IWM is off to a good start. Challenging traditional narratives and presenting new perspectives is how Holocaust studies remain relevant to future generations, for "It seems to us, that for the time being mankind does not comprehend what we have gone through and what we have experienced" (Zalman Grinberg, doctor, June 1945).[14]

The Holocaust Centre North, Huddersfield

Located in the Yorkshire city of Huddersfield is Holocaust Centre North (HCN). The exhibition within this site, *Through Our Eyes*, focuses on the stories of 16 Holocaust survivors who relocated to Yorkshire and influenced the creation of the exhibition.[15] As a source, *Through Our Eyes* illustrates how an exhibition can encourage and facilitate community engagement to preserve Holocaust memory.

The location of this centre, situated on the University of Huddersfield campus, is integral as it is surrounded by students and academics. The exhibition's focus is therefore centred around education, with school groups, university students, and members of the community visiting. Through mediums such as artefacts and touch screen interactives, visitors learn the stories of these survivors. In addition, the centre provides learning sessions following their exhibition tour for 8- to 16-year olds as well as adult sessions. These sessions include the use of objects, texts, Nazi propaganda, and images to learn and discuss aspects of Holocaust history to build upon their exhibition visit. The sessions also deal with misconceptions surrounding the Holocaust and the reality of ordinary people participating in these atrocities.[16]

According to Hannah Randall, the Head of Learning at the HCN, it is crucial to tell Holocaust stories not often mentioned. For instance, the exhibition and learning sessions illuminate the negative aspects of the *Kindertransport*, internment camps for Germans in Britain, and antisemitism in the United Kingdom. Through open dialogue on these topics, understanding can evolve, and collective memory can change. Randall raises the importance of Holocaust survivors' influence on the HCN. The original centre, founded by Holocaust survivors, established a theme of personal stories, with the use of survivors' objects and narratives, an advisory board of survivors, and the continuance of survivors joining educational sessions. The importance that the HCN places on Holocaust remembrance and survivor influence fosters a space for community engagement, learning, and reflection.[17]

Tom Howard deals directly with this topic by presenting a teaching resource and offering ways that teachers can educate openly and honestly about the Holocaust.[18] He details the British government obtaining knowledge in September 1942 of the mass extermination taking place in Europe and becoming public knowledge by year's end. While the Allies knew of the Jewish plight, the strategy remained focused on the war, backed by the belief that winning the war would halt the genocide. Howard suggests that talking openly about the positives and negatives of Britain's role in the Holocaust creates a better understanding.[19]

As a further foundation for the HCN's teaching methods, University College London conducted a national survey for secondary school students to better understand the Holocaust and the UK's relation to it. One of the questions the survey asked is, "What happened when the British government knew about the mass murder of Jews?" The most popular answer was "declare war on Germany" given by 34.4 percent of the students polled. The second most popular answer was "none of the above: knew nothing" at 23.8 percent. This is especially surprising, considering a large number of the students chose this answer.[20]

Howard argues that through the use of primary sources, counter-narratives arise in response to common Holocaust misconceptions, which is precisely how the HCN approaches its Holocaust learning programmes.[21] Through primary sources and conversation, the HCN aims to break down false narratives students might accept regarding the Holocaust and illustrate different sides of the story. To further establish an exhibition as a source for transmitting Holocaust memory, the source would benefit from examining education packs and follow up surveys with students. *Through Our Eyes* is an excellent example of how exhibitions can be a vessel for Holocaust education through community engagement, as well as presenting a source for how the narrative is taught.

Jewish Museum London

The Jewish Museum London examines the Holocaust from an entirely different perspective by focusing on the story of one man. *The Holocaust Gallery* depicts the life of Leon Greenman OBE, a British Jew born in East London who became a survivor of six concentration camps. According to Adam Corsini, the museum's Senior Collections Engagement Manager, this permanent exhibition has been at museum since 2010, after first opening in 1996 at the London Museum of Jewish Life's Finchley location.[22] When considering *The Holocaust Gallery* as a source, this case study will examine the impact of personal memory used alongside visitor feedback.

The first background wall of this exhibition is lined with a wallpaper of bright red flowers that fade to grey as the hope in Greenman's life diminishes. The narrative on the text panels accompanying photos of Greenman's family tells the story of life in London and Rotterdam. This includes meeting his wife Else Van Dam and moving to Rotterdam to care for her grandmother. In 1940, they welcomed their son Barney into the world. When the Nazis invaded the Netherlands in May 1940, Greenman still believed that possessing a British passport would protect his family. This hope vanished when friends entrusted with his family's passports destroyed them out of fear.

108 *Abigail Winslow*

On 8 October 1942, the Nazis arrested the Greenman family and transported them to Westerbork camp. The story continues with a quote that says, "Our only thoughts were for our baby." The Greenmans never received proof of their identity and endured forced deportation to Poland in early 1943. Upon arrival at Auschwitz-Birkenau, Greenman became separated from his wife and child, with no knowledge of their whereabouts, but maintained the hope of seeing them again.

As viewers follow Greenman's struggles in concentration camps, with his objects displayed in cases, a sense of connection is formed in the humanness of wanting the family reunited. When the viewer learns of the murder of Greenman's family in the gas chambers, it is gripping, even more so when reading that he never remarried. Despite the tragic losses he endured, Greenman dedicated his life to Holocaust education, sharing his experiences in the camps for others to learn about the severity of the Holocaust. The exhibition conveys Greenman's heartbreak, featuring toys and a little outfit belonging to Barney, and Else's wedding dress. These items are significant as Greenman retained and treasured them as vestiges of a broken past.

Due to Greenman's heavy involvement with the educational programme at the Jewish Museum London, it is safe to assume he contributed to the content within the exhibition.[23] Using personal memories in relation to the Holocaust is a common practice that museums employ when dealing with such a complex topic. Not only does this return a victim's identity; it also makes a connection with visitors by illustrating the humanity amidst the abhorrence.[24] As the years progress, the time between the present and the end of the Holocaust grows larger, increasing the importance of using first-hand accounts within exhibitions. In the words of Victoria Aarons and Alan L. Berger, the continued testimony of survivors "constitutes a resistance to encroaching anonymity and obscurity, their language a defense against forgetting." In this sense, eyewitnesses are "guardians of memory."[25]

To ascertain how the public engages, museums use visitor feedback. This is a common museum practice to understand the response to an exhibition. Museums use different forms of evaluation, with the first being front-end evaluation to test ideas before a project is fully formed, followed by a formative evaluation when the exhibition is a "prototype." The final stage is known as a summative evaluation which takes a more critical look at the exhibition, including asking specific questions concerning the project.[26] As a researcher, evaluating and using an exhibition as a source, this information can be vital for better evaluating how the public responds to an exhibition.

As an example, the following lines from *The Holocaust Gallery*'s summative evaluation feedback between 2017[27] and 2020[28] provides an illustration of the public response.

- "My family's ashes are in Auschwitz—Grandmother, Grandfather, Uncles, Aunties 'NEVER EVER FORGET.'" (Unknown, 2017)
- "Forgetting is easy. Remembering takes effort! Thanks for helping us remember" (Ian Herriott, 2017)
- "Your sacrifices will never be fully comprehended but the best I can try and do is to now prevent anything like from happening ever again." (Anon.)

These are sample responses regarding the exhibition, but when using evaluations to support an exhibition as a source, one should engage with the data. Positive, negative, and uncertain responses are often categorised, as well as remarks related to design, accessibility and interactives. This helps understand how the exhibition is perceived.

Holocaust exhibitions are overwhelming in nature, but what this exhibition does is simplify things by looking through the lens of one family. From *The Holocaust Gallery's* feedback, the intended use of personal memory to engage with the visitor succeeds and evokes strong emotions just as the curators intended.

Memorials

The Holocaust Memorial, Hyde Park, London

The Holocaust Memorial in the Hyde Park Memorial Garden was the first of its kind in the UK.[29] Erected in 1983, the Board of Deputies of British Jews funded the memorial to be placed in Hyde Park in Central London.[30] While Hyde Park receives heavy footfall from both Londoners and tourists, the design of the garden makes this memorial difficult to find, prompting the question of its location. This chapter uses *The Holocaust Memorial* as a source to show how the positioning of a memorial can greatly impact public reception.

Following the end of the Second World War, the collective memory of the Holocaust developed gradually.[31] National memory did not become established and transmitted in Britain until 40 years after the liberation, placing Britain as the liberator and protector of refugees.[32] The proposition of a Holocaust memorial in Hyde Park offered great promise as a step towards the broader education of Holocaust awareness, additionally funded by the Jewish community. This site of permanence provides a physical form of memory to the public.[33] Caroline Sharples and Olaf Jensen argue that due to *The Holocaust Memorial* being hidden, Holocaust memory was at risk.[34]

The positioning of the memorial hinders its impact. Inscribed on the stone are the words "Holocaust Memorial Garden." Beneath this is a verse from Lamentations 1:16, etched in both Hebrew and English: "For those I weep, streams of tears flow from my eyes because of the destruction of my people."[35] There are no other words, leaving viewers to dwell on the verse. The focus is on those lost in the Holocaust and does not include the survivors. This memorial steers the perspective away from a specific narrative, including one which might include Britain's involvement.[36] The words centre on the lives lost in the simplest and most impactful way it can. The design is effective as a memorial, if placed in the right location. Instead, as the first Holocaust memorial erected in Britain, a hidden existence did not establish a good start for Holocaust memory.

The National Holocaust Centre and Museum, Children's Memorial

Cemeteries are sacred spaces of remembrance, and one cannot help but be affected by them. Memorials can act similarly. *The Children's Memorial*, a large pile of stones that encourages visitors to add a stone in remembrance, is sombre, reminiscent of being in a cemetery. It illustrates how a Holocaust monument can prompt participatory commemoration as a living memorial.

The Children's Memorial is one of the first things visitors see at the National Holocaust Centre and Museum (NHCM) in Newark upon leaving the car park. The design is simple yet effective, as the multitude of stones initially creates a visual experience rather than an intellectual one.[37] Beyond the initial effect the mound creates, this memorial is an active one, beckoning viewers to add a stone to the many in recognition and in honour of just one of the 1.5 million children lost to the Holocaust. When placing a single stone, there is a feeling that comes over the viewer of the importance of remembering the nameless child; a sense that they once had a family who loved them. The emotion that this act of remembrance creates, even as a stranger, is enough to create a lasting memory.

The display of stones is comparable to the shoe displays at Yad Vashem and the US Holocaust Memorial Museum, in which large quantities are employed for effect. The stones are reminiscent of the individuals lost in the same way that the mounds of shoes are elsewhere. The power of a display such as this reflects those lost, and conveys the overwhelming numbers represented. This type of display firstly draws in the viewer by creating visual intrigue, and then allows the viewer to focus and contemplate the details of the memorial.[38] It also reflects the Jewish tradition of placing a stone on a gravesite in remembrance.[39] Whether the visitor is Jewish or not, they interact with this memorial by picking up a stone and adding to the pile, as a way of remembering the children.

The first Holocaust memorials erected after the Holocaust included towers and sculptures with traditional designs. The 1950s saw more experiential designs in sculptures that continue to transform and change depending on the designer.[40] *The Children's Memorial* departs from the more common abstract sculptures or traditional statues by allowing visitors to participate and honour the memory of children lost in the Holocaust. The memorial represents a unique experience of active Holocaust commemoration. Forever changing with the continued addition of stones to the pile, it creates an evolving nature that brings it to life, thereby making it a living memorial. *The Children's Memorial* offers an engaging experience through remembrance.

The Kindertransport Monument, Liverpool Street Station

Located outside of Liverpool Street Station in London is a statue of five children standing over a railroad track holding suitcases and identification tags. The monument also shows the few belongings the children brought with them, including a teddy bear, suitcases, and a violin. Every day, commuters and tourists walk past this memorial commemorating a site where the *Kindertransport* brought children to safety. Though many only see this memorial in passing, the story commemorates a significant time in British history. *The Arrival*, designed by Frank Meisler, educates the public daily.[41] This case study illustrates how memorials can be used as evidence for the transmission of collective memory.

Between 1938 and 1940, around 10,000 children escaped Nazi persecution to safety in the United Kingdom, in an initiative known as the *Kindertransport*. Historian Amy Williams has examined this monument and concludes that, "If we consider the wider contexts that Kindertransport memorials are situated within, their meanings can change."[42] The British government issued group visas for children after information came from Jewish organisations regarding the situation in Germany.[43] Both Jewish and non-Jewish children made the journey, predominantly on their own, from Austria, Germany, Poland, and Czechoslovakia.[44] While *The Arrival* reflects a traditional style of British monuments, the story surrounding its construction has more depth.[45]

Before *The Arrival* was unveiled, another *Kindertransport* memorial stood outside Liverpool Street Station. Designed by Flor Kent, *Für das Kind* (*For the Child*) was installed in 2003 as a permanent monument. The monument consisted of a girl's statue next to a glass suitcase filled with artefacts belonging to *Kindertransport* children. While this monument received favourable reviews, the positioning outside made the objects vulnerable to the sun. *Für das Kind* was then relocated and now resides at the NHCM, but this left a gap in *Kindertransport* memorialisation.[46] In 2006, Meisler's replaced Kent's as a commission by the Association of Jewish Refugees (AJR) and World Jewish Relief (WJR).[47] Andy Pearce argued that before the relocation, "the statue of the girl was affectionately known as 'the face of the station.'"[48] What *Für das Kind* established, and *The Arrival* continues, instils "memory in the collective consciousness as a place where a critical moment of the Kinder's evacuation took place."[49]

As one of the last Jewish children to escape Danzig and arrive at Liverpool St Station, Meisler held a special regard towards the creation of this monument. While it is true that these children escaped certain death in concentration camps, the story often focuses on reaching safety in Britain, not what they experienced. Finding a place in new homes often meant the neglect of their religion and cultural heritage. Many children suffered from separation anxiety leaving their parents, some experienced abuse, and others neglect.[50] For most of these children, they never saw their families again and survivor guilt among them became common.[51]

In Meisler's design, the children hold soft smiles with no hint of the separation anxiety, fear, or confusion many children experienced. Pnina Rosenberg argues that the way Meisler designed the memorial illustrates the hope and gratitude the children felt about being rescued.[52] The problem with showing the *Kindertransport* more positively is that it negates the 1.5 million children who died during the Holocaust, and the difficult circumstances many of the children faced upon arrival in Britain.[53] The fact that this memorial is a celebration reinforces the British narrative, which is focused more on the British contribution to saving Jewish children from the Holocaust and less on their experiences.

In contrast, Kent's original memorial offset this narrative, with the little girl appearing bewildered instead of hopeful. Wanting to honour Kent's work despite Meisler's memorial taking prominence, the WJR, who originally commissioned the piece, authorised another one to be placed inside the station in 2011. Today, this memorial with a similarly perplexed girl joined by a young boy and a suitcase sits atop a block, known as *Für das Kind—Displaced*,[54] with the former renamed as *Für das Kind—The Remains*.[55] This addition to Liverpool Street Station offsets Meisler's celebratory design by illustrating the difficulties the children faced through Kent's renewed sculpture. Both monuments work together to present a well-rounded representation of the *Kindertransport* to the visitors at this station rather than the more traditional narrative.

Sir Nicholas Winton Statue, Maidenhead Station

On Platform 3 of Maidenhead Railway Station, just outside London, sits a man on a bench. Leaning casually to his left side with his ankles crossed, he reads an open newspaper before him. On the back of the newspaper, a Union Jack protrudes under the words, "Winton Train." Just to the right of this, it states "Prague to London Liverpool St Station 1939 14 March to 2 August 669 children saved by Sir Nicholas Winton." On the inside of the newspaper, it reads along the bottom, "Kindertransport."[56] Designed and sculpted by Winton's neighbour, Lydia Karpinski, this memorial gives the impression that his presence lingers on at this station, so close to where Sir Nicholas Winton spent a large part of his life.[57]

Born in 1909 in London, Winton lived an exceptional life. In 1938, he planned a ski holiday but cancelled plans suddenly when a friend mentioned the plight of Czech refugees after Germany's annexation of the Sudetenland. Upon witnessing the conditions in person, Winton began a nine-month mission to bring the children safely to Britain with the help of volunteers. While not able to save all the children, they rescued 669.[58]

Another aspect of this memorial is the notoriety that Winton gained when featured on a television show called *That's Life!* A volunteer who assisted on the rescue mission, W.M. Loewinsohn, compiled all the information and data regarding the rescue into a scrapbook and presented it to Winton when no further rescues could be made. The scrapbook included a list of the children rescued and those who agreed to host them upon arrival to England. Only when he shared it with Elizabeth Maxwell, a historian in search of information connected to her Czech Jewish husband, did a series of events begin to unfold.[59] Maxwell then showed the scrapbook to Esther Rantzen, a talk show host for the television programme *That's Life!*

In February 1988, Winton received a call from the BBC asking him to come on the show, but his wife decided not to go and he proceeded on his own. The programme told his story to the public, with Rantzen showing parts of the scrapbook before the cameras panned to two of the rescued children in the audience. The second individual, Vera Diamant, was told by Rantzen that she sat next to Winton himself. Diamant turned to Winton and gave him a tearful embrace as everyone cheered. Winton and his wife returned to the show the following week but this time more aware of what might happen, only to find a standing ovation from an audience of individuals Winton rescued.[60] These two televised events evoked great emotion, so it is unsurprising that his story spread.

While Winton is a hero, his exploits remained largely unknown until the late 1980s because of the attention the television programme drew. In addition to the show, Maxwell's husband Robert owned the Mirror Group Newspapers and featured a three-page article in the *Sunday Mirror* entitled "The Lost Children," thereby reaching an even larger audience.[61] While Winton's efforts alone should have warranted a statue, without this wider knowledge, no one would have known the importance of remembering him. Indeed, William R. Chadwick argues in *The Rescue of the Prague Refugees 1938/39* that these mediums brought Winton notoriety and many accolades in the following decades, including a knighthood.[62]

The context behind this memorial illustrates how easily memorials might not exist if not for the circumstances. If the Maxwells and Rantzen had never taken an interest in Winton's story, it would have remained hidden in a scrapbook. Winton never desired attention and disapproved of how the television programme handled the story. This background is an excellent source for questioning the reasons behind the creation of a memorial, whether it is the importance of Winton's story or the popularity it accidentally generated.

Another way this memorial serves as a source is how the design engages with the viewer. Winton's wrinkled face behind the glasses is not unlike anyone else's grandfather, but it is the softness in the weathered face that humanises this memorial. Travellers might mistake the statue for being real if they pass by too quickly. This is, however, a deliberate design choice. Winton appears a typical traveller, but the words scrawled on the newspaper tell a different story. This is the power that a memorial can have because its simplicity depicts Winton as any other person, albeit one who chose to help those in need. Rather than a large, heroic figure, the statue represents a man easily unobserved. The ability to help others is in everyone, and this memorial continues that story while honouring Winton's impact on a few Jewish children's lives.

Conclusion

The case studies analysed here illustrate how museums and memorials offer different uses as sources for studying the Holocaust. While the general field is constantly changing, museums and memorials remain rich and plentiful with material. They are examples of how curators, foundations, artists, and governments can have an impact on Holocaust memory.

Despite the advantages these sources provide to Holocaust study, there are aspects which also hinder the research. A significant drawback to using museums and memorials as sources is that they are inherently biased. Depending on how the narrative is angled determines the memory being preserved. Another drawback to using museums as a source is that sometimes it takes time to contact museum professionals. The museum sector is fast-paced and largely under-resourced. It can take weeks to obtain the information about an exhibition, and sometimes there is no answer. When approaching a project, significant time should be allotted to research, site visits and communicating with curatorial and learning teams.

When exploring the creation of memorials and exhibitions, it can also be helpful to explore the funders for further foundation. The Association of Jewish Refugees (AJR), which has commissioned and funded several of the case studies mentioned in this chapter, has created a map of Holocaust remembrance sites across the United Kingdom, called the UK Holocaust Map.[63] This will not only make these sites more accessible, but they will also make it easier to find for those wishing to use these sites as sources for Holocaust study. According to Alex Maws, Head of Education and Heritage at the AJR, every country has their own national narrative. However, through the efforts of the AJR, the hope is that they will "move the needle in how the country remembers the Holocaust."[64]

In addition to the AJR's efforts, the British government has also ensured that it is firmly established within the calendar year. In 2001, government inaugurated 27 January as Holocaust Memorial Day (HDM) to promote Holocaust remembrance.[65] Originally run by the Home Office, the government established the Holocaust Memorial Day Trust (HDMT) in 2005 to facilitate the day on its behalf. As the HMD is not a physical memorial, the day is more dynamic with the ability to look at different themes to expand understanding, and it intends to increase the empathy of those participating in remembrance ceremonies across Britain. Although the day is an annual event, according to the Chief Executive of the HMDT, Olivia Marks-Woldman OBE, when people continue engaging with HMD every year they learn new facts, increasing their understanding of what it meant be a victim of the Holocaust or of a recent genocide.[66] The hope is that after the ceremonies, people will be prompted to take action within their own communities, to get to know one another through talks and workshops and set up commemorative observances for the next HMD. When impacted by the experiences the HMD illuminates, it inspires people to continue remembering and commemorating the victims and survivors of the Holocaust, even on their own. This annual event and its commemorations can be considered an important additional memorial for the continued transmission of Holocaust remembrance.

As this chapter has shown, there are many ways to study Holocaust memorials and museums, but the best method to grasp the emotions and thoughts they evoke is by visiting them. These mediums can affect people differently, which is part of the process in understanding their role relative to Holocaust remembrance. At the heart of these examples is memory, its uses, and how these mediums transmit different versions of the past, depending on their narrative or design. Holocaust memory may look differently by country, but exhibitions and memorial sites are the physical evidence of how this memory is being preserved and shared with the public. Museums and memorials are powerful influencers of Holocaust memory. Understanding the position these mediums have towards society further enhances their importance.

Notes

1. J.E. Young, *The Texture of Memory: Holocaust Memorials and Meaning*, London: Yale University Press, 1993, p. xi.
2. Ibid., p. 2.
3. Ibid., p. 6.
4. *The Journey: Children of the Holocaust*, 2008, [Exhibition] The National Holocaust Centre and Museum, Newark, 2008–Present.
5. Ibid.
6. G. Kavanagh, *Dream Spaces: Memory and the Museum*, New York: Leicester University Press, 2000, p. 14.
7. A. Landsberg, *Prosthetic Memory: The Transformation of American Memory in the Age of Mass Culture*, New York: Columbia University Press, 2004, p. 2.
8. J.H. Falk, *Identity and the Museum Visitor Experience*, New York: Routledge, 2009, p. 133.
9. Ibid., p. 135.
10. *The Holocaust Galleries*, Imperial War Museum, London, October 2021–Present.
11. J. Bulgin, *The Holocaust*, London: Imperial War Museums, 2021.
12. J. Bulgin, "Re-presenting the Holocaust at the Imperial War Museum," David Cesarani Holocaust Lecture, Royal Holloway, University of London, 24 January 2022.
13. Ibid.
14. *The Holocaust Galleries*, Imperial War Museum, London, October 2021–Present.
15. *Through Our Eyes*, The Holocaust Centre North, Huddersfield, 6 September 2018–Present.
16. H. Randall, interview with author, 24 May 2022.
17. Ibid.
18. T. Howard, "British Responses to the Holocaust: Student and Teacher Perspectives on the Development of a New Classroom Resource," in S. Foster, A. Pearce, and A. Pettigrew (ed.), *Holocaust Education: Contemporary Challenges and Controversies*, London: UCL Press, 2020, pp. 114–34.
19. Ibid., pp. 115–7.
20. S.J. Foster et al., *What Do Students Know and Understand about the Holocaust? Evidence from English Secondary Schools*, London: UCL Institute of Education, 2016.
21. Howard, "British Responses to the Holocaust," p. 115.
22. A. Corsini, email to author, 16 May 2022.
23. Ibid.
24. R.M. Ehrenreich, and J. Klinger, "War in Context: Let the Artifacts Speak," in W. Muchitsch (ed.), *Does War Belong in Museums? The Representation of Violence in Exhibitions*, Bielefeld: Transcript Verlag, 2013, p. 146.
25. V. Aarons and A.L. Berger, *Third-Generation Holocaust Representation: Trauma, History, and Memory*, Northwestern University Press, 2017, p. 43.
26. C. Heath and M. Davies, *Why Evaluation Doesn't Measure Up*, available online at https://www.museumsassociation.org/museums-journal/opinion/2012/06/01062012-why-evaluation-doesnt-measure-up/#.

27 Jewish Museum London, *Leon Greenman Gallery Book Quotes 20.2.2017*, 2020.
28 Jewish Museum London, *Leon Greenman Visitor Book Feedback February 2020_anon*, 2020.
29 R. Seifert, D. Lovejoy and Partners, *The Holocaust Memorial*, Hyde Park Memorial Garden, 1983.
30 A. Williams, *Memory of the Kindertransport in National and Transnational Perspective*, Ph.D. Thesis. Nottingham Trent University, 2020, p. 199, available online at http://irep.ntu.ac.uk/id/eprint/41429/.
31 C. Sharples and O. Jensen, "Introduction," in C. Sharples and O. Jensen (ed.), *Britain and the Holocaust: Remembering and Representing War and Genocide*, Palgrave Macmillan: Basingstoke, 2013, p. 6.
32 O. Jensen, "The Holocaust in British Television and Film: A Look over the Fence," in Sharples and Jensen (ed.), *Britain and the Holocaust*, p. 117.
33 A. Huyssen, "Monument and Memory in a Postmodern Age," in J.E. Young (ed.), *The Art of Memory: Holocaust Memorials in History*, New York: Prestel, 1994, p. 12.
34 Sharples and Jensen, "Introduction," 2013, p. 5.
35 Seifert, Lovejoy and Partners, *Holocaust Memorial*, Hyde Park Memorial Garden, 1983.
36 Williams, *Memory of the Kindertransport in National and Transnational Perspective*, p. 199.
37 J. Hansen-Glucklich, *Holocaust Memory Reframed: Museums and the Challenges of Representation*, New Brunswick (NJ): Rutgers University Press, 2014, p. 131.
38 Ibid., p. 135.
39 The National Holocaust Centre and Museum, *Children's memorial*, available online at https://www.holocaust.org.uk/childrens-memorial.
40 H. Marcuse, "Holocaust Memorials: The Emergence of a Genre," *American Historical Review*, 115:1, 2010, pp. 88–9.
41 F. Meisler, *The Arrival*, Liverpool St Station, 2006.
42 Williams, *Memory of the Kindertransport in National and Transnational Perspective*, p. 182.
43 R. Göpfert and A. Hammel, "Kindertransport: History and Memory: In Memoriam Erna Nelki," *Shofar: Special Issue: Kindertransporte 1938/39—Rescue and Integration*, 23:1, 2004, pp. 21–2.
44 J. Craig-Norton, "Contesting the Kindertransport as a 'Model' Refugee Response," *European Judaism: A Journal for the New Europe*, 50:2, 2017, p. 24.
45 A. Williams, *Memory of the Kindertransport in National and Transnational Perspective*, p. 183.
46 Ibid., p. 211.
47 M. Allard, "Modelling Bridges Between Past and Current Issues of Forced Migration: Frank Meisler's Memorial Sculpture Kindertransport—The Arrival," *Jewish Historical Studies*, 51:1, April 2020, p. 88.
48 A. Pearce, *Holocaust Consciousness in Contemporary Britain*, New York: Routledge, 2014, p. 216.
49 Allard, "Modelling Bridges Between Past and Current Issues of Forced Migration," p. 88.
50 Craig-Norton, "Contesting the Kindertransport as a 'Model' Refugee Response," pp. 25–6.
51 Göpfert and Hammel, "Kindertransport: History and Memory: In Memoriam Erna Nelki," p. 25.
52 P. Rosenberg, "Footsteps of Memory: Frank Meisler's Kindertransport Memorials," *Prism* 6:5, 2014, p. 93.
53 Williams, *Memory of the Kindertransport in National and Transnational Perspective*, p. 267.
54 F. Kent, *Für das Kind—Displaced*, Liverpool St Station, 2011.
55 Williams, *Memory of the Kindertransport in National and Transnational Perspective*, pp. 211–2.
56 L. Karpinski, *Sir Nicholas Winton Statue*, Maidenhead Train Station, 2010.
57 Sir Nicholas Winton Memorial Trust, *Memorials: Places of Interest and Memorials*, available online at https://www.nicholaswinton.com/memorials.
58 B. Winton, *If It's Not Impossible: The Life of Sir Nicholas Winton*, Leicestershire: Troubador, 2014, p. 156.
59 Ibid., p. 118.
60 BBC, *Holocaust Hero Nicholas Winton on That's Life*, available online at https://www.bbc.co.uk/archive/nicholas_winton_on_thats_life/zbmxhbk.

61 P. Callan, "The Lost Children," *Sunday Mirror*, London, 28 February 1988, pp. 19–21.
62 W.R. Chadwick, *The Rescue of the Prague Refugees 1938/39,* Leicestershire: Troubador, 2010, p. 58.
63 A. Maws, interview with author, 13 May 2022.
64 Ibid.
65 Holocaust Memorial Day Trust, *about Us*, available online at https://www.hmd.org.uk/about-us/.
66 O. Marks-Woldman OBE, interview with author, 28 June 2022.

9 Using Church Documents for Holocaust Study

Michael Dickerman

Christianity in one form or another has been the dominant religion of Europe—and of Germany—for millennia. When Adolf Hitler came to power in 1933, perhaps 40 million Germans were Protestant and 20 million were Catholic, from a total population of 65 million.[1] If for no other reason than the overwhelming percentage of the population that belonged to Protestant and Catholic Churches, the role the churches played during the run-up to and perpetration of the Holocaust was a critical force throughout German society that—for the most part—gave its allegiance to Adolf Hitler and the Nazi Party.[2]

The potential influence of the churches in German society raises difficult questions. What if the Protestant Church had harnessed the power of Christian ethics to ostracise those who would support an extremist group that vilified the innocent and deified its leader? What if the Catholic Church had threatened to withhold the sacrament of the Eucharist from Catholic members of the Nazi Party, or even excommunicated Nazi Party members? Could either effort, let alone both, have stopped Nazism in its tracks and made room for a more centrist government? We will never know the answers to these questions, but the very fact that we even ask them is of significance.

This chapter will describe the structure of the Protestant and Catholic Churches in Nazi Germany and assess the value of church documents in studying and understanding the Holocaust. In doing so, it will address three source-related issues unique to the Catholic Church: the status of the Vatican Archives; the impact of the play *The Deputy* on the reputation of Pope Pius XII (an issue that is no less impassioned today than it was when it first burst onto the scene in the early 1960s); and selected documents of Vatican II.

The Protestant Church[3]

The first anti-Jewish piece of legislation promulgated by the Nazi regime had a significant impact on the Protestant Church. On 1 April 1933, that is, shortly after Hitler came to power on 30 January 1933, the government passed the "Law for the Restoration of the Professional Civil Service," the intent of which was to begin the process of legally excluding Jews from German society. It did this by stating that non-Aryans (that is, Jews) must immediately be removed from their jobs in the civil service. This type of language excluding the Jews was known historically as the Aryan Paragraph, a form of regulation that blocked non-Aryans from becoming members of, or participating in, various German establishments, parties, clubs, groups, or working in certain positions.[4] The German civil service included not only people working for various levels of

DOI: 10.4324/9781003248620-12

government but also teachers, doctors, lawyers, and, because churches were considered state institutions, the clergy. The application of the Aryan Paragraph to the churches meant that Jews who had converted to Christianity (the so-called "Jewish Christians" or "non-Aryan Christians"), and had been fully accepted into the church by virtue of their baptism and profession of faith, could no longer continue in their positions as pastors or other church officials.[5] This rejection of their Christian status and their expulsion from the church ultimately came to apply to Jewish Christian parishioners, with suggestions that they worship separately from "real" Christians.

The significance of the application of the Aryan Paragraph to the German churches cannot be overstated, as it resulted in the government determining who was or was not Christian. By ignoring baptism, confession of faith, and the churches' welcome into the Christian community, it effectively nullified conversions of Jews to Christianity, and usurped what had always been the role of the church, namely, to determine who is a Christian. The Nazis "mandated that race transcends all other signifiers of [Christian] identity, including baptism."[6]

Thus developed a divide among the Protestant churches[7]: some wanted to apply the Aryan Paragraph to churches, while some were opposed.[8] The former created a movement—the *Glaubensbewegung Deutsch Christen*, the "German Christian Faith Movement"[9] (hereafter, the "Movement")—that demanded that the Aryan Paragraph apply to all Protestant churches as part of its broader goal to de-Judaise the churches and integrate Nazi ideology with Christian theology.[10] In addition to wanting to eliminate Jewish Christians from their clerical ranks and congregations, the Movement sought to Aryanise Jesus as a warrior against Jews and Judaism, eliminate the use of the Old Testament in Christian services, and rewrite the New Testament to eliminate all references to Jesus's Jewish roots.[11]

In perhaps the clearest example of the lengths to which the Movement sought to de-Judaise Christianity, in May 1939 it established the Institute for the Study and Eradication of Jewish Influence on German Church Life. Its mission was to redefine "Christianity as a Germanic religion whose founder, Jesus, was no Jew but rather had fought valiantly to destroy Judaism, falling as victim to that struggle."[12]

The documents associated with the Movement reflect not only its theology but also, indirectly, the ideology of the Nazi regime itself. Documents relating to the German Christian movement "functioned to help other Hitler-era Germans who read them. And who almost without exception identified themselves as Christian believers, comprehend what was happening around them as fully compatible with their Christian faith."[13]

In opposition to the Movement's Nazified version of Christianity, the *Bekennende Kirche*, the "Confessing Church" (formerly, the "Pastors' Emergency League") was formed. Churches affiliating themselves with the Confessing Church rejected the Movement's Nazification of Christianity and were determined to reject the application of the Aryan Paragraph to Protestant churches—thus pushing back against government interference in church authority—and reject any efforts to eliminate the Old Testament, to rewrite the New Testament, and so forth. However, it was neither an outspoken champion of the Jews, nor a virulent critic of the Nazi regime over its treatment of the Jews. The Confessing Church was standing up only for *Jewish Christians*,[14] as well as for the autonomy of the Protestant church's authority to determine who was or was not Christian.

The Catholic Church

Unlike the German Protestant Churches (and Protestantism globally), for which there is no single spokesperson on behalf of all the churches, the infrastructure of the Catholic Church is a model of worldwide organisation. With each level of religious authority responsible to the one above it—deacon, priest, bishop, archbishop, cardinal, and pope—the Catholic Church functions as a single unit. That does not mean that there are not differences among clergy, as would be expected in any global entity. But the most important decisions rest in the hands of a very small group of men, with the pope the ultimate arbiter.

The very same hierarchy that disseminated various decisions by the pope to priests and parishioners also worked to move information in the other direction: from the parishioners and priests to the pope (or, perhaps more accurately, to the Vatican). It was this means of communication that brought news of the Holocaust to the Holy See, making it one of the first major institutions to know what was happening to the Jews and others.[15] A brief timeline is in order.

The so-called "Thousand Year" Third Reich lasted for 12 years, neatly divided into two six-year periods: the first, from 1933 to 1939, was prior to the Second World War, and the second, from 1939 to 1945, was during the war and the Holocaust. That same division applies to the popes who were in office: during the first six-year period, Pius XI (who began his papacy in 1922) was pope, and during the second, Pius XII (who reigned until his death in 1958). Thus, for study of the Holocaust, the focus is on Pius XII.

However, in some ways, understanding the years and related documents of Pius XII requires that we begin with Pius XI, and his Secretary of State, Eugenio Pacelli. When Hitler came to power, he and Pius XI sought an agreement, the pope looking for Hitler's commitment that he would not interfere with the Church, and Hitler looking for assurance that the Catholic church (which had its own German political party, the Central Party) would not oppose, criticise, or interfere with his government. The agreement—the *Reichskonkordat*—was negotiated and signed by Secretary of State Pacelli on 20 July 1933 on behalf of Pius XI and the Vatican.

This last point is important for two reasons. The first is that upon the death of Pius XI in 1939, it was his Secretary of State, Eugenio Pacelli, who was elected his successor with the papal name of Pius XII. The second reason is that the Vatican took its commitment to the terms of the *Reichskonkordat* very seriously. When it was signed early in Hitler's regime, it meant that no opposition to the German government—not even verbal criticism—could come from any Catholic clergy, from priest to pope. As part of that restriction, the church dissolved its political party. The Concordat was meant to apply not only to Pius XI, but to all future popes until it would be abrogated. Thus, it was that Pius XII felt himself restricted by the Concordat during the Second World War and the Holocaust, and rejected any suggestions that circumstances required that it be nullified.

During the first six years of the Third Reich, the Concordat weighed heavily on Pius XI. The reason was that from the very beginning Hitler violated the terms to which he agreed, while the Vatican continued to abide by its obligations. These violations became so egregious that Pius XI issued an encyclical on 14 March 1937, called *Mit Brennender Sorge* ("With Burning Anxiety"). It was a strong statement calling out the Nazi government for its violations of the Concordat and undercutting some of the most basic tenets of Nazi ideology.[16]

There are two points to be noted about this encyclical. The first is that its tone and directness was never found in any encyclicals issued by Pius XII, which were written in much more diplomatic and, therefore, guarded language. The second is that despite the flagrant violations by the Hitler regime—which continued during Pius XII's papacy—and the precedent that Pius XI established for Pius XII to push back, the latter continued to feel personally bound by the Vatican's restrictions under the Concordat. As a result, all levels of Catholic clergy were similarly restricted.

Another document whose origin was attributable to Pius XI, but which overlapped the time of Pius XII, was the so-called "hidden encyclical." In June 1938 Pius XI was seriously ill, but he was intent on issuing an encyclical directly addressing the issue of racism as inimical to the very heart of Christian theology. He assigned the job of drafting the encyclical to an American Jesuit, John LaFarge, asking him to base his draft on a book he had written, and which the pope had read and admired. LaFarge called the drafted encyclical *"Humani Generis Unitas"* ("The Unity of the Human Race"). It is not clear what happened to the draft or whether Pius XI saw it at all, but it does appear that Pius XII ordered it to be put aside and not finalised or issued.[17]

The significance of this draft encyclical is that Pius XI authorised it, while Pius XII blocked its publication, contributing to how Pius XI and Pius XII are regarded today. The combination of *Mit Brennender Sorge*, coupled with Pius XI's intent to make some kind of definitive statement about race, has contributed to him being very positively compared to Pius XII, who was silent when he knew efforts were being made to exterminate an entire people from the face of the earth.

An example of the language that Pius XII employed in many of his encyclicals and other communications is the much-disputed papal Christmas message of 1942.[18] The dispute surrounding this message is whether Pius's words were adequate to the reality of the Final Solution that was at operating at full speed throughout that year. What is undisputed is the fact that Pius's radio message contained very few words about the Holocaust in its 26 pages of text.[19] Pius referred to "those hundreds of thousands who, without any fault on their part, sometimes only because of their nationality or race, have been consigned to death or to a slow decline." While some see this as a statement that would clearly be understood by listeners as a reference to the Jews, others argue that by never mentioning the Jews Pius was too vague to fulfil his moral obligation to protest vigorously the atrocities to which the Jews were subject.

Assessing the Value of Church Documents in Studying the Holocaust

In the summer of 1964, *The Journal of Bible and Religion* published an article by Canadian historian John S. Conway entitled "The Historiography of the German Church Struggle."[20] That article—almost verbatim—became the Introduction to his 1968 book, *The Nazi Persecution of the Churches, 1933–1945*.[21] He begins his essay by observing that "in almost all the accounts by English-speaking authors of the Nazi era in Germany only slight attention is paid to the affairs of the Churches."[22] He compares this with "the very numerous and very thorough studies of the Churches' life which have appeared in German."[23]

With this as background, he explores the motives behind these German writings. Conway emphasises that sources on the German Churches and the Holocaust, like sources on all topics, are influenced, explicitly or implicitly, by the motives of their authors. To read documents and sources about the churches in Nazi Germany, and to derive value from doing so, requires that the reader understand the motives behind the documents. Conway sets forth five different motives that drove this mass of material by German writers.

The first of these was the effort to "come to terms with the recent events in German history."[24] Although those events are not as recent today as they were when Conway was writing, his point still holds. Quoting another scholar, Arthur C. Cochrane, that "the true story of the Church in Germany ... is to a large extent a sad tale of betrayal, timidity and unbelief,"[25] Conway contends that it is still difficult to conceive that a country as cultured as Germany could become the country of Hitler and the Nazis, especially in light of the central role the churches played in German society. Trying to understand this was a principal motivation behind the German-language works.

The second motive was "to place on record the witness of all those who fell victims of the Nazi tyranny" such as Dietrich Bonhoeffer and Hans and Sophie Scholl, and "to justify the actions" of the Confessing Church.[26]

Related to the second motive, the third was

> to point out the errors, theological and political, of the 'Deutsche Christen' [the German Christian Faith Movement], and to document the manner in which the 'Bekennende Kirche' struggled against the whole weight of the Nazi state machinery to preserve the truth of the Christian Gospel.[27]

Conway notes that a "similar movement was to be found in the Catholic Church," namely, to make clear the extent of persecution of the Catholic Church, and thereby provide "the material on which the record of opposition to the Third Reich could be documented."[28]

Conway's fourth motive was, in his view, "undoubtedly the desire of these authors" in both the Protestant and Catholic churches "to demonstrate to the outside world that not all Germans had fallen for the errors of Nazism."[29] He also cautions that "all the books written in English before the war were wholeheartedly" on the side of the Confessing Church, whereas "since 1945 ... not a single theologian or Church historian has sought to defend in general ... the 'Deutsche Christen' or the theological deductions they made from their political decisions."[30] While this may no longer be as true as it was when Conway wrote it, general favouritism of a particular Church—e.g., the Confessing Church—can drive not only the number of books written about it but also the interpretation of facts relevant to it.

Finally, Conway writes about what he considers to be perhaps the most important motive behind these writings: that the authors "were conscious of the need to direct and guide the pattern of their Churches' life and thought for the future."[31]

With all these, Conway has laid out for us not only specific motives that generated the efforts by German-language authors to understand the role of the churches within German society as it perpetrated the Holocaust but also—and to the point of this chapter—to make clear on a more general level that church documents can be understood and therefore be of value to the study of the Holocaust only by asking what the author—whether an individual or an institution—sought to accomplish by the document. Knowing that, in turn, requires a full understanding of the author, the time and circumstances in which the document was being considered and drafted, and the broader implications of the message embedded or presented explicitly in the document.

In reaction to the almost always self-serving nature of the authors of the German-language writings on the Churches, Conway observes:

> in seeking to demonstrate their opposition to the Nazi state and to those in the Churches who had shown sympathy with Nazi aims, these historians were not free from the grievous fault of suppressing certain facts and blurring over the record of their own former sympathies and their own participation in the political processes which had brought the Nazi state into power.[32]

We are reminded here that the motive behind the writing of a source can compromise the objectivity and accuracy of that writing.

Considering the impact that motives have on the usefulness of Church documents in understanding the relationship between the churches and the Holocaust, Conway writes of historians who came after the initial burst of German-language writings and objected to "these received views" of the churches in the Nazi regime. Among the motivations of this new group of historians was "the motive of historical accuracy."[33] Another was based on theological grounds: "Against all the self-justifying of a Church, ready to compromise with political evil for the sake of expediency, these critics raise the uncompromising claims of the Gospel itself."[34]

The Importance of Christianity and the Churches in Nazi Germany[35]

The role of churches as social institutions includes providing a sense of community and belonging, an opportunity for social engagement and the exchange of information about individuals in the community, the organisation of charities and the means for other acts of kindness, a place of comfort in times of crisis, and a place in which various life cycle events occur or are recognised. Many of these functions can also be provided by fraternal, social, charitable, and other secular organisations. What is unique about the social role of churches is that all these individual roles are grounded in the dissemination and ritualisation of a particular theology and its concomitant moral and ethical precepts.

The theological and moral roles of churches are magnified in times of great societal stress. The general responsibility of teaching and guiding individuals and groups in the religion's theology over weeks, months, and years is compressed to address the immediate sources of stress, and to focus on the application of the underlying theology to real-life fears and moral decisions. Thus, in times of societal stress, the church's role expands, and in some cases and places, becomes—or has the opportunity to become—the primary determinant of parishioners' responses to a new environment with its own moral and ethical demands. More specifically, German churches played an "important role in shaping people's attitudes and actions vis-à-vis National Socialism, including anti-communism, nationalism, traditional loyalty to governing authorities (particularly among Protestants), and the convergence of Nazi anti-semitism with deep-seated anti-Jewish prejudice."[36]

It is hardly surprising that anti-Judaism was a deeply embedded component in Christian Germany (as it was throughout Europe), reinforced as it was from the pulpits with the authority of religious leaders, if in no other way than simply by the weekly reading and preaching of the Gospels. Church documents are filled with references to the "othered" Jews who have suffered, and continue to deserve suffering, for their millennia-old blindness to the Christian truth.

Therefore, there were several conditions that gave rise to how the Nazis influenced the churches' responses toward Nazism. German churches, no less than any other German institution or the German people themselves, were influenced by the confluence of events (e.g., the loss of the First World War, the Weimar Republic, the economy, etc.) that contributed so much to the rise of the Nazi Party and caused the sense in German society that nothing could be done to regain Germanic greatness. This resulted in a desperate need for change, not just around the edges of society, but change that would constitute a revolution. This also resulted in an equally desperate need for a great man—an *Übermensch*—to bring about that revolution. It was this societal cry for fundamental change and a heroic leader that parishioners brought to the pews, and to which the church had to appeal.

When reading Protestant church documents, it must be remembered that some will reflect the theological position of the Lutheran Church (the largest of the Protestant denominations) requiring obedience to government. Thus, the reluctance of many to push back on the Nazi government—or any government—is grounded in a theological precept. Also, when reading documents of the Catholic Church, it is important that they are not read through the prism of post-Vatican II reforms. Prior to 1963, the Catholic Church had a completely different relationship with and view of non-Catholics (and especially Jewish non-Catholics) than is the case today. We must be careful to judge the actions of Catholic religious leaders—and understand their related documents—based on the religious environment in which those actions were taken, not the post-Vatican II environment in which we read them.

Documentary Issues Unique to the Catholic Church

The Vatican Archives

Documents pertaining to the Holy See are maintained in the Vatican Archives, going back many centuries. Among millions of documents and artefacts, the Archives contain all documents related to each pope, including encyclicals and other official church pronouncements, letters, diaries, speeches, radio addresses, and the like. As a general rule, the documents of a particular pope are held in the archives for 75 years after the pope's reign and are only then released for purposes of scholarly research. Because of the significance of the events during the papacy of Pius XII there was intense pressure applied to the Vatican to release them earlier than would otherwise be the case.

As a result, in 1964 Pope Paul VI authorised four Jesuit historians to compile and publish *Acts and Documents of the Holy See relating to the Second World War* (ADSS).[37] An 11-volume work, it reveals much but certainly not all about Pius XII during those critical years.[38] Some historians have expressed concern about using this source. The documents that were selected are only a fraction of the millions of pages of Pius XII-related documents held in the Archives, and the choices as to which documents to include in the ADSS may have excluded some of the documents more damaging to Pius XII and the Vatican.[39] Thus, Pope Francis ordered the full archives of Pius XII to be opened to scholars beginning on 2 March 2020. However, by the second week in March access had to be closed due to the Covid-19 pandemic. The

Archives were reopened 12 weeks later. As of this writing, little has yet to be published based on the newly available documents with the single major exception of a work by historian David I. Kertzer in 2022.[40] Thus, we might be years away from being able to make use of this, the ultimate source on Pius XII and the Holocaust.[41]

The Play

Any discussion of documents about Pope Pius XII and the Holocaust would be remiss not to include reference to a play, *The Deputy* (*Der Stellvertreter*) that was first performed in Berlin on 20 February 1963.[42] Its author was a 31-year-old Protestant German playwright named Rolf Hochhuth. This was his first play. *The Deputy* was a dramatic portrayal of the author's understanding of the actions and motivations of Pius XII regarding the Jews during the Final Solution. As presented by Hochhuth, Pius was a cold, egotistical, uncaring man, more concerned with his possible role in history as the person who would mediate the end of World War II than the almost unimaginable attempted annihilation of the Jews, something that he knew beyond question was happening. He is seen drowning in vague, diplomatic generalities, refusing to take a stand against Hitler, insisting that the *Reichskonkordat* signed by Germany and the Vatican in 1933 requires silence.[43]

Most unusual—perhaps unique in the annals of modern theatre—is the controversy the play generated. In some cities, it was met with protests (2,500 people protested it in Stuttgart), while in others it was outright banned.[44]

Further, and most germane to this chapter, the play had an extraordinary impact on Pius's reputation around the world.[45] On his death in 1958, he was lauded as a hero of the Jews by (among others) the Synagogue Council of America and Golda Meir, then the Israeli Foreign Minister.[46] Although there were some questions quietly being asked about his actions during the Holocaust, they were held mainly by a small group of scholars. But after *The Deputy* was performed, the questions about Pius XII exploded, questions that had never been voiced before: what did he know? Why did he never mention the Jews? What was his primary responsibility: to avoid antagonising Hitler and thereby increase the chances that the Catholic Church would survive the war, or to care for millions of innocent victims whose death in the most horrible way were being perpetrated by an overwhelmingly Christian nation? It all came down to this: did Pius do all that he could and should have done to protect the Jews from the Final Solution? And it was *The Deputy* that was the catalyst for these, questioning a reputation, asking compelling questions, and triggering as difficult a moral examination as one can imagine.

Controversy surrounding Pius XII remains as strong today as it was when it first came to the fore in the 1960s. Was he a saint for the efforts he made on behalf of the Jews, or a moral failure for not confronting Hitler, especially in light of the Final Solution? And while it might be years until enough scholars have sufficient time in the Vatican Archives to give us the full picture of what Pius did or did not do for the Jews, there is no question that it was *The Deputy* that set the controversy in motion.

Vatican II

There is yet another set of important Catholic sources for studying the Holocaust, though the first of them was not promulgated until 1965. On 11 October 1962, Pope

John XXIII convened all bishops to the Second Vatican Council (Vatican II) to consider various issues of the church, including relations with the Jewish people.[47] Sixteen documents were enacted following the close of the Council on 8 December 1965, under the auspices of Pope Paul VI. There are three documents that are of particular relevance to this chapter.

Nostra Aetate ("In Our Time"), entitled "Declaration on the Relation of the Church to Non-Christian Religions," is the Council's foundational document.[48] It was a breakthrough pronouncement that rejected many of the longest held anti-Judaic church doctrines that had, over the millennia, caused so much suffering.

We Remember: A Reflection on the Shoah, written by the Commission for Religious Relations with the Jews, was announced by Pope John Paul II on 16 March 1998.[49] It sought to reconcile the church with the role it, Christians, and Christianity played in the Holocaust. Though surely well-intended, it met with concerns by many in the Jewish community globally which saw the preparation and release of the document *Response to Vatican Document "We Remember: A Reflection on the Shoah,"* by the International Jewish Committee on Interreligious Consultations.[50] This was issued shortly after *We Remember*. The two documents should be read together.

Then, in November 1999, the Bishops' Committee for Ecumenical and Interreligious Relations issued *Catholic Teaching on the Shoah: Implementing the Holy See's We Remember*.[51] As the title indicates, this is guidance for teaching *We Remember* in Catholic Schools.

Conclusion

Adolf Hitler, although baptised a Catholic, was not a Christian, at least, not in its most basic sense. He and his Nazi ideology (and the regime which based itself slavishly on both) were, in fact, anti-Christian, showing support for Christianity as a temporary means of maintaining the allegiance of the overwhelmingly Christian German nation. If given enough time there is every reason to believe that Hitler, nationalism, and hate would have replaced Jesus, the Gospels, and love as a form of religion. Steps in that direction were already being taken in what the Nazis expected would be the very beginning of their mooted Thousand Year Reich: the pledge of loyalty unto to death to the Führer; the gross violations of the Concordat between the Catholic Church and the Nazi government; the rise of the German Christian Movement; the support of the Confessing Church for Jewish Christians but not for Jews; the harassment, arrest, and murder of religiously observant Catholics, and the decision made by Pius XII to remain silent in the face of overwhelming evil. The intent of Nazism to replace Christianity can be seen in the nature of the beliefs and rituals of Nazism. Professor of Religion Mary M. Solberg writes:

> One has only to view National Socialist rallies to get a sense of their quasi-religious fervor. The German Christian chronicler Arnold Dannenmann writes that adherents of the National Socialist movement, as they organized for change throughout Germany, "were carrying out a religious task." He goes on, "The Führer Adolf Hitler ... was utterly aware of his divine mission," and "the thousands of gatherings that took place during the National Socialist movement's struggle to take power in Germany actually fulfilled a religious purpose." From the German Christian viewpoint, the "experience of the times"—binding together the whole German people—was "God-given."[52]

It was not just the Nazis' perversion of Christianity and their intention to supplant it that was significant, but also the willingness of the German people to not only accept Hitler as their leader and accede to his anti-Christian ideology but also to act in ways that were the antithesis of Christian doctrines, committed primarily against the very people of Jesus, his disciples, his family, and his followers. And yet, there seems to have been little sense that by exterminating the Jews they were somehow betraying their church-taught beliefs and would thereby have strayed beyond redemption. Did the killers ask themselves if what they were doing would isolate them from their church and their God? Did the families of the killers welcome them home with even the slightest concern about the loathsome violations committed by their loved ones against the most basic and important of the teachings of Jesus? Yes, no doubt some did, but it is fair to assume that most killers and families failed to recognise the chasm that had opened between their actions and their religious upbringing.

This is the context in which church documents were written, and the context which historians must examine to find their meaning and insights. But ultimately it all comes down to whether and to what degree these documents and sources are useful in studying and understanding the Holocaust. Might one consider them of great significance? Or could one argue that in an era fraught with the horrors of the death camps, concerns about the rights of converted Jews to worship in a church should be ignored—or at least not considered to be a necessary component without which no study of the Holocaust is complete?

A strong argument can be made that an understanding of Church-related documents and sources about them is absolutely critical to any effort at understanding the Holocaust, if by "to understand" one means going beyond the who, what, where, and when of the Holocaust, as important as they are, and to see the "why" of it as the most critical question to be answered. If we are trying to understand why virtually an entire population living in a highly cultured and religious country decided to give itself over to a regime of unrivalled evil, then an examination of the role of the Church in that country is required. Religion is at once private and communal. Churches play a central role in both of those elements, helping the individual to form certain beliefs and, at the same time, providing a community of like-minded worshippers. Religious beliefs of the national Christian population of Nazi Germany, and the role of the churches in crafting those beliefs and disseminating their related system of morality, provide insights into at least one reason that the population behaved as it did. If it allows us to know nothing more than what people were being told each Sunday by an institution of great influence, it is worth our consideration. There are few areas of study of the Holocaust that can provide a window into what ordinary Germans believed about good and evil, about commitment to one another, and about the sanctity of human life like that which is provided by church documents.[53]

Most of the documents discussed here show us the "faith-chaos" that befell the Protestant and Catholic churches when Nazi ideology—including anti-Christianity—began to seep into the churches, befouling all who were touched by it and who voluntarily, even eagerly, sought ultimately to embrace it. The documents represent a critical step in the rise and power of the Nazi movement, when the institutions and beliefs that had held Christian Europe together were unable (or perhaps, unwilling) to stand up to decidedly non-Christian institutions and beliefs. The Holocaust could not have happened if Germans (and Christians in occupied countries throughout Europe) had held fast to their Christian beliefs and had refused to abandon them for the obvious anti-Christianity of Nazism. Perhaps examining the church documents of the time will help us better understand why no such refusal occurred.

Notes

1 See "Christianity and the Holocaust," available online at https://www.ushmm.org/collections/bibliography/christianity-and-the-holocaust. The estimated number of Jews at the time was between 560,000 and 600,000.
2 On church membership, see R.P. Ericksen and S. Heschel (ed.), *Betrayal: German Churches and the Holocaust*, Minneapolis: Augsburg Fortress Press, 1999, p. 10.
3 The Protestant church in Germany is called the *Deutsch Evangelische Kirche* (the "German Evangelical Church.") It is an umbrella name for the Lutheran, Reformed, and United churches of Germany in a confederation of 28 autonomous regional churches with little organisation among them. See M.M. Solberg, *A Church Undone: Documents from the German Christian Faith Movement*, Minneapolis: Fortress Press, 2015, p. 19, n. 30. See also D.L. Bergen, *Twisted Cross: The German Christian Movement in the Third Reich*, Chapel Hill: University of North Carolina Press, 1996, p. 5.
4 https://www.yadvashem.org/odot_pdf/Microsoft%20Word%20-%205774.pdf.
5 For a broader discussion of the Aryan Paragraph as it applies to the churches, see Bergen, *Twisted Cross*, pp. 88–100; and Solberg, *A Church Undone*, pp. 53–79.
6 S. Heschel, "Sacrament Versus Racism: Converted Jews in Nazi Germany," in I. Kacandes (ed.), *On Being Adjacent to Historical Violence*, Berlin: De Gruyter, 2022, p. 89.
7 This is one component of the so-called *Kirchenkampf* ("church struggle"), namely, the conflict between the German Christian Faith Movement and the Confessing Church. See M.D. Hockenos, "The Church Struggle and the Confessing Church: An Introduction to Bonhoeffer's Context," *Studies in Christian-Jewish Relations*, 2:1, 2007, p. 3.
8 It should be noted that most pastors did not join with either the German Christian Movement or the Confessing Church. See J.S. Conway, *The Nazi Persecution of the Churches, 1933–1945*, Vancouver: Regent College, 1968, p. xix.
9 This is not to be confused with the "German Faith Movement," a neo-pagan movement opposed by the German Christian Faith Movement and the Confessing Church.
10 This was an example of the Nazi concept of *Gleichschaltung*, or "coordination," the government's effort to Nazify every aspect of German society.
11 Further, it "sought to incorporate the twenty-eight Protestant regional churches into a united German Evangelical Reich church." See Hockenos, "Church Struggle," p. 4.
12 S. Heschel, *The Aryan Jesus: Christian Theologians and the Bible in Nazi Germany*, Princeton: Princeton University Press, 2008, p. 1.
13 Solberg, *A Church Undone*, p. 13.
14 R.P. Ericksen, *Complicity in the Holocaust: Churches and Universities in Nazi Germany*, Cambridge: Cambridge University Press, 2012, p. 28.
15 M. Phayer, *The Catholic Church and the Holocaust, 1930–1965*, Bloomington: Indiana University Press, 2000, pp. 43–50.
16 For the full text, see https://www.vatican.va/content/pius-xi/en/encyclicals/documents/hf_p-xi_enc_14031937_mit-brennender-sorge.html.
17 In this regard, see G. Passelecq and B. Suchecky, *The Hidden Encyclical of Pius XI*, New York: Harcourt Brace, 1997.
18 The full text of this message can be found at https://www.papalencyclicals.net/pius12/p12ch42.htm.
19 Phayer, *The Catholic Church*, p. 49.
20 J.S. Conway, "The Historiography of the German Church Struggle," *Journal of Bible and Religion*, 32:3, July 1964, pp. 221–30.
21 Conway, *Nazi Persecution*, pp. xiii–xxxi.
22 Ibid., p. xiii.
23 Ibid., p. xiv. Conway writes: "A bibliography compiled in 1958 [of German-language works] ... contained no fewer than six thousand items."
24 Ibid., p. xv.

25 A.C. Cochrane, *The Church's Confession Under Hitler,* Lexington: Westminster Press, 1962, p. 16, quoted in Conway, *Nazi Persecution,* p. xv, and n. 2, p. 409.
26 Conway, *Nazi Persecution,* pp. xv–xvi.
27 Ibid., p. xvi.
28 Ibid.
29 Ibid., p. xvii.
30 Ibid., pp. xvii, xix.
31 Ibid., p. xviii.
32 Ibid., p. xx.
33 Ibid., p. xxi.
34 Ibid., p. xxiii–xxiv.
35 Doris Bergen observes "an often overlooked point [in the study of German society in the Hitler years is] the centrality of religion in National Socialist society ... Christianity permeated Nazi society." See Bergen, *Twisted Cross,* pp. 8–9.
36 "Christianity and the Holocaust," available online at https://www.ushmm.org/collections/bibliography/christianity-and-the-holocaust.
37 The acronym is based on the title in French. All volumes can be found in French at https://www.vatican.va/archive/actes/index_en.htm.
38 See P. Blett, S.J., *Pius XII and the Second World War, According to the Archives of the Vatican,* New York: Paulist Press, 1997. Especially helpful as an introduction to the Archives is the Preface by T.F. Stransky, and Blett's Introduction.
39 For a detailed report on the reliability of the ADSS, see "The Vatican & the Holocaust: Preliminary Report on the Vatican during the Holocaust" by The International Catholic-Jewish Historical Commission (October 2000), at https://www.jewishvirtuallibrary.org/preliminary-report-on-the-vatican-during-the-holocaust-october-2000-2#1. See also J. Kornberg, *The Pope's Dilemma, Pius XII Faces Atrocities and Genocide in the Second World War,* Toronto: University of Toronto Press, 2015, pp. 76–78; and H. Wolf, *Pope and Devil, The Vatican's Archives and the Third Reich,* Cambridge (MA): The Belknap Press of Harvard University Press, pp. 11–8.
40 D.I. Kertzer, *The Pope at War: The Secret History of Pius XII, Mussolini, and Hitler,* New York: Random House, 2022.
41 It should be noted that Pope Francis has authorised digitising 170 volumes of requests from Jews for help World War II. See https://www.nytimes.com/2022/06/24/world/europe/pope-vatican-jews-second-world-war.html.
42 R. Hochhuth, *The Deputy,* New York: Grove Press, 1964.
43 Following the script is a 65-page historical analysis written by Hochhuth which, he contends, confirms the various representations he has made throughout the play.
44 E. Bentley (ed.), *The Storm Over the Deputy,* New York: Grove Press, 1964.
45 Although controversial, Pius XII is currently being considered for sainthood by the Catholic Church. He was declared a Servant of God by Pope John Paul II in 1990 and deemed Venerable by Pope Benedict XVI in 2009. The next step—Veneration, which requires the attribution of a miracle—has been delayed pending further examination of the Vatican Archives.
46 *We Remember* included a lengthy footnote (n. 16) which cites additional statements by Jewish leaders commending Pius XII for his actions on behalf of the Jews during the Holocaust.
47 For an excellent source on Vatican II, see J. Connelly, *From Enemy to Brother: The Revolution in Catholic Teaching on the Jews, 1933–1965,* Cambridge (MA): Harvard University Press, 2012.
48 For the full text of *Nostra Aetate,* see https://www.vatican.va/archive/hist_councils/ii_vatican_council/documents/vat-ii_decl_19651028_nostra-aetate_en.html.
49 For the full text of *We Remember,* see https://www.bc.edu/content/dam/files/research_sites/cjl/texts/cjrelations/resources/documents/catholic/We_Remember.htm.
50 For the full text of *Response,* see https://www.bc.edu/content/dam/files/research_sites/cjl/texts/cjrelations/resources/documents/jewish/response_We_Remember.html.

51 For the full text of *Catholic Teaching,* see https://www.usccb.org/beliefs-and-teachings/ecumenical-and-interreligious/jewish/upload/Catholic-Teaching-on-the-Shoah-Implementing-the-Holy-See-s-We-Remember-2001.pdf.
52 Solberg, *Church Undone,* p. 38.
53 Solberg has suggested that there are crucial questions that have yet to be answered: "What *is* the church, and what should be its role within society? What should the relationship be between Christian people and their governing authorities? ... [and] Perhaps most poignantly, who is the neighbor—and what does it mean to love that neighbor as myself?" Ibid., p. 42.

10 Contemporary Newspapers as Sources for Approaching Holocaust Study

Eve E. Grimm

The News and Newspapers

The English word "news," sometimes alleged to be an acronym for the letters North, East, West, and South (suggesting information coming from all points on the compass) is actually derived from a much earlier form of the word "new," signifying contemporaneity of information. In essence, news stories describe singular events, often without discussion, as "reports" rather than commentary or analysis. These are obtained by professional information gatherers called variously reporters, journalists, or stringers, who work either for an organisation that will publish their findings, or who will sell the stories to that organisation in a freelance capacity. For an item to be accepted, it must be deemed "newsworthy," that is, it should find resonance with an audience such as to warrant press attention or coverage. Newsworthy stories are generally those upon which consumers will remark. Those involving local matters, conflicts, the environment, sport, business, and celebrities are common news topics.[1] Government pronouncements about laws, taxes, public health, and crimes have always been considered news.

The modern newspaper as the conveyance for passing news to the community was the most important form of communication until the invention of wireless technology in the early twentieth century—and even then, the reach of newspapers probably exceeded wireless until the middle of the century.[2]

In Britain, *The Times* had been published under that name since 1788. In 1814, it began daily editions, with printing on both sides of a page. News gathering techniques developed as the century progressed. By the late 1840s, telegraph networks linked cities, allowing the prospect of overnight news reporting, while technological developments in the manufacture of cheap paper, known as newsprint, enabled larger print runs and cheaper prices. Increasing literacy rates throughout the century saw more readers, a growing demand for news, increased competition among newspaper proprietors, more pages in each edition, a wider coverage of topics, and a consequent augmentation of advertising revenue upon which newspapers began to rely.

Newspapers in the New World had as long a history as in Britain, particularly in Boston, New York, and Philadelphia. As in Britain, technological advancements during the nineteenth century, such as the telegraph and faster printing presses, also helped to expand press coverage across the country and played a large role in the process of "Americanisation" as the United States experienced rapid economic and population growth through massive waves of immigration from Europe. By 1900, major newspapers such as the *New York Times, Boston Globe, Philadelphia Inquirer,*

DOI: 10.4324/9781003248620-13

and *Chicago Tribune* had become leading and highly respected national newspapers with international reputations.

Newspapers in other parts of the world, particularly Europe, followed a similar trajectory to those of Britain and the United States. More people than ever before could read, and newspapers penetrated the remotest regions. It has been written that European societies at the outset of the First World War were "better informed than any previous generation."[3] Before then, newspapers were largely free and independent, coming from a century in which their popularity had never been greater. The outbreak of war, however, saw a setback. Censorship and propaganda intruded on newspapers as proprietors and editors hastened to align with the war aims of their respective countries. Failure to do so could result in the paper being shut down, or the principals involved being deemed less than patriotic. The war thus presented a severe challenge for newspapers, where rationing of newsprint, massive enlistments, and the closure of news sources in various countries saw the number of papers decrease. Despite this, circulations remained high in most countries (other than for those experiencing revolution and defeat), and journalists looked forward to a time when they could return to the freer days from before 1914.

The Newspaper Press and the Holocaust: General Features

The historical record of Western newspaper coverage of the Holocaust has been far from positive. Considering the press of the United States, for example, historian David S. Wyman has concluded that "very many" Americans, "probably a majority," were unaware of the Final Solution until well into 1944 because "the mass media treated the systematic murder of millions of Jews as though it were minor news"—despite the fact that "extensive information" about the Holocaust arrived on news desks throughout the war.[4] The very title of Deborah Lipstadt's major study of the American press—*Beyond Belief*—provides her thesis, in which she shows that the press had complete knowledge of the Holocaust almost as it was taking place, but kept the details from the American people.[5] To underscore the argument, Laurel Leff, in a focused study of the *New York Times*, argues convincingly that the most influential newspaper in the United States consistently downplayed, and even supressed, credible news about the Holocaust and hid it from the American people.[6]

By contrast, as recounted by Andrew Scharf as long ago as 1964, in Britain "few facts of Nazi anti-Semitism were left unstated by the British Press," which was itself "uniformly disgusted by those facts."[7] He tempers this, however, with the statement that there was also "a frequent failure to appreciate the full significance for the Jews under Nazi rule of all that which was known and deplored."[8] Scharf does not place this at the feet of the newspapers; rather, cultural and political currents within British society, which predated the rise of the Nazis in Germany, played a role in conditioning British attitudes towards Jews and willingness to accept or reject the news printed in the papers.[9]

A more damning assessment of the British newspaper press is that of historian Colin Shindler, who, in writing about *The Times*, has concluded that in the paper's estimation the Holocaust was "a minor, marginalised, amorphous item underpinned by a modicum of genuine disbelief and selective indifference"; as a result, items on the topic were "not perceived to be a priority in terms of news coverage."[10]

In Canada, as shown by Rebecca Margolis, scholars have concluded that "large-circulation English-language newspaper coverage of the liberation of the Nazi death camps failed to identify the Jewishness of the vast majority of those targeted for systematic annihilation."[11] Another key actor with a free press—and not occupied by Nazi Germany—was Mandate Palestine, where the press received information sufficient to inform readers "that the Nazis were systematically exterminating the Jews of Europe" and that "they knew about the gas chambers, too." As a rule, however, "the papers played down these stories."[12] Reading the situation in hindsight, the newspapers preferred to give top priority to local Palestine news, and "failed to display as much compassion for the Jews of Europe as one would like to find."[13]

Of the newspaper presses in the major English-speaking Western countries, according to historian Paul R. Bartrop, only Australia showed a willingness to accept the news coming out of Europe. Often, months would pass without reference to the Jewish situation, but when reports arrived, the newspapers were prepared to publish them and anticipated that they could be contextualised by the Australian public. His finding was that this was due to a tacit appreciation of the fact that from 1942 onwards oppression of the Jews formed a distinct element of Nazi policy and was different from other persecutions.[14]

A well-known aphorism holds that newspaper journalism is "the first rough draft of history,"[15] a place where news and notes—sometimes with interpretations and explanations, sometimes not—first appear in the popular domain. What does this mean where the Nazi period and the persecution of the Jews is concerned? Unquestionably, the Nazi period can be divided neatly into the two halves of pre-war and wartime, with quite different newspaper responses characterising each.

In the first half, broad statements in newspapers around the world were made concerning Nazism's Jewish victims, subjected to measures ranging from dismissal from government positions to economic dispossession (a process known as "Aryanisation"), to more brutal forms of intimidation such as beatings or imprisonment in concentration camps. The period on and after 9–10 November 1938, colloquially termed *Kristallnacht*, saw a vast number of stories and comments in the newspaper press, universally condemning Nazi antisemitic actions. In some countries, such as Australia, Canada, and the United States, discussion focused (with varying degrees of intensity) on the question of Jewish refugees from Nazism seeking to leave Germany and commence new lives as immigrants. Responses over this issue ranged from sympathy and welcome to hostility and rejection.

The pre-war period presented a series of challenges for the newspaper press globally: how should Germany's internal policies regarding its Jews be reported? As this was a human rights issue of the first magnitude, taking place in a European country renowned for its levels of high culture, was the issue one worthy of impartiality? Indeed, was there a place for anti-German or anti-Nazi condemnation, in a world emerging from the Depression and seeking a return to international normality?

Within days of the German attack on Poland in September 1939, the first measures were taken by the invaders against Jews. Across the next six years, all over Europe, millions of Jews were killed in conformity with Nazi antisemitic policy, the intention being nothing less than the annihilation of every Jew in Europe. How was this news transmitted to publics around the world—frequently the same publics allied in fighting the war against Germany? The newspaper press was the principal vehicle for news dissemination, so whatever was happening to the Jews had to compete with war news from the front, as well as new domestic arrangements and changes caused through involvement in the conflict. News about the Jewish situation was also dependent upon just how much news was being received, its source, and how far it conformed to what wartime security permitted. Finally, during the war years it was often unclear about the exact nature of the Nazi killing process, making it difficult to be able to inform readerships with accuracy.

Renowned journalist and Harvard scholar Marvin Kalb has identified five key reasons behind what he sees as "insensitive, unprofessional journalism"[16] when recording the Jewish situation in Europe. In summary form, these are Nazi regulation of the press, which "controlled the foreign press and dominated the German press"; the Allied focus "on winning the war, rather than saving the Jews"; bureaucratic and public antisemitism; "the enormity of the crime," which led to many people being unable to believe "that the German people would be engaged in the systematic extermination of the Jews"; and finally, "the nature of journalism itself," which was not brave enough to pursue and publish "quite fantastic stories about millions of Jews being gassed and burned to death."[17] He has concluded that with hindsight "we can second-guess the editorial limitations of the time—and say, tsk, tsk, you blew the story."[18]

These important issues are not easy to address. An examination of the role of the newspaper press is necessary if only to determine the extent to which publics around the world were apprised of the situation in Europe as it pertained to the Jews. From that information, it can be discerned how governments responded and, perhaps, what localised reactions from readers were to what they saw.

Those in the forefront of gathering and forwarding this news were war correspondents, journalists with a history dating back to William Howard Russell, an Irishman recognised by many as the first modern war correspondent.[19] Covering the Crimean War for *The Times* between 1853 and 1856, he witnessed the Siege of Sevastopol and the Charge of the Light Brigade, and later covered events during the Indian Mutiny, the American Civil War, the Austro-Prussian War, and the Franco-Prussian War. By the time the Nazis came to power in Germany in 1933, a long tradition of war correspondents had arisen. While life under the Nazis during the 1930s did not equate with war, for many of the journalists sent to cover the Hitler regime the dangers in that totalitarian society hovered around a sense of extraordinary menace. This often flowed on through the war years for those able to remain in Germany after September 1939.

One who did not remain was the American Dorothy Thompson, who worked in Munich before Adolf Hitler's ascent to office. In 1931, she interviewed him, and in a subsequent book written about the experience she raised alarm bells about the dangers should he win power.[20] Disparaging Hitler was a dangerous tactic, and in August 1934 she was the first American journalist to have her credentials cancelled and was expelled from Germany. This sent a clear but terrifying message to other journalists working in Germany: toe the Nazi line or be forced out.

One journalist who was always worried about expulsion was William L. Shirer. Between 1934 and 1940, he lived and worked in Germany, operating for the Berlin bureau of the Universal News Service until 1937, and then as European bureau chief of CBS radio based in Vienna. Throughout this time, Shirer was an acute observer of Nazi policies regarding the harassment of Jews. In 1935, he reported on the Nuremberg Laws and continued his reports the following year when additional restrictions on Jews were made. There was, however, only so much on which he could report, as his outgoing dispatches were watched carefully by the Nazis as a condition of his credentials being respected. Shirer was concerned that he could suffer the same fate as Dorothy Thompson, and his reporting was therefore fenced in by a form of self-censorship; this was to become much more formalised once war broke out, when state-imposed censorship was introduced.[21]

Thompson and Shirer are two of many journalists, from before and during the war, who sent reports back to their various newspapers or radio networks (and often doubled for both). Many of these were Americans: names such as John Gunther, H.R. Knickerbocker, Vincent Sheehan, and Howard K. Smith, among others, played an important role in alerting opinion in American and world opinion to the dangers of Nazism. Possibly the most famous was Edward R. Murrow, who gained prominence reporting from Britain during the early war years through nightly radio broadcasts beginning with the words "This is London." Remaining active until America's entry into the war in 1941, he was later one of the first reporters to enter Buchenwald concentration camp on 12 April 1945, broadcasting the shocking news of what he witnessed.[22]

Of course, he was only able to do this once the Nazis had been defeated, which brings up another issue when it comes to newspaper reporting about the Holocaust (and thus for obtaining certain types of information): how could news about the Holocaust be obtained when there was no possibility of reporters accessing it or being permitted to send reports home?

Assessing Newspaper Coverage

The Holocaust exposed fundamental questions about the nature of newspaper reporting. If we ask how newspapers can be employed to gain an understanding of that horrible event, we need first to inquire as to what the function of a newspaper should be at all.

The main purposes of newspapers are to inform, interpret, and entertain. Most newspapers contain stories representing the opinion of their controlling management or ownership, as well as that of their editors.[23] A newspaper's primary function is to inform its readership, usually on matters of local, national, and international interest. Ideally, the content of such information should be diverse in nature and based on sources which readers would not otherwise have access to on their own.

Given this, it is sometimes the case that newspapers move beyond reporting the facts of a matter and instead work to shape the views of their readers on certain subjects. This can lead to accusations that the newspaper press exceeds its responsibility to report the news, and, instead, to making its own. As a result, many newspapers have editorial or opinion pages which interpret events and seek to influence readers (including governments) as to their own take on events.

Moreover, while the major function of a newspaper company is to sell newspapers, the revenue raised through sales is minimal. Most mass-circulation newspapers, if relying on paper circulation alone, would barely cover publication costs; hence, the selling of advertising space is a vital part of any newspaper's operations. The greater the circulation, the more exposure advertisers achieve—and thus the higher the price charged to those advertisers by the newspapers. It is this relationship that keeps most newspapers functioning. Despite this, most mass-circulation newspapers see a prescribed social position for themselves within the community, and philosophical considerations play a definite part in helping to determine this. Once revenues have been guaranteed, a newspaper can afford to give full rein to the promotion of issues, guarding the public good, informing governments as to the state of community awareness, and drawing the public's attention to matters of which it should be aware.

The question arises as to how intrusive the state can be in controlling what the public reads—especially when a country is at war. A newspaper can employ war correspondents to gather information, but when the country is at war this type of reporting ceases and reliable news sources can dry up. Often, the most that newspapers can hope to do is engage journalists originating from neutral countries or pay for stories from other publications or news agencies (referred to as wire or cable services in the 1930s and 1940s), organisations that gather news reports and sell them to subscribing news bodies.

Beyond the function of a newspaper and the sources of its news, additional concerns arise, whether in peace or war. How much foreign news should be reported in any single issue of a newspaper? How is it to be selected? In the modern world, what priority should be given to stories coming from different countries—for instance, stories from the United States, Britain, or France, as distinct from Peru, Liberia, or Portugal? Most newspapers, in the 1930s as in our own day, were dominated by what are now referred to as "hot button issues," and nothing was hotter than whatever was coming out of Nazi Germany.

The presentation of news during wartime faced a major dilemma: censorship. For combatant countries, wartime regulations made mail, telegrams, pamphlets and books, newspapers, radio broadcasting, the film industry, plays, and photographs, subject to censorship—or, if not that, then at the very least, some form of restriction. Such censorship was designed to stop information deemed crucial to national security from falling into enemy hands.

In democratic countries, press censorship was largely self-regulating though operating within very strict guidelines. Newspapers were issued with government-imposed guidelines about topics subjected to censorship and control, but any information of potential military significance would be removed. Stories considered suitable for publication after having been submitted to the censor were permitted to be published: any deemed not suitable were held back.

With the security of the nation at stake, the press was expected to take sides and not remain neutral. This often resulted in press stories embellishing the information they received to make the enemy appear in the worst possible light. As a Norwegian professor of journalism has written in relation to more recent conflicts, "it is not just the events and actions themselves ... that determine media coverage, but that the 'news slant' and rhetoric applied to the stories are influenced by the prevailing enemy image."[24] In other words, the worse the enemy image, the better it serves the war effort. When it came to reporting about the Holocaust, carried out during a period of total war, this provided an ideal opportunity to demonise the Nazis and give added motivation for defeating the Hitler regime. The key question, however, was whether the reader would take the stories being disseminated as true, or simply as wartime propaganda.

A final consideration when assessing newspapers as sources for the study of the Holocaust pertains to the very scale of the event. The Second World War surpassed every previous conflict in history; as a result, any examination of how it was covered in the global press would be a massive project necessitating many volumes, having to take into account not only the combatant nations but also the press of the neutrals, the underground presses of the occupied countries, and sectional newspapers whose aim was only to report news on specific topics such as in local or ethnic communities.

Given this, it is simply not possible to assess the role of the global newspaper press accurately in a single study—just as newspapers could not definitively encapsulate the essence of the Holocaust by themselves. That task was (and is) too great.

Using Newspapers in Holocaust Research

For a long time, newspapers were not considered reliable sources for historical research, rejected for their immediacy, the lack of measured scholarship which underlay the work of reporters, and the preference for sensational, headline-grabbing accounts that were not necessarily representative of a broader picture.

Despite this, the newspaper press during the period of the Holocaust was important in that it conveyed not only the facts of a situation but also perceptions of that situation by those being interviewed or witnessing it with their own eyes. By the time a journalist selected his or her topic, wrote up their story, and then filed it, the editorial team swung into action to get the piece into the papers and onto the streets. It must always be borne in mind, however, that the material produced in a newspaper does not always tell the full story—nor can it, given the haste with which it most often must appear. Perhaps the best one can say is that the newspaper record provides historians the opportunity to examine what was offered to the public at a particular time; it is in that context alone that judgements can be made, and not with the benefit of hindsight. We know what happened next; readers and journalists at the time did not.

Historians of the Holocaust, therefore, must remain careful when it comes to using newspapers as factual material. Those who write newspaper stories are just as liable to error as those who generate other contemporary material such as diaries or letters. Moreover, newspapers and reporters during the Holocaust period had severe limitations holding back their ability to be one hundred percent authoritative in every respect: time pressure, limited access to information, and available space to elaborate on a story could lead to an inaccurate slant on a much bigger or more important theme. The process of writing history using newspapers, therefore, can lead to a subjective selection of material which might not have even been completely accurate at the time—and can, of course, lead to distortion in the historical account.

Newspapers can serve as useful primary sources, enhancing part—though by no means all—of the record. They can be used to establish general outlines, or narrative factual details concerning people, places, and events. When using newspapers for studying the Holocaust, a useful technique—beyond simply reading the stories and accepting or rejecting what they have to say—is through a content analysis, measuring such things as the number of column inches employed by the editors or the size and nature of the headline. While this can help to assess the degree of importance given by a paper to the event being reported, however, it is far from perfect. The Holocaust scholar must take cognisance of what the story contains as well as how it is presented.

To remain viable, newspapers must have a solid readership, guaranteed by the paper's appeal to their ways of thinking and sympathetic to their biases. In that sense, perhaps, newspapers, in addition to being "the first rough draft of history," are also a measure of public opinion—not perfect, perhaps, but often the only way to tell what the public view might be of any situation. In many countries during the Holocaust period, opinion polls did not exist, so governments could only look to what appeared in the press, whether as editorials or letters to the editor. Those studying the Holocaust using newspapers should not read too much into it regarding how the whole population viewed events; again, the question of how representative the expressed views could have been needs to be taken into consideration.

There are undoubtedly certain disadvantages as well as rewards in using newspapers in Holocaust study. The biased opinions of journalists and editors—political viewpoints, cultural prejudices, or national chauvinism—flavour their assessments. They can also deliberately seek to influence their audience into their way of thinking, operating from similar motives. For example, the proprietor of London's *Daily Mail*, Lord Rothermere, was concerned to support the principles of appeasement, and during the Munich Crisis of September 1938 suppressed the aggressive role Nazi Germany played.[25] Again, those employing newspapers as a source when studying the Holocaust must be aware of such possibilities, just as they should also be conscious of the fact that what they are using reflects the time in which it was created. The Holocaust and Third Reich period of the 1930s and 1940s was in many respects, of an altogether different socio-cultural and intellectual calibre than that of today, with attitudes and values often a quantum leap from each other.

The Australian Press and the Holocaust

While discussions about the newspaper press during the Holocaust have, as shown earlier, frequently centred on the failure of the newspapers to expose their readers to the reality of Nazi mass murder, little has been written on the uses that can be made of newspaper accounts when writing today about the Holocaust. As a practical illustration of how one scholar has approached the task, Paul Bartrop's analysis of the Australian press during the final year-and-a-half of the Second World War offers useful insights into the uses than can be made of newspapers when researching the Holocaust.[26]

The Australian press reported on changes in Germany from the beginning of the Third Reich in 1933. Throughout the 1930s much coverage was given to the issue of Jewish refugees attempting to enter Australia.[27] During the war years, competition for column inches often saw issues concerning the Jews of Europe to be less important than other news, particularly when Australia was threatened with invasion in 1942—a period coterminous with the implementation of the Final Solution. Although news about the atrocities directed against Jews had been reported from 1939, it took the revelations from about 1944 for Australian newspapers to vent their full indignation.

Four leading newspapers from Melbourne, Sydney, and Adelaide, respectively *The Age*, *The Argus*, the *Sydney Morning Herald*, and *The Advertiser*, all used international news reports from the Australian Associated Press (AAP) foreign cable service and agencies such as Reuters. Other state newspapers, such as the *Courier-Mail* (Brisbane), the *West Australian* (Perth), and the *Mercury* (Hobart), also relied on the same news outlets. Identical coverage often appeared verbatim in all papers on the same day, though individual editors chose what they used from the overseas wires. All Australian newspapers relied on the same sources of overseas information, except in infrequent cases where an individual correspondent had been sent, or stringers hired, overseas. Occasionally, news about the Holocaust was generated locally, as in rare cases when rescued Jews who arrived in Australia during the war spoke about their experiences to one or other of the newspapers.

At the end of January 1944, a report in *The Argus* declared that more than 3,000,000 Jews had been killed since the Nazi rampage began, with "not more than a few hundred thousand starving people ... left out of 3,300,000 Jews in Poland."[28] When news came in March 1944 that the Jews of Hungary were now at risk, *The Argus* reported on that the German News Agency had "boasted" that "more than 1,000,000 Jews in Budapest will now be 'politically and economically eliminated, along with unreliable Hungarian elements.'"[29] The Australian public was now under no illusions as to what this implied but there were no further reports about the fate of the Hungarian Jews for a further three months.

On 27 November 1944, horrifying news appeared in *The Age*, the *Sydney Morning Herald* and *The Advertiser*. *The Age* account, headed "Death by Torture/An Organised Campaign," reported that at Auschwitz-Birkenau "up to 1,765,000 were murdered in ... torture chambers" between April 1942 and April 1944.[30] *The Advertiser* reported accounts of "Demoniacal terrorisation and extermination of Jewish men, women and children, including the use of Jewish women as human guinea pigs in scientific obstetrical experiments."[31] None of the major Australian newspapers had previously recounted atrocities committed against Jews so graphically.[32]

In April and May of 1945, after Germany was defeated by Allied forces, the results of the Holocaust were finally revealed. War correspondents provided graphic images of the brutality being uncovered and within days, Australian newspapers were displaying their disgust, either as editorial opinions, juxtaposition of stories, or the writing of emotive headlines. Soon after the liberation of Buchenwald, the editor of *The Advertiser* published an editorial damning the regime that created such a place.[33] He then highlighted the fact that although Nazi atrocities were already known in Australia, no-one had expected the reality to be as reports now coming in revealed: "Buchenwald is a testimony to Nazi devilry that excludes every possibility of doubt, and admits of no word of palliation."[34] An editorial in the *Sydney Morning Herald* the next day echoed the theme of the German people's moral debasement, claiming that the concentration camps represented "convincing evidence of national degeneracy."[35]

As the first newsreels of Belsen, Dachau, and Buchenwald began showing in Australian cinemas, *The Argus*, along with other newspapers, urged all Australians to see them. *The Argus* warned that every adult Australian should view such films "as a matter of duty," as they would convince viewers once and for all of the truth of the atrocities—"That is why the people should view for themselves the evidence upon which the guilty 'master race' is to be convicted."[36] Later references sprang from either of the two strands of revelation or retribution, and subsequently it was the press that provided the commentary Australians received about the Nuremberg Trials and other post-war developments.

Because Australian newspapers depended for their news on overseas wire services, "reports were usually piecemeal, frequently late, and often incomplete," and as a result the picture that formed for the Australian public "was therefore patchy, built over nearly six years of war."[37] Once Western reporters could see the evidence for themselves, detailed accounts began to be published in April and May of 1945, but "every piece of news published seemed to have coalesced into what may be described as an educated understanding of what was happening to Jews in Europe between 1939 and 1945."[38]

Learning about the Holocaust from Newspapers

The Holocaust encompassed an enormous amount of activity taking place in many areas. It is unclear how much of it was reported. Nor would we know of the destruction where no-one survived to tell the tale. How can one establish what happened in a community where a population which once numbered several thousand has been totally obliterated? From whom does one obtain eyewitness testimony, if all the eyewitnesses have been killed? How does one examine written records, where none were kept? Are there any advantages for the historian who visits a location if—as often happened—it had been completely destroyed by the Nazis? Many hundreds of small villages throughout Eastern Europe were literally expunged from the face of the earth. We cannot know how the Holocaust manifested itself in these communities. Unless there were reporters embedded with the armies of the perpetrators, there was no-one to witness what occurred.

Some items in newspapers, such as eyewitness accounts and editorials, are considered primary sources; for us today, they can be very useful to help understand historical events. However, when the original sources of a story are lacking, and we have only a reporter's ingenuity or third-party testimony on which to rely, enormous care must be taken by the researcher. Historians generally use newspapers for learning facts about specific events or looking for long-term trends. Sometimes the evidence to support the facts laid out in a report simply is not present, and it would be immense folly for a scholar to fabricate possibilities without verification. All newspaper articles, therefore, should carry the warning *"caveat emptor"*—let the buyer beware!

Readers of newspapers have certain expectations: that is their right as consumers of news. In all newspapers, those cover accuracy, impartiality, reliability, relevance, validity of the source, the expertise of the journalists, and, in highly charged situations, knowledge of the author's identity.

When it comes to articles that are based on what the reporter has witnessed directly, it is important to consider the broader context of what has been written, such as the intended audience; whether the reporter, or indeed the publisher itself, might have a specific bias; and then, taking it further, what the editor's justification is for publishing the piece. Another practical aspect is where the article is placed in the newspaper. It could be considered front page news, or, given that editors are human, perhaps considered less important. Even after accepting these elements and putting a reporter's writing to the test, however, as a source for studying the Holocaust it must always be borne in mind that while newspapers are valuable as sources, they must not be relied upon as the only vehicle from which to reconstruct history.

Newspapers have a role to play in the research process; sometimes, a most important, and even vital, role. But this must not blind us to the limitations that newspapers can present when undertaking research, as well. They, like all other sources when studying the Holocaust, must be treated not only with respect but also with caution.

Notes

1 For a comprehensive examination of how a consciousness of news gathering and reporting evolved from earliest times to the period of the Enlightenment, see A. Pettegree, *The Invention of News: How the World Came to Know About Itself*, New Haven: Yale University Press, 2014; taking the story further, see R.R. John and J. Silberstein-Loeb (ed.), *Making News: The Political Economy of Journalism in Britain and America from the Glorious Revolution to the Internet*, Oxford: Oxford University Press, 2015.
2 The history of newspapers is large. For a good introduction, see G. Boyce, J. Curran, and P. Wingate (ed.), *Newspaper History from the Seventeenth Century to the Present Day*, London: Constable, 1978; and A. Smith, *The Newspaper: An International History*, London: Thames and Hudson, 1979.

140 Eve E. Grimm

3 F. Keisinger, "Press/Journalism," *1914–1918 Online International Encyclopedia of the First World War*, available online at https://encyclopedia.1914–1918-online.net/article/pressjournalism.
4 D.S. Wyman, *The Abandonment of the Jews: America and the Holocaust, 1941–1945*, New York: Free Press, 2007, p. 321.
5 D.E. Lipstadt, *Beyond Belief: The American Press and the Coming of the Holocaust, 1933–1945*, New York: Free Press, 1986.
6 L. Leff, *Buried by the Times: The Holocaust and America's Most Important Newspaper*, New York: Cambridge University Press, 2005.
7 A. Scharf, *The British Press and Jews under Nazi Rule*, London: Oxford University Press, 1964, p. 193.
8 Ibid.
9 For additional insights into this phenomenon, see also T. Kushner, *The Persistence of Prejudice: Antisemitism in British Society during the Second World War*, Manchester: Manchester University Press, 1989.
10 C. Shindler, "The 'Thunderer' and the Coming of the Shoah: *The Times* of London, 1933–1942," in R.M. Shapiro (ed.), *Why Didn't the Press Shout? American and International Journalism during the Holocaust*, New York: Yeshiva University Press, 2003, p. 169. The prewar situation has been dealt with in F.R. Gannon, *The British Press and Nazi Germany, 1936–1939*, Oxford: Clarendon Press, 1971; and K. Galbraith, *The British Press and Nazi Germany: Reporting from the Reich, 1933–9*, London: Bloomsbury Academic, 2020. Neither of these works focus only on the Jewish issue, though inevitably there is some treatment of the subject in both.
11 R. Margolis, "A Review of the Yiddish Media: Responses of the Jewish Immigrant Community in Canada," in L.R. Klein (ed.), *Nazi Germany, Canadian Responses: Confronting Antisemitism in the Shadow of War*, Montreal and Kingston: McGill-Queen's University Press, 2021, p. 116.
12 T. Segev, "It Was in the Papers: The Hebrew Press in Palestine and the Holocaust," in Shapiro (ed.), *Why Didn't the Press Shout*, p. 612.
13 Ibid., p. 613.
14 P.R. Bartrop, *The Holocaust and Australia: Refugees, Rejection, and Memory*, London: Bloomsbury Academic, 2022, p. 190.
15 As shown by author Jack Shafer, the origin of this term is disputed. By most accounts it was first popularised by the former publisher of the *Washington Post*, Philip L. Graham, in April 1963. Deeper research has shown that the term was used as far back as 1943. See J. Shafer, "Who Said It First? Journalism Is 'the First Rough Draft of History,'" *Slate*, 30 August 2010, available online at https://slate.com/news-and-politics/2010/08/on-the-trail-of-the-question-who-first-said-or-wrote-that-journalism-is-the-first-rough-draft-of-history.html
16 M. Kalb, "Introduction: Journalism and the Holocaust, 1933–1945," in Shapiro (ed.), *Why Didn't the Press Shout*, p. 5.
17 Ibid., pp. 5–8.
18 Ibid., p. 8.
19 For a history of war correspondents, see the early study by Philip Knightley, *The First Casualty: The War Correspondent as Hero, Propagandist, and Myth Maker from the Crimea to Vietnam*, London, Andre Deutsch, 1975.
20 D. Thompson, *I Saw Hitler!*, New York: Farrar and Rinehart, 1932.
21 There are two good accounts of Shirer's life and career, apart from his own extensive work. See especially K. Cuthbertson, *A Complex Fate: William L. Shirer and the American Century*, Montreal and Kingston: McGill-Queen's University Press, 2015; and Steve Wick, *The Long Night: William L. Shirer and the Rise and Fall of the Third Reich*, New York: St. Martin's Press, 2011.
22 On Murrow, see J. Persico, *Edward R. Murrow: An American Original*, New York: McGraw-Hill, 1988.
23 A 2022 study of newspaper ownership in the United States and Britain during the 1930s has argued that six of the most powerful media owners worked to pressure their respective governments into adopting policies that would minimise the threat of fascism, feeding directly (and reinforcing) isolationist and appeasement sentiments. See K.S. Olmsted, *The Newspaper Axis: Six Press Barons Who Enabled Hitler*, New Haven: Yale University Press, 2022.

24 R. Ottosen, "Enemy Images and the Journalistic Process," *Journal of Peace Research*, 32:1, 1995, p. 100.
25 R. Crockett, *Twilight of Truth: Chamberlain, Appeasement, and the Manipulation of the Press*, London: Weidenfeld and Nicolson, 1989, pp. 56, 78–80.
26 I am indebted to Paul Bartrop for his willingness to share his research with me for this chapter, as well as his insights during our discussions about how he approached the task of using Australian newspapers when undertaking his investigation.
27 Bartrop, *The Holocaust and Australia*, especially chapters 2–10, *passim*.
28 *The Argus*, 26 January 1944, p. 16.
29 Ibid., 25 March 1944, p. 1.
30 *The Age*, 27 November 1944, p. 1.
31 *The Advertiser*, 27 November 1944, p. 4.
32 Bartrop, *The Holocaust and Australia*, p. 187.
33 *The Advertiser*, 19 April 1945, p. 4.
34 Ibid.
35 *Sydney Morning Herald*, 21 April 1945, p. 2.
36 *The Argus*, 25 May 1945, p. 2.
37 Bartrop, *The Holocaust and Australia*, p. 190.
38 Ibid.

11 Using Yiddish Sources in Studying the Holocaust

Freda Hodge

What is Yiddish?

Yiddish is a language of medieval West Germanic origin derived from the word for "Jewish," applying, in its origin, specifically to Ashkenazi Jews—that is, Jews from Central and Eastern Europe and their descendants. Despite its derivation, Yiddish integrates many languages including words from German, Hebrew, Aramaic, and additional Slavic and Romance vernaculars. It is usually presumed that the earliest forms of Yiddish originated during the ninth and tenth centuries in Central Europe, as Ashkenazi Jews from France and Italy migrated to Germany's Rhine Valley. The earliest chronicled references date from the twelfth century. Unlike other languages of Germanic origin, written Yiddish uses the Hebrew alphabet.

As Jewish communities spread throughout Eastern Europe, Yiddish accompanied them and thrived as their vernacular.[1] For many Jews in Western Europe, however, it held a low status as a language of poverty and oppression.

For at least the last 1,000 years, therefore, Yiddish was spoken by most Ashkenazi Jews, starting in what is now Germany but spreading to much of Eastern Europe as Jews left Germany, and moved eastward into areas of the Polish-Ukrainian Commonwealth when religious persecution began to take hold. While Hebrew was the sacred language used in the synagogues and for prayer, Yiddish continued to serve as the language of everyday discourse, business affairs, and secular matters. For many centuries, traditional education in Jewish communities was conducted in Yiddish, and as Jews migrated to different countries, various dialects developed. For Sephardic Jews from non-Ashkenazi origins, for example, Yemenites and Moroccans, Ladino, also known as Judeo-Spanish, became the vernacular.[2] Yiddish has remained a medium of instruction in some Orthodox Jewish schools today, though, of the Jewish day schools offering Yiddish as a subject, most use the majority primary language for teaching purposes, with Yiddish employed only for specified coursework.

Prior to the Holocaust (referred to in Yiddish as *Churban* or Destruction), there were between 11 and 12 million Yiddish speakers worldwide, by far the majority of all Jews. It was estimated that there were 9.5 million Jews living in Europe, mostly in Eastern Europe. This figure represented over 60 percent of the world's Jewish population, estimated at 15.3 million.[3] There were also over 4.5 million Jews in the United States, a vast number of whom had arrived during the latter part of the nineteenth century and the early twentieth century, escaping from pogroms and other forms of persecution in Eastern Europe. The Holocaust, however, saw a huge collapse in the number of Yiddish

DOI: 10.4324/9781003248620-14

speakers—up to 85 percent of the six million Jews murdered by the Nazis people spoke Yiddish as their everyday language.

Other forces were also at work, such as acculturation and assimilation, especially in the United States, which further diminished the number of Yiddish speakers, as they acquired the local vernaculars. A further consideration came with the establishment of the State of Israel, where Hebrew—the language of prayer—has been revived and employed as the Jewish national language. Still, to this day, some Yiddish words have entered everyday mainstream usage throughout the English-speaking world. The English vernacular includes words like *shlep* (pull or drag), *shtik* (pranks or tricks), and *maven* (expert), perhaps without their users knowing the Yiddish derivation of the words they are speaking.

The Role of the Yiddish Press

The importance of Yiddish newspapers in depicting Jewish life, language, and culture cannot be underestimated. They were vital in uniting a people living for hundreds of years in a very widespread diaspora. The first Yiddish newspaper appeared in Amsterdam in 1675 under the name *Gazeta de Amsterdam* (*Amsterdam Gazette*), serving a community in the Netherlands which had provided refuge to Spanish and Portuguese Jews after their expulsions in 1492 and 1495, respectively. The paper was bilingual, featuring both Yiddish and Ladino. Yiddish newspapers also became an integral part of the lives of Jews in Germany and Eastern Europe: as Jewish populations grew the numbers sustained dozens of journals and newspapers. The Jewish press was indispensable for the stateless Jews who lived in small *shtetlach* (villages) as well as in larger cities governed by authorities whose attitude towards Jews ranged from benevolence to discrimination, to exploitation. Given that Jews for the most part had no voice in government, Yiddish newspapers enabled Jews to keep abreast of the political forces and state decrees controlling their lives.

When it came to the relationship between Jews, the gentile population, and the state, the Yiddish press helped to mould Jewish opinion as well as serving as a bridge between rural and urbanised Jews, and between those across the religious-secular divide. It included philosophical discussions and matters of Jewish culture, literature, and the arts. Politics was of enormous interest and importance to the Jews who were always at the mercy of different regimes, and the Yiddish press provided a voice for Jews who attempted to protect the rights of others by serving as their voice. Within the diaspora environment, many Jews considered that their dispersion globally made it difficult for them to feel that they were part of a single people, sharing the same political aspirations as well as their ancient culture and beliefs. By the nineteenth century, the Yiddish press spanned the political spectrum from socialist, communist, and anarchist, to moderate and traditional, easing this feeling of disconnection. Indeed, newspapers and journals were the closest unifiers, in the absence of a national home for the Jewish people, during 100 years of homelessness. In America, for example, *The Forward*, established in 1892 (and still being published today in Yiddish, though also available in English), was both useful and enlightening as a teaching aid covering important social and political matters.

There sometimes arose friction in different countries between Jewish religious and secular expression, or cultural and civic status. Despite these differences, a reading of the Yiddish press, published in many countries in Europe and elsewhere, gives insight into a specifically Jewish world view—of their lives, their thoughts and ideologies, and their relationship with non-Jews. Some decline in the use of Yiddish during the nineteenth century occurred because of the changing conditions and rulers' new political policies. However, it was the press that still cultivated and enriched the Yiddish language and culture by publishing the works of writers such as Mendele Mocher Seforim, Sholem Aleichem, J. L. Peretz, and others who were among the most renowned authors in the Yiddish canon.[4]

Coverage in the Yiddish press about the pogroms in Eastern Europe in the 1880s informed the readership about the fate of their fellow Jews. Yiddish remained the language of comfort and connection among Jews despite the mass migrations to the United States following the pogroms. Although refugees from Eastern Europe were eager to absorb English to enable them to integrate more comfortably into their new home, the continuing use of *mame loshen* (mother tongue) among their fellow recent arrivals remained their daily language; with it, they could share with their fellow Yiddish speakers the difficulties in coping with the vast number of changes they had to accommodate in their lives as they established themselves in the new country.[5]

Yiddish newspapers proliferated in the United States and served an eager audience, just as a lively Jewish press, in both Yiddish and Polish, had developed in Poland. These papers reflected Jewish life in Poland and the Jewish struggle against antisemitism. In short, it has been concluded, anyone "wishing to study the history of Eastern European Jewry and the flowering of its culture could not do better than to study the history of the Yiddish press in the present century."[6]

The onset of the Second World War, and the rapid advent of the Final Solution, devastated Jewish life in Europe as the Germans conquered large swathes of Eastern Europe.[7] Despite the desperation in which they found themselves, those committed to the maintenance of Jewish existence established an underground press, not only to disseminate news among the Jewish inhabitants of the ghettos and concentration camps but often also to pass on information that could contribute to their chances of survival. Jewish youth groups producing newspapers represented a wide range of political organisations and movements such as *Hashomer Hatzair*, *Betar*, *Dror-Hechalutz*, and the Bund. They described life in the ghetto, feelings about the *Judenrat* (Nazi-imposed Jewish Councils), and publicised wide-ranging political discussions. Overall, the newspapers of the Yiddish press served to bolster the courage and determination of Jews to survive.

Personal Testimonies in Yiddish

In the immediate aftermath of the Holocaust, much scholarly work focused more on the events of the war itself than on the experiences of the Jewish people. Historians who had little awareness of the lesser known elements of the Shoah revealed only limited interest in the Holocaust until the early 1960s when the trial of Adolf Eichmann took place in Israel. At this same time, the world awoke to the historical importance of individual testimonies, while the Jewish press, which emerged in the American Zone in occupied West Germany, added another dimension of knowledge about the Shoah useful for researchers. Personal testimonies and newspapers revealed a more Jewish-focused approach to the Holocaust which had at that time been largely passed over by academic scholars.[8]

The early testimonies and newspapers in Yiddish illustrate the nature of Jewish identity and culture before, during, and immediately after the Holocaust. The history of the Displaced Persons' (DP) camps was only recorded later in scholarly studies.[9] Even before the war's end, Jews incarcerated in ghettos and concentration camps surreptitiously began to create records—mostly in Yiddish—describing their ordeals at the hands of the Nazis. The Germans forbade the possession by Jews of any writing material, so victims wrote on hidden scraps of paper and kept secret diaries and letters telling of their experiences.

The Ringelblum Archive

One of the most notable amongst the secret archives recording ghetto life until 1943 was *Oyneg Shabes* (*Oneg Shabbat*, "Sabbath Joy"), established by Jewish historian Emanuel Ringelblum in the Warsaw Ghetto. He and his volunteers collected a vast number of materials, mostly in Yiddish, chronicling the life of the inhabitants in all its tragic detail. Ringelblum's archive saw him working with some 60 others to collect documents, photographs, diaries, artwork, and objects used in daily life as well as samples from the press, tickets, German posters, and much more. It became one of the most important Jewish archives to emerge from the war. The end of the Warsaw Ghetto Uprising in May 1943 saw the entire collection hidden with hopes that it would be recovered after the war, but unfortunately, only part of the archive was retrieved later. Among those working alongside Ringelblum was Rokhl Auerbakh (also spelled Rokhl Oyerbakh and Rachel Auerbach), who was one of only three surviving members of the *Oyneg Shabes* group. After the war, she initiated the excavation of the archive. Not all of it, however, was retrieved from the hiding places where Ringelblum and his volunteers had hidden them.

The loss of part of the invaluable record of Jewish life was great, but the Ringelblum archive contains crucial historical material. Others incarcerated in the Warsaw Ghetto kept diaries; they were determined that the world should know the truth about the Holocaust and the murder of the Jews. In 2007, an American historian, Samuel D. Kassow, painstakingly pieced together not only the story of the Ringelblum archive chronicling its establishment and the methodology of amassing its content through the use of *zammlers* (collectors); he also analysed the nature of the archive through a comprehensive treatment of the Yiddish material it contains. Kassow's study is an invaluable source for teaching about the minutiae of ghetto life under the Nazis.[10]

Underground Yiddish Accounts

Although the Second World War temporarily destroyed mainstream Yiddish journalism as it had flourished in Eastern Europe before 1939, a cultural and historic link between the pre-war Jewish press, and that of the war years, was to be found in the underground publications produced and surreptitiously printed and distributed by the partisans and youth groups. These all reflected the different political streams existing in Jewish communities throughout Eastern Europe before the war. They disseminated everyday news, especially about Nazi activities. Youth group newspapers included *Tsukunft* (*The Future*), *Der Yiddishe Kemfer* (*The Jewish Struggle*), a partisan paper entitled *Poalei Tzion Smol* (Workers of Zion-Left), *Dror-Hechalutz* (*Liberty*), *Poalei Zion* (*The Pioneer*), and others from *Hashomer Hazair*, which produced a prolific number of newspapers. These Yiddish papers contained information about the immediate concerns of the ghetto population, and as such, they discussed imminent Nazi plans and events (such as could be anticipated in advance).

146 *Freda Hodge*

At the end of the war, 1,000 of testimonies written in Yiddish were collected by Historical Commissions established by Jewish leaders, frequently in the DP camps, among survivors known collectively as the *She'erit Hapletah*.[11] Their self-appointed mission was to record the history of the Holocaust from the point of view of the survivors themselves. However, it was not only testimonies recording the horrors of the Holocaust: thousands of photographs, documents, and newspapers of the *She'erit Hapletah* also chronicled evidence of German brutality. A vast quantity of this material was used as evidence in the Nuremberg trials, with most of the evidence written in Yiddish (though other languages, inevitably, were also used). Today, these firsthand records of Nazi war crimes give a graphic account of the horrors experienced by Jews in the concentration camps and in hiding, with partisan testimonies describing the inner workings of the units hidden in the forests and elsewhere.

Fortunately, many of the testimonies have now been translated into English by individual historians as well as institutions such as Israel's Yad Vashem, the University of Southern California (USC) Shoah Foundation, and, importantly, the Yiddish Scientific Institute in New York known as YIVO (*Yidisher Visnshaftlekher Institut*). As the preeminent body safeguarding Jewish history and language—especially in relation to Yiddish and Eastern Europe—YIVO has a large archive pertaining to the Holocaust and the Second World War and still collects material pertinent to this history. Today, testimonies originally in Yiddish and now in English translation have been a boon to historians and teachers of the Holocaust.

The Post-war Yiddish Press

As the Jewish *lingua franca*, Yiddish enabled the survivors to communicate even in the conditions of the DP camps, where many languages were spoken. Approximately 82 percent of the survivors were to be found in the American Zone of West Germany and although this was a period of great personal upheaval for the survivors, it did not take long for various newspapers to appear in the camps. The survivors were determined to endure and recreate their lives. Even in translation, the early testimonies and newspapers retain the authenticity of the raw Holocaust experience and an iteration of identity.

The multi-faceted Yiddish press that emerged in the DP camps represented the major political parties, which once again flourished as the highly politicised *She'erit Hapletah* resurrected earlier Zionist parties as well as those of other ideological affiliations. These included, but were not restricted to, the Left *Poale Zion* (Zionist Socialist), *Mapai* (General Zionist), *Folkspartei* (People's Party), *Hashomer Hazair* (Zionist Youth Movement), *Betar* (Revisionist Youth Movement), *Hanoar Hazioni* (Zionist Youth), *Agudat Yisroel* (Orthodox Religious), and *Mizrahi* (Religious Right Zionist). The religious component of *She'erit Hapletah* was comparatively small and spanned the range from Orthodox to Progressive Judaism.

Between 1945 and 1948 more than 100 publications, mostly in Yiddish, appeared in the liberated zones of Europe. Almost all had a particular allegiance, whether religious or political. The following titles reflect several major publications in the DP camps:

- *Dos Fraye Vort* (*The Free Word*), Feldafing Camp Paper appearing from 1945
- *Fun Letzen Khurben* (*From the Recent Catastrophe*), Central Historical Commission, appearing from 1946

- *Landsberger Lager Tsaytung* (*The Landsberg Camp Paper*), appearing from 1945
- *Nitzotz* (*The Spark*), an underground newspaper of the *Irgun Brith Zion*, originally in the Kovno Ghetto, reappearing in Kaufering (a series of sub-camps of Dachau) from 1944
- *Techiyat Hametim* (*Resurrection*), appearing in Buchenwald from 1945
- *Undzer Veg* (*Our Way*), Central Committee of Liberated Jews in Bavaria, appearing from 1945

As well, local papers from various camps began to appear mostly in 1946. In his article "The Yiddish Press's Time Is Not Yet Up," Israeli author Moshe Ishon[12] states that the Yiddish language is connected to the soul of the Jewish people: his contention is that the more we try to break the link between them, through various alternatives, the more we lose the unique soul inherent in the language.

Of course, not all survivors spoke Yiddish, though a majority did. In the aftermath of the war, survivors were generally either refugees from Eastern Europe; survivors of the ghettos, death camps, labour camps, and death marches; had lived in hiding or with false identities; or had subsisted in the forests with (or often hiding from) partisan groups. After the war, in the DP camps, the number of these survivors was increased by the arrival of Jews who had survived the Holocaust years in the Soviet Union, having escaped to Russia across the Polish-Soviet border early in the war.

During the war, the long tradition of the Yiddish press continued, even under the worst Nazi repression. After liberation, in the DP camps, the press flourished once again, serving as a mouthpiece for the survivors—a voice, as it were, to bridge the gap between the Americans and the survivors who had to negotiate to improve their conditions and persuade the Americans that they wished to be treated as a separate nation, and not as citizens of the countries from which they originated.[13]

Holocaust Research Using Yiddish

Western historiography about the Holocaust includes tens of 1,000 of scholarly works, but an argument can be put that the approach of many historians omits the voice of the Jewish survivors who experienced the Holocaust at firsthand—much of which was recorded in Yiddish in the immediate aftermath of the war. Oral and written testimonies from survivors constitute a vital record of the overall Holocaust experience. Such accounts make a highly informative resource for present-day teachers and are now often available in English translation. The present author, for example, translated 30 testimonies in her book *Tragedy and Triumph* in which the survivors describe their experiences, in various circumstances, living under Nazism.[14] This is but one example of many. Others include translated testimonies focusing specifically on rescuing the voice of the survivors. These include such early works as *The Redeemers: A Saga of the Years 1945–1952* by Leo W. Schwartz,[15] and *I Did Not Interview the Dead* by David P. Boder.[16] In addition, testimonies in translation from Yiddish can be found in specialist studies dealing with broader issues: one such illustration is to be found in the examination by Lawrence L. Langer of the psychological effect of trauma as well as in the works of Paul R. Bartrop and Terrence Des Pres attempting to create a composite picture of survival in the concentration and death camps.[17] Such works, however, are but the tiny tip of a very large iceberg.

The act of surviving was extraordinary, and those who survived the Holocaust realised that the Jewish experience could best be understood from the survivors' depictions of their own lives in adversity. They were a disparate group of people linked largely by Yiddish, their common language. In the ghettos and the death and labour camps, they continued to speak the tongue their communities had spoken for centuries, along the way creating additional terms and codewords for their protection. While it is possible to compose a history of the Holocaust without considering the voice of those who lived through it and were its victims, those studying the experience can create for themselves a more solid appreciation of the entire phenomenon of the Third Reich, in all its forms, by also studying the Jewish perspective, written by those who saw these events from their exclusive standpoint as its main victims.

There is at present, however, a paucity of research on the richness of Yiddish, which survived as a binding force for the Jews, and of how the shared vernacular could lift their spirits and maintain their dignity.

Philip Friedman, a highly regarded Polish Jewish historian born in Lvov (Lviv) in 1901, served as a director of the Central Jewish Committee in Poland after the end of the war. Its mission was to gather data as a record of German war crimes and especially the heinous treatment of the Jews, particularly in the ghettos. Friedman, who wrote in Yiddish, undertook a detailed study about ghetto creation, "The Jewish Ghettos of the Nazi Era."[18] He showed how even under the degrading and dehumanising conditions in the ghettos, the Jewish inhabitants refused to succumb to the conditions imposed by the Nazis and attempted to maintain their humanity and separate identity. The struggle to avoid death, find food, and fend off disease, did not stop the establishment of underground groups by Jewish youth who sought to sabotage the German war effort and to save as many Jews as possible. They engaged in armed resistance along with the partisans and were determined to maintain the safety and spirits of the ghetto inhabitants.[19]

The Kovno ghetto reveals one example of how extensive the effort was to maintain Yiddish cultural life. Underground groups helped to establish clandestine schools for the children, created libraries and soup kitchens, and upheld Jewish culture by staging theatrical and musical shows. This boosted morale, and with the price of tickets kept low, even the poorest were able to attend and enter a world where—at least for a while—the miseries of ghetto life could be forgotten. The Nazis permitted the staging of shows and concerts, attending them for their own amusement. There were many talented musicians among the ghetto residents who, with great difficulty, put together a fine symphony orchestra that held concerts whenever possible.[20] The Kovno ghetto is only one example of the resilience of the Jewish people who maintained their culture and dignity to the best of their ability. Among the testimonies about ghetto life, there are many which describe the nature of this rich ghetto culture, persevering under the worst possible conditions.

One constant, however, remained to boost morale: a clandestine Yiddish press created and distributed by the underground kept people informed about events outside the ghetto. They reflected the inner life of the Jewish population, their values and hopes.

This was a world unknown to those outside the ghetto. Who else but the participants in all these events could have known the truth about life behind the walls? The Jewish point of view was seen through their eyes, demonstrating a determination to record Jewish history under the Nazi regime and explain the role of the Jews in opposing the Nazis which neither the Germans nor the Allies fully comprehended. It is here that Yiddish sources have an important role to play for those studying the Holocaust. To understand fully the Jewish experience, it is not sufficient to look *only* at German (or other perpetrator) documents, their obfuscations and attempts to conceal the truth, but also the interaction between the Nazis and their victims.

No programme for teaching the history of the Holocaust would be complete without research into the aftermath of the war for the Jewish survivors, who still faced enormous obstacles in creating their future. Most were to be found in the DP camps where they organised themselves for the purpose of representation and advocacy to the American administration. Here, they sought acceptance as a separate nation in their own individualised DP camps, where they would have a degree of local autonomy. They were eventually successful in their requests, and with this, they considered their future.

The establishment of an elected body to steer the remarkable vitality and resilience of the survivors in a positive direction resulted (as shown earlier) in the creation of numerous Historical Commissions whose tasks included the collection of as much evidence as possible to confirm the Nazis' heinous role in the Holocaust. They were aware that the world was largely indifferent to the fate of the Jews, and that it was up to them to record the truth about their experience during the war. Moreover, they desired also to record everything about Jewish culture both before and during the Holocaust—a culture of which Hitler had tried to eliminate completely all signs that the Jews had lived a rich and creative life in Europe for the past 1,000 years. The Historical Commissions pursued their goals by retrieving documents (including those left behind by retreating German forces), photographs, songs, and poetry from the ghetto period, and by sending out *zammlers* (collectors) to gather testimonies from as many survivors as would agree to talk about their experiences. Many were willing and even eager to communicate the nightmare of their own lives in the ghettos and death camps.

The material they collected came at a time before the survivors' memories had begun to fade or become confused, or to be influenced by the enormous amount of information flowing their way. The tone of most of the testimonies is straightforward, unembellished, and contains information about the personal experience of the writer and details about Nazi personnel and how they conducted themselves. The focus of various testimonies, to consider only a few of an almost endless number of perspectives, ranged from a description of daily living in the Mielice labour camp; the last road for 1,200 Bialystok children; the Braslav region under the Nazi regime; life and survival in the White Russian forests; and subsisting in Auschwitz with two small children. The survivors did not hold back from expressing openly what happened to those who collaborated with the Germans or betrayed fellow members of resistance organisations in the ghettos or camps. At the opposite end of the scale, heroic deeds were acknowledged and remembered by the survivors. Israel Kaplan, the editor of *Fun Letzen Khurben*, a 10-volume journal whose full title was *Fun Letzten Khurben: tsaytschrift far geshikhte fun yidishn leben beysn nasi rezhim* (*From the Recent Destruction: A Journal of the History of Jewish Life under Nazi Rule*), underscored the need to tell the story of the Jewish experience, relating to the emotional and mental ramifications for Jews under Nazi rule.[21] In every edition of the journal, Kaplan's top priority was documenting and recording survivor testimonies and cultural evidence. He published repeated requests to survivors to write testimonies and pass them on to the Historical Commissions.

Jewish refugees wrote these descriptions while waiting in the DP camps, and they were initially published between 1946 and 1948. Historically very significant, these accounts, both from adults and children, were not available in English until translated in 2018. The freshness of the accounts, so soon after the ordeal they describe, is a testament to their veracity.

By far, the survivor testimonies gathered by the Historical Commissions in Yiddish were the most important of the historical documents reflecting the Jewish experience of the Shoah. Indeed, Kaplan was also deeply interested in the expressions and witticisms created in the ghettos and concentration camps. In every edition of the journal, he included a section entitled *Dos folks-moyl in natsi klem* (*The Jewish Voice under the Nazi Regime*). In this section, he included new colloquialisms and expressions as well as songs, poems, and other aspects of folklore.

The new words had been designed to outwit the Germans and were often laced with acerbic wit or sarcasm. The assumption of a culture in common enabled communication between the captives and stimulated a reminder of the former home-that-was and the communities from which the Jewish prisoners had come. In the labour camps, where people were humiliated, dehumanised, and physically abused, the use of a private code language boosted their morale and enhanced their sense of a shared identity. The Jewish slave labourers were constantly guarded and watched over by armed SS and collaborationist auxiliaries from the occupied countries, but the ability to deceive them through the language to which they had no access restored the prisoners' sense of pride and was even seen as a form of vengeance. There was a lexicon relating to different officers, the worst torturers among them, and certain hazardous situations. The code served the prisoners in the ghettos as well, and many new words were coined there. Kaplan made a study of this phenomenon overall and wrote a book describing how the codes were used, translated into English in 2018.[22] Some groups, like the Greek Jews (who had Ladino as their vernacular), were often disadvantaged because Yiddish was the colloquial speech of so many speakers.

Overall, testimonies concerning different aspects of life under the Nazis were recorded in large numbers by the Historical Commissions. Most of the early testimonies they collected were written in Yiddish and were thus only of interest to researchers understanding that language until many years later. Importantly, it was not until they were translated from Yiddish that they became accessible to many Holocaust scholars; however, Yiddish testimonies did appear as early as 1944 with the appearance of Yankel Wiernik's *A Year in Treblinka* (*A Yor in Treblinka*).[23] Other testimonies appeared in various languages, but perhaps the best known was Elie Wiesel's *Un Der Velt hot Geshvigen*, a deeply personal reflection written in Yiddish. It was to go through various renderings until finally appearing in English in 1960 as *Night*.[24] All such works presented the perspective of the individual Jew who contemplated the effects of their experiences personally. As Philip Friedman has written, "without these testimonies, we would know almost nothing about the way of life in the ghetto, about the way they earned a living, the cultural life, the fate of the people there, their creation and their destruction, about the folk creations (folklore, etc), in the ghetto and the concentration camp, about the inner, psychological aspect of the external events."[25] Friedman also contends that the testimonies are essential for understanding the Final Solution since the picture given by German documents and other non-Jewish sources is far from complete without them.

The historian Joseph Kermisz has also claimed that these testimonies are invaluable "as a source of teaching Jewish history in the time of the occupation."[26] It should not be overlooked that they were also very important as a source of healing and rehabilitation. Many survivors saw them as a memorial to the six million dead, the only grave for those who no longer had a voice.

The Limitations of Yiddish for Holocaust Research

Liberation did not bring permanent relief for the Jewish survivors, as it did not take long before they realised the stark reality of their situation—a situation that made their future look very bleak. The anguish of facing an uncertain future, without family, without a home, and without a country made the survivors rely on the individual resilience that had helped keep them alive. Michael Brenner succinctly describes the situation of the survivors: "the Jewish survivors of the Holocaust were in reality stateless people, desperate to begin a new life, hopefully, with family."[27] Living in the DP camps, mainly in the American zone, the leaders among the Jewish survivors realised that the anger and disappointment among *She'erit Hapletah* in the face of the world's indifference should be channelled in more positive directions. Attempts had to be made to restore a sense of hope in the future and the growth of a national spirit to ensure the rebuilding of the Jewish people and nation.

That said, while there are enormous advantages to be gained for Holocaust researchers by reference to Yiddish sources, it must be acknowledged that there are also certain drawbacks for the scholar who seeks to utilise such materials. The first must be its relative inaccessibility for younger scholars. Yiddish language courses, though existing (and perhaps growing) in certain parts of the world, require highly specialised instructors, which presents a problem. Indeed, after the war, when large numbers of Yiddish-speaking Eastern Europeans migrated to Israel, an aggressive campaign against the language was waged by Zionist groups and pro-Hebrew activists, fearing it would prevent the revival of Hebrew.[28] Since the establishment of the state of Israel and the near-concurrent destruction of Yiddish Europe, Hebrew has replaced Yiddish as the Jewish world's *lingua franca*, along with a ubiquitous presence of English. Yiddish has to a large degree become a "foreign" language for Jews, meaning it is much less likely to be spoken at home, taught in schools, or employed in daily discourse except among a small (and diminishing) population.

While this means there are few teachers of Yiddish, it also, *ipso facto*, means there will be fewer translators of Yiddish materials to enable younger scholars (in particular) to access sources originally written in that language. That said, translation services exist online, while YIVO in New York offers helpful advice to those who seek it. While it does require extra effort to access many Yiddish sources, the reward to be gained is profound and enlightening. In 1989, an American, Aaron Lansky, founded the Yiddish Book Center in Amherst, Massachusetts, an organisation he created to help preserve books and other Yiddish language publications as well as the culture and history those books represent. Lansky had realised that this was a cultural legacy in danger of destruction by a largely disinterested Jewish community. To date the Center has collected over a million works in Yiddish, having developed into an organisation offering many services such as digitisation, translation, and education programmes.[29]

Despite the limitations imposed by the practical realities of working with sources in Yiddish, the pitfalls of not doing so are profound—the most vital of which is that an incomplete picture of the Holocaust will be created if only Nazi sources are used. The Holocaust was unquestionably an unmitigated disaster for the Jewish people, but focusing on this only, without taking cognisance of the immensely rich and expressive culture that was destroyed, will not allow for an appropriate degree of understanding of the world that was lost in the years between 1933 and 1945.

Notes

1. An excellent introduction to the history of Yiddish can be found in a series of essays and documents—in English and Yiddish—edited by J.A. Fishman. See his *Never Say Die! A Thousand Years of Yiddish in Jewish Life and Letters*, The Hague: Mouton, 1981. See also D. Katz, *Words on Fire: The Unfinished Story of Yiddish*, New York: Basic Books, 2007; M. Weinstein, *Yiddish: A Nation of Words*, New York: Ballantine Books, 2001; and D.E. Fishman, *The Rise of Modern Yiddish Culture*, Pittsburgh: University of Pittsburgh Press, 2005.
2. Although once vibrant, Judeo-Spanish/Ladino is now restricted to a much narrower community of speakers. See T.K. Harris, *Death of a Language: The History of Judeo-Spanish*, Newark (DE): University of Delaware Press, 1994.
3. https://encyclopedia.ushmm.org/content/en/article/jewish-population-of-europe-in-1933-population-data-by-country.
4. See especially L. Weiner, *Yiddish Literature in the Nineteenth Century*, 2nd edition, New York: Herman Press, 1972. This remarkable account was first published in 1899 and is here reproduced with a new (and highly detailed) introduction by Eliar Schulman. A taste of other nineteenth-century Jewish literature can be found in J.M. Hess, M. Samuels, and N. Valman (ed.), *Nineteenth-Century Jewish Literature: A Reader*, Stanford: Stanford University Press, 2013.
5. On the continued use of Yiddish after arrival in the new country, see, for example, H.R. Diner, *Roads Taken: The Great Jewish Migrations to the New World and the Peddlers Who Forged the Way*, New Haven: Yale University Press, 2015; also, H.R. Diner, *Lower East Side Memories: A Jewish Place in America*, Princeton: Princeton University Press, 2000.
6. M. Tzanin, *The Criterion: The Yiddish Press*, 12, 1994, pp. 5–8.
7. The literature on the Final Solution is immense and too voluminous to list here. As a starting point, though, the following are indispensable: D. Cesarani, *The Final Solution: The Fate of the Jews, 1933–1945*, London: Macmillan, 2016; R. Breitman, *The Architect of Genocide: Himmler and the Final Solution*, New York: Knopf, 1992; D. Cesarani (ed.), *The Final Solution: Origins and Implementation*, 1994; and H. Friedlander, *The Origins of Nazi Genocide: From Euthanasia to the Final Solution*, Chapel Hill: University of North Carolina Press, 1997.
8. Indeed, one of the first major scholarly studies dealing with the topic was Raul Hilberg's *The Destruction of the European Jews*, Chicago: Quadrangle Books, 1961. Hilberg had great difficulty getting this book published, with most mainstream and academic publishers deciding that the topic of the Holocaust was unworthy of public interest.
9. In a large literature, see especially, D. Nasaw, *The Last Million: Europe's Displaced Persons from World War to Cold War*, New York: Penguin Press, 2020; and M. Wyman, *DPs: Europe's Displaced Persons, 1945–51*, Ithaca: Cornell University Press, 1998.
10. S.D. Kassow, *Who Will Write our History? Rediscovering a Hidden Archive from the Warsaw Ghetto*, Bloomington: Indiana University Press, 2007.
11. She'erit Hapletah (Hebrew, "surviving remnant") is a biblical term from the Books of Ezra (9:14) and 1 Chronicles (4:43). It was the term used by the survivors of the Holocaust to refer to themselves. In this regard, see A. Königseder and J. Wetzel, *Waiting for Hope: Jewish Displaced Persons in Post-World War II Germany*, Evanston (IL): Northwestern University Press, 2001.
12. Moshe Ishon served as a representative for Israel's Jewish Agency in New York from 1977 to 1980. In 1981, he became the chief editor of the Israeli newspaper *HaTzofe*, a position which he held until 1997.
13. On the nationhood aspect and its relationship to the Yiddish language, see P. Kriwaczek, *Yiddish Civilization: The Rise and Fall of a Forgotten Nation*, London: Weidenfeld and Nicolson, 2005.

14 F. Hodge, *Tragedy and Triumph: Early Testimonies of Jewish Survivors of World War II*, Clayton (Victoria): Monash University Publishing, 2018.
15 L.W. Schwartz, *The Redeemers: A Saga of the Years 1945–1952*, New York: Farrar, Strauss and Young, 1953.
16 D.P. Boder, *I Did Not Interview the Dead*, Urbana: University of Illinois Press, 1949.
17 L.L. Langer, *Holocaust Testimonies: The Ruins of Memory*, New Haven: Yale University Press, 1993; P.R. Bartrop, *Surviving the Camps: Unity in Adversity during the Holocaust*, Lanham (MD): University Press of America, 2000; and T. Des Pres, *The Survivor: An Anatomy of Life in the Death Camps*, New York: Oxford University Press, 1976.
18 P. Friedman, "The Jewish Ghettos of the Nazi Era," *Jewish Social Studies*, 16:1, January 1954, pp. 61–88.
19 The best-known example of this, of course, lay in the Warsaw Ghetto Uprising of 19 April-16 May 1943. Commanded by Mordecai Anielewicz and Yitzhak Zuckerman, its other leading members included Rachel Zilberberg, Mira Fuchrer, Zivia Lubetkin, Marek Edelman, Dawid Wdowinski, and Tosia Altman, among others. For all of them, Yiddish was their primary language. See H. Dreifuss, "The Leadership of the Jewish Combat Organization During the Warsaw Ghetto Uprising: A Reassessment," *Holocaust and Genocide Studies*, 31:1, Spring 2017, pp. 24–60.
20 A good general history of the Kovno ghetto is D.B. Klein (ed.), *Hidden History of the Kovno Ghetto*, Washington, DC, United States Holocaust Memorial Museum, 1997. For a first-person account, see Abraham Tory's remarkable chronicle of life in the ghetto: A. Tory (ed. M. Gilbert), *Surviving the Holocaust: The Kovno Ghetto Diary*, Cambridge (MA): Harvard University Press, 1990. It was written originally in Yiddish and translated into English for this edition by Jerzy Michalowicz.
21 I. Kaplan, *Tog-tteglekher Historisher Arbeit*, Munich: Historical Commission, 1947.
22 I. Kaplan, *The Jewish Voice in the Ghettos and Concentration Camps: Verbal Expression under Nazi Oppression*, Jerusalem: Yad Vashem, 2018.
23 Y. Wiernik, *A Year in Treblinka: An Inmate Who Escaped tells the Day-to-Day Facts of One Year of His Tortuous Experience*, New York: General Jewish Workers' Union of Poland, American Representation, 1944.
24 E. Wiesel, *Night*, New York: Hill and Wang, 1960. This was first written in Yiddish, Wiesel's native language. In its first incarnation, it ran to more than 800 pages. A version of this, published in 1956 in Argentina, *Un di velt hot geshvign* (*And the World Remained Silent*), was substantially shorter at 245 pages. Wiesel then halved the manuscript further in French, finally publishing it in 1958 as *La Nuit*. The book was then further translated into English as *Night* and published in 1960.
25 P. Friedman, *Di Elementen Fun Undzer Khurban-Forshung* (*The State of our Holocaust Research*), New York: YIVO, n.d. p.7.
26 J. Kermisz, *Metodologishe Onvayzungen tsum Oysforshen dem Khurbn fun Poylishe Yidntum* (*A Guide to the Methodology used in Research about the Destruction of Polish Jews*), Lodz: Tsentraler Yiddisher Historishe Komisye, 1945, p. 2.
27 M. Brenner, *After the Holocaust*, Princeton: Princeton University Press, 1999, p. 22.
28 https://apnews.com/article/9d46cc421298178d834b94bc067c1821.
29 A. Lansky, *Outwitting History: How a Young Man Rescued a Million Books and Saved a Vanishing Civilisation*, Chapel Hill: Algonquin Books, 2004.

12 Researching the Holocaust in a Digital World

Rachel Tait-Ripperdan

Introduction

In 1994, Rabbi Robert A. Jacobs, Executive Director of New York's Leo Baeck Institute, wrote: "How very fortunate we are to live in a time when electronic capabilities enable us to provide bibliographic references that will allow subsequent generations of scholars to find the materials they seek with no more than a few keystrokes."[1] The occasion of his writing was the creation in the Leo Baeck Institute of a database recording the Jewish archival holdings of the five new states of Germany after the demolition of the Berlin Wall. This project aimed to reunite dispersed records and increase accessibility to scholars across the world by compiling existing finding aids and commencing an examination of the collection to determine which materials would need to be short listed for digitisation due to deterioration.[2] Today, the Leo Baeck Institute offers online bibliographies and finding aids that can be consulted as well as a series of fully digitised collections accessible to the public. Their collections are an exciting example of how the digitisation of Holocaust resources has led to the democratisation of access and the preservation of delicate materials that would otherwise have perished.

In the past 80 years, the production and replication of cultural and educational resources in digital format have changed the field of Holocaust Studies in profound ways that are still being fully examined. This rapid advancement in technological abilities has created new opportunities to experience and participate in the field but has also presented scholars with challenges and concerns that must be addressed, lest the new technology serves as more of a hindrance than a help in the investigative process. At a time in which information is measured in zettabytes rather than pages, this transition is obviously a technological one. New methods of storage, preservation, and access make it a methodological and social one, as well. There has been much debate through the years over the experience that digital natives who have grown up with technology bring to the classroom versus digital immigrants who came to technology later in life.[3] Scholars Joshua Sternfeld and Sharon Ringel suggest that all users of digital resources are in need of a new theory of digital historiography which combines traditional historiography, computational studies, and archival theory.[4]

The physical library and archives used to be the place for researchers to find the information for which they looked. Those searches were often chaperoned by librarians and archivists. While some ungraciously refer to those guides as "gatekeepers," implying that they were guarding the information from the public, the purpose was for research to

DOI: 10.4324/9781003248620-15

be assisted by someone who had a deep knowledge of the collection and the research process, not just the subject. Today, however, one only needs a smartphone and a data plan to access a virtual galaxy of information. While this has democratised both the production and access of information to some extent, the system is not without flaws, as anyone who has attempted to use a broad internet search for research can attest.

In this context, it is important to articulate fully what is meant by digital research, specifically within the field of Holocaust Studies. This area of study does not just constitute digital archives like those held by Jerusalem's Yad Vashem, nor is it only databases of articles and e-books like JSTOR. It encompasses both primary, archival resources as well as secondary and tertiary sources. Primary resources in this context have generally been digitised from their physical formats, a process that is much more complex than often is realised. They may include diaries that survived the writer's internment in a concentration camp, testimonials and oral histories of survivors and witnesses, government documents, newspaper articles, photographs, necrologies, and more. Secondary and tertiary resources, on the other hand, may be digitised or born digital, that is, those materials that were created in a digital format, as is often the case with modern academic journals. In some instances, the aforementioned secondary and tertiary sources may exist in both physical and digital formats, such as scholarly monographs that are published and distributed as both physical books and e-books.

Some reflection upon the history of digitisation can keep students of history from continually rediscovering "the promise of 'digital history,' with all its attending hopes, visions, and ambitions for reinventing and reshaping historical research."[5] Computing within the humanities is not a contemporary endeavour, nor was it entirely new even during World War II and the Holocaust. In fact, the field as we know it was built upon technologies that were developed much earlier, such as the photostat machine (similar to what we now know as the photocopy machine), microphotography and microform, the punch card and tabulating machine, and data communication precursors, such as information theory and the telegraph. As is often the case with war, focused funding and manpower led to great technological strides forward during World War II. The punch card and tabulating machine, for example, played very important roles. On one hand, the punch card technology was utilised to counter Axis—and specifically, Nazi—domination through the creation at Bletchley Park of the Colossus, a computer that utilised punch cards, pulleys, and thousands of vacuum tubes to decrypt high-level German messages sent by the machine called "Tunny" using the Lorenz cipher system.[6] By the end of the war, the Colossus computer had been further improved, with ten of them at work deciphering Nazi codes.[7] The general public would not learn of the existence of the Colossus computers until the 1970s.[8]

On the other hand, punch card technology in the form of the Hollerith Machine has been linked to the destruction of the Jewish population during World War II. These machines, which were originally created to assist with the United States Census in 1890, were utilised by the Nazis to gather and create a national register of political, religious, and racial information about potential "enemies" of the Nazi Party, including Jews, Roma, Sinti, and Freemasons.[9] It was not until 2001 that the full story of International Business Machines (IBM) Corporation's role in this was examined by Edwin Black, who compiled copious documentary evidence to scrutinise intentional collusion between IBM and the Nazi Party.[10] These two examples demonstrate that technology itself may be neutral, but the ends to which people use it seldom are.

History and Evolution of Digital Research

Before World War II had even ended, Dr. Vannevar Bush, the Director of the United States Office of Scientific Research and Development (OSRD), wrote in *The Atlantic* magazine that scientists must turn their skills to "the massive task of making more accessible our bewildering store of knowledge."[11] He had many suggestions for doing so, from wearing miniature forehead cameras that would allow the user to capture anything of interest they looked at or read, to personal microform workstations called "Memex" that would allow for the creation of digital trails of research paths that could be stored and retrieved with ease. Toward the end of his essay, he wrote:

> Presumably man's spirit should be elevated if he can better view his shady past and analyze more completely and objectively his present problems. He has built a civilization so complex that he needs to mechanize his records more fully if he is to push his experiment to its logical conclusion and not merely become bogged down part way there by overtaxing his limited memory.

The use of technology to tame the enormity of human thought has led to the creation of many marvels. It is interesting to note that Bush presided over the Manhattan Project and the creation of the atomic bomb, which puts his words about viewing mankind's "shady past" into a darker perspective. Bush's advocacy for government funding of scientific research would lead to the development of the National Science Foundation (NSF) in 1950, an agency that would provide grant funding to hundreds of researchers, including several within the field of Jewish Studies.[12] In part due to the relatively minimal losses compared to some countries elsewhere, and later due to Cold War geopolitical tension, the United States would lead the rest of the world in post-war technological innovation for some years.[13]

Bush was hardly the only researcher advocating for the mechanisation of the research process, though he may have been one of the most creative. In 1948, Murray G. Lawson referenced Bush's article while presenting his own paper, "The Machine Age in Historical Research," to the annual meeting of the American Historical Association. Lawson accused his colleagues of technological conservatism and insisted that they needed to take more advantage of the technological advances of their time, looking to the business world for examples of how to do so. He closed his exhortation by stating that historians either needed to "accept the challenge and attain to new heights of achievement or else reject it and be swamped by the tidal wave of accumulated and expanding knowledge."[14] There were, however, already thriving pockets of scholars dedicated to incorporating new technologies into historical research, including within the fields of Jewish and, later, Holocaust Studies.

The American Jewish Historical Society President Abraham Rosenbach, and the Jewish-American historian Samuel Oppenheim, made use of the photostat machine to duplicate records that created collections of materials that would be utilised by future historians studying Jewish history.[15] Microform was used to archive Jewish congregational records in the 1930s, punch cards were used for census taking, and automated machine translation was already being discussed in the early 1940s.[16] Yehoshua Bar-Hillel, born Oscar Westreich in Vienna, received his PhD in Philosophy from Hebrew University and took a position at the Massachusetts Institute of Technology (MIT) in the early 1950s. He would be one of the first scholars to work in-depth in the field of mechanical translation and would form a computational linguistic group in Jerusalem.[17] Although he was sceptical of the abilities of machine translation, his work continues to impact the field of digital humanities.[18]

Within the field of computational linguistics, Italian Jesuit priest, Father Roberto Busa, gained IBM sponsorship for a computer-generated literary analysis of the works of Saint Thomas Aquinas in 1949.[19] His work would ultimately impact that of Jewish researchers within the field of computational humanities when he assisted in the establishment of a literary data processing centre at Hebrew University from which many digital projects in Jewish Studies would come.[20] Shortly thereafter, in 1954, Professor Ze'ev Ben-Hayyim, leading Israeli linguist and second president of the Academy of the Hebrew Language, would propose a plan to "create a complete computerised database of all the Hebrew texts up to the eleventh century, and a large selection of Hebrew literature from the eleventh century to the founding of the state of Israel."[21] While this project would take years to complete, the final product has since appeared online.[22]

Established in 1953, Yad Vashem, the World Holocaust Remembrance Centre, was proposed to the Jewish National Fund in 1942 as a memorial to the Jews who had been murdered in Nazi-occupied areas.[23] Although Yad Vashem would lag behind in the digitisation process, in time it would become one of the largest and most important digital resources for Holocaust research, including the Central Database of Shoah Victims' Names, and the Righteous Database, which includes stories of those who helped to save Jewish lives during the Holocaust.[24] Launched in 1967 and headed by Munich mathematician Aviezri Fraenkel and computer scientist Yaacov Choueka, The Responsa Project was a massive undertaking with the goal of building a full-text retrieval system for rabbinic case-law rulings.[25] This project is also still extant and can be accessed by the public, although the ability to save or print content is limited to subscribers.[26] At the Fifth World Congress of Jewish Studies in 1969, Henry C. Ekstein presented his ideas for organising and funding an international data bank of resources, including rare manuscripts and images, that would be connected via a telecommunication network to the most important research centres around the world.[27] By the late 1960s, when Ekstein presented his idea about a world wide data bank, packet-switching networks were in development and would lead to the eventual development of the internet.[28] The creation of the World Wide Web in 1989 would revolutionise the ways that people communicated, shared content, and learned. By the end of the millennium, internet access was the norm for over half of the United States; by 2016, the trend had turned global with an estimated 3.408 billion users.[29] Countless new projects would be developed during the upgrowth in internet access.

Examples, Benefits, and Challenges of Key Digital Resources for Holocaust Studies

As demonstrated, the current hype of what we now colloquially call "digital humanities" is not new. However, the last 20 years have brought increased interest in the field, characterised by a focus on data analysis and visualisation, mass digitisation, and new ways of accessing and using information. In part, this is because we are now living in a truly digital world. According to a report by the International Data Corporation (IDC), the amount of data created, captured, and replicated is expected to grow from 33 zettabytes in 2018 to 175 zettabytes by 2025.[30] Perhaps equally as enlightening as that number is the estimation of digital interactions per person per day: from 1,426 in 2020 to an anticipated 4,909 in 2025.[31] Google Books, launched in October 2004, had digitised over 40 million books as of 2019 and The Internet Archive states their goal as to "provide Universal Access to All Knowledge."[32] The beauty of digitisation lies in the freedom of access and democratisation of research and the production of scholarship. Despite all this, though, there are clear challenges to widespread digitisation. Furthermore, the field of Holocaust Studies carries its own unique set of challenges which are sometimes lessened and sometimes magnified by the digital trend.

Perhaps the most complex of the challenges in Holocaust Studies is the wide dispersal of content due to its diasporic nature. During and after World War II, both the Jewish people and their stolen textual materials were displaced and forcibly relocated to various countries around the world.[33] *Landsmanshaftn*, organisations of Jewish immigrants meant to provide social structure to those set adrift from their homelands, formed where groups of survivors made their new homes, and it is in those multitudes of locations where locally created archives sprang up. As groups sometimes battled for the rights to looted books and documents, those resources were often gathered by institutions local to the new Jewish communities growing nearby. Although there have been efforts to gather resources into central locations like Yad Vashem and the United States Holocaust Memorial Museum (USHMM), there has been turbulence over who has the right to those resources. An excellent example of this challenge is the work of Hans-Günther Adler. Born in Prague into a German-Jewish family, Adler was deported in 1942 to the Terezín ghetto. He documented his experiences of the Holocaust while imprisoned. After his release, he lived in Prague and later London; his works were scattered between these locations and later picked up by no fewer than five (sometimes competing) repositories.[34]

This example of the fragmentation of Holocaust materials demonstrates the complexity of the task of consolidating—or even locating—collections. In 2010, the European Holocaust Research Infrastructure (EHRI) was funded by the European Union to create an integrated database that linked diverse Holocaust archives from all around the world. Project leaders have written numerous articles discussing the intricacies of the project.[35] EHRI has identified more than 2,100 institutions that hold Holocaust materials in at least 59 countries; the materials thus far have appeared in at least 23 languages.[36] In addition to coping with the dispersal of the collections, they have had to deal with the different metadata standards that are often used by the wide variety of archival bodies that have collected materials of interest.

Metadata is generally defined as "data about data" and can include a variety of relevant information about a given object, such as title, author, date, size, and provenance.[37] It is used by libraries and archives not only to organise and catalogue materials but also to draw connections between collections. There are many different standards in use internationally; in addition, the standards have changed over time to reflect both changes in principles and technologies.[38] Within the digital world, metadata grows even more complex. One of the key purposes of digital repositories is to increase access to the content, but it is not simply a matter of just merging entities. Smaller, less-well-funded and staffed archives may use entirely different metadata languages or even "homegrown" methodologies. Even larger institutions such as Yad Vashem, USHMM, and Cegesoma—who all use the same technical standards—record the provenance of their materials in different fields and to different levels of detail.[39] In fact, when EHRI surveyed interested and interesting archives in the early stages of the project development, they learned that "half of the archives that responded to the survey said that they do not use archival standards at all. Among these were also some of the major archives in Holocaust research."[40]

An additional hurdle in digitising Holocaust materials is that they often vary in language, script, and audience. The field includes a wide array of primary documentation, encompassing diaries, letters, photographs, and other personal materials. Unlike secondary sources, these primary objects were seldom created to be studied by scholars; rather, they were intended to record and memorialise the experiences of the creators. As an example, Yizkor books were produced for Jewish prayer rituals of collective mourning; by providing a space for them to record communal histories of people, locations, and community life, they serve as necrologies and memory resources for Jewish survivors who had been violently displaced from their homes.[41] Because these materials are personal narratives of those who lived through extreme trauma, there are variations in the stories that are told within, sometimes not agreeing with each other. This is perfectly acceptable when considering the original intent of the books but presents challenges in historical veracity if the context is neglected.

Since the Yizkor books were intended to be used for a specific, liturgical purpose, they were often published in small runs and with production quality that was not intended to hold up to regular usage.[42] Because they were communal works, they were often written in a variety of languages and scripts.[43] However, collections of Yizkor books have proven to be in demand for multiple reasons. The first relates to the purpose for which they were intended: as sources of record for survivors attempting to track details of people and places lost to the war.[44] The other group of users are researchers interested in the insight these materials provide into the cultural, commercial, and political activities of villages that were wiped out during the Holocaust. Since the materials are fragile and in demand, they made an excellent target for transcription and digitisation; a project that was begun by JewishGen and continued by the New York Public Library. Approximately 600 Yizkor books have been fully digitised and many of them, even those in Hebrew and Yiddish, are full-text searchable.[45] This demonstrates not just an impressive digitisation undertaking, but an excellent advancement in technology; when the books were initially digitised, they were not optical character recognisable (OCR) due to the complexity of the multilingual nature of the books.

As is evidenced in the previous examples, digital databases are used to preserve a multitude of resources by a wide range of administrators. It is not a simple matter of applying methodologies consistent with the physical formats of the same materials, either, given that contextual indicators that one takes from a physical item are missing or separated from the content itself. This is one of the main criticisms that is often levelled at digital resources by scholars who have experience rooting through folders and boxes of original documents preserved in physical archives around the world. Jane E. Klinger, Chief Conservator at the United States Holocaust Memorial Museum, presents an example of the dilemma of missing context with regard to Holocaust materials that have been digitised. As she explains, how an "object was used and damaged during the war years—through being hidden, through use, or through neglect—are important parts of the story it has to tell."[46] However, when digitising materials, those contextual clues cannot always be captured due to limitations of available technology and funding, lack of perceived need, skill of the contractors in charge of the project, and the condition of the material itself.[47] Certainly such qualities, such as smell and texture, cannot be replicated via digitisation, although they can be noted within the metadata by observant archivists. Even if they are included in the metadata, however, the disconnect between "thing" and "digitised thing" leads to an inevitable loss in sensory research methods.

Finally, it is necessary to consider the commercial role in the presentation of digital Holocaust memory. While it is tempting to hope that open access to archival materials is the great democratiser in academia, Annika Björkdahl and Stefanie Kappler warn against accepting without qualification the idea that digitisation will right all the systemic wrongs in the scholarly community. They argue that the decontextualising of local memory into global discourse "corresponds to a global economy in which memory-makers and consumers interact politically, socially, and financially."[48] In other words, when memory equals money, people with money own memory.

The selection of materials for digitisation projects is complex and the funding is often fleeting.[49] When creating a digital collection, each item that goes into that collection is carefully chosen based on some pre-established criteria, such as condition, availability elsewhere, and demand. Decisions of what is included and excluded from collections are ultimately still made by people and institutions who often have social and national positions of privilege. While this is not intended to disparage those who make collection development decisions—most librarians and archivists do—often the ultimate decision of what to include comes down to choosing what is going to get people in the door or hits on the website. Materials that are less unique, socially relevant, or politically acceptable will be shuffled back into their boxes, perhaps to be pulled out for consideration again at some point in the future.

Increasingly, commercial publishers are becoming involved in the field of digitisation. There are some excellent primary and secondary commercial databases that are invaluable when doing research in Holocaust Studies, such as JSTOR, Gale Archives Unbound, ProQuest Historical American Jewish Newspaper, and EBSCO Jewish Studies Source. However, content in these databases is behind a paywall for those researchers who do not have access to an institution that can afford to subscribe to them. While it has always been the case that some materials are locked behind a position of academic privilege, it is worth noting that in a time where funding is becoming increasingly dire, more of these resources than ever before will be digital but still inaccessible to those who cannot afford to access them.[50]

Future of Digital Research in Holocaust Studies

There is little question that at least the immediate future of research will be heavily focused on the digital realm. The year 2020 saw a response to the COVID-19 pandemic that led to global lockdowns on travel. Universities around the world turned to online learning in a move that had professors scrambling and students struggling.[51] There was little choice, at the time, as society endeavoured to embrace the "new normal" and weather the storm. It became increasingly apparent that researchers would need to rely on digital resources in lieu of travelling to physical locations; in addition, it was clear to libraries and archives that, to survive economically, they would need to improve and advertise their digital collection access.[52] The words "unprecedented" and "innovative" were used repeatedly in responses, adding to the urgency of the times. While the full impact of this response to the pandemic is still unclear, many libraries have switched their focus from physical monographs to e-books, and archives have turned furiously to digitisation. This sea change has led to upheaval within the realm of interlibrary loans as libraries struggle to keep up with the need for easy access by borrowing resources from other institutions. This is a challenging endeavour as many publishers do not allow the lending of their e-books through existing interlibrary arrangements, leading to further frustration from researchers.

During this time, it also grew readily apparent just how much was missing from the digital record. Researchers were faced with the dilemma of altering their research agenda or settling for sources that were available online but not fully relevant to their needs. As travel gradually reopens, it is time to revisit the physical archives and remain vigilant in pursuit of research that is significant, not just that which utilises the most easily accessible sources. The future of Holocaust research depends upon serendipitous discoveries within both the digital and the "hidden archives." To this end, increased focus on shared metadata standards and the unification of dispersed records as seen within the EHRI and Yerusha databases should be given higher priority than the piecemeal digitisation of collections.[53]

Perhaps of most critical importance to the future of the field at this time is the inevitable passing of the generation that survived the Holocaust. The year 2021 alone saw the passing of over 15,000 Holocaust survivors; as of this writing, the average age of remaining survivors is 85 years old.[54] Thankfully, the digital revolution has given us excellent tools for preserving survivor testimonies, including video, interactive websites, virtual reality, and even artificial intelligence (AI). There are several key archives that incorporate audio and visual oral history collections from survivors and witnesses, including the United States Holocaust Memorial Museum, the Zekelman Holocaust Center, Jewish Family and Children's Services Holocaust Center, the British Library, and the Association of Jewish Refugees Refugee Voices. One of the most prominent of these collections is that of the University of Southern California (USC) Shoah Foundation. The USC Shoah Foundation was established in 1994 by Steven Spielberg after the appearance of his film *Schindler's List*.[55] As he spoke to survivors of the Holocaust, he realised that there was a need for preserving oral testimonies of survivors around the world. Although accessing the full collection requires creating a free account, the Visual History Archive contains over 54,000 eyewitness testimonies from survivors. In addition to the main database of testimonies, IWitness is the educational branch of the USC Shoah Foundation. Here, educators can sign up for resources about developing assignments that incorporate virtual testimonies. In addition, they can invite students to a group in order to curate a custom curriculum using IWitness resources.

Although watching virtual testimonies can be impactful to students and researchers, USC Shoah Foundation saw the need for deeper engagement in light of the passing of survivors. To that end, in 2020, it implemented the development of a project using virtual reality and AI. This project, called *New Dimensions in Testimony*, is fully interactable and 3D. In it, volunteer Holocaust survivors are interviewed and recorded from every possible angle; the questions they are asked are in-depth, meant to take into account any question that an interviewer may ask. After this process, the questions and answers are recorded in a database that uses AI to consider all possible algorithms in which an answer may match a question. Once this is complete, the hologram is ready to be questioned by students, visitors, and researchers. The algorithm will improve with use, allowing the AI to respond more appropriately to questions over time.[56] While the technology is still in its early stages, the potential for future iterations is auspicious. It seems appropriate that these archives allow for those who could have died 80 years ago in the most horrific of circumstances to live on in our memories forever.

Conclusion

At a time when mass digitisation is considered by some to be a moral imperative and by others to be the downfall of authentic research, there are still many who do not understand the ways in which materials are either born digital or digitised, the selection process that takes place to build a collection of digital materials, the methods of preservation, and the disunification of materials from their original contexts. These are important methodological considerations that must be considered when using any source, including digital. As pointed out by Danish scholar Nanna Bonde Thylstrup, the digitisation process is complex and often political in nature and should be viewed as "emerging sociopolitical and sociotechnical phenomena that introduce new forms of cultural memory politics."[57] While the democratisation of information through digital archives that allow for access to content around the world serves the nobler motivations of academia, the system is not without flaws. The digital divide, the gap between those who have access to modern technology and those who do not or who have restricted access, remains an ongoing issue within the realm of digital research.

In addition, the field of Holocaust Studies has challenges unique to itself, including the dispersal of sources, the multitude of languages in which the history is recorded, and the specific intent for which many of the resources were created. There is a need for students of the Holocaust to understand not just the history of the field but also the history of the preservation of the resources of the field; a "digital historiography" of sorts that allows us to move forward with truly new innovations that enhance future understandings of the subject. Finally, we must not forget that the process of digitisation is governed by available funding and value judgements that determine which sources make it to digital and which remain housed in physical archives around the world. While it would be counterproductive to ignore those resources that are available online through various databases and collections, it would be equally foolish to forget that there are still physical resources awaiting study and serendipitous discoveries that wait to be made.

Notes

1 R.A. Jacobs, "Jewish Archival Holdings in the Five New States of Germany: Creating an Inventory," *Judaica Librarianship*, 8, 1994 p. 22.
2 Ibid., pp. 19–21.
3 C.L. Riley, "Beyond ctrl-c, ctrl-v: Teaching and Learning History in the Digital Age," in T. Weller (ed.), *History in the Digital Age*, New York: Routledge, 2013, pp. 149–69. See C. Evans and W. Robertson, "The Four Phases of the Digital Natives Debate," *Human Behavior and Emerging Technologies*, 2:3, 2020, pp. 269–77 for an overview of the stages of the digital native debate.
4 J. Sternfeld, "Archival Theory and Digital Historiography: Selection, Search, and Metadata as Archival Processes for Assessing Historical Contextualization," *American Archivist*, 74:2, 2011, p. 544; S. Ringel, "Interfacing With the Past: Archival Digitization and the Construction of Digital Depository," *Convergence: The International Journal of Research Into New Media Technologies*, 27:5, 2021, p. 1309.
5 G. Zaagsma, "Exploring Jewish History in the Digital Age," keynote, POLIN Conference, 4 October 2021, p. 2.

6 B.J. Copeland, "Colossus: Its Origins and Originators," *IEEE Annals of the History of Computing*, 26:4, 2004, p. 39.
7 T.H. Flowers, "The Design of Colossus," *Annals of the History of Computing*, 5:3, 1983, pp. 239, 247.
8 A.E. Sale, "Colossus and the German Lorenz Cipher—Code Breaking in WWII," paper, International Conference on the Theory and Applications of Cryptographic Techniques, 14–18 May 2000, p. 417.
9 "Hollerith Machine," Jewish Virtual Library, available online at https://www.jewishvirtuallibrary.org/hollerith-machine.
10 E. Black, *IBM and the Holocaust*, New York: Crown Publishers, 2001.
11 V. Bush, "As We May Think," *The Atlantic*, July 1945, p. 101.
12 V. Bush, *Science, the Endless Frontier: A Report to the President by Vannevar Bush, Director of the Office of Scientific Research and Development, July 1945*, available online at https://www.nsf.gov/od/lpa/nsf50/vbush1945.htm. Although Bush would not be Director, the NSF was founded in 1950 and provided grants to several of the researchers discussed below, including Busa (1960), Bar-Hillel (1960), Ben-Hayim (1969), and Choueka (1969).
13 D.P. Gross and B.N. Sampat, *Inventing the Endless Frontier: The Effects of the World War II Research Effort on Post-War Innovation*, Cambridge (MA), National Bureau of Economic Research Working Paper 27375, 2020, p. 2.
14 M.G. Lawson, "The Machine Age in Historical Research," *American Archivist*, 11: 2, 1948, p. 142.
15 Zaagsma, "Exploring Jewish History in the Digital Age," p. 4.
16 Ibid.
17 A. Margalit, "Bar-Hillel: The Man and His Philosophy of Mathematics," *Iyyun: The Jerusalem Philosophical Quarterly*, 39, 1990, p. 7.
18 Y. Bar-Hillel, "Some Theoretical Aspects of the Mechanization of Literature Searching," in W. Hoffman (ed.) *Digital Information Processors*, New York: Interscience, 1962, pp. 406–43; S. Nirenburg, "Bar Hillel and Machine Translation: Then and Now," *Proceedings, Fourth Bar Ilan Symposium on Foundations of Artificial Intelligence*, 1995, p. 303, available online at https://www.aaai.org/Papers/BISFAI/1995/BISFAI95-027.pdf.
19 R. Busa, "The Annals of Humanities Computing: The Index Thomisticus," *Computers and the Humanities*, 14, 1980, p. 84.
20 S.E. Jones, *Roberto Busa, S.J., and the Emergence of Humanities Computing: The Priest and the Punched Cards*, New York: Routledge, 2016, p. 163.
21 "Historical Dictionary Project," The Academy of the Hebrew Language, available online at https://en.hebrew-academy.org.il/historical-dictionary-project/.
22 "Ma'agarim: The Database of the Historical Dictionary Project," The Academy of the Hebrew Language, available online at https://maagarim.hebrew-academy.org.il/Pages/PMain.aspx.
23 A. Margalit, *The Ethics of Memory*, Cambridge (MA): Harvard University Press, 2002, p. 22.
24 R. Barkai, "So That Future Generations Will Know ... " *Yad Vashem Jerusalem Quarterly Magazine*, 73:5774, December 2013, pp. 6–7; The Central Database of Shoah Victims' Names, available online at https://yvng.yadvashem.org/; The Righteous Among the Nations Database, available online at https://righteous.yadvashem.org/.
25 Y. Choueka, "Computerized Full-Text Retrieval Systems and Research in the Humanities: The Responsa Project," *Computers and the Humanities*, 14:3, 1980, p. 154
26 See https://www.responsa.co.il/home.en-US.aspx.
27 H.C. Ekstein, "How to Increase Effectiveness of Research in Jewish Studies," *Proceedings of the Fifth World Congress of Jewish Studies*, 5, 1969, pp. 3–7.
28 L.G. Roberts, "The Evolution of Packet Switching," *Proceedings of the IEEE*, 66:11, 1978, pp. 1307–8.
29 M. Roser, H.Ritchie, and E. Ortiz-Ospina, "Share of the Population Using the Internet," Our World in Data, available online at https://ourworldindata.org/internet.
30 D. Ryndning, J. Reinsel, and J. Gantz, "The Digitization of the World From Edge to Core," International Data Corporation white paper #US44413318, 2018, available online at https://www.seagate.com/files/www-content/our-story/trends/files/idc-seagate-dataage-whitepaper.pdf, p. 2.

31 Ibid., p. 13.
32 H. Lee, "15 Years of Google Books," Google Blog, 17 October 2019, available online at https://www.blog.google/products/search/15-years-google-books/; About the Internet Archive, see https://archive.org/about/.
33 G. Amit, "'The Largest Jewish Library in the World': The Books of Holocaust Victims and Their Redistribution Following World War II," *Dapim: Studies on the Holocaust*, 27:2, 2013, pp. 107–28.
34 T. Blanke and C. Kristel, "Integrating Holocaust Research," *International Journal of Humanities and Arts Computing*, 7:1–2, 2013, pp. 42–3.
35 R. Speck, et al., "The Past and the Future of Holocaust Research: From Disparate Sources to an Integrated European Holocaust Research Infrastructure," arXiv, 2014, p. 168, available online at https://arxiv.org/abs/1405.2407.
36 S.A. Erez, et al., "Record Linking in the EHRI Portal," *Records Management Journal*, 30:3, 2020, p. 366.
37 K. Long, "An Entirely Too Brief History of Library Metadata and a Peek at the Future, Too," American Library Association, available online at https://www.ala.org/rusa/sites/ala.org.rusa/files/content/sections/history/resources/History_metadata.pdf.
38 D.F. Spidal, "Treatment of Holocaust Denial Literature in Association of Research Libraries," *The Journal of Academic Librarianship*, 38:1, 2012, pp. 26–32; D. Kalita and D. Deka, "Searching the Great Metadata Timeline: A Review of Library Metadata Standards From Linear Cataloguing Rules to Ontology Inspired Metadata Standards," *Library Hi Tech*, 39:1, 2021, pp. 190–204.
39 S. A. Erez, et al., "Record Linking in the EHRI Portal," *Records Management Journal*, 30:3, 2020, pp. 366–369.
40 T. Blanke and C. Kristel, "Integrating Holocaust Research," *International Journal of Humanities and Arts Computing*, 7:1–2, 2013, p. 48.
41 S. Kricsfeld and A. van de Kamp-Wright, "Death and Mourning in Judaism: Kaddish, Yizkor, and Yahrzeit," *The Jewish Press*, July 2021, available online at https://www.omahajewishpress.com/news/death-and-mourning-in-judaism-kaddish-yizkor-and-yahrzeit/article_fc267a7c-ea31-11eb-87c9-db390d2a5529.html; F. Jones and G. Siegel, "Yizkor Books as Holocaust Grey Literature," *Publishing Research Quarterly*, 22, 2006, pp. 52–62.
42 Jones and Siegel, "Yizkor Books as Holocaust Grey Literature," p. 53.
43 Ibid.
44 Ibid., p. 58.
45 "Yizkor Books: Home," New York Public Library LibGuides, available online at https://libguides.nypl.org/yizkorbooks.
46 J.E. Klinger, "Exploring the Limits of Digitization," European Holocaust Research Infrastructure, available online at https://www.ehri-project.eu/exploring-limits-digitization.
47 Ibid.
48 A. Björkdahl and S. Kappler, "The Creation of Transnational Memory Spaces: Professionalization and Commercialization," *International Journal of Politics, Culture, and Society*, 32, 2019, p. 384.
49 M. Sandle, "Studying the Past in the Digital Age: From Tourist to Explorer," in T. Weller (ed.) *History in the Digital Age*, London: Routledge, 2012, p. 133.
50 H.R. Gur, "Along With Row Over its Next Head, Yad Vashem Faces Cash Crunch Due to Pandemic," *The Times of Israel*, 30 November 2020, available online at https://www.timesofisrael.com/yad-vashem-faces-cash-crunch-due-to-pandemic-political-gridlock/.
51 "COVID-19 Educational Disruption and Response," UNESCO, 24 March 2020, available online at https://en.unesco.org/news/covid-19-educational-disruption-and-response.
52 For some examples of responses, see "Holocaust Remembrance and Education During COVID-19," Yad Vashem: The World Holocaust Remembrance Center, 14 July 2020, available online at https://www.yadvashem.org/blog/holocaust-remembrance-and-education-during-covid19.html; "The Library's Innovative Response to COVID-19," University of Chicago Library, 12, April 2021, available online at https://www.lib.uchicago.edu/about/news/the-librarys-innovative-response-to-covid-19/; "Mitigating COVID-19: The Contribution Research Libraries Are Making," Association of Research Libraries, 16 March 2020, available online at https://www.arl.org/news/mitigating-covid-19-the-contribution-research-libraries-

are-making/; C. Bradley-Sanders, "Working Remotely, Working Effectively: Improving Collection Access During a Global Pandemic," *Collections: A Journal for Museum and Archives Professionals*, 17:2, 2021, pp. 119–27.
53 Zaagsma, "Exploring Jewish History in the Digital Age," p. 13.
54 N. Dvir, "Over 15,000 Holocaust Survivors Passed Away Last Year," *Israel Hayom*, 26 January 2022, available online at https://www.israelhayom.com/2022/01/26/over-15000-holocaust-survivors-passed-away-this-year/.
55 "The Shoah Foundation Story," USC Shoah Foundation, available online at https://sfi.usc.edu/#.
56 L. Stahl, "Artificial Intelligence Preserving Our Ability to Converse with Holocaust Survivors After They Die," CBS News, 27 March 2022, available online at https://www.cbsnews.com/news/holocaust-stories-artificial-intelligence-60-minutes-2022-03-27/.
57 N.B. Thylstrup, *The Politics of Mass Digitization*, Cambridge: MIT Press, 2019, p. 4.

13 Persistence of Memory Through Artefacts

Melissa Minds VandeBurgt and Bailey Rodgers

Introduction

The Nazis actively stripped the identities of millions; the study of artefacts mitigates the erasure of personal histories of those who survived and those who did not. Certain artefacts, such as the railway cars and piles of shoes that have been displayed all over the world, are instantly recognisable symbolic memorialisation of the horrors of the Holocaust. Additional material culture, such as smaller personal artefacts, allows students of the Holocaust to glean historical and social context, as well as ethnographic insight, directly from those who experienced it. Artefacts provide pertinent historical evidence that is both poignant and tangible, deepening one's understanding of identity, expressions of resistance, and memory.

Over the past 40 years, museums and archives dedicated to the Holocaust have provided a platform for scholars from multiple disciplines to theorise, experiment, and illustrate both the value and the limitations of artefacts as a primary vehicle for the study of the Holocaust. Traditionally, scholars of the Holocaust have focused their enquiry on documents and testimony. Material culture, including artefacts and relics, provides insight into a person, family, religious group, or civilisation—in some instances, all four. More recently, the study of material culture is multidisciplinary, with social scientists, anthropologists, archaeologists, and historians utilising artefacts to contribute to the historical narrative. The process of collecting, preserving, and interpreting artefacts is critical to informing contemporary cultures of the past and an important research strategy in Holocaust Studies. For most victims of the Holocaust, the primary historical record of their lives was not written; rather, it exists in the artefacts, the physical objects that remained after they were gone.

This chapter is an exploration of the use of artefacts to enrich the study of the Holocaust and an investigation of the benefits and limitations of using material culture to address scholarly enquiry. The history of artefacts in Holocaust Studies is presented as well as definitions of what material culture is and how it can be applied. There is a comprehensive overview of the challenges archivists and museum professionals face in the collection, preservation, and display of artefacts. Finally, the chapter provides examples of the types of artefacts Holocaust scholars may come across in their studies. The objects themselves hold agency and are survivors unto themselves.

The Historiography of Artefacts in Holocaust Literature

In the last 30 years, scholarship on the Holocaust has shifted from strictly political and military history to a more holistic approach, incorporating disciplines from the arts,

DOI: 10.4324/9781003248620-16

sciences, and humanities into the study. During court investigations and prosecution of the perpetrators in the late 1940s, government documents became available by the Allied forces and historians would later use these documents for their research. In 1961, American political scientist Raul Hilberg published *The Destruction of the European Jews,* which is still regarded as one of the most notable pieces of Holocaust literature.[1] In the years following, most scholarship focused on the Nazi rise to power and reflections on the post-war era, with little crossover between the two.[2] Germany was struggling to come to terms with shared memory and identity in a post-Nazi era. By the 1980s, there was large public debate between historians and left- and right-wing politicians on how the Holocaust should be remembered in the German state. The debate was highly politicised, lasting a decade, and would become known as *Historikerstreit* ("historians' quarrel"). The *Historikerstreit* highlighted the "relationship between historical consciousness and identity" as well as history's contentious relationship with politics.[3] After the public debate concluded, historians became more interested during the 1990s in how and why the Holocaust happened and how ordinary Germans contributed to the event, leading to even more debates and disagreements.

In 1992, historian Christopher Browning published *Ordinary Men*, which argued that everyday German citizens were indifferent to the suffering of Jewish communities.[4] In a counterargument in 1996, Daniel Goldhagen published *Hitler's Willing Executioners: Ordinary Germans and the Holocaust,* a piece of literature that was, and is still considered, controversial.[5] Using the anthropological perspective, Goldhagen argued that everyday German citizens supported and participated in the Holocaust because of the antisemitic culture that was rampant in the country before the rise of the Nazi Party. Browning's and Goldhagen's books are cornerstone pieces of literature in Holocaust Studies with differing arguments, but one similarity is certain: the sources used to support their arguments were textual.[6]

The appearance of these two works saw an intensification in interdisciplinary studies of the Holocaust. Archaeologists, anthropologists, artists, and psychologists have since begun using artefacts to answer broader questions with respect to their fields.[7] In the last two decades, there has been a shift in using artefacts to glean more awareness of the experiences and suffering that occurred during the Holocaust period. Studying material culture can create a link between those who have been lost in the past and those in the present.[8] Moreover, the study of material culture allows for a deeper understanding and knowledge of events related to the Holocaust. Examining individual suffering and the affairs leading up to that suffering can allow us to experience something that can "transform us and involves reflection and learning."[9] Using artefacts in this manner can create new interpretations of the past that may have been overlooked.[10]

Material Culture

Archaeologist Leland Ferguson provides a particularly simple definition of material culture as "the things that people leave behind."[11] Many disciplines use material culture to analyse and interpret human interaction with the physical world. The fields of anthropology and archaeology are based on the study of artefacts to understand human civilisation and behaviour, as are many of the social sciences. Historians, with a long-established custom of using documents and testimonies for research, are using material culture to rethink and expand upon traditional narratives. Historian Thomas J. Schlereth describes material culture studies as the "study through artifacts and other pertinent historical evidence of belief systems—the values, ideas, attitudes, and assumptions—of a particular community or society, usually across time." Schlereth's definition, generally agreed upon across disciplines, asserts that "the common assumption underlying material culture research is that objects made or modified by humans, consciously or unconsciously, directly or indirectly, reflect the belief patterns of individuals who made, commissioned, purchased, or used them, and, by extension, the belief patterns of the larger society of which they are a part."[12]

Material culture studies become particularly poignant when applied to a horrific event such as the Holocaust. The Holocaust was a systematic effort to erase the Jewish people as well as additional groups that did not fit the Aryan definition; it was a clear act of genocide. The term "genocide" was coined by lawyer Raphael Lemkin in his book, *Axis Rule in Occupied Europe*, in 1944. Lemkin's definition of genocide did not only entail the mass murder of people, but also the methodical attack on a group of people's cultural identity, specifically their material culture.[13] In 1933, he conceptualised the term "vandalism," defining it as the "malicious destruction of works of art and culture because they represent the specific creations of the genius of such groups."[14] In *Axis Rule*, Lemkin emphasised that "prohibiting or destroying cultural institutions and cultural activities" is a critical component of genocide.[15] The methodical destruction of a group's material culture is termed "cultural genocide."[16] It is the attempt to target a specific culture and eradicate an entire population from the historical record.

Museums have used material culture to educate on the Holocaust for decades, but it has recently come into its own in Holocaust Studies. Artefacts are now deliberately studied beyond their representational meaning and contribution to the story of the Holocaust. Practicing a biographical approach to the study of an artefact communicates the agency of the artefact beyond its provenance. The provenance and object biography work in tandem to "create close, contextual consideration of the shifting relationships of things and people as they circulate into and out of different social situations."[17] In addition to understanding who created and/or owned an object throughout its life cycle, Holocaust scholars and conservators use material culture practices and methodologies to determine how the object has influenced people in dialogue with people's influence on the object through time. The comparative study allows students of the Holocaust to move beyond the supposition of an artefact's symbolic meaning to a linear and temporal understanding of the object throughout its life cycle. Consider the following series of questions: Was it damaged? Was it repaired? If so, when? Was the damage from the period? Does the damage contribute to the story and therefore needs to remain (blood, dirt, etc.) or is it mould from being stored in a damp basement since the end of the war?[18]

The same scholarly enquiry can apply to archival documents as well. Historians have traditionally focused on text rather than considering the object containing the text as an object with a biography of its own. How was it made? Was it made while in a camp? In hiding? How did the creator acquire the materials to make it? There is value in understanding the materiality of the object; its fabrication can contribute to the scholarly enquiry of a person, place, and/or event.[19] Historians using artefacts in their scholarly pursuits expand their research opportunities beyond the traditional archival setting. Studying artefacts can marry traditional archival research with cultural studies and provide students of the Holocaust with broader insight and perspective and will help researchers and students better communicate their findings.[20]

Challenges

Artefacts have a clear value for Holocaust Studies and education, but they also pose a host of challenges and limitations for collecting institutions. The primary challenges revolve around ethical and legal issues in the acquisition and collection of artefacts. Institutions rely on tools such as a collection management policy, which defines what is and what is not in scope for collecting during the acquisition process. Guidelines and documentation requirements proving the provenance of a potential acquisition would also be defined in an institution's collection management policy. Though the definition of "provenance" varies slightly among different cultural heritage fields, it is generally understood as information on the origins of the artefact to provide proof of authenticity of the item or collection of items.[21] Most major institutions will walk away from a potential acquisition if the provenance or chain of custody of an object is questionable.

The acquisition of artefacts initially came through first-person sources: survivors, refugees, members of the resistance, Allied troops, and military aid workers. Tracing the object's chain of custody was relatively simple in these first-person accounts. As the decades pass, tracing the chain of custody becomes more difficult as acquisition professionals are dealing with second-, third-, and fourth-generation accounts. Provenance can be tricky, even in cases where there is no ill intent on the part of the potential donor. The provenance may be questionable when based on a 20-year memory from a grandchild of a survivor, for example, "My grandmother saved this diamond ring through her internment in three concentration camps." While there is no intention to misrepresent the history of the artefact, it could still likely be family lore. Memory and interpretations of artefacts and their symbolism can be tricky and sometimes unreliable.[22] Conservators often verify authenticity based on material and date. A simple example would be a Star of David badge or an armband made of polyester. While authentic badges and armbands of the Star of David provide important context to the required identification of Jews throughout the Nazi era and would be useful in Holocaust education, polyester was not a material used during the period and clearly identifies the artefact as a reproduction.[23] Conservators often play a role in verifying provenance through scientific examination and practice during the acquisition process.

Sadly, there has been and continues to be a large black market for artefacts associated with the Holocaust. Collection Management Policies also provide the ethical framework for handling Nazi memorabilia, looted materials, forgeries, and commemorative objects or propaganda. The laws pertaining to buying and selling Nazi memorabilia vary from country to country, making provenance a particular challenge. While many of the larger collecting institutions in the United States do not collect standard Nazi materials such as armbands and daggers, there is an effort to collect personal artefacts from perpetrators. The United States Holocaust Memorial Museum (USHMM), as part of a larger European Union effort, is acquiring materials from perpetrators to help expand our understanding of the Holocaust. An example of a 2021 USHMM acquisition is a photo album from an officer who worked at the Sobibor extermination camp in Poland. The guard's photo album documents the daily life of officers at the camp, which helps to confirm testimonies from the very few survivors of Sobibor.[24] It is through the accounts of witnesses, bystanders, survivors, and perpetrators that we gain a holistic historical account. A single artefact, such as the Nazi photo album, can document multiple people's experiences, provide ethnographic insight directly from those who experienced it, and support or discredit other research tools, such as personal testimonies.

Once an artefact enters a museum or archive, conservators are intimately involved with the object throughout its life cycle. Post-accession, conservators determine what conservation protocols are necessary, including cleaning and repairs. Critical to material culture studies, conservators contribute to the verification of provenance, develop a detailed biography of the object, stabilise the physical condition, and ensure that the proper context is provided to artefacts when on display.[25] Conservators determine the limitations of exhibiting material culture by prioritising the physical preservation of the object over an object's potential impact while on display. Conservators apply constraints to curators, such as limiting the time an artefact can be on display, as well as ensuring strict light and physical conditions are met.

Museums provide the most accessible venue for the public to engage with the material culture of the Holocaust. It is here that curators have the difficult task of shaping the story of the Holocaust and those involved using objects as the narrators. The artefacts become the agent of the people. It is while on display that the provenance and biography of the artefacts provide context to the object and the person or persons it is representing. Curators typically use highly stable, large-impact objects to provide material evidence of the sheer scale of crimes committed against humanity, and smaller more personal items to elicit empathy and human connection. In an interview with USHMM's Exhibit Experience Manager Ramee Gentry, she described three categories of artefacts: visually impactful but short on narrative and historical substance; rich in narrative and historical substance but visually boring; and visually impactful and rich in narrative and historical substance.[26] Curators work to create a balanced experience intended to lead visitors to the larger lessons of the Holocaust.

Some of the most recognisable objects identified with the Holocaust are those related to mass deportation—the railcars and the heart-wrenching piles of suitcases or shoes confiscated by the Nazis as the victims entered the camps. They are staples of any museum exhibition spaces dealing with the Holocaust.[27] Both speak to the horrors of the Third Reich and the confiscation of not only the Jews' material objects, but also of their physical bodies. They are a part of the material culture of the Holocaust and part of the collective memory of two very distinct groups of people—the victims and the perpetrators. Using cultural artefacts as a form of memory is done on both an individual and collective level.[28] The object is a surrogate for a person or persons; it is a survivor unto itself.

One of the greatest challenges curators must confront is how to express the extent of the atrocities committed during the Holocaust and avoid glorifying the events. In the interview mentioned above, Ramee Gentry argued that "horror for the sake of horror is problematic."[29] Students of the Holocaust should seek more than the visceral impact of display.

Nazi Destruction of Jewish Material Culture

Material culture, such as bullet casings, have served as evidence of mass murder and genocide. The warehouse at the Auschwitz-Birkenau Memorial and Museum holds the personal belongings of the 1.3 million prisoners taken to the camp. Hair, suitcases, shoes, toothbrushes, and many other items are on display at both the Auschwitz

Museum and the United States Holocaust Memorial Museum to demonstrate the scale of atrocities committed.[30] Studying the destruction of artefacts may seem counterproductive, but there are insights that prove to be important to the study of the Holocaust. The scale on which Nazis destroyed sacred and precious Jewish cultural objects was massive. The objects that remain, specifically books and religious relics, provide tangible evidence that people can see and experience.

In April 1933, the world began to witness the first results of the antisemitic propaganda campaigns being spread by the Nazis. The Nazi German Student Association wrote a nationwide proclamation to promote a literary "cleansing" by fire. The local chapters of the association spread the word through the press and provided readers with a list of authors that were considered "un-German."[31] Finally, after a month-long campaign, one of the largest book burnings to occur in modern history took place. Thirty-four universities across Germany participated in the event, with thousands of people in attendance watching an estimated 80,000–90,000 volumes burned. In Berlin alone, it was estimated that 40,000 people attended. During the burnings, the student groups who organised the events would march alongside the fire and take an oath to combat and persecute any literature that did not promote Nazi ideologies. In the years to come, more and more attacks on Jewish communities would continue.[32]

One of the most infamous examples of the calculated destruction of Jewish relics is *Kristallnacht*, or the Night of Broken Glass. On the night of 9–10 November 1938, paramilitary forces and civilian supporters of the Nazi Party took to the streets and destroyed thousands of synagogues, Jewish-run businesses, homes, and cemeteries. There was a clear focus on destroying objects of religious significance to Jews. Book burnings and the destruction of Jewish-related artefacts continued throughout the Nazi regime.

The destruction of *Kristallnacht* confirmed that religious materials associated with Judaism and the Jewish people were under great threat. Many Jews salvaged what they could from the devastated synagogues throughout Germany in the days following the November pogrom, with fragments from sacred Torah scrolls and objects used in religious practices or rituals among the possessions taken as Jews fled Nazi persecution. Within the Jewish religious tradition there is a distinction between what is considered sacred as distinct from an object used in religious practice or ritual. The word of God (the Torah) or anything else that has God's name in any iteration is considered sacred. Though there is continued debate over the treatment and display of religious and sacred objects as they pertain to Holocaust museums and archives, conservators and curators at both the USHMM and the Canadian Museum of Human Rights adhere to a strict policy not to display sacred objects in which God's name is viewable.[33] Curators often display *tikim* (singular, *tik*), the ornamental cases protecting the Torah, or fragments of Torah saved after *Kristallnacht*, but the fragments are always arranged to ensure respect for Judaic religious practices.

During times of conflict, deliberate attacks on material culture are carried out in an attempt to erase the adversary's identity and collective memory.[34] The literature that was burned at the first book burning was seen by the Nazis as a dangerous tool that threatened to undermine the ideologies that were at that time being carefully constructed and broadcast nationally. Books are objects of human endeavour that hold information and ideologies, and these challenged the power and control of the Nazi Party. The destruction of the literature and religious relics was not a by-product of what was to come. Rather, it was a thought-out and systematic effort contributing to the erasure of the Jewish people. The objects that survived provide pertinent historical evidence of the "belief patterns of individuals who made, commissioned, purchased, or used them, and, by extension, the belief patterns" of both the victims and perpetrators.[35] While the *history* of the destruction is perhaps less relevant than what remained, it is the scale of the destruction that inherently provides value to the artefacts that survived.

The Artefacts

Whether fleeing or being forcibly relocated, the personal belongings people choose to take with them provide contextual clues to ethnographic and cultural details that might have been previously overlooked. When researching and considering the objects that individuals carried with them during the war, people often "assume that the refugees and victims were carrying clothing and some food, whatever transportable valuables they had left, official documents such as passports and family records, and work records including job histories and recommendations."[36] The victims of the Third Reich took practical things, but they also took things of personal value, such as photographs, family heirlooms, religious objects, and objects related to identity and memory. The extreme behaviours provoked by war illustrate how an individual's social being is determined by their relationship to the objects that represent them, and how such objects become metaphors for the self, providing a way of knowing oneself through things both present and absent.[37]

Victims of the Nazi regime were stripped of their personal belongings as they were forced into camps and provided nondescript camp uniforms. The blue and grey striped prisoner uniform is one of the most recognised artefacts of the Holocaust and is imbued with the horrors of the concentration camps. The artefacts discovered during the liberation of the camps add contextual, ethnographic details to victims, survivors, and perpetrators. At the USHMM and Auschwitz Museum, shoes found after liberation are used as physical metonyms to provide evidence of the forced mass deportation to camps. The shoes that remain hold the physical and metaphorical imprint of their original owners. The context in which the shoes are presented to visitors has transformed the individual represented into the collective identity of victims. The perpetrators' confiscation of the shoes also contributes to the biography of each of the artefacts. A single object can materially relate to numerous, often unidentified, individuals (victim, survivor, and perpetrator). Multi-perspectivity is required to effectively reconstruct the narrative of the Holocaust and provide a more comprehensive understanding of how people and events intersect.[38]

Throughout the estimated 44,000 incarceration sites, each camp's layout and purpose was determinant of the access to materials and personal items. Owing to the different nature of labour camps, concentration camps, and extermination camps, personal items were created more in the former than in the latter two. Despite the challenges faced by prisoners, however, there have been drawings and personal artefacts collected from extermination camps such as Auschwitz, and concentration camps like Dachau. These drawings and personal artefacts provide strong evidence of the horrific living conditions of the camps, the physical state of the prisoners, the verification of specific prisoners interned, and the resources available. The book *Dora, Auschwitz, Buchenwald, Bergen-Belsen: Croquis Cladenstins* contains a series of sketches created by artist Léon Delarbre during his incarceration at four concentration camps in 1944. The collection of drawings is what is called evidentiary Holocaust artwork and has been used to illustrate the decline of the prisoners' physical condition while imprisoned.[39]

Prisoners interned in camps were subject to strict social hierarchies and forced into rigid categories. The classification system was demonstrated by the colour of the triangle sewn onto the prisoner's uniform, indicating to the guards and other prisoners why a person was incarcerated. These strict social rankings created disparities throughout the classes of prisoners, which formed "a hegemonic system dominated by a core of elite prisoners."[40] The social rank of a prisoner could also determine access to food and trade goods, which contributed to their socio-economic power as well as their survival.[41] The classification system was designed to oppress and strip the identity of the prisoners. In a system that is meant to dehumanise and take identity away, how does one maintain their own agency? In labour camps specifically, owning personal materials was a constant battle among the inmates. Access to goods depended upon the job assigned to the prisoners and the different privileges associated with that assignment. Affinity was strong within the different nationalities at the camp, but not among the collective group.[42] With this being the case, the possession of objects was sacred and of the highest value. Personal objects could be used for trading or contribute to survival and coping mechanisms.[43] Further, the objects reflected the agency of the creator's persistence and resistance to hold onto their individual identities. During an interview, Jane Klinger, Chief Conservator at the USHMM, provided an example of the persistence to hold onto individual identity. One of the objects that Klinger came across in a collection was a Star of David that was made of electrical wire and pieces of plastic. The creator would have had to collect these materials over several months in order to create the Star. Personal artefacts, such as this example, are a response that prisoners had to the perpetrators at large and showcase their determination to hold onto their identity.[44]

The personal objects collected from the survivors of Ravensbrück include handwritten history and translation books, a pocket mirror, children's toys made from scavenged material, and drawings. Their creation symbolises the resistance to withstand the dehumanisation of being interned at the camp and is a reflection of the identity of their creators.[45]

One of the many objects created in Ravensbrück is a small book that details seventeenth-century Polish history. The book is wrapped in polka dot linen and the inscription on the inside is handwritten with what appears to be a pencil. There is eyewitness testimony stating that during quiet hours in the barracks, some women would teach lessons about Polish history and culture.[46] The simple initiative of writing down a history that was actively being destroyed is an act of resistance, remembering, and reclaiming national identity.

Artefacts made in the camps exemplify the tenacity to reclaim identity. For some prisoners, these artefacts are all that remain of them, and their identities are imprinted on the objects. For others, the artefacts represent hope, such as the children's toys and educational books. Holocaust archaeologists have an opportunity to explore these broader themes and ideas, re-establish identities for the victims who perished, and add social and historical context to scholarly records. Indeed, the field of Holocaust archaeology is a subsection of modern conflict studies and uses artefacts primarily to support its various hypotheses. It is an examination of how conflicts in the twentieth and twenty-first centuries have left a lasting legacy on the geopolitical landscape and the collective social memory, demonstrating the impact material culture has on both.[47]

Modern conflict has shaped human behaviour in society and has changed how scholars view the past.[48] The study of the Holocaust is now entering a new era where first-hand living memory is disappearing. The landscape and the structural remains of the Holocaust such as ghettos, internment camps, extermination camps, infrastructures, mass graves, and euthanasia sites are troves of information networks. These networks show the movement of people, the roles of individuals in Nazi policies, and the physical products of human activities during conflict.[49] Archaeological excavations have diverse opportunities for further investigations but can be fraught with limitations and challenges.

One of the challenges facing academics and archaeologists is the physical decay of structures, as well as shifting political and cultural attitudes.[50] While this is true of all the work done in archaeology, within the context of the Holocaust the structures created in the camps were not built to withstand time. This may be a challenge but studying the landscape of the camps and treating them as an artefact can display the spatiality and power dynamics of camp life. Additionally, performing such excavations can, in fact, protect these historic sites from potential destruction.

Historical studies tend to be linear, telling a story with a beginning, middle, and end. Archaeologists need the historical background to support hypotheses during excavations, but their research lies within the artefacts excavated at these sites. Holocaust archaeology can thrive on the tension of the linear, negotiating between the contextual articles, memory of those who experienced, and the material culture that is left behind.[51] Archaeological excavations are not new to the field of Holocaust Studies. Forensic investigations were conducted for trials after the end of the Second World War in order to collect evidence. Surveys for academic research did not take place until the 1980s. Some projects since then have been criticised for failing to account for the beliefs of affected groups.[52] Conducting archaeology at internment and concentration camp sites is indeed a public affair, involving government officials, caretakers of memorials, the immediate surrounding community, and the families that lost loved ones at the sites. Whenever a survey takes place, archaeologists are literally, and figuratively, digging up a country's dark past. For the families involved, it can be like reopening a wound, having to face the pain that their loved ones experienced. Archaeologists in recent times have asked for professional spiritual advisors, such as rabbis and priests, to be present at excavation sites to maintain respect.

Holocaust archaeology is just one example of a field that is heavily grounded in using artefacts for research. Artefacts are interwoven into the emotional and historical fabric of not only the creators but throughout the world in the post-Second World War era. Scholars have a responsibility to uphold the care of the items used to contribute to the historical record. These materials hold a fragility and weight in proof of the reality of the horrors of the Holocaust and affect how the modern world works today. Using artefacts in studies is no easy feat, but the rewards far outweigh the challenges faced by scholars.

Conclusions

The memory of the Holocaust has been carefully established to honour the victims and survivors. Academics today continue to research the events that transpired and how to proceed with remembering. In recent decades, particular attention has been given to the areas of those who are absent from the written record, such as LGBTQIA+ people.

Their experiences have been traditionally overlooked in Holocaust studies, due to continued persecution and oppression after the end of the war.[53] The perpetrators were those in power and the artefacts created during that time are the victims' and survivors' responses. The role of agency and looking at artefacts can be the key to filling the gaps, as they are palpable proof and offer additional historical, social, and ethnographic perspectives.

Scholars, students, and the public interact with artefacts to connect with the past. Material culture helps people remember historical narratives and contribute to identity. Seeing certain artefacts, such as recognisable boxcars or small personal belongings, can evoke an emotion that establishes a tangible thread to past events. The connection made can then allow for reflection and contribute to an understanding of the past as well as their own personal sense of being and belonging. The institutions embedded in society, such as museums, libraries, and archives, can "help us remember past events in the historical narrative that characterises our cultural identity."[54] These institutions offer a platform that encourages scholars to theorise and illustrate the importance and limitations of using artefacts in historical narratives. As researchers contribute to Holocaust narratives, the collection, preservation, and interpretation of the artefacts remain critical to continue informing contemporary cultures about the Holocaust.[55]

Notes

1 R. Hilberg, *The Destruction of the European Jews*, Chicago: Quadrangle Books, 1961.
2 D. Stone, "Recent Trends in Holocaust Historiography," *Journal of Holocaust Education*, 10:3, 2001, pp. 1–24.
3 M. Nolan, "The Historikerstreit and Social History," *New German Critique*, 44, 1988, p. 53.
4 C.R. Browning, *Ordinary Men: Reserve Police Battalion 101 and the Final Solution in Poland*, New York: HarperCollins, 1992.
5 D.J. Goldhagen, *Hitler's Willing Executioners: Ordinary Germans and the Holocaust*, New York: Random House, 1996.
6 Nolan, "The Historikerstreit and Social History;" also, P. Graves-Brown, A. Piccini, and R. Harrison, *The Oxford Handbook of the Archaeology of the Contemporary World*, Oxford: Oxford University Press, 2013.
7 N.J. Saunders, "Material Culture and Conflict: The Great War, 1914–1918," in N.J. Saunders (ed.), *Matters of Conflict: Material Culture, Memory, and the First World War*, Abingdon (UK): Routledge, 2004, pp. 5–25.
8 C.S. Colls and R.M. Ehrenreich, "Value in Context: Material Culture and Treblinka," *Current Anthropology*, 62:5, 2021, pp. 539–68.
9 Ibid.; also, S. Pollock, "The Subject of Suffering," *American Anthropologist*, 118:4, 2016, pp. 726–41.
10 D. Stone, "Holocaust Historiography and Cultural History," *Dapim: Studies on the Holocaust*, 23:1, 2013, pp. 52–68.
11 T. J. Schlereth, "Material Culture Studies and Social History Research," *Journal of Social History*, 16:4, 1983, p. 112.
12 E.A. Brewer and P. Fritzer, "Teaching Students to Infer Meaning Through Material Culture," *The Clearing House: A Journal of Educational Strategies, Issues and Ideas*, 84:2, 2011, pp. 43–6.
13 L. Bilsky, "Cultural Genocide and Restitution: The Early Wave of Jewish Cultural Restitution in the Aftermath of World War II," *International Journal of Cultural Property*, 27:3, 2020, pp. 349–74.
14 E.C. Luck, "Cultural Genocide and the Protection of Cultural Heritage," *J. Paul Getty Trust Occasional Papers in Cultural Heritage Policy*, 2, 2018, p. 17, available online at https://www.getty.edu/publications/occasional-papers-2/.

15 R. Lemkin, *Axis Rule in Occupied Europe: Laws of Occupation, Analysis of Government, Proposals for Redress*, Washington, DC: Carnegie Endowment for International Peace, 1944, p. 84.
16 Luck, "Cultural Genocide and the Protection of Cultural Heritage."
17 C.J. Hodge, "A Guide to Object Biography," *Stanford University Archeology Collections*, 2017, available online at https://suac.stanford.edu/sites/g/files/sbiybj12066/f/suac_2017_guide_to_object_biography_0.pdf.
18 J. Klinger, interview conducted by Bailey Rodgers, 27 April 2022.
19 J.B. Rydén, "When Bereaved of Everything: Objects from the Concentration Camp of Ravensbrück as Expressions of Resistance, Memory, and Identity," *International Journal of Historical Archaeology*, 22, 2018, pp. 511–30.
20 P. Graves-Brown, et al., *The Oxford Handbook of the Archaeology of the Contemporary World*; W. Lower, "A Response to Dan Stone's 'Holocaust Historiography and Cultural History'," *Dapim: Studies on the Holocaust*, 23:1, 2013, pp. 81–6.
21 S. Sweeney, "The Ambiguous Origins of the Archival Principle of 'Provenance'," *Libraries & the Cultural Record*, 43:2, 2008, p. 193.
22 D. Dean, *Museum Exhibition: Theory and Practice*, Abingdon (UK): Routledge, 1997; D. Stone, "Holocaust Historiography and Cultural History."
23 R. Gentry, interview conducted by Bailey Rodgers, 10 May 2022.
24 Z. Levine, interview conducted by Bailey Rodgers, 4 May 2022.
25 J. Klinger, interview conducted by Bailey Rodgers, 27 April 2022
26 Gentry, interview, 10 May 2022.
27 Graves-Brown, et al., *The Oxford Handbook of the Archaeology of the Contemporary World*; Lower, "A Response."
28 R. Heersmink, "Materialised Identities: Cultural Identity, Collective Memory, and Artifacts," *Review of Philosophy and Psychology*, 2021, pp. 1–17.
29 Gentry, interview, 10 May 2022.
30 Graves-Brown, et al., *The Oxford Handbook of the Archaeology of the Contemporary World*; Lower, "A Response."
31 United States Holocaust Memorial Museum, "Book Burning," *Holocaust Encyclopedia*, available online at https://encyclopedia.ushmm.org/content/en/article/book-burning.
32 See, for example, M. Glickman, *Stolen Words: The Plunder of Jewish Books*, Philadelphia: Jewish Publication Society of America, 2016; R. Knuth, *Burning Books and Leveling Libraries: Extremist Violence and Cultural Destruction*, Westport: Praeger, 2006; and J. Rose, *The Holocaust and the Book: Destruction and Preservation*, Boston: University of Massachusetts Press, 2001.
33 O.B. Stier, "Torah and Taboo: Containing Jewish Relics and Jewish Identity at the United States Holocaust Memorial Museum," *Numen*, 57, 2010, pp. 505–36.
34 H. Kalman, "Destruction, Mitigation, and Reconciliation of Cultural Heritage," *International Journal of Heritage Studies*, 23:6, 2017, pp. 538–55.
35 E.A. Brewer and P. Fritzer, "Teaching Students to Infer Meaning Through Material Culture," *The Clearing House: A Journal of Educational Strategies, Issues and Ideas*, 84:2, 2011, pp. 43–6.
36 R.M. Ehrenreich and J. Klinger, "War in Context: Let the Artifacts Speak," in Wolfgang Muchitsch (ed.), *Does War Belong in Museums? The Representation of Violence in Exhibitions*, Bielefeld: Transcript Verlag, 2013, pp. 145–54.
37 J. Hoskins, *Biographical Objects: How Things Tell the Stories of People's Lives*, Abingdon (UK): Routledge, 1998, p. 195; N.J. Saunders, "Material Culture and Conflict: The Great War, 1914–1918," in N.J. Saunders (ed.), *Matters of Conflict: Material Culture, Memory, and the First World War*, Abingdon (UK): Routledge, 2004, pp. 5–25.
38 M. Bernard-Donals, "Synecdochic Memory at the United States Holocaust Memorial Museum," *College English*, 74:5, 2012, pp. 417–36.
39 L. Delarbre, *Auschwitz, Buchenwald, Bergen-Belsen: Croquis Clandestins*. Paris: M. de Romilly, 1945.
40 A.T. Myers, "Between Memory and Materiality: An Archaeological Approach to Studying the Nazi Concentration Camps," *Journal of Conflict Archaeology*, 4, 2008, p. 325.
41 Ibid.; H. Mytum, "Materiality Matters: The Role of Things in Coping Strategies at Cunningham's Camp, Douglas During World War I," in H. Mytum and G. Carr (ed.), *Prisoners of War: Archaeology, Memory, and Heritage of 19th- and 20th-century Mass Internment*, New York: Springer, 2013.

Persistence of Memory Through Artefacts 177

42 Rydén, "When Bereaved of Everything," pp. 511–30.
43 Ibid.; H. Mytum, "Materiality Matters."
44 Klinger, interview, 27 April 2022.
45 For additional information and insights on Lund University's Ravensbrück Archive, visit https://www.ub.lu.se/hitta/digitala-samlingar/witnessing-genocide. The collection of materials made at Ravensbrück was compiled and later donated to Lund University, Sweden and Kulturen museum in Lund. In addition to these materials, 500 oral histories were collected from survivors.
46 S. Helm, *Ravensbrück: Life and Death in Hitler's Concentration Camp for Women*, New York: Knopf Doubleday, 2015.
47 Saunders, "Material Culture and Conflict;" C.S. Colls, "Holocaust Archaeology: Archaeological Approaches to Landscapes of Nazi Genocide and Persecution," *Journal of Conflict Archaeology*, 7:2, 2013, pp. 70–104.
48 N.J. Saunders, "Excavating Memories: Archaeology and The Great War, 1914–2001," *Antiquity*, 76, 2002, pp. 101–8.
49 C.S. Colls, *Holocaust Archaeologies: Approaches and Future Directions*, New York: Springer, 2015, p. 199; Saunders, "Material Culture and Conflict."
50 T. Zwick, "Memory and the Mississippi: The Authority of Artifacts at Auschwitz-Birkenau," *UCLA Historical Journal*, 15, 1995.
51 Myers, "Between Memory and Materiality," p. 325.
52 Colls, "Holocaust Archaeology."
53 J. Newsome, "Liberation Was Only for Others: Breaking the Silence in Germany Surrounding the Nazi Persecution of Homosexuals," *The Holocaust in History and Memory*, 7, 2014, pp. 53–71.
54 R. Heersmink, "Materialised Identities," p. 1.
55 Our deepest gratitude to Ramee Gentry, Jane Klinger, Robert Ehrenreich, Katie Lanza, Zachary Levine, and Michael Levy of the United States Holocaust Memorial Museum for lending their expertise, sharing their insights, and their willingness to meet with us on this chapter.

Part III
The Popular Domain

14 Learning About the Holocaust Through Movies

Paul R. Bartrop

Film and the Holocaust

The Holocaust was arguably the greatest moral challenge Western civilisation ever faced. It threatened to overturn the general course the West had been taking over the previous thousand years. How have filmmakers addressed the issue? A multiplicity of issues confronts filmmakers seeking to recreate the Holocaust on the screen. Given that the film medium is going to be the most likely source of knowledge regarding the Holocaust in the future, it is important that students, teachers, and the public have some knowledge of how a considered appreciation of motion pictures can be utilised; this way, they can begin to understand the historical and contemporary implications of the Holocaust experience.

Over recent years, since the start of the twenty-first century, a considerable number of works have been produced dealing with a wide variety of themes relating to film and the Holocaust.[1] In some cases, these have examined movies from the perspective of their content *as movies*, that is, from a film critic's eye view, rather than looking at what the films have attempted to achieve as historical texts. However, some excellent studies have addressed the issues through an in-depth analysis of movies as legitimate sources of history, and the degree to which they can (or cannot) be effective in helping to generate some degree of understanding of this—arguably the most challenging and incomprehensible event in modern world history.

Filmmakers undertaking movie projects based on historical events, regardless of the topic, employ what is known colloquially as creative license. This is an important consideration when we contemplate the connections to be made between real-life events and movies. For the most part, it is simply not possible for filmmakers to recreate with complete accuracy everything that happened in any historical situation, so liberties must be taken—perhaps not with the truth, but rather with representations of it (though often the former, unfortunately, might also be the case). While filmmakers might have a commitment to telling the general outline of a story, in doing so they are often forced to select specific vignettes, themes, or exchanges as the best means to express themselves within a two-to-three-hour timeframe, using contrived dialogue and artificially constructed sets. This way, the ambiguous caption "based on" (or sometimes, "inspired by") a true story can lend credibility to even the most tenuous of movie tie-ins.

Of course, there is a danger here: those who would detract or deny the veracity of the history being portrayed could well see that flaws in a movie generated by creative license can negate the entire account. In response to such a possibility, Robert A. Rosenstone, the doyen of authors who have addressed this issue, has asked "if the bulk of what

DOI: 10.4324/9781003248620-18

historical films show on the screen is fiction, how can we consider them to be history?" He answers his own question:

> The best and more serious kind of historical film does "history" only in so far as it attempts to make meaning out of something that has occurred in the past. Like written history, it utilizes traces of that past, but its rules of engagement with them are structured by the demands of the medium and the practices it has evolved—which means that its claims will be far different from those of history on the page.[2]

In other words, in exercising their creative licence movie makers do not set out to lie or deceive; rather, they are confined by the limits of their medium. Conscious of the fact that they cannot "do it all," as a result they will seek to create an understanding or interpretation of a particular historical event in accordance with the tools at hand. Historians employing the written word also "compose," though their use of footnotes to justify or to validate their assertions ensures that their claims are more accurate.

The study of film as history is not new; nor, of course, is the study of film as *Holocaust* history. Filmographies covering the Holocaust are immense in size and growing each year.[3] For each film studied, the essential tools remain the same, as examination proceeds from an analysis of the subject matter that explores issues such as film content, period representation, historical and social construction, character empathy, moral responses, and textual composition. Where the Holocaust is concerned, the filmmakers must be wary that they do not fall into the trap of maudlin sentimentality, as this can detract from the impact that a movie on the Holocaust can have on an audience—especially an uninformed or under-informed audience, such as those found among younger viewers today.

The skills of the filmmaker, like those of the historian, can produce works that enhance understanding of past events. What the educator does with movies of this nature is a matter for further discussion, though there is little doubt that movie representations will have to be considered more and more in the future, as educators address a population that derives most of its understanding of the world through visual sources, rather than textual ones.

Recent years have seen a sharp increase in people's interest in the Holocaust. Vast libraries of books, movies, and documentaries have been produced, and new works keep coming every week. This notwithstanding, interest in learning *about* the Holocaust does not seem to have been translated into an interest in learning *from* the Holocaust and remembering those who were its victims. Motion pictures are, however, one way in which this trend can be countered. It can be argued that helping younger generations learn about the Holocaust through critical consumption of film might be a way to engage them emotionally as well as intellectually.

Films play an important role in helping to provide a sense of "place" and "period" for viewers. They are not documentaries, nor do they try to be. This is one of the major concerns some people have regarding movies that take historical episodes as their theme; namely, that because films employ actors speaking manufactured lines, on movie sets that are recreations of what might have been, they have as little validity as if they were fiction. Yet historic events portrayed in film are often just as much an interpretation of historical realities as other forms of analysis (indeed, of historical writing). Certainly, they evoke images and emotions that have an immediacy rarely found in all but the most outstanding written forms.

A Plethora of Movies and Themes

In 1966, historian Jacob Robinson observed that:

> The usual course of any particular community is even and uneventful; ordinarily, little of historical significance takes place, except in those rare times when a peak of military, political, intellectual, and moral activity is reached. Thus, on a continental scale, each year brings a few people, a few ideas, a few groups, to the fore. But the era of Nazi oppression was quite different. Then, in the span of only twelve years, every single Jewish community in Europe perforce was faced with the greatest crisis possible to a group—the crisis of existence. Every single Jewish community perforce reached its peak of activity, called upon its deepest spiritual resources, brought forth its ultimate answers to the questions of life and death, of relations between man and God.[4]

The challenge for the Holocaust scholar, he wrote, is thus "to rescue from oblivion a history as eventful and rich as that of a thousand years."

Given the event-laden historical richness Robinson described, filmmakers have a huge palette on which to practice their art. For the most part, they have covered an immense range, both of general themes and specific topics, all as creative as their medium allows, as the following examples demonstrate.

To begin chronologically, the pre-war period of the 1930s, which saw increasing persecution against Jews in Nazi Germany, has been expressed in various ways on the screen. Movies discussing the spread of Nazi antisemitism include *The Mortal Storm* (Frank Borzage, 1940), *The Seventh Cross* (Fred Zinnemann, 1944), *'38—Vienna before the Fall* (*38—Auch das war Wien*, Wolfgang Glück, 1987), *Invincible* (Werner Herzog, 2001), and *The Garden of the Finzi-Continis* (*Il giardino dei Finzi-Contini*, Vittorio de Sica, 1970).

With the Final Solution in progress during the war years, how have filmmakers approached the highly confronting responsibility of portraying the process by which the Holocaust took place? Various means were adopted by the Nazis in bringing their murderous plans to fruition: isolation, ghettoisation, planning, concentration, and the actual killing process itself. The range of movies is as varied as the means employed by the Nazis to effectuate the Final Solution itself, but some movies stand out, such as *Ghetto* (*Vilniaus Getas*, Audrius Juzenas, 2006); *Conspiracy* (Frank Pierson, 2001); *La Rafle* (*The Round Up*, Roselyne Bosch, 2010); *Auschwitz* (Uwe Boll, 2011); *Out of the Ashes* (Joseph Sargent, 2003); and *Betrayed* (Eirik Svensson, 2020).

The question of resistance during the Holocaust has always been controversial. Many films have focused on resistance, ranging from those featuring Jews fighting in the forests of Eastern Europe (*Defiance*, Edward Zwick, 2008), to death camp and ghetto rebellions (*Uprising*, Jon Avnet, 2001 and *Escape from Sobibor*, Jack Gold, 1987), to covert "special operations" (*Black Book* (*Zwartboek*, Paul Verhoeven, 2006). Filmmakers have sought to approach an increasingly vexed question: how effective were resistance activities during the Holocaust? Other resistance movies include *Army of Crime* (*L'armée du Crime*, Robert Guédiguian, 2009) and *Rosenstrasse* (Margarethe von Trotta, 2003).

Filmmakers have addressed some of the moral questions posed by the Holocaust by exploring the moral dimensions of trying to stay alive—or in lieu of that, of attempting to maintain dignity and a quality of life in the face of all-pervasive death. In this regard, some of the most important movies produced have been *Korczak* (Andrzej Wajda, 1990); *The Ninth Day* (*Der Neunte Tag*, Volker Schlöndorff, 2004); *The Grey Zone* (Tim Blake Nelson, 2001); *God on Trial* (Andy de Emmony, 2008); and *Son of Saul* (*Saul fia*, László Nemes, 2015).

For those who were not captured or incarcerated, the Holocaust brought challenges beyond that of survival, and filmmakers have sought ways to depict the tension filled world of those who lived through the Third Reich without suffering its worst excesses. Often, viewers see both incredulity and trauma caused through living under the Nazis, in movies such as *Good* (Vicente Amorim, 2008); *Jew-Boy Levi* (*Viehjud Levi*, Didi Danquart, 1999); *Swing Kids* (Thomas Carter, 1993); *Amen* (Costa-Gavras, 2002); and *Free Men* (*Les hommes libres*, Ismaël Ferroukhi, 2011).

Death during the Holocaust, in most cases, requires no explanation; survival does, however, and some filmmakers have dealt with aspects of survival—either through the various ways in which Jews sought to hide from the Nazis, or through the acts undertaken by rescuers (both Jewish and non-Jewish) who sought to save lives despite the risks. The opportunities presented to filmmakers by these topics are many, and they have showcased a broad range of areas in which Jews and others embraced life despite the Nazis' murderous intentions.

Many Jews seeking to escape the fate intended by the Nazis attempted to do so through hiding; simply by removing themselves from the mainstream of life, they hoped that they could avoid the gaze of the Nazis and thereby find some way of riding out the Holocaust as it swirled around them. Accordingly, some movies have taken concealment as their theme: hiding in secret rooms *The Diary of Anne Frank* (George Stevens, 1959); being hidden "in plain sight" *Divided We Fall* (*Musíme si pomáhat*, Jan Hřebejk, 2000), and *Le Chambon: La Colline aux Mille Enfants* (*The Hill of a Thousand Children*, Jean-Louis Lorenzi, 1997); literally burying themselves underground (*Debajo del Mundo*, Beda Docampo Feijóo, 1987); and, ultimately, simply hiding where no-one else could see (*In Darkness* (*W ciemności*), Agnieszka Holland, 2011, and *The Pianist*, Roman Polanski, 2002).

The theme of rescuing has also been an important motif for filmmakers. Possibly the best known of all Holocaust movies, *Schindler's List* (Steven Spielberg, 1993), falls into this category, though there are several others that also illustrate this aspect of the Holocaust—from neutrals, to Germans, and even to Jews who sought to rescue other Jews. Such movies include *Varian's War* (Lionel Chetwynd, 2001); *Süskind* (Rudolf van den Berg, 2012); *Persona non Grata* (Cellin Gluck, 2015); *Perlasca: Un eroe Italiano* (Alberto Negrin, 2002); and *Good Evening, Mr. Wallenberg* (*God afton, Herr Wallenberg*, Kjell Grede, 1990).

The innocence of children is also a recurrent theme. These films provoke images that can be tragic, heroic, sometimes humorous, and almost always result in empathy on the part of the viewer. There are two core elements in which filmmakers have approached the experience of children during the Holocaust; first, considering the incomprehension children faced given the events swirling around them (and how they dealt with their situation); and second, through an examination of fantasy as an approach able to convey some degree of understanding to this seemingly incomprehensible subject.

When filmmakers address the experiences of children during the Holocaust, they are looking into the very core of innocence—and all too often, do so from the perspective of how children dealt with the utterly overwhelming situation in which they found themselves. Such movies include: *The Book Thief* (Brian Percival, 2013); *Wunderkinder* (Marcus Otto Rosenmuller, 2011); *Europa, Europa* (Agnieszka Holland, 1990); *Au Revoir les Enfants* (Louis Malle, 1987); *Fanny's Journey* (*Le Voyage de Fanny*, Lola Doillon, 2016); and *Fateless* (*Sorstalanság*, Lajos Koltai, 2005).

Other filmmakers, on the other hand, have sought to showcase the horrors of the Holocaust through the literary device of fantasy. Moving away from a narrative approach when examining Holocaust experiences, they have composed accounts not grounded in fact, but which, nonetheless, draw viewers' attention to the horror in a way that younger audiences (in particular) can appreciate. There are iconic movies in this genre, such as *Life is Beautiful* (*La vita è bella*, Roberto Benigni, 1997); *The Boy in the Striped Pajamas* (Mark Herman, 2008); *Jakob the Liar* (Peter Kassovitz, 1999); *The Island on Bird Street* (*Øen i Fuglegade*, Søren Kragh-Jacobsen, 1997); *The Devil's Arithmetic* (Donna Deitch, 1999); and *Jojo Rabbit* (Taika Waititi, 2019).

The Holocaust was a historical phenomenon into which could be folded the full range of human experiences. Filmmakers, recognising this, have found expressions of the human condition to explore it. Three such forms of expression—sport, humour, and music—show not only how filmmakers have approached the specific instances they showcase, but also the effectiveness of such forms of expression as a window to understanding.

Some have sought to depict elements of the Holocaust through the lens of sport—albeit all too often under the Nazis, a somewhat corrupted interpretation of what sport entails. From the flawed Olympic ideal of the 1936 Berlin Games (*Berlin 36*, Kaspar Heidelbach, 2009); to the perversion of the spirit of fair play embedded in European football (*The Third Half* (*Treto Poluvreme*), Darko Mitrevski, 2012 and *Two Half Times in Hell* (*Két félidő a pokolban*), Zoltán Fábri, 1962); to champion boxers from the pre-war years now fighting for their lives in the Nazi concentration camps (*Triumph of the Spirit*, Robert M. Young, 1989, *Surviving Auschwitz* (*Victor Young Perez*, Jacques Ouaniche, 2013), and *The Survivor*, Barry Levinson, 2021), movies dealing with sports-related themes stemming from the Holocaust present their own way of adding to our understanding of the awful fate that befell Jewish athletes during the Nazi period.

While the very notion of humour in a discussion of the Holocaust might seem to be offensive, several movies have attempted to develop an understanding of the Holocaust through recourse to such devices as satire, metaphor, and pun. Such movies force the question of how—and whether—humour can be effective as an approach to appreciating the horror and complexity of the Holocaust. These include (but are not restricted to) *The Great Dictator* (Charles Chaplin, 1940); *To Be or not to Be* (Ernst Lubitsch, 1942, and the 1983 remake directed by Mel Brooks); *Me and the Colonel* (Peter Glenville, 1958); *Train of Life* (*La Train de Vie*, Radu Mihăileanu, 1998); and *Genghis Cohn* (Elijah Moshinsky, 1993).[5]

As with the theme of humour, so also have several filmmakers employed music as a vehicle from which to approach the Holocaust. Some movies examine motifs from before the war (*The Harmonists* (*Comedian Harmonists*, Joseph Vilsmaier, 1997) and *Gloomy Sunday* (*Ein Lied von Liebe und Tod*, Rolf Schübel, 1999)); during the war, in which music was employed in the service of collaboration from a neutral country (*Tears of Stone* (*Tár úr steini*, Hilmar Oddsson, 1995); at Auschwitz during the killing phase of the Holocaust (*Playing for Time*, Daniel Mann and Joseph Sargent, 1980)); and after the war (*Taking Sides* (*Der Fall Furtwängler*, István Szabó, 2001)).

With the end of the Holocaust came a cessation of overt Nazi persecution, but this did not mean the trauma ended. Filmmakers have long sought to find ways by which to make sense of this period, with three themes predominating: the immediate end of the Holocaust and what it meant for the survivors; the appearance of some people who denied the reality of the Holocaust in the years that followed; and the international quest for justice after the fact.

Liberation, for many, was merely a release from Nazi imprisonment. The emotional and physical wounds took a long time to heal, and, in many cases, never managed to do so completely. Films dealing with the end of the Holocaust include one explaining the liberation of Bergen-Belsen (*The Relief of Belsen*, Justin Hardy, 2007); one chronicling the painful return home from Auschwitz (*The Truce* (*La Tregua*), Francesco Rosi, 1997); and others that consider how the immediate end of the Holocaust impacted the former prisoners' lives (*The Search*, Fred Zinnemann, 1948, and *Almost Peaceful* (*Un Monde Presque Paisible*), Michel Deville, 2004).

While memories of the Holocaust lasted a lifetime for those who lived through it, antisemitic voices, within a single generation, began to question—and then deny—that it had ever happened. All such expressions had at base a political motive, and all sought to promote or perpetuate the "myth" of a Jewish conspiracy that sought to defraud the world. A range of movie dramatisations of such a confrontation have been made, presenting another way in which filmmakers have employed the Holocaust to highlight broader issues relating to memory, imagination, and antisemitism. These include *Never Forget* (Joseph Sargent, 1991); *Skokie* (Herbert Wise, 1981); *Evil in Clear River* (Karen Arthur, 1988); and *Denial* (Mick Jackson, 2016).

Even as the Holocaust was in progress, the Allies declared that the perpetrators would be brought to justice once the war had been won. The theme of anti-Nazi trials, therefore, has featured among filmmakers to highlight the shock of the Holocaust. Such movies also make for strong courtroom drama. These range from a recreation of the Nuremberg trials of 1945–1946 (*Nuremberg*, Yves Simoneau, 2000); a more fictionalised version of the same event (*Judgment at Nuremberg*, Stanley Kramer, 1961); the 1961 trial of Adolf Eichmann (*The Eichmann Show*, Paul Andrew Williams, 2015, and *Hannah Arendt*, Margarethe von Trotta, 2012); and a thoroughly imaginative interpretation of the latter trial in which the event is used as a backdrop to a broader examination of the moral issues such trials raised (*The Man in the Glass Booth*, Arthur Hiller, 1975).

A final consideration from filmmakers relates to how to approach the key legacies of the Holocaust. For some, this has led to an examination of how the experience transformed the sense of self (for both survivors and perpetrators); for others, the core legacies of the Holocaust have seen an ongoing opportunity to ask key questions regarding the nature of the experience and what it meant both for the future of the individual and for society.

Of the many legacies left by the Holocaust, one relates to the question of personal identity. Considering the experience, many asked, where do I stand now? Who am I? And who can I be? This type of question has proven to be a deep well from which filmmakers have drawn inspiration. For Germans no less than for Jews, the Holocaust represented a searing reconsideration of their place in the post-Holocaust world, as several filmmakers have attested. Such films include *Habermann* (*Habermannův mlýn*, Juraj Herz, 2010); *Ida* (Paweł Pawlikowski, 2013); *The Pawnbroker* (Sidney Lumet, 1964); *Father* (John Power, 1990); and *The Music Box* (Costa-Gavras, 1989).

In addition, other films have looked at some of the questions posed in light of the challenges provoked by the Holocaust. Should Nazis be pursued (*Labyrinth of Lies* (*Im Labyrinth des Schweigens*, Giulio Ricciarelli, 2014 and *The Reader*, Stephen Daldry, 2008)? Should the role of local communities during the war years be investigated (*The Nasty Girl* (*Das schreckliche Mädchen*, Michael Verhoeven, 1990)? What does the Holocaust experience say about faith in a just, compassionate, and loving God (*The Quarrel*, Eli Cohen, 1991, and *God on Trial*, Andy de Emmony, 2008)? Indeed, what does the future hold if the memory of the Holocaust is lost (*Everything is Illuminated*, Liev Schreiber, 2005)?

The Holocaust: The Jewish Experience

While a list of films—even a short one—can identify the range of themes and topics filmmakers have covered, an illustration can show how two films dealing with the same theme can be utilised to enhance understanding. In this case, we can examine Nazi mass murder and resistance from Jews faced with their own imminent destruction. Both *Escape from Sobibor* and *The Grey Zone* assume a substantial degree of creative license, but in so doing each one attempts to create a compelling scenario that can be admired as a plausible speculation of how events played out. Both movies are set against a backdrop of intrigue, moral ambiguity, mass murder, rebellion, and, ultimately, a form of deliverance.[6]

Escape from Sobibor tells the story of the uprising at Sobibor on 14 October 1943, from the perspective of the two principal leaders, Leon Feldhandler and Alexander Pechersky. The screenplay was adapted from a closely researched study of the same name written by a non-Jewish author from the United States, Richard Rashke, in 1982. Much of Rashke's work, in turn, was assisted by survivors of the camp and the uprising. Three of them—Thomas "Toivi" Blatt, Stanislaw "Shlomo" Szmajzner, and Ester Terner Raab—worked as technical consultants on the film.

In the film, Feldhandler is a Jewish slave labourer working in the camp. A leader among the prisoners, his moderation in the face of Nazi brutality, and his counsel to new arrivals to bide their time before undertaking any precipitate revenge measures, is his way of trying to endure the horrors of camp life. He has not given up hope, though he realises that death stalks around every corner.

One day, a transport arrives that includes several Soviet prisoners of war. All are Jewish: their officer is Alexander ("Sasha") Pechersky. The movie builds its tension as plans for a mass escape are made, now utilising Pechersky's strategic and military abilities. This escape, embracing the entire camp population of 600, will have to be made; it is realised that if only a partial escape was attempted, those remaining afterwards will be slaughtered. The film's scenes of the escape itself, which take some ten minutes of run time, are the stuff of high drama and daring.

By way of contrast, *The Grey Zone* tells the story of the uprising of the XII *Sonderkommando* at Auschwitz on 7 October 1944. The screenplay was adapted from director Tim Blake Nelson's 1996 play of the same name, which had in turn been inspired by the memoir *Auschwitz: A Doctor's Eyewitness Account*, written by Dr. Miklos Nyiszli, a Hungarian Jew who was forced to work directly with the notorious "Angel of Death" Dr. Josef Mengele.

The film begins with a small group of *Sonderkommando* men planning an insurrection that, they hope, will destroy at least one of Birkenau's four crematoria. They are receiving firearms from Poles from outside, and gunpowder from a nearby munitions factory where female prisoners are smuggling it to the men among the bodies of their dead workers.

When a new trainload of Hungarian Jewish prisoners arrives, all are immediately sent to be murdered. After they are gassed, a young girl is found alive beneath a pile of bodies. Soon after, the insurrection begins and Crematoria I and III are destroyed with the smuggled explosives, but there is a huge loss of life among the prisoners. All those who subsequently survive the explosions and the fighting are then captured; they are later executed by the SS, in a highly dramatic penultimate scene. After all captives are shot, the rescued girl, who has been watching developments, begins to run toward the main gate of the camp, but she is shot. The film closes with an emotive voice-over recitation by the dead girl.

Both *Escape from Sobibor* and *The Grey Zone* culminate with the depiction of the respective revolts in October 1943 and October 1944. While the directors of each take liberties to convey the drama of the story they are trying to tell, nonetheless the filmmakers' art provides a rich interpretation of what the events might have looked like. Moreover, each movie permits viewers to assess for themselves how they will respond to the images they see on the screen: mostly, either as action movies with "good guys" battling "bad guys," or as moral dramas in which there are no black-and-white figures, only those of varying shades who inhabit the grey zone.

The most fundamental questions regarding filmic portrayals of historical issues can be addressed through a viewing of such movies: first, is the movie true to the historical reality (so far as it can be understood) upon which it is based? Second, is the movie useful in providing an understanding of what death camps can "look" like? And third, how effective can graphic depictions of prisoner revolts in these same camps be for a new generation of viewers seeing such images for the first time?

Beyond these two movies, it must not be overlooked that some others, though operating from the best of intentions, nonetheless miss the mark when it comes to artistic reliability. *Auschwitz*, by Uwe Boll, is a German film that was intended to show the overwhelming lack of knowledge in German schoolchildren regarding the Third Reich period. However, Boll boldly steps over the "socially acceptable" boundary and creates a film that shows the parts of Auschwitz that no one else has been willing to recreate. He is the only director of a feature film to include a scene that goes inside a gas chamber during a Nazi gassing of Jewish victims.

Boll was inspired to make the film by the thought that recent movies about the Holocaust softened the reality of what had happened through looking at heroes and resisters such as Claus von Stauffenberg (*Valkyrie*, Bryan Singer, 2008) or Oskar Schindler (*Schindler's List*), or through fantasy stories such as *Life Is Beautiful* or *Jakob the Liar*. (If dealt with today, we might also add *The Boy in the Striped Pajamas* and *Jojo Rabbit*.) As a result, Boll's film is relentless in its depiction of the viciousness of life in a death camp, using brutally realistic imagery. What matters for Boll is the meaning behind the movie, which has been designed to force viewers to remember the horror of the Holocaust and remain conscious of genocide as a major moral and tangible problem still plaguing the world today.

Colour, Black-and-White, and Schindler's List

One of the problems facing Holocaust educators and researchers is that documentary footage illustrating the event was invariably shot in black-and-white. For people today, this significantly reduces levels of empathy with the subject. People who were once real are reduced to black-and-white images, with scenes somewhat artificial for a student's level of colour-familiar understanding—a generation, it must be said, that has simply not known black-and-white imagery as anything but an aberration, whether in television or movies. Thus, when they are exposed to such images, there seems to be a disconnect between what they are watching and any sense of authenticity.

What are we to make of this? According to historian Mark M. Smith, the modern era has really made humans more sight- and colour-sensitive than at any other time. In his view, "the importance of sight in the modern era, at least in the West, is beyond doubt not least because lots of other forces in addition to the invention of print served to empower vision."[7] Thus, in the words of philosopher David Michael Levin, "our Western culture has been dominated by an ocularcentric paradigm, a vision-centred interpretation of knowledge, truth, and reality."[8] What this has led to of course, is not just a fixation with seeing; it is a question of seeing *in colour*. And this reality is compounded when we consider that there are at least two generations who have grown to maturity unaccustomed to seeing in anything *but* colour.

Why should this be an issue today? The answer is quite simple: the domination of screen portrayals of virtually everything in a young person's world, who view their sense of reality through a screen—and that screen, invariably, is in colour.

Today, motion pictures filmed in black-and-white media often have a nostalgic, historic, or anachronistic feel. In films about the Holocaust, the best-known example, par excellence, is *Schindler's List*. Other films, such as the non-Holocaust film *Pleasantville* (Gary Ross, 1998)—which nonetheless focuses on issues relating to prejudice and racism—play with the concept of black-and-white, using it to selectively portray scenes and characters that are either more outdated or dull than the characters and scenes shot in full colour.

In movies set in modern times, a director's choice to use black-and-white might seem experimental, even gimmicky. In *Schindler's List*, however, the black-and-white presentation effectively evokes the Second World War era and deepens the impact of the story. Black-and-white presented Spielberg with the opportunity to use sparing colour to highlight key scenes and signal shifts in time. For example, the opening full-colour scene, one of only a handful in the movie, fades into the next scene (and the rest of the film), in black-and-white. The shift plunges viewers into late 1939, bringing them symbolically closer to the events and characters in the story. The artistic and psychological convention of bringing the audience back in time works well partly because it captures the way many people visualise the Second World War—through black-and-white images and film footage of the 1930s and 1940s. Although contemporary viewers are accustomed to full-colour images and tend to consider such images to be more realistic than those in black-and-white, the monochrome of *Schindler's List* conveys an alternate but no less realistic version of life. The style links the film to the period and serves to deepen viewers' immersion in the historical setting.

The artistic advantage of black-and-white is that it heightens the impact of the film's violence and highlights the duality of good and evil. The lighting and contrast enhance the brutality of each violent scene. In some terrifying scenes, such as the liquidation of the Krakow ghetto, the lighting is kept dark, conveying a sense of panic and confusion. The white faces of the dead in the streets contrast starkly against the murky background. *Schindler's List* might not have had the same visual and emotional impact had Spielberg made the film in colour.

What makes *Schindler's List* so special? It is the meaning and love that Spielberg puts into every frame. Among the many masterful scenes in the film, one deserves special mention: the razing of the Krakow ghetto, where viewers' attention is drawn to a little girl in a red coat, who, filmed in colour, stands out among the black-and-white gloom. The scene embodies the savagery of the Holocaust and the humanity of its victims, and it is the single most-remembered sequence spoken of when people recall the movie.

Movies beyond the Jewish Experience

The Holocaust overturned many of the essential tenets of Christian belief,[9] along the way presenting a much more profound doctrinal shock for Christianity than for Judaism. This has been expressed through film, leading to the question of whether films about the Holocaust focusing other than on Jews can be just as effective as those with a specifically Jewish orientation.

Christians have been portrayed in Holocaust movies in a variety of ways since the inception of the genre, though care should be taken to distinguish between *Christians* and *non-Jews*. In the early days of anti-Nazi films, during the 1940s, filmmakers were cautious about the use of racial or religious descriptors; thus, for example, *The Mortal Storm* does not refer to Christians or Jews at all, but Aryans and non-Aryans; likewise, Charlie Chaplin, in *The Great Dictator*, does mention Jews as such, but does not mention Christians.

Yet there have been many movies since which have embraced the relationship between Christians and the Holocaust. The important thing to note is that movies about the Holocaust featuring Christians run the full range of images, from heroes to villains, from rescuers to bystanders, from perpetrators to victims.

Fred Zinnemann's *The Seventh Cross* was one of the very few movies made during the Second World War addressing the Nazi concentration camps. Made in 1944 but set in 1936, it tells the story of seven men who escape from a fictitious concentration camp, Westhofen (possibly a mask for the actual camp at Osthofen, near Worms, which operated between 1933 and 1934). It focuses on an escaped prisoner, George Heisler, and his efforts to find someone he can trust to help him. At first, no one seems prepared to go out of their way, until, bit by bit, expressions of hope become manifest. Like it or not, George is forced to rely on the kindness of strangers—good Germans who see his plight and are willing to risk their own personal well-being as well as that of their families. Further, we see here the fear and claustrophobia of being trapped within Nazism's totalitarian system, and perhaps gain an insight into the factors that inhibited people's freedom of action even had they wanted to assist. These are not necessarily Nazis, but tortured souls who had legitimate reasons, in such a confronting totalitarian society, for not helping—not the least of which was putting one's family and loved ones at risk.

While the temptation, after nearly five years of war, could have been to exploit the story of *The Seventh Cross* for full propaganda value, the filmmakers chose instead to depict George Heisler's search for decency and goodness among the German people. The film concludes that not every German was a Nazi; by extension, just as George could find hope among the Germans, so also could Germany find hope among the nations of the world. Rather than demonise the German people, the movie finds a positive message upon which their future could be built. What the movie attempts to show is that the actions that constitute "doing the right thing" are universal and timeless.

The Seventh Cross, moreover, cannot be classed as a Jewish film, even though it takes as its backdrop an escape from a Nazi concentration camp. A common perception is that where Nazi concentration camps are featured in movies, Jews must be also featured; this, of course, is far from accurate, as movies such as *The Ninth Day* and *Bent* (Sean Mathais, 1997), among others, testify. If not a Jewish movie, nonetheless the film shows the nature of the system George Heisler was forced to confront. Overall, *The Seventh Cross* is an ideal illustration of what the moral issues were—and remain—for those who would minimise the relevance of the Nazi period for humanity today.

In like manner is *Good*, a British film telling the story of German literature professor John Halder, a solid citizen beset by family problems—children, a concert pianist wife who relies on John for domestic peace and quiet so she can practice, and an aged mother with Alzheimer's. John takes solace from several sources: his writing, his teaching, his Jewish best friend Maurice Glückstein, and, increasingly, a student *femme fatale* named Anne. Thinking little of the Nazi Party to begin with, John becomes seduced by promises of payment, privileges, and career advancement after his novel—dealing with compassionate euthanasia—attracts attention from the Reich Chancellery. Before he realises it, he is offered work as a consultant with the SS and granted an honorary position with officer rank. At no time does he ever consider he is being compromised, even as he is drawn deeper and deeper into moral collaboration with the Nazi movement.

The major arena in which this is played out is through his changing relationship with Maurice, his comrade in arms in the trenches during the First World War. John is aware that Nazi rule is increasingly strangling the Jewish community but does not really contemplate what this signifies for Maurice—even though we see the many ways in which the situation leads to his friend's physical and emotional deterioration. John finds himself torn between an increasing sense of duty (as a "good" man obeying the law) and his relationship with Maurice.

Toward the end of the movie, John, now in an SS uniform, is working in the office of SS leader Adolf Eichmann. He visits a concentration camp, improbably seeking Maurice. In a moment of illumination, John imagines that he sees him, gaunt and tortured, now just another Jewish concentration camp prisoner. Only at the very end of the movie, as John contemplates the Jewish victims around him, is he able to question the meaning of what he is seeing. Incredulous, he stands with his arms outstretched, wondering how it all got this far—and why he had not seen it before now.

John Halder's tragedy, like that of so many other Germans, was that he had no idea that in trying to be a "good" citizen, conforming to the norms of society, and not in any way projecting himself as a radical Nazi, he had, in fact, not only abetted the regime, but also legitimised it.

Another movie of the genre that considers "goodness" in the Holocaust is *Amen*, based on the controversial 1963 play *The Deputy* by Rolf Hochhuth and directed and co-written by Costa-Gavras in 2002. Examining the political and diplomatic relationship between the Vatican and Nazi Germany during the Holocaust, it focuses on Kurt Gerstein, a Waffen-SS officer employed in the SS Hygiene Institute. Upon witnessing the Nazi mass murder of the Jews using Zyklon-B gas, he tries to alert the world to what is happening—in particular, through seeking the urgent assistance of Pope Pius XII. An idealistic Jesuit priest, Riccardo Fontana—a scion of an elite and influential Italian family with ties to the Vatican—joins Gerstein and appeals personally to Pius, but the Pope is depicted as making only a timid and vague condemnation of Hitler and Nazi Germany.

As with other movies looking at the non-Jewish response to the Holocaust, *Amen* is strong on morality and condemnation over the inaction of those who knew what was happening but elected to do nothing. In this sense, the Holocaust is employed as a vehicle for the exploration of broader themes of relevance to all humanity, drawing attention to the dangers of apathy and indifference in the face of monstrous evil.

Film: Whether and When to Use It

In the pursuit of scholarly appreciation of historical issues, the words of the French-Jewish historian Marc Bloch, in *The Historian's Craft*, remain relevant today: "When all is said and done, a single word, 'understanding,' is the beacon light of our studies … . We are never sufficiently understanding."[10] Helping younger generations learn about historical events through critical consumption of film might be a way to approach such understanding, while engaging them emotionally as well as intellectually. Unquestionably, young people today are likely to glean much (if not most) of their knowledge about the wider world (and history, especially) through films, both before and after their formal education.

Yet it is important to bear in mind that movies can only approximate life, filtered (literally) through the lens of the filmmaker. Such films might therefore be effective, but they might also be titillating, exploitative, or just plain wrong in their representations. Nonetheless, a few questions can be asked in the hope that deeper insight can be achieved. When viewing a movie about the Holocaust, how useful is it in developing an understanding of the causes and nature of the events it describes? Does it have any obvious biases? Was the filmmakers' point of view obvious?

In an article published in 2007, leading educators Alan S. Marcus and Thomas H. Levine argue strongly for the use of film in teaching about history (and in the current context, that certainly includes the Holocaust):

> Helping students learn history through critical consumption of film may offer a fine antidote to common criticism of history education. Commercial films are designed to entertain; they can engage students emotionally as well as intellectually. Feature films offer the potential to motivate students, to help students gain access to diverse perspectives, develop empathy with characters and situations in contexts different from their own, and to connect their lives, values, and concerns with those of people in the past. Films may help students construct their own insight about different eras and cultures, particularly when analysed as primary sources reflecting the time period and culture in which they were made.[11]

It is worth reiterating that young people in the West—today and in the future—are more likely to encounter the Holocaust in films than in any other setting. There is thus a need for them to understand how films can support a more sophisticated learning of the event. By enhancing the development of such an understanding, motion pictures—the most likely source of Holocaust literacy they will encounter in the future—can equip them with ways of learning and contextualising what happened, and why knowing and thinking about it is important.

Notes

1 See especially L. Baron, *Projecting the Holocaust into the Future: The Changing Focus of Contemporary Holocaust Cinema*, Lanham (MD): Rowman and Littlefield, 2005; H. Gonshak, *Hollywood and the Holocaust*, Lanham (MD): Rowman and Littlefield, 2015; A. Insdorf, *Indelible Shadows: Film and the Holocaust*, 3rd ed., Cambridge: Cambridge University Press, 2003; J.E. Doneson, *The Holocaust in American Film*, 2nd ed., Syracuse: Syracuse University Press, 2002; T. Haggith and J. Newman (ed.), *Holocaust and the Moving Image: Representations in Film and Television since 1933*, London: Wallflower Press, 2005; and R.C. Reimer and C.J. Reimer, *Historical Dictionary of Holocaust Cinema*, Lanham (MD): Scarecrow Press, 2012. Two excellent article-length essays are S. Wood, "Film and Atrocity: The Holocaust and Spectacle," in K.M. Wilson and T.F. Crowder-Taraborrelli (ed.), *Film and Genocide*, Madison: University of Wisconsin Press, 2012, pp. 21–44; and J.C. Friedman, "The Holocaust in Feature Films: Problematic Current Trends and Themes," in J.C. Friedman and W.L. Hewitt (ed.), *The History of Genocide in Cinema: Atrocities on Screen*, London: Bloomsbury Academic, 2017, pp. 103–16. When looking at film and the Holocaust as part of larger studies, see also D.H. Magilow and L. Silverman, *Holocaust Representations in History: An Introduction*, London: Bloomsbury Academic, 2015; and B. Zelizer (ed.), *Visual Culture and the Holocaust*, New Brunswick (NJ): Rutgers University Press, 2001.
2 R. Rosenstone, *History on Film/Film on History*, Harlow (UK): Pearson Education, 2006, p. 161.
3 For just one example, see the unique (and in some respects, controversial) perspective of R. Brownstein, *Holocaust Cinema Complete: A History and Analysis of 400 Films, with a Teaching Guide*, Jefferson (NC): McFarland, 2021.
4 J. Robinson, "Research on the Jewish Catastrophe," *Jewish Journal of Sociology*, 8:2, December 1966, p. 192.
5 Humour is, of course, a double-edged sword, as Jews have found for centuries; there is a very big difference between laughing *with* and laughing *at*, especially when one is the subject of the humour. Hence, as shown by film historian Valerie Weinstein, Nazi filmmakers utilised comedy during the Third Reich, but for the purpose of emphasising Jewish differences that would separate and alienate Jews from the mainstream. See V. Weinstein, *Antisemitism in Film Comedy in Nazi Germany*, Bloomington: Indiana University Press, 2019.
6 Related movies that can also be considered here include *Sobibor* (Konstantin Khabensky, 2018) and *Son of Saul* (László Nemes, 2015).
7 M.M. Smith, *Sensing the Past: Seeing, Hearing, Smelling, Tasting, and Touching in History*, Berkeley: University of California Press, 2007, p. 22.
8 Cited in ibid., pp. 21–2.
9 For just one essay in an otherwise huge literature, see, for example, P.R. Bartrop, "The Ten Commandments, the Holocaust, and Reflections on Genocide," in S.L. Jacobs, *Confronting Genocide: Judaism, Christianity, Islam*, Lanham (MD): Lexington Books, 2009, pp. 209–21.
10 M. Bloch, *The Historian's Craft*, Manchester: Manchester University Press, 1954, p. 143.
11 A.S. Marcus and T.H. Levine, "Exploring the Past with Feature Film," in A.S. Marcus (ed.), *Celluloid Blackboard: Teaching History with Film*, Charlotte: Information Age Publishing, 2007, p. 3.

15 How Holocaust Documentaries Defined Documentary Cinema

Yvonne Kozlovsky Golan

Documentary cinema is cinema that feeds on grave, everyday materials from social, environmental, and political reality.[1] According to filmmaker John Grierson, it can be defined as cinema that engages in "the creative treatment of actuality"—it arranges and describes reality but also designs it aesthetically.[2] Charles Musser explains documentary film as a modern alternative to the tradition of visual instruction,[3] and as a history of dialogue and form.[4] Through documentary film, using one voice (the narrator's), in a consolidated unit in time and a single time and space, reality can be explicated, relying on experts and witnesses, photographs and film clips. These can be edited and arranged in a coherent, textual manner into an alternate narrative to describe the historical reality—all as the director, or those on behalf of whose name they shoot the film, comprehends this narrative.

This chapter will discuss nascent documentary cinema following the Second World War. The first group of documentaries (1945–1946) was filmed by the Western Allies and the Soviet Union, which liberated the camps in the west and the east, after which the footage was edited by filmmakers ahead of the Nuremberg Trials. As they entered the camps, photographers would film their traumatic encounter with the camp's inhabitants and the place. The second group of documentaries, beginning in the mid-1950s and spanning the next few decades, was made by French filmmakers who consolidated these materials into substantive, iconic, artistic insights. Both groups of documentaries have influenced Holocaust representation and other arts down to the present.

The images filmed became ground zero for cinema and the media's depiction of the Holocaust post-Auschwitz.[5] They examined both the boundaries of the medium and the historical event in an in-depth, original manner.[6] The common objective was to inculcate the lessons of the Holocaust and to preserve the dimension of truth in documentary cinema in different ways.[7]

Thus, this chapter will focus on the representation and depiction of the Holocaust in documentary films since 1945, and its treatment of the ethical, ideological, and political meanings and implications of the filmmaker's perspective.[8] This chapter is divided into two parts: (1) the Allies Experience (1945–1946), between discovery and recognition, and focusing on the central film, *Nazi Concentration Camps*; and (2) the French Experience (1957 onwards) considering the cinematography of reality.

The Allies Experience

In January 1946, during the early stage of the Nuremberg Trials, the Allies chose to bolster their case through a clear and unequivocal instrument. The film *Nazi*

DOI: 10.4324/9781003248620-19

Concentration Camps (1946) was directed by United States Lieutenant-Colonel George Stevens, who had already made his reputation in Hollywood before joining the Signal Corps.[9] The film was made from materials collected by the Russians when they liberated Auschwitz-Birkenau, and from footage shot by the British in other camps, such as Bergen-Belsen.

Nazi Concentration Camps is considered the first visual evidence presented to the Nuremberg tribunal of the extermination of Jews and the horrors of the wartime concentration camps. Yet Jews were absent from the film, in the sense that they were not mentioned. Rather, the film presented an image of camp inmates—a general term for all who were interned. The assumption was that there was a principled, political decision from above to refrain from focusing on the Jewish issue and to focus instead on the humanitarian aspect, without transforming the Nuremberg Trials into a specific mechanism to achieve justice for the Jews. The prosecutors, led by American judge Robert H. Jackson, believed that under the circumstances and due to the intensity of the event, the tribunal should be presented with the results of the Nazis' crimes rather than dealing individually with witnesses and testimonies. The guiding principle was to point to the universality of the Nazi crimes while treating them as particular to the Nazis only.

The film made use of several modes to move the plot forward. The first was expository, aiming to convince and educate the international public about the lessons of the Holocaust, as if stating "never again." It exposed the viewer to the reality the camera confronted when the cameraperson entered the camp together with the Allies, and directed itself at the audience, sometimes through the voice of the narrator as the "Voice of God." The narrator translated the situation for the viewer in terms of a historical event that has just ended.[10] The film also utilised an observational mode, in the sense that the cameras wandered through the heart of the camp and allowed the survivors to pass before them, so that viewers could form an impression of events at the camp at the time of liberation, without any interference by the creators.

Nazi Concentration Camps was the central (and key) documenting movie and also the generic name for a collection of films shot as the Allies entered Central Europe from Normandy, progressing towards Eastern Europe. These films were very important in building Holocaust awareness and embedding the events in the memories of the films' global audiences. Precisely because these were the first documentary films of their kind, it is interesting to see how their aesthetics were used as a transferential means intended to elicit feelings about traumatic social phenomena. Aesthetics were used to describe and explain "dry" historical facts by means of creative photographic thinking and a figurative representation of death and human destruction.[11] The importance of the films, whose crew was subordinate to the American Secret Service (OSS) immediately before the Nuremberg Trials in 1946, is expressed in different spheres and times.[12]

Since they were the first of their kind, they became a prototype for all later Holocaust films. Post-war producers concluded that these films most accurately and authentically depicted the human catastrophe that took place in the concentration camps.[13]

It is safe to assume that by entering the camps immediately upon liberation, George Stevens did in fact capture the "natural" immediacy of camp life without any external interference that would tip the balance one way or another. The films failed to address the question of whether the local population knew precisely what was happening inside the camps: however, by providing visual information that helped viewers understand what happened, they served as a first step in the endless task of attempting to understand that which humanity cannot otherwise grasp.

Since no other portrayals of the camps and what happened there were available—certainly none as strong as those displayed on the screen for the first time before Western eyes—audiences naturally internalised the image of the Muselmann (a camp inmate who has lost the will to live) and projected it on any Holocaust survivor they might subsequently encounter. The image of the survivor became synonymous with the emaciated figure on the verge of collapse, and never a normal, ordinary person. Similarly, the audio-visual impression of the "human landscape," as filmed on the day the camps were liberated and shown over and over in different forums, was deeply etched in the world's consciousness, and quickly inducted into the permanent album of images through which world cinema sought to describe the Holocaust and its horrors. The archetypal icon of the prisoner, with the striped uniform, round cap, and hunger-ravaged body, became a staple of every motion picture that told the story of the camps.

Other scenes in the film that could not escape notice taught viewers about additional aspects of camp life, for example, the scene in the Buchenwald concentration camp where survivors take off their caps in unison before the photographer, as though obeying some kind of routine command. This scene conveyed more clearly than any written law that removing one's cap before a higher authority in the camp—a kapo, a block senior or a Nazi guard—was a necessary condition for staying alive. Every "educated" prisoner realised this within their first few hours in the camp.[14]

The cameras taken into the death camps produced 18,000 feet of film, 6,000 of which was brought to Nuremberg and presented for some 50 minutes. Most of the footage was silent, edited and dubbed with a narrated script in English. Undoubtedly, the "Stevens' Irregulars" tried to capture the moment before liberation, the horror of the day before as perceived by the survivors. Obviously, however, the liberators only arrived after the Nazis had fled the camp, and so no actual brutality could be captured by the eye of the camera or described in words. Instead, the camera displayed the tools of that cruelty and the wounds they inflicted: a twisted leg, whip scars, broken noses, empty eye sockets, or split skulls. Viewers could see the liberated inmates' great cry of pain and relief on the screen, but those same inmates had no voice. In the absence of sound footage, the pain observed by the film's audience was transformed from an accessible pain to an imaginative guess at what kind of pain the survivor might have experienced. The survivor's personal pain was silenced—there was no language to identify them as the member of a particular nation, there was no sound to their story.

Cruelty in its various forms was dramatised for the camera by prisoners/survivors playing roles. The audience could draw conclusions about the abuse through the torture implements that were filmed, such as a finger crusher, a truncheon, a club covered in barbed wire, a pillory, stocks. The "neutral," English narration contributed first and foremost to the universalisation of both the pain and the survivor, without regard to the latter's ethnic or national origin. In the same measure, it distanced the cruelty from German soldiers as the source of evil (since they are not in the picture at all) and universalised them too, together with their cruelty and punishment methods in the camp. From the cinematic point of view, the power of the survivor's visual appearance was neutralised by the director's decision not to use the survivor's voice. As a result, the survivor's image was a silent, perfect icon that served their new, compassionate benefactors, the liberating troops; the photographer who commemorates the survivor's wretchedness forever; and the mercy of a world that does not want to see such images ever again.

From the outset, a decision was made to shoot *Nazi Concentration Camps* in black-and-white, primarily for technical reasons. Stevens's commanders assumed there might not be facilities for screening colour footage in every venue where his films would be screened, whereas they were completely confident that black-and-white 35-mm cameras could be found everywhere, so they filmed in black-and-white.

Given the extensive publicity accorded to this film, together with other liberation films made in the same mould, the integration between black-and-white photography and a place that is not a place had a very significant impact on the way we evaluate the credibility of photos of the past and remember the Holocaust. It also influenced patterns of production and direction that would shape fictional and even documentary Holocaust films in the future.

The French Experience

The "raw" cinematic course, which American writer Susan Sontag called a cinematic watershed dividing cinema before and after the war,[15] led, primarily in France, to a new cinematic wave starting in 1956 with French Director Alain Resnais's work *Night and Fog* (*Nuit et Brouillard*). He was followed by Marcel Ophuls with *The Sorrow and the Pity* (*Le Chagrin et la Pitié*, 1969) and *The Memory of Justice* (1976), and finally by Claude Lanzmann with his timeless work *Shoah* (1985), as well as additional films deriving from this body of work. These films dealt with absolute evil in differing ways. The common denominator between them was first and foremost the process component in describing the events, an element that was absent in the liberation films, in addition to films and images the Nazis shot of their victims in different states. Second, they gave a human countenance to the survivors and the key figures of the time and allowed them to speak in their own voices and give testimony. And third, the films utilised a cinematic mechanism through which the viewer was exposed to the historic event not just as a linear narrative but as a *reflexive* narrative in which the viewer participated emotionally and cognitively.

Night and Fog, Alain Resnais, France, 1956

In 1956, at a time when France had frozen remembrance of the war and its collaboration with the Nazis, it was the film *Night and Fog* which violated this code of silence and became the force that formed Second World War remembrance in France, with all its ills.[16] Like the liberation films,[17] *Night and Fog* entered the camps. This time it was a decade later, and a meaningful layer of consciousness was added to the horrific photographic combinations which come from documenting the camps the Nazis left behind them.

While the cinematography may have appeared naturalistic, in actuality it bore significant visual baggage. This reflected not only the director's ethical stance towards visual testimony, beginning with the horrific journey in the trains to Auschwitz and ending in the mass graves in Bergen Belsen, but also programmed how the viewers were supposed to react to what they saw, without explaining to them how and why. The film's narrator described the journey: "No day, no night, hunger, thirst, suffocation, madness. Death makes its first act. Its second made on arrival in the night and fog." From the creator's perspective, the viewer was supposed to pass moral judgement not only on the film, but on themselves, as the observer of real death on the screen. In fact, the deed of active viewing caused the viewer "to judge not just the filmmaker's ethical behaviour towards death, but also their ethical reaction to the visual activity represented on screen—both in its form and its content."[18] Thus, the film was exponentially more unsettling and pushed the viewer's nerves to their limit.

The basic concept of the cinematography and editing was composed of a collection of camp shots arranged into a narrative: gates, fences, residential blocks, and train stations. A precise description of reception at the camp, extreme close-ups of male nudity, shaving, tattooing numbers, and the hierarchy from the simple inmate up to the Camp Director. Nazi documentation was in black and white. Resnais disoriented the viewer, who was focused on the image, by suddenly diverting the camera to the present and to colour cinematography, familiarising the viewer with the camp: the hospital shacks, the prison and punishment cells, and the immediate surroundings—"a real city," a killing city with the crematorium and chimney on the backdrop of a pastoral landscape. The film opened with the words of the narrator Jean Cayrol, himself a former political prisoner at Mauthausen:

> Even a peaceful landscape, even a meadow in harvest with flights of crows and grass fires, even road [*sic*] for cars and peasants and couples, even a resort village with marketplace and steeple, can lead to a concentration camp. Struthof, Oranienburg, Auschwitz, Neuengamme, Belsen, Ravensbrück, Dachau were names like any others on maps and in guidebooks ... the blocks are visited only by a camera.

In fact, the film attempted to decipher the Nazi death apparatus through cinematography and editing based on cutting and erasing. Thus, the cinematic mechanism was an art that paralleled the concentration camp mechanism. The Final Solution was an artistic act of terror, designed by the Nazis.

As the camera entered the block and passed by the bunks, the narrator asked:

> What hope do we have of truly capturing this reality? ... No description, no image can reveal their true dimension ... We can but show you the outer shell, the surface. We pretend to take up hope again as the image recedes into the past as if we were cured once and for all of the scourge of the camps. We pretend it all happened "only once" at a given time and place. We turn a blind eye to what surrounds us and a deaf ear to humanity's never-ending cry.

The multitude of photographs Resnais collected from the "Nazi inheritance," ranging from still life images of the camp to shots of horror such as decapitated heads alongside corpses, overwhelmed the viewer and in hindsight made the film iconic in every sense. It outdid the first films shot at liberation in terms of narrative, content and form and inherited the title "prototype" of documentary films on the Nazi horrors of the Holocaust in particular, and the art of film, in general. The film made no mention of those who were murdered by the Nazis, it did not contain French accomplices (except one moment where a French policeman's hat could be seen on the platform). It would appear there were no culprits either—in the absence of a confession of guilt by the responsible parties. "So, who is guilty," the narrator asked, directing himself to the viewer. Humanity has murdered humanity. Thus, the Holocaust narrative has shifted from differential group particularism (Nazis) to the human and universal.

The Sorrow and the Pity, Marcel Ophuls, France, 1969/1981

If *Night and Fog* directed the gaze outside the French borders, *The Sorrow and the Pity* directed the gaze inwards. Marcel Ophuls's film is a narrative that described the life of a small city called Clermont-Ferrand. The director interviewed 34 local men and women and formed an impression of the occupation period. His questions to them were general, inquisitive, and outwardly non-judgmental.[19] But the film was indeed subjective and addressed remembrance of the occupation and not its history. The resultant picture reflected a historical reality that was not flattering to the French: complicity, indifference to the pain of others and an aspiration for normalcy under occupation were what mattered to them.[20] Below the surface stirred long-time anti-semitism, which became more acute and gained legitimacy under the auspices of the Vichy regime. In the opinion of Brett Bowles, Ophuls has thus created a new form of documentary film, "dedicated to subverting official media propaganda and exposing the blind spots of the collective national memory."[21] In this enterprise of domestication, the testimony is of fundamental importance.

In fact, in the view of philosopher and cinema critic François Niney:

> Marcel Ophuls' films are entirely built on the virtue and perversion of the word, the word that seeks or refuses itself, that explains or denies, that explains or betrays, accuses or excuses what is being spoken about. There are those who know more than they say, and there are those who, in speaking, discover that they are saying more than they wanted to or thought they were capable of saying.[22]

To achieve this objective, Ophuls used several techniques unique to his period, altered and violated the accepted rules of the documentary genre *cinéma vérité*, which seeks, with the help of light hardware, to capture a raw reality.[23] He utilised cinematography and editing that actively interferes, discussion alongside interviewing and confrontation with the interviewees.

He initiated interviews with a diverse grouping of witnesses, whether survivors, members of the opposition and underground, testimonies of Vichy supporters and those who justified or denied the past, members of the government, and regular people. He came to them and interviewed them in their comfort zones so they would not feel under attack. Once they were confident and at ease, he trapped them in his net with piercing questions, the answers to which were normally akin to placing a mirror in front of their shocked faces. To this, he added the technique of montage, in alternating tones, to create the right atmosphere.

Like Alain Resnais, Ophuls utilised additional techniques: first, segments from periodical archives served as quotations from the past, and he confronted interviewees with open questions throughout the film. For example, there was an interview with Pétain government leaders "before" and "after-now," or the choice to juxtapose the song *Ça Sent Si Bon La France* by Maurice Chevalier alongside archive footage showing an excited throng marching in reverence to Marshal Pétain, or a military march with ridiculous circus music in the background. Second, the truth was exposed by connecting different responses to the question "did you see Germans in your city?"

This was met by "no, I did not," from the coffee shop proprietor, compared with the pharmacist from the shop next door who responded, "the streets were flooded with Germans and steel hats marching through the streets." Third, the dialogue and interviews were based on a narrative dynamic built on pauses in the tone of speech and narration, which caused fluctuating disequilibrium in the pace of the discussions and the order of events. The dramatic pauses confused the interviewees who had difficulty discerning what side the interviewer was on, and they were caught unprepared. The result was the answers that nail the viewer to their chair.

Ophuls intentionally refused to mystify the events and instead confronted the interviewees with questions relating to ethics and French responsibility for their past and the fate of the country's Jews. One highlight was a segment with a shop owner who was interviewed and affably ignored the question of the "disappearance" of the Jews around him. In response to the question "where are they?", he stated, "they left or were deported." The interviewer complimented the interviewee and goaded him on, asking as an aside about a notice he published in the newspaper, announcing that he was not Jewish (his name was Klein) so he would not be identified mistakenly.

On the path to denying the mystification of France as a perfect nation devoid of problems, Ophuls insisted on demonstrating the gap between memory of the past and the past as it actually occurred. Thus, *The Sorrow and the Pity* offers another alternative to the history of German occupation: remembrance of the occupation without engaging in its history.

Despite the film's length (about four hours!), *The Sorrow and the Pity* was screened in 1969 in theatres and drew approximately 600,000 viewers. Critics in prestigious newspapers such as *Le Monde*, *Le Figaro*, *L'Observateur*, and *Le Canard* went out of their way to praise the film and describe it as a spectacle and the Vulgate of documentary film. However, for 12 years television screening of the film was blocked. Yet, this did not prevent the film from serving as an impetus for change in historiographic research and an important cultural catalyst cited both by historians who followed in its path and filmmakers who quoted it.[24] What was important to Ophuls was to demonstrate the residues history and politics left on human beings. He contradicted de Gaulle, who was engaged in building the image of a heroic France that liberated itself. *The Sorrow and the Pity* proved the time had come for desacralisation of the past. The film's important contribution was in confronting remembrance of the past and institutionalising the art of documentary film as a means of conveyance, discussion, judgement, and remembrance. Historian Marc Ferro declared it the "October Revolution" of documentary filmmaking.[25]

Despite the important questions they raised about personal responsibility, the two French films described above chose to omit the central subject of antisemitism, focusing instead on universal suffering. Some 30 years later, Claude Lanzmann presented a new approach to coping with the horrors of history, simultaneously developing several issues of critical importance to the phenomenon itself.[26] In time, his work became the cornerstone of documentary cinema research.

Shoah, Claude Lanzmann, France, 1985

In 1985, the nine-and-a-half-hour film *Shoah* collected survivor testimonies as evidence of the Holocaust, salvaged these testimonies from oblivion, and delivered them straight into public awareness and consideration.[27]

In an interview following the premiere of his final film, *The Last of the Unjust*, Claude Lanzmann stated, "The term Shoah is an impermeable term that cannot be cracked, or precisely defined." He added that it "encapsulates concepts such as anxiety, terror, fear, and death."[28] Lacking a more suitable universal term, he named his documentary *Shoah*. Lanzmann used the film to channel the term *Shoah*, in all its complexity, into an intellectual statement conceivable through the universal languages of sight and sound that connected this mythical term to antisemitism and to Israel.

His work focused on trauma and moments of heroism during the Holocaust, exploring a narrative of death and the birthing of life despite it.[29] At the same time, it shifted from abstract historical thinking to expressive ideas, documenting the personal experiences of flesh-and-blood human beings—survivors, perpetrators, and bystanders—transforming them into living witnesses.

French historian Lucette Valensi stated that *Shoah* was a work of history presented by a cinematographer.[30] According to Valensi, "[t]hree crucial works contributed to the acknowledgment of the annihilation of the Jews, more than any historical research: that of Primo Levi, the works of Raul Hilberg and Claude Lanzmann's *Shoah*."[31]

In *Shoah*, Lanzmann examined the past in terms of the present by exploring layers of emotion, current thinking patterns, and the physical sites that were active during the Holocaust. The film can be viewed as a documentation of the horrors of the Nazi extermination plan and an exposition of the darkest side of human nature.[32] Lanzmann was determined to avoid theoretical statements and intellectual discussions, mirroring Raul Hilberg's approach to conceiving the reality of the Holocaust by explaining the details of concrete events without falling into generalisations. Lanzmann employed this method, but, aware of the risk of drowning viewers in a sea of information, he touched upon reality using remnants from then and there (railway tracks and trains) and employing survivors in the dramatic role of witness. He documented their concrete, active remembering, examining the elements from which evil incarnate is comprised—prejudice, stereotypes about Jews as the collective murderers of Jesus, and myths about Jewish wealth and power. All this was presented against a backdrop of breathtaking rural scenery, creating a disturbing contrast between the innocence of nature and the cruelty of humanity. The viewer's rage was channelled toward the forces that conspired to create this murderous regime: physical force, bureaucratic efficiency, complicity, and indifference. The interviewees seemingly underwent a process of change toward the end of their testimony, a direct outcome of the spiritual and mental crises they experienced during filming—that is the very magic of the cinematic moment and its ability to capture and transmit these changes in their fullest authenticity.[33]

Lanzmann explained that omitting archival materials was part of his strategy. Most archival images were of German origin, produced by the Wehrmacht's *Propagandakompanie* (WPr), and presented the perspective of the aggressor rather than the oppressed—they were mocking and degrading.[34] Archival footage, authentic as it may be (such as the shot by the *Sonderkommando* in the pasture where they cremated bodies), requires evidence. Lanzmann claimed that archival footage was not evidence. Rather, it was testimony and memory from which evidence is made: "I did not produce *Shoah* to respond to Holocaust deniers or those belittling its magnitude: with those we do not argue, I never thought to do so. An incredible chorus of voices—Polish and German Jews—constructs and establishes in my film the true memory and testifies to the crime that was committed."[35] Bystanders and perpetrators testified to their perceptions and beliefs as well as to their experiences. Lanzmann believed that had it not been for Christian antisemitism and the ostracising of Jews, the extermination would not have occurred.

Some critics and colleagues have claimed that Lanzmann's works do not live up to historical standards, that they were commissioned and sponsored by the State of Israel and as such are tainted by structured diversion and a lack of historical accuracy.[36] Film director Jean-Luc Godard scrutinised the film, claiming it "showed nothing," and he dismissed Lanzmann as "a provocateur." According to Godard, "[t]he cinematic medium betrayed his ethical responsibility to display Nazi extermination camps."[37] Writing about the film, in which he participated as an interviewee, esteemed Polish resistance fighter Jan Karski stated that *Shoah* was not a historical film *per se*, because it isolated the suffering of the Jews from that of other victims, dwelling only on the singularity of the Holocaust. He dubbed the film one-sided and said viewers did not learn of the help provided by the Polish people to the Jewish struggle inside and outside the ghettos. Karski objected to the underlying message that everyone abandoned the Jews to their fate, when in fact it was the governments that abandoned them—not all of humanity.[38]

Film critic Serge Toubiana and others claimed that the Holocaust and Israel were the two matters which concerned Lanzmann most.[39] He affected the way in which we view the Holocaust, shed light on the young State of Israel by raising ground-breaking questions, and was eventually recognised as a warrior director—then and now—fighting for the study of truth and liberty, until eventually becoming a moral authority, a rare conscience of our time. Indeed, Lanzmann invented a genre that was neither documentary nor epic film. He created his own rules by choosing and arranging visual and auditory imagery documented in reality, interpreting characters and their motivation to cooperate and share their stories, and finally, by supplying meaning through a study of testimony, culminating in an aesthetic, realistic, and at times critical experience that Lanzmann called memory.[40]

"It is a work of art, not the truth. I refuse to call *Shoah* a documentary. A documentary explores something that occurred before filming. Here, there was nothing before."[41] The object, Lanzmann claimed, is memory, and speaking is the act of remembering. The crux of the matter was speaking and meeting the need to interpret the essence of the Holocaust while using the death motif as an unapologetic foundation for the life and revival of the Jewish people. This was much more important than mere historical explanation;[42] *Shoah*, he stated, is a film that objects to representation, because all testimonies presented therein indicate the nature of extermination that cannot be represented.

Last of the Unjust, Claude Lanzmann, France, 2013

In 2013, Lanzmann returned with a new film, which would also be his last, *The Last of the Unjust*. This film presented interviews conducted in 1975 with Benjamin Murmelstein,[43] the last remaining *Judenrat* leader from the Theresienstadt ghetto. The interviews were among those Lanzmann had filmed for *Shoah* earlier but had been cut and stowed away for many years, for fear they would not suit *Shoah's* narrative structure. As in Lanzmann's previous films, the component of memory as first-hand survivor testimony was central to the film.

The film's title alludes to André Schwartz-Bart's award-winning novel, *The Last of the Just* (1959),[44] and it focuses exclusively on interviews with Murmelstein.[45] The importance of the film is inherent in the unique, intensely personal testimony it presents. In 2013, when Lanzmann edited the film, Murmelstein was no longer among the living, and Lanzmann decided the time had come and the film could finally be released. Unwittingly, he became Murmelstein's spokesman, presenting his own view of him and perhaps also defending him. While 28 years earlier, in *Shoah*, Lanzmann had been an outsider with the rhetoric of an uninvolved observer, like Susan Sontag's *Promised Lands* (1974) or Chris Marker's *Description of a Struggle* (1960),[46] now Lanzmann preferred to refer to his films as "essay films." Lanzmann had reformed his ways. He allowed the witness's voice to be heard with the objective of involving and impacting the audience, changing viewers' minds about the past in general and the role of the *Judenrat* in particular. To this end, he needed to employ historiographical practices.[47]

The film raised questions about the interviewer and issues of ethics and morality, of Murmelstein's responsibility and guilt. Could Murmelstein be blamed for his conduct? Was it subversive? Did he collaborate or manipulate to preserve his community and survive personally? How can we examine decisions he made alone or with his colleagues? Yet throughout the interview it seemed that Lanzmann, the interviewer, somehow found himself identifying with the hero.

In his previous film, *Shoah*, Lanzmann had been careful to avoid using archival materials, arguing that only solid testimony from survivors should be taken into consideration, in contrast to historians who consider survivor testimony as a secondary and not a primary source. Yet in *The Last of the Unjust*, he chose to use archival material to tell the story of the ghetto, while in actuality he directed the historical narrative with his camera. In this sense, *The Last of the Unjust* was both a continuation and a divergence from Lanzmann's *oeuvre*: from a formal viewpoint, the film moved between past and present. The filmmaker visited the site of the Theresienstadt ghetto and read aloud from a page on its history, supplying the historical context for Murmelstein's narrative, or from texts taken from Murmelstein's own book, *Theresienstadt: Eichmann's Model Ghetto*, which he published in Italy in 1961 to present his testimony in as objective a manner as possible. He selected shocking passages in which Murmelstein described events in minute detail in a way that conveys great pain and rage. Based on familiarity with Lanzmann's *oeuvre*, this incomprehensible act was further clarified in the film through the relationship that developed between the two and Lanzmann's desire to bring Murmelstein's testimony to life: that is, not only to see his testimony, but to describe it. In a certain sense, this is a more personal film than his others—*Shoah*, *Sobibor*, and the *Karski Report*.[48]

Murmelstein summarised in the film: "All were martyrs but not all were saints." That is to say, we were all engaged in crime and politics, the boundaries of morality expanded or narrowed as needed. Sometimes children were sent to their deaths, and sometimes invalids. The conscience was true in any particular moment.

Conclusion

These seminal films, which were also called visual testimony, have become cornerstones of global documentary film on the Holocaust and on ethics and morality in general.

The objective of the American films was to establish themselves as the saviours of Western culture in Europe, which had been ravaged by Nazism. Footage of the war and the liberation served this objective well and provided answers to the questions of "why and what" they were fighting for. Unwittingly, the liberation footage also became iconic and created a new visual language for the representation of abstract narratives such as evil and cruelty, hunger and suffering. Yet, this only presented part of the picture, which was at the margins of the Final Solution. All the previous stages—planning of deportation and slavery in the camps—were absent. The narration was immediate and touched upon harsh scenes from the camps and their inmates. The narrator dubbed the "objects on display" and in many cases, spoke in their names. The filmmakers cannot be blamed for this. The shock the photographers and soldiers experienced upon entering the camps was too intense. This was the best they could do under the conditions on the ground and the tight schedule ahead of the Nuremberg Trials in 1946. The shots taken, as close to death as possible, became embedded in the public's memory and consciousness as the definition of "Holocaust."

The French experience was different. Early French filmmakers sought to redirect the period's history to mentalities and cultural representations of the war. The films corresponded with each other and created a continuum of questions about the French individual's responsibility and guilt in the Holocaust, as well as about complicity with the Germans in all aspects of society during the Vichy period. In *Night and Fog*, a chronological continuum of extermination was described, from the train platforms to the death chambers. The voice of the survivors was not heard, but the sophisticated cinematography spoke in their names. The questions raised separated us (the French) from them (the Nazis) but did not ask questions about who the survivors were and why they were interned. The photographs used were taken from the German archive and were in fact shot by the aggressors.

Ophuls in *The Sorrow and the Pity* was the first to confront his surroundings and created a film that, in its entirety, is an internal confrontation with the French. It was a film about their willing subjugation to the occupation and the destructive outcome, as well as a focalisation about the Nazis and other regimes he viewed as bloodthirsty, such as the Americans in Vietnam as presented in his subsequent film, *The Memory of Justice* (1976).

French cinema, despite its egocentricity, influenced European cinema overall and contributed a more developed style of Holocaust representation, moving forward. This was a more nuanced, subversive style. On one hand, just as before, the harsh sights were hard for the eyes to bear. On the other, they unsettled the heart and elicited thought, anger, guilt, sorrow, and pity.

As the years passed, the films produced became more specific. In his film *Shoah*, Lanzmann shifted the focus of these questions to Jewish relations with the Poles and their surroundings, and later within the Jewish experience itself, touching on the highly sensitive issue of the role of the *Judenrat* in complicity with the Nazis, through his tragic hero in *The Last of the Unjust*. Unlike his predecessors, he created a new genre, based on the memories of survivors, which were transformed into testimony. He refused to use Nazi photographic material and searched for the survivors' internal viewpoint. This method, together with that of his predecessors, had a great impact on documentary cinema.[49]

Finally, we can ask: what is the documentary film's power and ability to reflect truth? What technique(s) can best help us distil that truth? In what context were statements made? Richard Meram Barsam uses the example of *The Triumph of the Will* (Leni Riefenstahl, 1935), and notes how a film with a political message was concealed within a documentary film using covert and overt editing techniques. Riefenstahl's work was utter falsehood, yet it represented the truth for a distinct group of Germans. Is that sufficient, Barsam asks, to call the film a documentary? Should a film be deemed documentary only when it strives for absolute truth? When, and at what stage of the production process, does the creator succeed in creating a distorted and one-sided truth of myth and propaganda, and when, and under what conditions, is that not the case?[50] Thus, documentary film's complexity, and its importance as a tool perceived as objective, raises questions about the filmmaker's choices with respect to the representation of historiographic, legal, philosophical, ethical, political, and aesthetic issues.[51]

These matters also raise questions such as: What relationship can documentary films offer us between knowledge, pleasure, and horror, and how are they different from fictional films? How are verbal historical testimonies, as well as expert testimonies, used in documentary films? What criteria should be adopted with respect to objectivity, procedures of interpretation, choice, and organisation of facts? What is the filmmaker's responsibility towards the audience and the film's subject? How should directors be held accountable for their presence and influence to the people who place faith in them, not just behind the camera but also in front of it? To answer these questions fully, we must determine whether there is a difference between the two mediums and if there is any point in this distinction.

Finally, as viewers, we must also take some responsibility and be critical when watching documentaries: whether they are institutional and funded, private or biased. We must equip ourselves with sensitivity, patience, and empathy; we must learn to analyse both the work's content and form, to enquire about its context within the historical period, geographical space, and the location in which it unfolds. We must get to know the individuals who turned thought into action (the Nazis and collaborators), those who acted and were acted upon (the victims), and search for the human spirit behind and in front of the camera: the film's human heroes in the frame and on the screen. It is important to be discerning and ask ourselves what, in the end, is the work's statement for me and my surroundings, what truth did the work seek, and what did it find? And most importantly, what is the work's essence and what can we take from it in our lives now and in the future?

Notes

1 O. Landesman and L. Melamed (ed.), *Truth or Dare: Selected Essays on Documentary Cinema*, Tel Aviv: Am Oved, 2021, pp. 11–16.
2 J. Grierson, "The Documentary Producer," *Cinema Quarterly*, 2:1, 1933, p. 8.
3 J. Glick, "Documentary's Longue Durée: Reimagining the Documentary Tradition" (interview with Charles Musser), *World Records*, 2, 2018, available online at https://worldrecordsjournal.org/annotations/02-04/.
4 P. Arthur, "Extreme Makeover: The Changing Face of Documentary, *Cineaste*, 30:3, 2005, p. 19.
5 J.L. Godard, *Godard on Godard: Critical Writings by Jean-Luc Godard*, New York: Da Capo Press, 1985.
6 E. Pery, *Cinema and the Nazi Death Apparatus*, Jerusalem: Resling Publishers, 2020, p. 19 (Hebrew).
7 For further reading, see A. Insdorf, *Indelible Shadows: Film and the Holocaust*, New York: Random House, 2003.
8 I. Avisar, *Screening the Holocaust: Cinema's Images of the Unimaginable*, Bloomington: Indiana University Press, 1988.
9 He later became famous in the 1950s for such films as *A Place in the Sun* (1951), *Giant* (1956), *Shane* (1953), and *The Diary of Anne Frank* (1959).

10 R. Yosef, "The Responsibility of the Gaze: Reflections on Ethics and Documentary Film following Bill Nichols," *Mikan: Journal for Hebrew and Israeli Literature and Culture Studies*, 13, 2013, pp. 182–85 (Hebrew).
11 U. Weckel, "The Influence of the Film Die Todesmuhlen on the German Public: The Failure of Shock Education?" in Y. Weiss and G. Margalit (ed.), *Memory and Amnesia: The Holocaust in Germany* Tel Aviv: Hakibbutz Hameuchad, 2005 (Hebrew).
12 The group of films was comprised of the following: Imperial War Museum; *German Concentration Camps Factual Survey*, 1945; *Bergen-Belsen Concentration Camp, Germany 1945 No. 5 Section*, Army Film and Photographic Unit; *Nazi Concentration Camps and Sites of Atrocity in Austria and Germany*, 1945 US Army Signal Corps—Colonel George Stevens and staff, US Army/Movietone News; Pathé News; Universal News, *Cameramen at Concentration and Extermination Camps in Poland, 1944–1945, Auschwitz*, Mikhail Oshurkov.
13 K. Gladstone, "Separate Intentions: The Allied Screening of Concentration Camp Documentaries in Defeated Germany in 1945-46: Death Mills and Memory of the Camps," in T. Haggith and J. Newman (ed.), *Holocaust and the Moving Image: Representations in Film and Television Since 1933*, London: Wallflower Press, 2005, pp. 50–64.
14 P. Levi, *The Drowned and the Saved*, New York: Simon & Schuster, 1988.
15 S. Sontag, *On Photography*, New York: Delta Books, 1977.
16 A.P. Colombat, *The Holocaust in French Film*, Lanham (NJ): Scarecrow Press, 1993, p. 150.
17 V. Sobchack, *Carnal Thoughts: Embodiment and Moving Image Culture*, Berkeley: University of California Press, 2004, p. 244.
18 Ibid.
19 S. Zand, *Film as History: Imagining and Screening the 20th Century*, Tel Aviv: Am Oved, 2002, p. 236 (Hebrew).
20 Cinéma et Politique, *The Sorrow and the Pity: Another Version of Occupation* (Documentary Film), 2021 [French]
21 Ibid.
22 Ibid.
23 Ibid.
24 Zand, *Film as History*, p. 236.
25 Ferro was a keen critic of Soviet cinema and how it influenced the development of film as a medium. See, for example, M. Ferro, *Cinema and History*, Detroit: Wayne State University Press, 1988.
26 I. Avisar, "Time and Testimony in Claude Lanzmann's Shoah," *Nativ* 2:2, 1989, pp. 63–7.
27 C. Lanzmann, "Le lièvre de Patagonie," *HaArnav MiPatagonia*, Jerusalem: Keter, 2009, pp. 156–64.
28 U. Klein, "Holocaust is not a French Word," *Haaretz*, 28 October 2004, available online at https://www.haaretz.co.il/gallery/1.1528670.
29 C. Russell, *Narrative Mortality: Death, Closure and New Wave Cinema*, Minneapolis: University of Minnesota Press, 1995.
30 G. Koch, "The Aesthetic Transformation of the Image of the Unimaginable: Notes on Claude Lanzmann's Shoah," *October*, 48, 1989, pp. 15–24; also, D. Herzog (ed.), "Documenting the Liberation of the Camps: The Case of Alexander Ford's Vernichtungslager Majdanek—Cmentarzysko Europy (1944)," *Lessons and Legacies*, 7, 1991, pp. 125–34.
31 Lanzmann, "Le lièvre de Patagonie."
32 Avisar, *Screening the Holocaust*, p. 44.
33 Ibid., p. 65. Lanzmann's book, *An Oral History of the Holocaust*, recounts an interview with a Polish couple in Grabów. Locals claimed the Holocaust was the will of God, a punishment for the Jewish murder of Christ. See C. Lanzmann, *Shoah: An Oral History of the Holocaust: The Complete Text of the Film*, New York: Pantheon Books, 1985, p. 130. In 2001, Bill Nichols analysed the six modes of which the film is comprised: poetic, expository, observational, participatory, reflexive, and performative. See B. Nichols, *Introduction to Documentary*, Indiana: Indiana University Press, 2001, pp. 1–20, 35–41, 42–60, 99–138, 160–67).
34 Lanzmann, "Le lièvre de Patagonie," p. 346.
35 Ibid., p. 392.
36 L. Frenk, "Shoah: Film and History," *Zmanim: History Quarterly*, 38, 2003, pp. 76–89; also, Anon., "Remember," *Israel Zechor Association and Treasure of Wisdom*, 1987, pp. 197–200.

37 L. Saxton, "Namnésis: Godard/Lanzmann," *Mita'am, Journal of Literature and Radical Thought*, 9, 2007, pp. 106–204, available online at http://www.text.org.il/index.php?book=0714031; and L. Saxton, *Haunted Images: Film, Ethics, Testimony and the Holocaust*, London: Wallflower, 2008.
38 J. Karski, "Shoah," in S. Liebman (ed.), *Claude Lanzmann's Shoah*, Oxford: Oxford University Press, pp. 171–174.
39 C. Lanzmann, E. Marty, and S. Toubiana, "Discussion of the film at the Mémorial de la Shoah Museum in Paris," 21 September 2006.
40 E. Cowie, *Recording Reality, Desiring the Real*, Minneapolis: University of Minnesota Press, 2011, pp. 37–9.
41 C. Lanzmann, Discussion of the Film Shoah at the Hebrew University of Jerusalem, 2013, YouTube video, available online at https://www.youtube.com/watch?v=0wr-2iPsdbc.
42 I. Adilovic, "Values and Jewish Faith Following the Holocaust: Emmanuel Levinas, Jean Améry, Emil Fackenheim and Arthur Cohen," *Maof Uma'ase*, 9, 2003, pp. 7–38 (Hebrew).
43 A.L. Mintz, *Popular Culture and the Shaping of Holocaust Memory in America*, Seattle: University of Washington Press, 2001.
44 D. Karpel, "Claude Lanzmann's Journey to Clear the Name of the Head of the Judenrat of Theresienstadt," *Haaretz Weekend Supplement*, 16 January 2014 (Hebrew).
45 U. Klein, "'Last of the Unjust:' Claude Lanzmann's Requiem for Self," *Haaretz*, 27 January 2014 (Hebrew).
46 O. Landesman, "When Lanzmann, Marker and Sontag Visited Israel," *Takriv*, 6, 2013 (Hebrew).
47 H. Greenspan, *The Awakening of Memory: Survivor Testimony in the First Years after the Holocaust, and Today*, Washington, DC: United States Holocaust Memorial Museum, 2000.
48 G. Johnson and A.O. Scott, "Eichmann's Rabbi Gazes Backward. Lanzmann's 'The Last of the Unjust' Hears a Wily Survivor. The Last of the Unjust," *New York Times*, 6 February 2014.
49 For further reading, see Y. Kozlovsky Golan, "Benjamin Murmelstein, a Man from the 'Town As If': A Discussion of Claude Lanzmann's Film *The Last of the Unjust* (France/Austria, 2013)," *Holocaust Studies, A Journal of Culture and History*, 23:4, 2017, pp. 464–82. Y. Kozlovsky Golan, "The Role of the Judenräte in Serving Nazi Racial Policy: A Discussion of Claude Lanzmann's film 'Last of the unjust'," *Slil: A Journal of History, Cinema and Television*, 2019, pp. 72–98 (Hebrew); Yvonne Kozlovsky Golan, "Through the Director's Lens: Claude Lanzmann's Oeuvre: Commemorating the First Anniversary of his Passing," *Antisemitism Studies*, 4:1, Spring 2020, pp. 143–68.
50 R.M. Barsam, *Filmguide to Triumph of the Will*, Bloomington: Indiana University Press, 1975, pp. 30–55.
51 See especially B. Nichols (ed.), *Movies and Methods: An Anthology*, vol. 1, Berkeley: University of California Press, 1976; ibid., vol. 2, 1985; and B. Nichols, *Representing Reality: Issues and Concepts in Documentary*, Bloomington, Indiana University Press, 1991.

16 Humanising the Holocaust: Literature as a Source for Studying the Holocaust

Kinsey Brown

Literature is one of the most enduring forms of expression in the documented history of humanity. In its many forms, literature is the backbone of the development of the modern world: the worlds of mythology converge and lead to the establishment of organised religion; fables reinforce cultural norms, dictating acceptable behaviours by ingraining themselves into the minds of unwitting children; and folk heroes ascend beyond fiction, rising to become cultural icons shaping the very fabric of society. People are hard-wired to tell stories as a way of interacting with the world around them. Literature is a powerful tool of rebellion, documentation, and accountability: in the case of Holocaust literature, it is a stage upon which survivors and broader humanity can represent and reckon with the trauma of a previously inconceivable genocide.

Out of necessity, this chapter limits the scope of the texts evaluated. As Sue Vice has shown, this can lead to a disparity in Jewish authorial representation,[1] but it also raises questions about the importance of authorial credentials and life experience. Alan Rosen argues that Holocaust history deals with the "factual and interpretive coordinates"[2] of the event, which tend to focus on the whole: six million Jewish people murdered, a continent left in ruins, and a new world order dictated by military might and international political relations. The magnitude of the deaths is simultaneously horrifying and overwhelming, a challenge for the human brain to conceptualise on such an unprecedented scale. Literature offers an entry point to understand this overwhelming suffering through empathy. A novel's focus on the individual perspectives and experiences of narrators prioritises subjectivity and emotion, allowing a reader to empathise directly with the subjects of that novel.[3] This empathic connection allows the author to express truth through the experience of reading.

This chapter considers how the personal backgrounds of novelists can affect the way the Holocaust is manifested in literary works. Authors with Jewish backgrounds tend to focus on the Holocaust as the ideological and physical extermination of the Jewish people and the intergenerational trauma that has passed into the modern consciousness. Authors of other backgrounds have also wrestled with the enduring philosophical scars of the genocide through a variety of lenses such as German perspectives featured in *The Reader*, French interpretations of accountability centred in *Sarah's Key,* and American anxieties over the definition of genocide in *Sophie's Choice*.

The power of storytelling can transcend the factual (and often less satisfying) historical record. Holocaust literature should be read responsibly and contextually as a literary representation of the event itself. A discussion between Howard Reich and Elie Wiesel has reflected on the failure of literature to encompass the full nature of Holocaust remembrance:

DOI: 10.4324/9781003248620-20

The failure, [Weisel] seemed to be saying, was not really a failure of language, nor of our attempts to harness it, but of humanity itself. Language is simply our means of coming to terms with that larger failure, a quixotic but essential attempt to explain the unexplainable. "Logically I should have given up on language."[4]

Weisel and Reich assert that Holocaust literature is essential, but it is not a factual record; literature is an art form, a way for society to collectively process the unspeakable suffering of the Holocaust. However, the representational nature of Holocaust literature can lend an air of unreality to the Holocaust itself when read without historical context; there is already a major schism occurring in younger generations who have become so far removed from the event that they doubt its occurrence. Educators cannot afford to blur the lines any further by allowing a reader to misinterpret fictional literary representations as historical facts.

There has been academic debate surrounding the distinction between fiction and memoir in Holocaust Studies,[5] and scholars and teachers need to emphasise the differences between these two literary styles because any conflation of the two can lead to either literal interpretations of fiction or symbolic interpretations of survivor recollections. Both misinterpretations contribute to an over-arching rejection of the legitimacy of the Holocaust: fiction interpreted as fact can lead readers to disillusionment when they find out their favourite characters never existed, and memoir interpreted as metaphor can allow a reader to remit witness accounts to the realm of fantasy. This chapter will discuss the advantages and difficulties of utilising fiction as a source for studying the Holocaust by identifying thematic and authorial trends in a selection of Holocaust novels: *Night* (Elie Wiesel), *Schindler's Ark* (Thomas Keneally), *Sophie's Choice* (William Styron), *The Reader* (Bernhard Schlink), *Sarah's Key* (Tatiana de Rosnay), *The Devil's Arithmetic* (Jane Yolen), and *The Boy in the Striped Pyjamas* (John Boyne).

Thematically, Holocaust fiction tends to focus on specific ideas of good versus evil, morality, and ethical behaviour. While these ideas may be considered reductive when used in the study of history, their consistent presence in Holocaust literature displays the artistic importance of storytelling in humanity's attempt to rationalise the Holocaust after the event. The novels analysed here do not attempt to document objective facts or undebatable timelines; each novel utilises a specific lens to analyse the Holocaust and process the implications of the event within their own cultural and social understanding of the world, wherein the authors attempt to wrestle meaning from the murder of millions so that readers may benefit from their observations.

Elie Wiesel, Night

Elie Wiesel was a Romanian-born Jewish Holocaust survivor who endured Auschwitz and Buchenwald, where he witnessed the deaths of his family. His identity is essential when we consider that he physically experienced the horrors which Holocaust literature attempts to simulate. And yet his most impactful book, *Night*, is not a memoir, but a novel. Its events are thought to mirror Wiesel's experiences as a teenager, but the account focuses heavily on the internal machinations of the narrator's psyche rather than the exact details of his surroundings. The narrator watches the inhabitants of his small town doubt the reality of the Holocaust even as it is happening to vulnerable members of their community, like Moshe the Beadle, who acts as a symbolic canary in the coal mine for a town who will not heed his cries. In a matter of days, the narrator and his family are taken to Auschwitz, where the boy must witness the horrors of the camp and live through what he perceives as the death of God himself.

Night is an essential novel in Holocaust study, but it exemplifies some of the major pitfalls of a literal interpretation of Holocaust literature. The narrator is often read as a manifestation of Wiesel himself, who lived through Auschwitz at a similar age. Wiesel has published memoirs, but his fictionalised novel has received the most critical and popular attention of all his works. Wiesel seemed to resist the parallels made between his character and his own experiences: in the preface to *Day*, the final book of the *Night* trilogy, Wiesel proclaimed that "a novel about Auschwitz is not a novel—or else, it is not about Auschwitz."[6] *Night* is unique in the trilogy as a fictionalisation of Wiesel's personal experiences in the camps, and yet, he claimed the work is not a novel. Auschwitz was not a setting in a novel, and the feeling of being confined there cannot be truthfully conveyed through literature—so Wiesel creates a work of Holocaust fantasy that can only simulate the unimaginable horror of his experiences. The work is specifically designed to evoke the feelings experienced in the camp and is not intended as a journalistic retelling of Wiesel's time at Auschwitz: the emotions, not the timeline, are the most crucial element of the narrative.

Despite Wiesel's personal connection to the work's subject matter, *Night* was first published in French, a "cartesian language dominated by reason, logic, and clarity."[7] Indeed, the bulk of his work was written in French because, in his view, that language "lends itself to narrative."[8] French was a fresh start, an intellectual lens through which Wiesel could analyse his own emotions via its more logical linguistic framework. One aspect of this syntactical shift was Wiesel's need to adapt the mystical elements of Jewish culture to the fact-driven narrative style of Western literature. This contributes to the fast and somewhat disjointed pacing of *Night*, where fractures in the narrative represent the splintered perceptions of the narrator. These fractures contribute to the goal of the work which is to transport the audience through empathy rather than a factual timeline. *Night* is thus an exercise in empathy intended to bring his audience into the mental state of an anonymous child narrator imprisoned in the camp. *Night* is thus not a novel about Auschwitz—it is about the emotions of a young boy, forced to bear witness to the destruction of his people. The decimation and despair were so inconceivable to the outside world that the only possible way to convey an understanding of the victim's state of mind is to evoke those feelings through the art of Holocaust fantasy.

Wiesel's transformation of his life experiences into fantasy is the only possible way to give his readers insight into the depth of emotion he experienced in the camps. *Night* does not offer a conclusive account of the inner workings of a concentration camp, only the emotional state of a single boy. The specificity of the novel's perspective embodies Wiesel's idea that the Holocaust's enduring legacy is not in the facts of the genocide, but in the emotional and cultural impacts the event had on the Jewish people. The deaths are shocking though quantifiable, but the experience of surviving Auschwitz is impossible to articulate through numbers or even language. Therefore, Wiesel follows the age-old tradition of bearing witness through storytelling to offer an unflinchingly brutal look into his time in the camps that is bolstered by symbolic elements intended to convey the emotional horrors he endured. The essential statement of this work is that the Holocaust was not just a genocide; it was an attempt to wipe Judaism from the face of the earth.

Thomas Keneally, Schindler's Ark

Thomas Keneally is an Australian author of Irish descent. Oskar Schindler, an opportunistic businessman and the main character of Keneally's novel, sees a way to make money under the economic oppression of the Nazi regime: give Jews a place to work in exchange for whatever money they have left. As the war progresses, Schindler uses his influence within the Nazi regime to organise an escape for his workers to save them from deportation and death. The novel was received very positively and received the Booker Prize in 1982,[9] to the dismay and confusion of the author himself, and many others in the literary community.[10] Some (Kenneally among them) insist that the novel is not a work of fiction, but rather a novelised version of factual events:

> I am delighted with the Booker McConnell Prize, but it is also preposterous to me ... The facts are there, but I make use of fictional techniques in character development, the manner in which an incident is relayed. There is some fictionalization when there is not a record of the dialogue. I do a reasonable reconstruction. I had a responsibility to those who cherish the memory of Oskar, many of whom read and corrected the manuscript.[11]

Despite Kenneally's protestations, his novel is an excellent example of mythmaking in the wake of the Holocaust. The story exemplifies one way in which Germans resisted the Nazi regime, though not always for the reasons one would expect. A modern audience would expect Schindler to reject Nazism because of its antisemitic hatred and violence, but in reality, his actions stemmed from capitalist exploitation of the Jewish people. Modern audiences also struggle mightily with the idea that most of Germany's population could stand aside, passively acquiescing in the extermination of millions of people. Oskar Schindler does not become a hero until it benefits him financially, and yet, in this novel, he is painted unilaterally as a hero. The ends seem to justify the means, and Schindler's legacy emerges in mythic proportions at the end. While it is important to remember Germans who had the bravery to stand up against the Nazi regime, Schindler's story ends with him exalted as a hero. And yet, Schindler does very little beyond treating his employees like human beings: he is still a war profiteer, he remains a member of the Nazi Party, he still casually rubs elbows with the Nazi elite, and he never openly resists the actions of the regime.

Despite the problems with Kenneally's exaltation of Oskar Schindler, the plot of *Schindler's Ark* is based in fact and, therefore, reads as believable—like most myths, *Schindler's Ark* is based on the true actions of a man who actually lived. Keneally, however, imposes a redemption arc over the true events of the situation, which remain unknown. The novel is almost entirely based on witness testimony. Even the author questions the surety of the narrative, peppering the text with phrases like "we do not know."[12] These admissions seem candid and almost endearing within the context of the novel, inviting the reader to be part of this historical mystery. Instead of leading the reader to question the narrative, these interjections only solidify confidence in the authority and relatability of the narrator.

Schindler's Ark may not be based in fact, but it is intentionally crafted to be believable. It is, however, a myth, the post-war creation of a redeeming hero among the German gentile population. The problem is that people want to believe it. Students of Holocaust Studies so often ask themselves: would I have been courageous enough to stand up for what was right under the Nazi regime? Would I have saved people? *Schindler's Ark* reassures readers that yes, at least some people were willing to stand against the Nazis, and perhaps the reader could have been one of them. Despite the apathetic and exploitative characterisation of Oskar Schindler, gentile audiences are reassured by his existence because it proves that they too might be capable of standing in the face of oppression. Readers must be aware of how easy it is to slip into this argument from analogy and avoid idealising Schindler without considering how and why he became involved in rescuing thousands of Jewish people.

William Styron, Sophie's Choice

Other entries to the canon of Holocaust literature have used the Holocaust as a backdrop for social critique elsewhere in the world. *Sophie's Choice* is the result of an author from the American South, William Styron, reckoning with the larger implications of the Holocaust, particularly the parallels between the treatment of Jewish people in Nazi Germany and the continued oppression and murder of Black citizens in the United States. The novel also pursues a feminist critique of bystander's guilt, acknowledging the passive roles of women in male-dominated societies. The novel's title character, Sophie, is a Polish Catholic survivor of Auschwitz whose actions have been dictated by the male influences in her life. In America, her defining relationships are with Stingo, the novel's Southern aristocratic narrator, and Nathan Landau, a Jewish-American intellectual. This trio of central characters form a complex web of social critique: Sophie represents women passively indoctrinated into the Nazi cause; Stingo embodies the hypocrisy of non-Jewish Americans who condemn the Holocaust while continuing to profit from similar oppression of Black people; and Nathan is a manifestation of Jewish rage, a seemingly insane character whose actions hold deeper meaning when read in concert with the rest of the book's commentary. It is important to note that throughout *Sophie's Choice*, Sophie's emotions (as interpreted by Stingo) are privileged over Nathan's views of the world. A feminist reading of Sophie's character yields several important interpretations at the cost of reasonable Jewish representation.

Women living under the Nazi regime, even non-Jewish women, were at risk of direct violence if they dissented against the opinions of the pro-Nazi men in their lives. For Sophie, her way to survive the Nazi regime is to parrot the Nazi ideology imbued in her by the men who have controlled her life over the years: her father, her husband, and Auschwitz commandant Rudolf Höss. And yet, Sophie ends up with Nathan in New York, who seems to control her body, mind, and decisions in the same way the Nazis did, implying that she is never able to define herself as a person without a man to lead her. Even in death, Sophie aligns with Nathan's cause.

Ironically, the ultimate act of control through death is perpetuated by the only Jewish character in the novel. Nathan Landau is paranoid, a drug abuser, and consistently insists that Sophie contributed to the perpetuation of the Holocaust. The most fascinating part of this seemingly negative characterisation is that Nathan is not wrong; Sophie took a privileged position by working for Höss at Auschwitz, willingly adopted antisemitic views, and attempted to seduce him to save the life of her son. The fact that Sophie never knows if her son lives or dies illustrates the way Nazis manipulated people into perpetuating their own oppression. Nathan attempts to point this out several times but is shot down by the narrator, who feels personally offended by the parallels drawn between Sophie's situation and the passive role of white Southerners in American slavery and the continuing Jim Crow era.

An interesting parallel is drawn when Nathan points out Stingo's complacency in the horrors of slavery and the Civil War. Once again, Nathan is correct in his social critique: Stingo is a Southerner travelling on inheritance money, and given the timeframe of the novel, it's reasonable to assume that his family accrued that wealth by owning enslaved people. Stingo is living off the direct profit of atrocity, perpetuated and forgotten within America's borders. These complacent roles of Stingo and Sophie are critiqued openly by Nathan, but instead of siding with Nathan, the author portrays him as schizophrenic and unable to cope with reality. The tragedy of Nathan's and Sophie's joint suicide is portrayed as murder inflicted by Nathan, a senseless tragedy in which Sophie is portrayed as the victim of a liar, manipulator, and paranoid schizophrenic.

Literature scholar Rhonda Sirlin offers a different perspective on Nathan's role in the novel, arguing that "Nathan is quite literally mad with the knowledge of Auschwitz and is determined to make those around him as obsessed and demonic as he."[13] Based on this approach, Nathan's bizarre behaviour is "a necessary response to the excruciating horrors the twentieth century has wrought."[14] Nathan's ultimate act of suicide with Sophie does make sense from a nihilistic viewpoint: the world has entered a new phase of hatred and widespread death. Nathan lives in a country built on the foundations of a completely unacknowledged genocide. In this reading, Nathan sees the United States for what it is, and makes parallels between the legacy of slavery and the American perception of the Holocaust. Despite American condemnation of the genocide, Nathan sees the ways American politics and society have been corrupted by nationalism and racism.[15] In a final act of outrage and protest, Nathan removes himself (and Sophie) from a world that refuses to acknowledge the complex webs of societal pressure and complacency that allow genocide to occur.

Bernhard Schlink, The Reader

Bernhard Schlink is a German lawyer and academic.[16] *The Reader* is the result of a German author reckoning with his country's passive complacency to genocide as part of the German writing tradition known as *vergangenheitsbewältigung*, that is, "working to or struggling to overcome the past"—a genre of German literature that recalls, processes, and takes accountability for cultural and even familial connections to the perpetrators of the Holocaust.[17]

The novel is in three parts encompassing the life of German narrator Michael Berg. In Part I, Michael is 15 years old and has a covert affair with a 36-year-old neighbour named Hanna Schmitz. The primary focus is Michael's sexual awakening and the secrecy surrounding his taboo affair with Hanna. The Holocaust is never directly mentioned. In Part II, Michael is a young man in law school who is made to attend the Nuremberg Trials as part of his education. Here, he witnesses Hanna being charged and tried for her role as a concentration camp guard at Auschwitz, specifically, the burning of a barn containing hundreds of imprisoned women and children. Hanna is accused of writing an account of the fire, so she is asked to give a sample of her handwriting to compare the two. When Hanna adamantly refuses, Michael realises that she is illiterate and that this may have contributed to her refusal of a promotion that would have removed her from responsibility for overseeing the imprisoned women. Hanna's illiteracy becomes a central point of empathy between the narrator, Hanna, and the reader: her inability to read renders her a victim in her own right, diverting sympathy from the women she burned to be placed squarely on Hanna's seemingly naive shoulders.

During the trial, it is also revealed that Hanna continued her practice of having children read to her while working at Auschwitz. Hanna had "favourites"[18] who she kept from hard labour in exchange for nightly readings in her room. Despite her favouritism, the "weak and delicate ones"[19] still ended up being deported to the death camps. Michael ruminates on this fact, sympathising with Hanna's point of view once again: "Say it, Hanna. Say you wanted to make their last month bearable. That was the reason for choosing the delicate and the weak. That there was no other reason, and could not be."[20] Again, Michael's narration reflects a profound and pointed sympathy for Hanna's situation, hoping desperately that Hanna had good-natured motivations while working in a concentration camp.

Part III focuses on Hanna's and Michael's continued relationship in her later years. Michael records books on tape and sends them to Hanna, and he even agrees to visit her in prison, where he realises she is now an old woman who he cannot love romantically.

During the preceding sections of the novel, Michael's overwhelming love for Hanna overshadows the morally questionable fact that he is 15 and she is 36 when they begin their affair, foreshadowing the way his love will complicate his interpretation of Hanna's actions during the Holocaust:

> I wanted simultaneously to understand Hanna's crime and to condemn it ... When I tried to understand it, I had the feeling I was failing to condemn it as it must be condemned. When I condemned it as it must be condemned, there was no room for understanding ... it was impossible to do both.[21]

While *The Reader* successfully considers the mental workings of German characters, the Jewish perspective is all but ignored. Jews are props in Hanna's story, plot devices whose suffering acts as a background to Hanna's trauma. Michael meticulously hypothesises about Hanna's mental state, but the feelings and experiences of the murdered prisoners are never considered until the final pages of the novel when Michael meets an unnamed survivor of the fire. Their exchange over Hanna's final gift, a tea box filled with money which Michael wants to give the survivor, highlights the implications of Hanna's final request. She asks: "And how am I supposed to deal with it ... grant Frau Schmitz her absolution?"[22] The money is not just a gift, but a symbol meant to represent Hanna's desire to be forgiven. The survivor, unwilling to honour this request, puts the onus on Michael to donate the money to a Jewish organisation. This final scene is essential to understanding Schlink's slow-burning theme of *vergangenheitsbewältigung*: Germans cannot be directly forgiven for their actions, only through action can they be redeemed.

It is perhaps not surprising that the central theme of the novel is the analysis of intergenerational relationships in post-war Germany rather than a direct confrontation with the incalculable suffering inflicted upon the Jewish people. Law students attend the trial of a woman who contributed to the Holocaust, but the students did not live through the event and are torn between a desire to condemn and a desire to understand. Michael's mental gymnastics to absolve Hanna of blame mirror the author's own attempts to condemn and understand his country's legacy.

The Reader is a parable, a morality play, whose success or failure is determined by how much the audience can relate to the narrator and transfer the story's guiding principles into their own lives. While the work is completely fiction, the events of the story are certainly believable—a child is seduced by an adult, and she convinces them they are in love. That same child must then reckon with the legacy of his lover and his country. Michael chooses compassion for his lover rather than accountability, mirroring his own struggle to rationalise his involvement with Hanna given the atrocities she has committed. Only when Hanna is old and unlovable does he realise that he chose wrongly and that his continued support of Hanna was his own attempt to avoid confronting his guilt over being born into a genocidal country. The book raises questions about culpability and the intergenerational trauma of being born of the Nazis, but the personal nature of the work leads the author to omit all but one unnamed Jewish perspective, whose presence is restricted to the novel's three-page penultimate chapter.[23]

Tatiana de Rosnay, Sarah's Key

Tatiana de Rosnay is a writer of French and British parentage. Raised in Paris and educated in the United States, French, and American perspectives define her novel, and while the title character, Sarah, is Jewish, the author is not. *Sarah's Key* was initially published in French but was received positively: it sold over 11 million copies worldwide, and the text was translated into 15 languages.[24]

De Rosnay acknowledges that a part of her inspiration to write the novel was the fact that the Vel' d'Hiv Roundup was not taught in French schools until a speech in 1995 by then-president Jacques Chirac: "France," Chirac said, "land of the Enlightenment and of Human Rights, land of hospitality and asylum, France, on that day, committed an irreparable act. It failed to keep its word and delivered those under its protection to their executioners."[25] *Sarah's Key* is not about the murder process in the Shoah; it is about French participation in the Holocaust—because the novel is not focused on Jewish perspectives, *Sarah's Key* analyses the results of the deaths of Jewish characters and how those deaths impact the lives of those who are still alive and occupying the apartment where Sarah once lived. This is a theme echoed in *Sophie's Choice*, *The Reader*, and *The Boy in The Striped Pyjamas*—Jewish suffering is not the problem, the effect of Jewish suffering on non-Jews is the main conflict in these novels.

Co-protagonists Sarah and Julia live the same apartment in France almost 60 years apart. Sarah Starzynski and her family are deported from that apartment during the Vel' d'Hiv Roundup, and Sarah's brother is left there, locked in a cabinet. She survives but is separated from her parents. Sarah eventually escapes and is harboured by a non-Jewish couple, Jules and Geneviève Dufare, who take Sarah to Paris so she can access her apartment to free her brother from the cabinet. Here, they meet the non-Jewish Tézac family that has taken over the Starzynski's home. The final third-person narration from Sarah's perspective is the discovery of her brother's desiccated body. Years later, the narration continues from the point of view of Julie Tézac, an American journalist who has married into the family and lives in the Starzynski's former home. After being assigned to write about the Vel' d'Hiv Roundup, Julie embarks on a journey of self-discovery that supersedes themes of Holocaust remembrance or accountability; Julie's quest for liberation from her controlling husband is presented parallel to her investigation of Sarah's story. It is revealed that Sarah committed suicide and that the details of her life had been intentionally concealed by the Tézac family. Julia meets with Sarah's son in the final chapter of the book and is praised for naming her newborn after Sarah.

This novel offers an interesting perspective by acknowledging French collaboration in rounding up Jews during the Holocaust, with Sarah and her family victims of French police, not German soldiers or SS. Interestingly, the French characters in the book do not support the revelation of their involvement; Julie, an American journalist, is the only character willing to confront the reality of French involvement in the Holocaust. Julie's role as whistle-blower reflects de Rosnay's commentary on the historical denial of French culpability in the Holocaust.

The plot is believable but laced with tragedy and ends with a fanciful reconciliation between Sarah's son and Julie, who has appropriated Sarah's story as her own. Julie uses Sarah's journey as a way of breaking free from her oppressive French husband, whose domineering presence symbolises the culture of Holocaust revisionism in France. Tragedy seems to be woven into the plot as character development for the non-Jewish Julie. The novel's ending is intended to be a closed loop, a satisfying emotional catharsis that resolves all the loose ends of the modern storyline. While the ending may be emotionally satisfying for Julia, it is revealed that Sarah killed herself. Sarah does not get a happy ending, and even more disturbingly, she is never allowed to tell her own story; it is filtered through the lens of Julia's experiences. While the novel attempts to reckon with French involvement in World War II, it strays into the trap of satisfying, closed plots that are appealingly easy to market. Subplots of romance, troubled marriages, and feel-good female liberation divert from the core themes of Holocaust accountability and prioritise a positive resolution over an authentic representation of French involvement in the Holocaust.

Jane Yolen, The Devil's Arithmetic

Jane Yolen is a Jewish American author of over 365 children's books, illustrated and non-illustrated.[26] *The Devil's Arithmetic* was Yolen's first book on the topic of the Holocaust. Since its publication in 1988, Yolen has authored several other works focusing on the Holocaust, attempting to frame the event for children and teenagers through the incorporation of fairy-tale folklore.[27] *The Devil's Arithmetic* follows the mystical experiences of Hannah Stern, a pre-teen Jewish girl living in New York. In the opening pages of the book, Hannah is frustrated that she must attend a gathering with her family, claiming "[she] is tired of remembering."[28] During a Passover Seder, Hannah symbolically opens the door for the prophet Elijah and is transported through time to inhabit the body of Chaya Abramowicz in 1942. Hannah/Chaya is rounded up with the rest of the village and taken to a concentration camp. Hannah/Chaya knows of the horrors to come but finds solace with a group of girls her age: Rivka, Esther, and Shifre. One day, while digging trenches, a guard accuses the girls of shirking and begins to lead them to the gas chambers. Hannah/Chaya quickly switches places with Rivka, sparing Rivka's life at the cost of her own. With Chaya's death in 1942, Hannah is transported back to her family's Seder. At the dinner, Hannah's Aunt Eva calls her over, and Hannah realises that Rivka and Eva are the same person. It is revealed that Hannah was named after Chaya to acknowledge her sacrifice, and Hannah is filled with a new respect for Holocaust remembrance and Jewish tradition.

Yolen pre-empted her artistic choices for *The Devil's Arithmetic* in her 1987 article "An Experimental Act," published a year before the novel. In the article, Yolen discusses the usefulness of time-shift narratives as "a straight road into memory, an experimental act for an understanding of the past."[29] She argues that the time-shift format allows child readers to relate more closely to the events of the novel because the main character speaks and thinks in a contemporary style, just like the readers themselves. Given the overwhelmingly positive reception of *The Devil's Arithmetic*, it is clear that this technique struck a chord with young audiences: the book won the Jewish National Book Award for Children's literature in 1989 and is currently published as a Puffin Modern Classic novel.[30]

The Devil's Arithmetic represents a powerful artistic endeavour to bring young readers a step closer to the events of the Holocaust. While the plot is not necessarily believable given the fantastical elements of the narrative, Yolen does not need to be believable to achieve her goal of promoting empathy between young contemporary readers and her novel's subjects. Her writing style expands on the authorial goals of Wiesel's *Night* by highlighting the experiences of a single child to whom the reader can closely relate in age, with Yolen taking it a step further by mystically transporting a modern child into the experiences of one who lived through the Holocaust. Themes of sacrifice, Jewish mysticism and tradition, and the power of remembrance are at the forefront of *The Devil's Arithmetic*, and Yolen weaves these powerful themes into a Holocaust fantasy that resonates deeply with children and adults alike.

John Boyne, **The Boy in the Striped Pyjamas**

John Boyne is an Irish Catholic author of 20 credited works.[31] *The Boy In The Striped Pyjamas* is by far his most successful novel, having sold over 11 million copies in 58 languages.[32] Given novel's success, Boyne is credited as the highest-selling Irish novelist and most-translated Irish author of all time.[33] Despite the worldwide success of the novel, he has been heavily criticised for his representation of the Holocaust. In response, Boyne has engaged in online altercations with historians and museum professionals about the authenticity and ethical representation of his work.[34]

The Boy in the Striped Pyjamas follows the story of Bruno, a sheltered and privileged Berlin-born German boy whose father is a Nazi camp commandant. Bruno's family relocates to the country, where Bruno has very little understanding of his father's activities or the war at large. He eventually sees the concentration camps in the distance and learns from his sister that their home is called "Out-With" (Auschwitz).[35] Bruno begins to venture towards the fences, and befriends an imprisoned boy named Shmuel. The boys form a tight friendship from across the Auschwitz wire, and Bruno eventually ventures into the camp to play with his friend. Inside the camp, Bruno quickly realises that the conditions are far from his father's descriptions, and he is shocked by the suffering he sees. Bruno is then herded to a gas chamber and dies among the anonymous throng of people. Bruno's father later discovers how Bruno must have entered the camp and despairs at the realisation that he has murdered his son.

Boyne's novel attempts to emulate the empathy-evoking tactics of Wiesel and Yolen by employing a main character to whom readers can relate. The problematic aspect of this evocative format is that the "relatable" aspect of Bruno's character is his identity as a gentile. The novel implies that non-Jewish readers cannot relate to the suffering of the Jewish victims of the Holocaust, given that Boyne found it necessary to appropriate the experiences of millions of Jews to be filtered through the naive viewpoint of a privileged German child rather than centring the Jewish Shmuel as the main character. Bruno's overwhelming naivete effectively represents the innocence of a child while critiquing the ways that the truth of the Holocaust was concealed from the general German public during World War II, but Bruno's identity as the literal child of the oppressor adds an extra layer of irony to his situation. Bruno's death connects the suffering of the Jewish people to the suffering of the commandant after Bruno's death to convey the universality of the pain of loss, but in connecting the two, Boyne centres the perspectives of a fictional German family over those of the millions of real people who died at Auschwitz.

The tragedy of Bruno's death was repeated countless times, yet Bruno's death is portrayed as uniquely horrifying because he was not the intended victim. The end of the novel focuses closely on the emotional fallout on Bruno's family, specifically on his father's journey to the realisation that Bruno must have entered the camp and died there. Narrated in the third person, the short final chapter follows Mother, Gretel, and the commandant in the months following Bruno's disappearance. Mother waits for months anticipating his return before she goes back to Berlin, expecting Bruno to be waiting there. Gretel spends her time in her room crying because she misses her brother. The scene is short, but the concise and journalistic description of a grieving mother and sister evokes a deep emotional response. The rest of the three-page chapter is devoted to the commandant's fall from grace. After the disappearance of his son, the commandant becomes angry and falls out of favour with his soldiers. He eventually investigates the site of Bruno's disappearance and "followed it through, logically, step-by-step"[36] to the realisation that his son accidentally became a victim of the Nazi murderers. This revelation seems to break the man, who collapses and gives himself over to his duty because "he didn't really mind what they did to him anymore."[37] The humanisation of a single Nazi officer is the result of the novel, and despite this, he never does anything to resist the death machine of which he is part.

Conclusions

Literature is an essential tool for studying the Holocaust from the perspective of the individual to gain a deeper understanding of the social, cultural, and emotional impacts of the event. Literature written by Jewish authors specifically is especially important when considering the Jewish cultural context of the Holocaust, which was a unique cultural experience for the Jewish people. While five million non-Jews also died, the specific and persistent persecution of Jews by the Nazi regime was a targeted genocide. The unique perspective of Jewish authors should be centred in the study of Holocaust literature and considered when reading novels written by non-Jews.

For Jewish and non-Jewish authors alike, it is important to remember that fiction is a distinct genre from memoir, serving a different purpose in the literary canon. While fiction authors may draw in elements of testimony or memoir, works of fiction should be read as art pieces rather than factual reports.

Though it may be optimistic to separate the art from the artists, it is essential in studying Holocaust literature to track the connections between the author, narrator, and the larger themes being showcased. The Holocaust represents a unique event in human history, one that revealed the ease with which genocide can be perpetuated in the era of modern technology. This revelation spilled into the cultural consciousness of groups that were directly or tangentially related to the event itself: German, French, Irish, and American authors are all featured in this chapter because each community has felt compelled to reckon with the global implications of the Holocaust as it relates to their own culture. The Holocaust is reduced to a backdrop upon which the morality plays of non-Jewish authors play out. Given this appropriation of Jewish suffering, it is not surprising that the genre of Holocaust literature is fraught with controversy.[38] Many of the books analysed here examine themes that are completely unrelated to the suffering of the Jewish people during and after the Holocaust. While several of the books from non-Jewish authors have great literary value, the novels tend to overlook Jewish perspectives in favour of other themes; in *The Reader*, German intergenerational relations and culpability are examined at the cost of reasonable Jewish representation in the novel; in *Sophie's Choice*, the perspective of an American narrator is privileged above that of the novel's only Jewish character; and in *The Boy In the Striped Pyjamas*, Jewish suffering is appropriated by a child of the perpetrators themselves to elicit emotion from the audience.

Novels like *The Boy in the Striped Pyjamas* represent the most concerning sub-genre of Holocaust literature, where non-Jewish authors seem to utilise the Holocaust as a selling point for their works. The biggest concern in these cases is a blatant appropriation of Jewish suffering, re-tailored for a gentile audience incapable of comprehending the Shoah unless it is experienced by a character to whom they can relate or empathise. This raises a disturbing question: why do such audiences struggle to comprehend the Shoah unless it is applied to their own people? Are Jews still othered in Western society to the point that audiences cannot empathise with the tragedy of the Shoah?

Historical fiction can be a tricky subgenre when considered for academic study. Depending on the age and educational background of the reader, historical fiction can be misinterpreted as testimony, or a more factual representation of the event depicted. In the case of Holocaust literature, this may result in significant misrepresentations of historical fact.

Literature is useful in studying the widespread and complex impacts of genocide in Western culture, both in Jewish and non-Jewish communities. The novels reviewed reflected a non-Jewish urge to reckon with the Holocaust, to condemn it as a singularly horrific moment in history that cannot be allowed to repeat itself. While the themes of these novels have value in literary study, it is important to use literature responsibly through a contextual approach to the text. Author background should be considered, and questionable themes can be sources for further study and analysis. Thus, literature is a tool that must be wielded consciously and contextually in Holocaust Studies.

The art of literature can provide a uniquely meditative and humanising perspective on the Holocaust, where readers use empathy to access the viewpoints of people on all sides of the conflict. It can thus be concluded that the act of interpreting the Holocaust through art allows authors and audiences to reflect on the emotional, moral, and long-reaching effects of the Holocaust, both to individuals and to society at large.

Notes

1 S. Vice, *Holocaust Fiction*, New York: Routledge, 2000, pp. 1–2. Vice articulates that novels written in English are often written by authors who did not survive the Holocaust, which makes them ripe for fictional literary examination.

2 A. Rosen (ed.), *Literature of the Holocaust*, Cambridge: Cambridge University Press, 2013, p. 2.
3 Ibid., pp. 2–6. In his introduction to the volume, Rosen discusses distinctions between Holocaust historical study and Holocaust literary study.
4 H. Reich, *The Art of Inventing Hope: Intimate Conversations with Elie Wiesel*, Chicago: Chicago Review Press, 2019, p. 3.
5 Vice, *Holocaust Fiction*, pp. 4–7. Vice discusses a trend where critics seem to prefer testimonial content over interpretive literature and points out that the preference may stem from a lack of distinction between the genres.
6 E. Weisel, *Day*, New York: Hill and Wang, 2008, p. i.
7 E. Fine, *Legacy of Night*, Albany: State University of New York Press, 1983, p. 6.
8 Ibid.
9 "Schindler's Ark," The Booker Prizes, *The Booker Prizes Foundation*, 2022, available online at https://thebookerprizes.com/the-booker-library/books/schindlers-ark
10 Richard F. Shepard, "Nonfiction Schindler's List and a Fiction Prize," *New York Times*, November 22, 1982, available online at https://www.nytimes.com/1982/11/22/books/nonfiction-schindler-s-list-and-a-fiction-prize.html
11 Ibid.
12 T. Kencally, *Schindler's Ark*, New York: Atria Books, 2013, pp. 40, 190, 319, 351, 370.
13 M. Lackey, "The Scandal of Jewish Rage in William Styron's Sophie's Choice." *Journal of Modern Literature*, 39:4, 2016, p. 86.
14 Ibid.
15 For one example, see W. Styron, *Sophie's Choice*, New York: Random House, 1979, p. 75.
16 "Bernhard Schlink," Penguin Random House, *The Penguin Random House Network*, 2022, available online at https://www.penguinrandomhouse.com/authors/27183/bernhard-schlink/
17 P.A. Fritzsche, "What Exactly is Vergangenheitsbewältigung? Narrative and Its Insufficiency in Postwar Germany," in A. Fuchs, M. Cosgrove, and G. Grote (ed.), *German Memory Contests: The Quest for Identity in Literature, Film, and Discourse since 1990*, Woodbridge (UK): Boydell and Brewer, 2006, pp. 25–40.
18 B. Schlink, *The Reader*, New York: Vintage Books, 2001, p. 90.
19 Ibid.
20 Ibid., p. 92.
21 Ibid., p. 121.
22 Ibid., p. 161.
23 Ibid., pp. 160–63.
24 L. Daley, "Tatiana de Rosnay on 'Sarah's Key,' Boston memories, and her scary new novel," *Boston Globe*, February 22, 2021, available online at https://www.bostonglobe.com/2021/02/22/arts/tatiana-de-rosnay-sarahs-key-boston-memories-her-scary-new-novel/
25 Chirac's speech can be found at http://www.levendel.com/En/html/chirac-s_speech.html. On the Vel' d'Hiv Roundup of 16–17 July 1942, see C. Lévy and P. Tillard, *Betrayal at the Vel d'Hiv*, New York: Hill and Wang, 1969.
26 J. Yolen, "A Short Biography," *Jane Yolen: Author of over 400 books for children and adults*, May 16, 2022, available online at https://www.janeyolen.com/biography/
27 Ibid. *Briar Rose* (1992) is a retelling of Sleeping Beauty and *Mapping the Bones* (2018) mirrors the story of Hansel and Gretel.
28 J. Yolen, *The Devil's Arithmetic*, London: Puffin Books, 2004, p. 1.
29 J. Yolen, "An Experimental Act," *Language Arts*, 66:3, March 1989: p. 4.
30 "Past Winners," National Jewish Book Awards, *Jewish Book Council*, 2022, available online at https://www.jewishbookcouncil.org/awards/national-jewish-book-awards/past-winners?category=30737. See also Puffin Modern Classics," Education, *Penguin Random House*, 2022, available online at https://penguinrandomhouseelementaryeducation.com/series-landing-page/?seriesCode=DT2&seriesName=Puffin%20Modern%20Classics
31 See https://johnboyne.com/about/
32 Ibid.
33 Ibid.
34 In January 2020, John Boyne engaged in an online exchange with the verified Auschwitz Memorial Museum Twitter account. The Museum tweeted that *The Boy in The Striped*

Pyjamas "should be avoided by anyone who studies or teaches about the history of the Holocaust." Instead of addressing this critique, Boyne deflected any factual inaccuracies in his book. See B. Weich, "Auschwitz Museum embroiled in spat with 'Striped Pyjamas' author," *Jewish Chronicle*, January 7, 2020, available online at https://www.thejc.com/news/uk/auschwitz-museum-twitter-spat-john-boyne-author-boy-in-striped-pyjamas-film-1.495118
35 J. Boyne, *The Boy in The Striped Pyjamas*, Oxford: David Fickling Books, 2006, p. 24.
36 Ibid., p. 216.
37 Ibid.
38 Vice, *Holocaust Fiction*, pp. 2–7. Vice discusses examples of controversies with fictional representations of the Holocaust, including the film adaptation of Thomas Keneally's *Schindler's Ark*; the banning of Jim Allen's *Perdition*; and concerns over the authenticity of Binjamin Wilkomirski's *Fragments*.

17 Art as a Source for Studying the Holocaust[1]

Laura Morowitz

Introduction

In their highly subjective and often indeterminate nature, works of visual art are different from many other kinds of documents. Their use may be problematic and complex yet can offer powerful and illuminating truths. The very ability of art to speak the unspeakable, to bypass language, makes it a unique tool in teaching and learning about the Holocaust. Unlike so many documents reliant upon language, such as oral histories and trial records, there is no need for translation; the viewer may have direct access to them and may even view them first hand. In contrast to sources that may attempt to convey the overwhelming nature of mass murder, works of art testify to individuality, the richness of an individual consciousness, and thus bring home the tragic loss of a single, unique human being.

Among the most powerful sources are works of art made by those who perished, both professional artists and amateurs. They may serve as eyewitness sources as well as enabling our own subjective and deeply emotional understanding. Their power resides in the works themselves as well as in our knowledge of the tragic circumstances in which they were made. Some of these artworks seem like messengers beyond the grave; in many cases, the "survival" of artwork, when the artists themselves did not, is a constant source of pain in confronting these works. "If you live to leave this hell, make your drawings and tell the world about us," a fellow Auschwitz inmate implored artist Halina Olomucki, "We want to be among the living, at least on paper."[2]

Over 30,000 works of art survived the Holocaust.[3] Their survival, in nearly every case, is a small miracle. Small-scale objects and drawings were buried in the ground, bricked up in walls, smuggled out by being wrapped around limbs, stored in bodily orifices, and hidden in every other way imaginable. Many more works, perhaps ten times as many, were destroyed or lost. The size and media of the works were not "chosen" but rather made from the only conceivable materials available. Their dimensions are often very small, sometimes tiny, such as the 1 × 1 inch "postage stamps" made by Karl Shwesig in Gurs internment camp.[4] They testify to conditions of utter deprivation and danger. Slovene artist Zoran Music used the rust from his jail cell bars in Dachau to draw, while partisans created drawings consisting of twigs and blades of grass. At Auschwitz, toothpaste tubes were scavenged from the garbage cans of the SS and turned into tiny creations.[5] Indeed, our knowledge of the context in which works were made is central to our understanding of the works, and to what they teach us. In nearly every case, the works were made under duress, certainly in situations of poverty, difficulty, scarcity, and often terror.

DOI: 10.4324/9781003248620-21

Art of the Holocaust ranges from works in documentary style, to macabre surrealism, to abstraction and in every other conceivable visual language. "There are values that supersede aesthetic ones," Irving Howe noted of works from the Shoah, "and situations in which it is unseemly to continue going through the paces of aesthetic judgement."[6] Yet we can recognise the images of professional artists who often worked in the prevailing artistic languages of their time, such as Expressionism. In their desperate need to somehow capture and comprehend the reality around them, artists most often worked in figurative styles. Some of their works are simple and powerful, others astonishingly beautiful and accomplished. Bedrich Fritta, one of the leading artists imprisoned at Terezín (Theresienstadt) and director of its *Technische Abteilung* (Technical Department) for a time, drew in an Expressionist style that recalls the German painter and printmaker Otto Dix. Felix Nussbaum, discussed in detail below, drew on the macabre world of the sixteenth-century Dutch painter Hieronymus Bosch and the tradition of medieval *Todtentanz* ("dance of death," or *danse macabre*).

In using works of art as documents of the Holocaust, it is important to understand the function for which they were intended and their perceived viewers. Professional artists were often conscripted to produce works for their Nazi captors, for their personal enjoyment, or as "decoration" or "sign makers." Artist Halina Olumucki was commissioned to paint the walls of a building at Majdanek, and later to produce works at Auschwitz. In a drawing by Polish-French artist David Olère, we see him adding designs to a letter as an SS officer stands over him.[7] Carrying out these works could often help someone survive by assuring them more rations or other favoured treatment. When the artist Malva Shaleck refused to do the portrait of a collaborator at Theresienstadt, she was placed on a deportation list.[8] As shown below, these artists often created other work in secret, for their fellow prisoners. Such works might serve as recognition of a fellow inmate's humanity, an attempt to offer a small act of kindness in a world of brutality, a flash of black humour. Certain images were made in an attempt to connect with the outside world, as part of organised resistance acts, conveying specific information, or the level of suffering.[9]

As documents, works of art from the Holocaust can teach on three levels. They often provide crucial information on the settings and situations of the victims, informing us about things little known, or even that no person lived to tell. David Olère depicted things in his drawings that no photograph ever captured; his images of the inside of the gas chambers have been used as evidence in courtrooms. While imprisoned at Auschwitz, one of many concentration camps to which he was sent, Olère was forced to work as a *Sonderkommando*, ordered by the Nazis to dispose of bodies murdered in the gas chambers and burned in the crematoria. In his 1945 drawing, *Selection for the Gas Chamber*, we witness SS and kapos coming to the bunks to casually record those next slated for extermination.[10]

At the same time, works such as Olère's move us and teach us on an emotional level, offering insights and a visceral connection that cannot be had in any other way. We learn from them in our hearts and in our bodies, as well as in our minds. Further, artworks from the Holocaust, no matter their subject, inform us about the struggle to remain human, to hold onto beauty, creativity, tradition, to some form of resistance to annihilation. "My commitment to drawing came out of a deep instinct of self-preservation," wrote Czech artist Alfred Kantor in 1971, "and undoubtedly helped me to deny the unimaginable horrors of that time."[11] Kantor survived both Terezín and Auschwitz.

224 *Laura Morowitz*

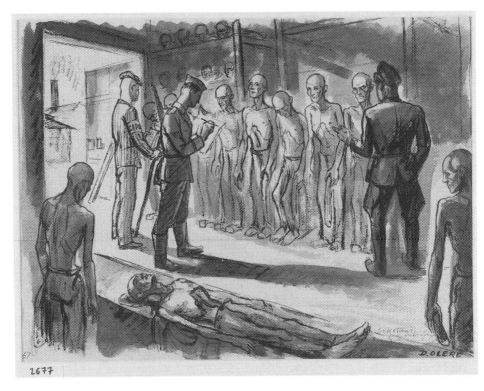

Figure 17.1 David Olère, *Selections for the Gas Chamber*, 30.8 × 42.4 cm, India ink and wash on paper, Memorial de la Shoah. Permission granted by Klarsfeld Foundation, Paris/NY.

Every work of art made by victims of the Holocaust is an act of resistance. Like the buried documents in the Ringelblum Archive in the Warsaw Ghetto, they testify to the lives of the persecuted and their urge to fight back against erasure. They serve both as a means and as a record, of survival. They are evidence of the artist's conviction to insist on the humanity of their fellow sufferers and often of themselves.

Subjects

Art of the Holocaust includes the full spectrum of subjects, from allegories to escapist dreamscapes to pure description. Not surprisingly, however, the images produced often focus on portraits, scenes of labour, brutality, daily life, sorrows, and death.

Portraits

A very large number of works produced during the Holocaust are portraits; indeed, a quarter of the works surviving from the camps consist of portraits.[12] Deprived of all other markers of identity—possessions, clothing, documents, even names—portraits testified to the existence of a person. A portrait is always a reference to an *individual*; indeed, there is no such thing as a portrait that neglects interest in the specific and unique. The very act of making someone's portrait repudiates the notion that their individuality has been obliterated. When we view these portraits, we must often do so with the heartbreak of knowing that the works escaped their fate while the individuals behind them did not.

Portraits were sometimes made for fellow inmates, to evoke a lost loved one, or to make them present for a moment. Interned in the Stutthof camp, artist Esther Lurie, born in Latvia and trained in Belgium, drew the portraits of fellow prisoners' boyfriends.[13] Sometimes portraits were the only reassurance to families that their loved one was still alive; in those cases, the artist might soften the signs of deprivation and violence to protect the relative. The scholar Mor Presiado notes that female artists sometimes beautified portraits as a way of obscuring the women's loss of femininity.[14]

Zofia Stępień-Bator, who drew fellow inmates in Auschwitz, noted later: "I attempted to make everything more pleasant. I did this because everything was so ugly, gray, and dirty ... In my portraits, the women were prettier, livelier, and all had more hair, there were no tragic expressions in their eyes."[15] For reasons both practical and psychological, artists often obsessively produced self-portraits. This was the case for artists alone in hiding or unable to entrust anyone to know about their covert act of drawing. Such images provided an outlet to the profound need to confirm one's own existence, through the work and through the recording of their individual physiognomy. For the viewer, confronting these portraits is an act of witnessing, especially when the portrait was the final trace of the artist's existence on earth.

Scenes and Recordings from Daily Life

Despite their harrowing situations, artists in the Holocaust were committed to recording their surroundings. As with Holocaust art in general, artists depicted their daily lives in every conceivable manner, from straightforward graphic depictions, to caricatures, to expressive abstractions. As documents, these works are beyond value and amongst the most vivid and informative records, we will ever have of the actual conditions, seen from the viewpoint of the victims, and are especially crucial and unique in two ways. For one thing, they show us things that are simply not recorded, imaged, or documented in any other way. Though fastidious documentarians, the Nazis left many events and moments uncaptured, sometimes as part of their work to cover their crimes, at other times because they simply did not think them important enough to document. Who was there, for example, to record the endless lines of victims being marched in to be gassed? The Nazis certainly had no interest in writing down or photographing moments of kindness or almost imperceptible resistance. Thus, these drawings give us access to elements and moments in the Holocaust that do not otherwise exist in record.

The second unique feature of these scenes is that the translation, or mediation, into art allows us to be able to view things we might not otherwise be able to bear. A photograph of the same subject might be too raw, too full of detail to witness.

Among the oft-repeated subjects and scenes depicted by Holocaust artists, Pnina Rosenberg lists the barbed-wire fences of the camps, interiors of prisoners' bunks (one of the few places where they might have been able to draw unobserved), attempts at bathing and bodily functions (particularly in the work of female artists), scenes of food (a not surprising preoccupation of the starving), and scenes of deportations.[16] These artists did not shy away from death and suffering all around them. In many of the ghettos, artists were called upon to record the conditions and activities, in a concerted attempt to document ghetto life.

226 *Laura Morowitz*

At times we might take what we see in these images as an intentional artistic distortion, the symbolic transcription of a nightmare. Yet they are in fact a document of the real. August Favier's *Block in the Little Camp at Buchenwald*, 1943, is one such image.[17] While a few dressed and recognisably human beings are visible in the foreground, the background shows the slats of bunks occupied by the bald, naked forms of skeletons, an array of the living dead attempting to stand or lie. This scene of hallucinatory horror is in fact a recording from life.

Escapist Scenes

For some artists, creating scenes of beauty, health, and freedom was a lifeline, often the only means of escape available to them and which they could offer others. Even in the most brutal of conditions, artists held on to their imaginations and produced surrealist flights of fancy or scenes of sunlit fields. Deported to Auschwitz on 3 April 1943, Czech artist Ewa Gabanyi created an album of 22 tiny drawings, entitled *A Calendar of Memories (Kalendarz wspomnień)*. The imagery that fills the phantasmagorical drawings includes fantastical landscapes, ornate balls, and majestic animals.[18] In ghettos, transit camps and in hiding, many artists created landscapes, either recalling distant places of beauty or transforming the harsh conditions around them into lyrical scenes[19] For perhaps a few seconds, these works provided an imaginary exit from hell.

Potential Problems with Using Works of Art as Documents

For all their astonishing value as documents of the Holocaust, works of art must be handled with care and we must be attuned to the potential issues that might arise in using them as such. While they *are* documents, they also transcend the category. What follows are some of the common difficulties that occur when dealing with visual art of the Shoah including the dangers of misinterpreting, oversimplifying, aestheticising, over-sentimentalising, or arriving at an emotional understanding at odds with historical realities.

First, *art is not a transparent record*. While it is tempting to see works of art as simple transcriptions of what the artist saw, they often are not. They speak in the language of art and often contain expressive distortion. Explanations like the following are cause for caution: "But these 'artists' were not interested in aesthetics or in creating a work of art, their principal aim was to record what *happened*. Mostly so that the perpetrators might be brought to justice."[20] We know from artists themselves that this was seldom the case. We know, through dozens of interviews, statements, and quotations, that the artists did not have the singular aim of recording things simply to bring the perpetrators to justice.

The relation between the "meaning" of a work and what is shown is also not transparent or fixed: a painting of man in red, for example, can mean many different things. Many students—and many historians—while skilled in the broader realm of visual literacy by simply living in a world overflowing with images, are not familiar with either formal analysis or iconographic decoding of paintings (and artists often refer to other works of art in their own creations). Viewers may tend to look for literal meaning in the images when their value lies elsewhere. An orderly, pleasant image may not reflect the conditions in which the artist lived, but instead bear testimony to their desire for escape, freedom, essential to the will to live. Malivina Schalkova's "Forced Labor in Theresien" 1943 shows a light-filled, agreeable scene, surely an attempt to provide a semblance of control over her surroundings that did not exist in actuality.[21]

Second, *art can be difficult to understand*. Works of visual art sometimes do not yield up their meanings easily. It can be frustrating to attempt to analyse a work which may not have a literal meaning. This is especially true for abstract works. But this very multiplicity or complexity of meaning is also part of the work's strength. Especially for students who may not read the language of an original document or literary text, artworks allow us "untranslated" access to an artist's vision, to truly see the world through their eyes.

Third, *our interpretation of a given work may not be a valid guide to the artist's own intentions*. If we wish to use a work of art from the Holocaust as a document, we must remain attuned to the circumstances and the intentions of the artist, as well as to the particular context of the work. What the viewer "feels" the artist was trying to say is not the same thing as knowing. As noted above, the most common or "easy" reading of a work may belie a more complicated one. When we insist on the fixed meaning of a work because that is how we "see" it, this might not foster real knowledge and could in fact stand in the way of it.

Some people might believe that learning about an artistic work or reading about it somehow "destroys" an authentic response or keeps people from responding to it on a "pure" level. If we are going to use the work as a documentary source, however, it is important that we learn as much about it as we can, not only about the artist (if information is available) but about the physical, emotional, sometimes economic, or mental or legal circumstances under which it was made. Was it traded for food? Meant to pass on vital information? A cry of pain? If we are fortunate enough to answer these questions our experience of the work is enhanced, not diminished, by this knowledge.

Finally, *works of art can trivialise or over-aestheticise the Holocaust*. This is a general caveat about works that take the Holocaust as their theme, and almost never applies to first-hand work made during the period. It may be true, however, of later works which include "documentary" elements such as photographs or objects or quotations. Memorials, for example, may speak in a heroic language that belongs to a pre-Holocaust world, and do little to communicate the raw suffering or sorrow of individual men and women. Many works that take the Shoah as their theme are over-simplified, or kitschy and do little to advance our understanding. Thousands of sculptures or paintings claim seriousness or profundity by taking on the theme of the Holocaust but teach us very little. This fact should make us appreciate even further the works made by survivors, both during and after the Holocaust, that possess the undeniable power of the witness.

Works of art from the Holocaust constitute a vast field, from eyewitness drawings, to memorials, to works created to serve Nazi ideology. Most such works are located in the United States, Israel, and Europe—but like Holocaust survivors, they are found throughout the world. The Yad Vashem Museum in Jerusalem alone has over 12,000 works, in a wide variety of media.[22] As with printed documents, the internet has radically altered our relationship to Holocaust art, providing access to excellent reproductions of images once only available in rare books or able to be seen in person. Those studying the Holocaust have virtual access to works by hundreds of artists addressing first-hand their experience of the Holocaust.

228   *Laura Morowitz*

Like all artworks, images from the Holocaust exist in two timeframes at once: the frame in which they were made, and the present in which we receive them. Both can be powerful ways to learn. We must always be careful about separating them.

Analysing Art of the Holocaust

To illustrate some of the themes involved in considering Holocaust art, we can examine closely certain works produced in varied sites and conditions from hiding, to ghettos, to transit and concentration camps, followed by works of post-memory.

Works of Art Made during the Holocaust

The most powerful documentary works of art were made by those who were victims, many of whom perished. Made both by professional artists and by amateurs, they are equal works of art and primary sources. Endowed with expressive power, we are moved by anyone's ability to make any works at all in those circumstances. In contrast to many photos from the Holocaust—almost always taken by someone in a position of power (or else, and very rarely, covertly)—these works allow us to "see" through the eyes of the oppressed. As such, they may be truthful without being an "objectively" accurate document. To be able to analyse and really understand the images requires that we know something of their circumstances. What does it show? For whom was it made? It is often very helpful if we know something about the artist, allowing us to know more about the work, but far too often we have little outside the work itself.

Works Made in Hiding

In the case of the powerful *oeuvre* of Felix Nussbaum (Osnabrück 1904-Auschwitz 1944) we know a great deal. Forced into hiding, he was imprisoned for a time in both St. Cyprien, escaped to Belgium, and was later caught and murdered at Auschwitz.[23] Due to his circumstances in hiding, he is one of the few artists who was able to create works in (slow drying) oil paint, supplied by his protectors and friends. Through work after work, with many self-portraits, we can chart the changes in his circumstances, his palpable fear, and his fierce struggle to survive against terrible odds, as in his *Self-Portrait with Jewish Identity Card* of 1943, where he holds the card and shows us his yellow Star of David, entrapped against a concrete wall.[24] Juxtaposed next to a leafless and limbless tree, Nussbaum included one sprouting new buds, a testimony to his refusal to give up hope. His paintings are of often allegorical and of incredible complexity and ambition, referencing the medieval *Todtentanz* (Dance of Death) and carnival to describe a world gone mad. His final work, *Triumph of Death* (1944), was created only months before his murder. Born in the town of Osnabrück, Germany, Nussbaum was studying art in Italy when the Nazis came to power, and he moved to Belgium in 1937. He was arrested in his apartment in May 1940 and taken for three months to the transit camp of St. Cyprien. Escaping, he returned to live in hiding in Belgium with his wife, artist Felka Platek, from 1940 until their arrest and deportation to Auschwitz in July 1944, where he was murdered on 9 August (a week after Felka).[25] What burns through his paintings is a terrible awareness of his fate and an unquenchable desire to live.

We see this in Nussbaum's *Self Portrait in St. Cyprien*.

Art as a Source for Studying the Holocaust 229

Figure 17.2 Felix Nussbaum, Self Portrait in the Camp, 1940, Credit: Found in the Neue Galerie N.Y. Photo credit: HIP/Art Resource, NY.

We must be careful not to assume it is an exact illustration; unlike many of the drawings below, it was not a recording done in a stolen moment on the spot. The question is not only what is it the artist "saw," but "what is it the artist wishes to convey?" Clues in the painting tell us, in the context of studying the Holocaust, that we are in a camp, and from Nussbaum's other works, that this is St. Cyprien. It reflects the real conditions of the camp, with the figures succumbing to disease, death, and despair. No sign of life or hope appears in the space, a barren, barbed-wire-enclosed expanse of sand littered with bones and skulls. At the left, a figure in rags sits, head in hands, at a rotting table before an ugly makeshift shelter. At the right, a half-naked figure defecates in a tin can and a bewildered, emaciated figure appears to be frozen in place. Dressed in dirty, frayed, and torn prison garb, Nussbaum nearly forces himself into our space. One of the most piercing aspects of the work, and one that closes the gap in time between the viewer and the artist, is Nussbaum's face, half in shadow. The direct stare from his right eye is nearly impossible to avoid. It is both a stare of accusation and grief, and a defiant assertion of his humanity. He is so directly present that we feel the life force and suffering of this man boring into our conscience.

Nussbaum has ingeniously stripped down the chaotic reality and filtered out the inessential to focus our attention on a few disorienting elements that quickly convey a place of utter despair, barbarism, and dehumanisation. We are at once aware of the horrifying conditions of imprisonment, and of the genius and consciousness of the artist who carefully composed the balanced composition and carefully observed self-portrait. There is no document, no photograph, and no description of St. Cyprien that brings us into that world like the swallowing eye of Felix Nussbaum, which fixes on us for eternity.

Works Made in Ghettos

Thousands of works of art were created in the many ghettos where Jews struggled to survive amidst disease, starvation, and despair. In the ghettos of Kovno, Lodz and Warsaw, among others, Jews kept alive their culture and artistic life against all odds, writing newspapers, performing plays and concerts, creating schools and libraries. Artworks produced in the ghettos served every conceivable function, from documenting scenes of unfathomable cruelty and terror, to providing a few minutes of escape, to bearing witness. In several of the ghettos, underground groups and organisations created archives where works were stored in hopes of future discovery.

Since it occupied a unique place as a "model ghetto"—one where nevertheless the vast majority of its inhabitants were deported to murder—we will start with art produced in the ghetto camp of Terezín (Theresienstadt), outside of Prague. The ghetto functioned between 1941 and 1945 and was intended to convince the outside world and agencies such as the Red Cross that such places were humane and liveable, with fully developed cultural programmes. Beneath the facade, however, 33,000 people died of disease and lack of food; of the 140,000 people who passed through its gates, 90,000 were deported East to killing centres and extermination camps. Of the 15,000 children sent to Terezín, barely a few hundred survived the war.[26]

Due to its unique propagandistic function, cultural activities were mandated at Terezín, and as a result thousands of visual works survive. Well-known actors, designers, and artists were sent there to staff the various workshops and studios. While creating the works demanded by their Nazi captors, many of these artists also created covert works that were used to document the actual conditions. Such was the case with a group of artists assigned to the *Zeichenstube* (Technical-Graphic Department), who managed to smuggle out works to the Red Cross. Upon discovery, SS lieutenant colonel Adolf Eichmann came to the camp and personally interrogated the artists; all of them were deported to their deaths, except for Leo Haas who managed to survive Auschwitz and Mauthausen.[27]

One of the best known of Terezín's prisoners was the brilliant Viennese-born Friedl Dicker-Brandeis. Dicker-Brandeis had studied at the Bauhaus and carried this pedagogy into her art workshops in Terezín, to which she was deported on December 16, 1942. She taught art to thousands of young girls there and managed to save the work of 660 of them, totalling 4,500 images, by smuggling them in two suitcases to Raja Engländerova, a fellow tutor there.[28] Encouraging their imagination and offering them art as a form of therapy and a temporary respite from suffering, the works created by "Friedl's girls" breathe with the life, creativity and beauty of the young girls who made them. Works like Helena Mändlová's (1930–1944) *Undated* (1943), a paper collage that forms a cityscape with stars, conveys a kind of hope and humanity. It was alongside many of her

Art as a Source for Studying the Holocaust 231

students that Dicker-Brandeis was deported to Auschwitz on 6 October 1944, where she was murdered three days later. Most of the children she taught were also deported and murdered. Like reading the *Diary of Anne Frank*, the heartbreak of viewing these works by Friedl's students comes from their innocence suspended in an eternal present and the knowledge of their murder and loss.

Though not taught by her, Helga Weissova lived in the building assigned to Friedl's girls and created over 100 drawings that she made with materials she had managed to transport from home. Helga arrived at Terezín at the age of 12 and remained until being deported to Auschwitz at the age of 15.[29] Her uncle hid her drawings inside the walls of the Magdeburg Barracks in Terezín.

Figure 17.3 Helga Weissova, *Transport Leaving Terezin*, 1943, coloured pencil on paper. Collection of the Museum of Jewish Heritage—A Living Memorial of the Holocaust, 214.88 NYC.

Weissova's *Transport Leaving Terezin* gives us something we would not otherwise have, a recording of the scene through the eyes of a child.[30]

It is at once a document and a view into Helga's existence. Leaving out details of setting and anatomy, Helga conveyed what most impacted her: the crowd gathered to say goodbye and prevented from doing so by the guards. We cannot know how reflective this is of the actual number of individuals, but its meaning is clear: The sense of two individuals torn from a community that mourns their deportation, the need to testify to their love and concern in the face of dehumanisation, the importance, even in this setting, of communal support. It resonates as the drawing, rendered in a clearly childlike manner, reminds us that this event is being experienced by a child, one whose overwhelming odds are that her destiny will be the same. This knowledge makes the scene doubly painful.

232 *Laura Morowitz*

In the ghettos of Vilna and Kovno, dozens of courageous artists continued to record the full spectrum of life behind the walls. A former professional artist, Esther Lurie (1913–1998) was commissioned by the Council of Elders (*Ältestenrat*) to create a visual documentation of the Kovno ghetto.[31]

Figure 17.4 Esther Lurie, Portrait of Chaim Nachman Shapiro, Kovno. Ghetto, 1942, ink on paper, 11.5 × 8.3. Collection of Yad Vashem Museum, Jerusalem. Gift of Avraham and Pnina Tory Collection. Photo credit: Yad Vashem Musuem, Jerusalem.

Lurie remembered:

> Henceforward I set out to sketch whatever seemed important to me; but this was not a simple or easy undertaking, for it was dangerous to do any sketching in the streets ... strangers agreed to permit me to paint from the window of their home ... The people of the house were friendly and concerned. "What should be done to make sure that your pictures will survive?" they used to ask.[32]

Favoured for her talents, her Nazi guard allowed her to have a studio, and acceded to her request to draw in the pottery studio. She had the foresight to order the creation of large ceramic pots, in which she hid over 200 of her watercolours and drawings, mostly 25 × 35 cm, during 1943 as the *Aktionen* and deportations increased. Some of the drawings were also photographed for the ghetto's secret *Slobodka* archive. In the summer of 1944, Lurie was deported to the labour camps of Stutthof and Leibitz, where she continued to draw, sometimes bartering her works for a bit of extra food, which helped her to survive. At the Eichmann trial, Lurie's 11 rescued works and 20 photographic reproductions were used as evidence.

The terror and sadness of the deportations were a common subject rendered by artists in the ghettos. Halina Olumucki's *The Liquidation of Dr. Korczak's Orphanage* (1941–1943) depicts the heart-breaking event in the Warsaw Ghetto. In front, the doctor carries a small child, followed by an endless line of children, the older ones holding the hands of the littlest, the only details their downturned eyes and mouths and their fearful steps.

Figure 17.5 Hirsch Sylis, Landscape in the Lodz Ghetto After Aktion 1942, crayon on cardboard 70.5 × 82 cm, Yad Vashem Museum. Photo credit: Yad Vashem Art Museum, Jerusalem.

Hirsh Szylis's *Lodz Ghetto After a Deportation* (1942) expresses the mood of loss through the heavy shadows, an overturned chair and abandoned cart in the courtyard, windows and doors gaping open to reveal a place emptied of human life but haunted by those who have disappeared.

234 *Laura Morowitz*

Works Made in Detention and Transit Camps

Amid the constant waiting and fear in the detention and transit camps spread throughout Western Europe, artists created works. In nearly all of them, exhaustion, despair, and boredom are palpable. The utter lack of privacy, constant hunger, and deprivation can be seen in scenes of figures huddled in dirty blankets or walking aimlessly among barbed-wire fences and decaying structures. In a few of the camps, such as Gurs in the south of France, the Red Cross was allowed in and brought supplies, allowing for artworks in more complex media. As viewers of these works, we feel a special desperation because we know the fate that awaits the subjects and the creators, even if they could not.

Pnina Rosenberg points out that in images drawn by women in the transit camps, such as Emmy Falck-Ettlinger (1882–1960) in Gurs, or Jeanne Lévy (1894–1944) in Drancy, we see scenes and interiors characterised by orderliness, often neat and clean. Such scenes are less reflective of reality than of a need to impose normalcy and control in places where they were utterly absent. Like the many "recipe books" women produced in the concentration camps,[33] these images testify to the attempt to cling to their lives and identities before imprisonment, to hold on to aspects of the self that were nearly impossible to maintain in those conditions.[34]

The German artist Karl Schwesig (1898–1955) was not Jewish but imprisoned for his political activities, including caricatures of prominent Nazis, and survived four camps in the south of France, including St Cyprien and Gurs. In addition to recording scenes of everyday life and landscapes, and portraits of fellow inmates, he produced a series of tiny, fake "stamps," 1 × 1.5 inches, now housed in the Leo Baeck Institute in New York.[35]

Figure 17.6 Karl Scheswig, 4 mock stamps from Gurs camp, 1940, 2.5 × 4 cm. Photo credit: Courtesy of Leo Baeck Insititute, New York.

Art as a Source for Studying the Holocaust 235

The stamps show the perversion of the concepts of *"Liberté, Égalité, Fraternité,"* for example, with the depiction of a giant boot kicking a Jewish man into the barbed-wire fence. These works document defiance, the ability to maintain irony, black humour, and social commentary in places intended to erase the human spirit.

Works Made in Concentration Camps

In the concentration and extermination camps spread throughout Eastern Europe, works of art were created under conditions of exhaustion, starvation, physical agony, and daily terror. That they were made, let alone that they were found, is nearly unfathomable. They depict details and emotions of utter darkness existing in no other documents.[36]

In the camps, artists were commanded to produce signs, maps, illustrations, and so on in the *Aufbaukommando* (Construction) and *Technische Abteilung* (Technical Divisions) departments, as well as for the "pleasure" of their captors, such as New Year cards or decoration of living quarters. Dinah Gottliebova Babbit (1923–2009) was forced to draw Roma women in Birkenau as examples of "ethnic types," while other artists were required to draw twins undergoing horrifying experiments. After her deportation to Auschwitz-Birkenau, Halina Olomucki (1919–2007) was employed in producing signs as a *Stubendienst* ("room orderly") but covertly made over 200 drawings, hiding them in the barracks, many beneath floorboards. To save himself between 1941 and 1943, the artist Franciszek Targosz convinced the camp commander of Auschwitz, Rudolf Höss, to allow the establishment of a museum at the camp for the amusement of the staff. The *Lagermuzeum* displayed the works of Nazi-approved art and looted objects, including portraits and ceramics that had been made by prisoners.[37]

We may never know the identity of the man who produced the Auschwitz Sketchbook and signed it only with his initials, MM. In a clear and simple drawing style, he produced 22 pages depicting every horror from selections, to beatings, to forced labour. Folios A through D show the full stages of murder from transport to the crematoria, with an SS officer casually smoking outside the building. In these drawings, as in those of David Olère, referred to earlier, we see a very rare image of things the Nazis kept well hidden. Someone, perhaps the artist himself, secreted the sketchbook in a bottle and buried it in the foundation of the hospital barracks, the *Häftlingskrankenbou* at Birkenau.[38] The artist Zoran Music also drew the corpses and crematoria of Dachau, using the only media available to him, the rust from the bars of his prison cell.

A few weeks after her arrival at Auschwitz on April 27, 1942, Ewa Gabanyi (1913–1942?) created a picture entitled *First Soup in the Camp*. It was one of 22 small drawings comprising a *Memories Calendar*, many of which show subject matter which is fantastical or difficult to understand. The overpowering need to produce this image in the camp testifies to the obsessive hunger that always drove the inmates. It is possible that even this scene reflects a desire rather than reality.

As noted, portraits in the camp were so precious they were often traded for a slice of bread, which at times meant the difference between life and death. Many of the artists who passed through Auschwitz somehow drew portraits of fellow inmates or their loved ones and managed to hide them, fulfilling the dying wishes of their fellow prisoners.[39] Halina Olumucki claimed that the faces of those she drew in the camp still haunted her years later:

> If I ever do an exhibition I will always exhibit some paintings, some portraits of those women ... because this is the obligation I took upon myself, that always those daughters of those women will be there, as they asked me back in Birkenau.[40]

In 1944 Susan Weiss had her portrait done by a fellow inmate, Manci Anis, in a labour subcamp of Buchenwald.

Figure 17.7 Manci Anis, Portrait of Susan Weiss, 1944. Coloured pencil and pencil on paper. Collection of the Museum of Jewish Heritage—A Living Memorial of the Holocaust, NYC. Gift of Susan Welber.

Rendered in pencil on a small piece of graph paper, Weiss hid the drawing under her mattress and later in her uniform during a death march, which she survived with her sister. In contrast, we know nothing about the artist beyond her name, not even Anis's fate. All we have left of her is this drawing. When we look at it, we see for a moment through Anis's eyes, we feel her powers of observation, her deep compassion, her connection, the lifeline of humanity she offered to Weiss. For those reasons, she is not forgotten, nor is her existence erased.

Other images made in the camps defy categorisation and seem to render things impervious to language. Josef Szajna's "The Roll Call Last Very Long ... My Feet Hurt a Lot" may not be recognised without its title, but once it is known to us, we realise how

Art as a Source for Studying the Holocaust   237

closely the artist captured the experience.[41] Rather than the realistic details, Szajna depicts the endless, boundless waiting, the psychological distancing. The prisoners are no longer fully human, but faceless, nearly bodiless entities, consisting only of their prison stripes, their utter lack of individuality. There is no time, no space. Like the existence in the camps themselves, the drawing defies rational description or full comprehension.

Works by Survivors of the Holocaust

Works of art made by survivors that post-date the Holocaust are no less documents, for they testify to first-hand witnessing of things seen and experienced. As Sylvia Blatter noted, such works are often even grimmer and more difficult to see because the artist may no longer need such distancing technique, and indeed was often using the works themselves to attempt to process unspeakable grief, terror, and mourning.[42] A far wider array of materials, and much more time, was available to attempt to capture their experiences in images. For those studying such works, it is important to remember that, like oral testimonies, the truth value of these documents might not lie in their descriptive accuracy or their correspondence to reality, but the truth of *their* experience. Any deviations from "fact" are the result of distance from the conditions under which the events were experienced, or of the need to give coherence to something traumatic and nearly unrepresentable.

While some artists, like Alfred Kantor, created detailed narratives right after liberation, other artists took years before they could begin to confront their

Figure 17.8 Edith Birkin, *The Death Cart in Lodz Ghetto*, acrylic on hardboard 914 × 712 mm. Copyright: Edith Birkin. Photo credit: IWM Imperial War Museums.

experiences.[43] In 1980, 35 years after her liberation from Bergen-Belsen, Edith Birken created this searing, nightmarish image of Lodz Ghetto. *The Death-Cart, Lodz Ghetto* renders the desperate, morbid environment of the ghetto in deep purples and blues.

The ghetto's occupants, who wrap the bodies for the death cart, are no less dead than they, their faces skeletal, their eyes hollowed out with terror. Every window and doorway is black. Skulls peer from the windows; we know it is only a matter of time until they, too, are loaded on the carts. In the doorway a woman stands holding a child, her face contorted into an endless scream. If the painting speaks in the language of Expressionism, it is hardly less truthful. Indeed, no photograph that surfaces will ever be able to match the visceral "reality" of Lodz at that time as well as Birkin's image.[44]

Zoran Music's *We are not the Last* is an etching made in 1970 and tells us virtually nothing about the specifics of the Holocaust.

Figure 17.9 Zoran Music, *We Are not the Last*, 1970, etching on paper 472 × 347 mm. Zoran Music@ AGDAP Paris and DACS London. Photo credit: Tate London.

Here Music's descriptive memory is replaced by an almost unbearable grief and torment, by a cry of universal anguish. The figure depicted is perhaps male, but, shaven and starving, who can presume? He or she lies on the ground, as much corpse as a living human being. And yet for all its lack of detail, it uncannily evokes the concentration camp as "another planet." What is the meaning of the title? Is it that he, his generation, is not the last to suffer? Is it meant as a warning? Or instead, is it an act of resistance to the Nazi project of annihilating the Jews, a message that even those millions of dead will not be the last of their people? It is impossible to know. Instead, music has created a visual embodiment, a tiny inkling, of what it feels like to be the living dead.

Conclusion

It is precisely the emotional power of art that makes it an important complement to learning about the Holocaust, and perhaps most so when it is simultaneously a document of experience. These visual documents never attempt to convey the totality of the Holocaust (and we should be wary of any work of art that tries). Instead, by nature of the visual arts, they convey the singularity of one person's perception, but connected to a form of human communication that precedes written language by centuries, if not millennia. Works of art made in the context of the Holocaust are documents, and always assertions of humanity in the face of dehumanisation.

If oral testimony does not give us the "truth" of the Holocaust, but only its effects on the survivor, certainly this is even more applicable in art, where "facts" do not exist, only their subjective transcription. Moreover, works of art exist in many time frames at once: the time of their making, and the always immediate time of our viewing and experiencing them. In a way that records, legal artefacts, and testimonies cannot, works of visual art give form to the indescribable and unfathomable, allowing us to grasp, even if just for the moment of viewing, a terror and loss that lie beyond language.

Notes

1 I am grateful to Lori Weintrob for her careful reading of this chapter and for her insightful questions and suggestions.
2 Quoted in G. Sujo, *Legacies of Silence: The Visual Arts and Holocaust Memory*, London: Phillip Wilson Publishers, 2003, p. 10.
3 S. Milton, "The Legacy of Holocaust Art," in J. Blatter and S. Milton (ed.), *Art of the Holocaust*, New York: Rutledge Press, 1981, pp. 36–43.
4 These are part of the Leo Baeck Institute Repository, AR 2273. Housed at the Centre for Jewish History, New York.
5 Milton, "The Legacy of Holocaust Art," p. 26.
6 I. Howe, introduction to Blatter and Milton, *Art of the Holocaust*, p. 11.
7 "Art of the Ghettos and Camps," *A Teacher's Guide to the Holocaust*. Florida Center for Instructional Technology, University of South Florida, available online at https://fcit.usf.edu/holocaust/arts/artVicti.htm.
8 P. Rosenberg, "Art During the Holocaust," *The Shalvi/Hyman Encyclopedia of Jewish Women*, The Jewish Women's Archive, available online at https://jwa.org/encyclopedia/article/art-during-holocaust.
9 P. Rosenberg, "Art in the Ghettos and Concentration Camps During the Holocaust," *Art and the Holocaust, Documenta*, available online at http://documenta-akermariano.blogspot.com/2014/01/5.html.

10 P. Rosenberg, "David Olère 1902–1985," *Learning about the Holocaust Through Art*, World Art and Beit Lohamei Hagetaot. 2001, available online at https://art.holocaust-education.net/explore.asp?langid=1&submenu=200&id=37. In 2018 the State Museum Auschwitz-Birkenau held an exhibit, curated by Agnieszka Sieradzka, devoted to Olère's work, entitled "David Olère. The one who survived from Crematorium III."

11 "Rendering Witness: Holocaust-Era Art as Testimony," *Museum of Jewish Heritage—A Living Memorial to the Holocaust*, 2021, available online at https://mjhnyc.org/exhibitions/rendering-witness-holocaust-era-art-as-testimony/.

12 Blatter and Milton, *Art of the Holocaust*, p. 28; P. Rosenberg, "Art During the Holocaust."

13 Rosenberg, "Art in the Ghettos and Concentration Camps."

14 M. Presiado, "A New Perspective on Holocaust Art: Women's Artistic Expression of the Female Holocaust Experience, 1939–1949," *Holocaust Studies: A Journal of Culture and History* 22:4, 2016, pp. 417–46.

15 Stępień-Bator quoted in ibid., p. 429.

16 Rosenberg, "Art in the Ghettos and Concentration Camps."

17 Collection of Robert Favier, 1943. Reproduced in Blatter and Milton, *Art of the Holocaust*, p. 153. The "Little Camp" consisted of a set of stables into which 2,000 prisoners were crammed.

18 P. Rosenberg, "Artists Confront their Past: Olère, Liberman-Shriber, and Bueno da Mesquita," *Learning about the Holocaust Through Art*, World Art and Beit Lohamei Hagetaot, 2001, available online at http://art.holocaust-education.net/learn.asp?langid=1&submenu=3&essayid=8#5t.

19 "Landscapes: The Art Collection," *Yad Vashem Art Museum*, available online at https://www.yadvashem.org/yv/en/exhibitions/art-landscapes/index.asp.

20 Quoted from "Holocaust Art," *Encyclopedia of Art Education*, available online at http://www.visual-arts-cork.com/definitions/holocaust-art.htm.

21 Malvina Schalkova, "Forced Labor in Theresienstadt", 1943. Watercolor, 12x 17 ½ ". Jerusalem: Ghetto Fighters House.

22 "The Art Collection," *Yad Vashem Museum*, available online at https://www.yadvashem.org/museum/museum-complex/art/collection.html.

23 E. Berger et al, *Felix Nussbaum: Art Defamed, Art in Exile, Art in Resistance: A Biography*, New York: Overlook Press, 1997.

24 The work is owned by the museum dedicated to the artist, the Felix Nussbaum Haus, Osnabrück, Germany. See https://www.museumsquartier-osnabrueck.de/.

25 I thank Lori Weintrob for relaying to me that Felka was murdered before Felix.

26 H.G. Adler, B. Cooper, A. Loewenhaar-Blauweiss, and J.D Adler, *Theresienstadt, 1941–1945: The Face of a Coerced Community*, New York: Cambridge University Press, 2017. Estimates on the number of children who survived Terezin vary from one hundred to one thousand.

27 P. Rosenberg, "Leo Hass (1901–1938)" Learning *about the Holocaust Through Art*, available online at https://art.holocaust-education.net/explore.asp?langid=1&submenu=200&id=14.

28 E. Makarova, *From Bauhaus to Terezin: Friedl Dicker-Brandeis and her Pupils*, Jerusalem: Yad Vashem, 1990.

29 "Helga Hošková-Weissová and Drawings: An Exhibition for the Artist's 80th Birthday," *Jewish Museum in Prague*, 2009, available online at https://www.jewishmuseum.cz/en/program-and-education/exhibits/archive-exhibits/88/.

30 "Artwork: Child's Drawing of Transport Leaving Terezin, 1943," Museum of Jewish Heritage Holocaust Curriculum, *Museum of Jewish Heritage: A Living Memorial to the Holocaust*, available online at https://education.mjhnyc.org/artifacts/artwork-childs-drawing-of-transport-leaving-terezin/.

31 Rosenberg, "Art During the Holocaust."

32 P. Rosenberg, "Esther Lurie (1913–1998)," *Learning about the Holocaust through Art*, available online at http://art.holocaust-education.net/explore.asp?langid=1&submenu=200&id=6#3f.

33 "Cookbooks and Recipes," *Holocaust Encyclopedia: The United States Holocaust Memorial Museum*. Last edited April 22, 2020, available online at https://encyclopedia.ushmm.org/content/en/article/cookbooks-and-recipes.

34 Rosenberg, "Art During the Holocaust."

35 *Karl Schwesig: Leben und Werk*, Galerie Remmert und Barth, Düsseldorf, Frölich and Kaufmann, Berlin, 1984.
36 M.S. Constanza. *Living Witness: Art in the Concentration Camps and Ghettos*, New York: The Free Press, 1982. For works made by women in the camps see the work of Mor Presiado.
37 Stefan Ludwik Aloszko, "Auschwitz: Art, Commemoration and Memorialisation: 1940 to the Present day," PhD thesis, University of Plymouth, 2011, 66–78, available online at https://core.ac.uk/download/pdf/29817233.pdf.
38 K. Uhl, "The Auschwitz Sketchbook," in D. Mickenberg, C. Granof, and P. Hayes (ed.), *The Last Expression: Art and Auschwitz*, Evanston: Northwestern University Press, 2003.
39 Among these artists are Franciszek Jaźwiecki (d. 1946), Xawery Dunikowski (1875–1964), and Mieczyslaw Koscielniak (1912–1993).
40 P. Rosenberg, "Halina Olomucki (1919-)," *Learning About the Holocaust Through Art*. Available online at https://art.holocaust-education.net/explore.asp?langid=1&submenu=200&id=5.
41 The image is reproduced in Blatter and Milton, *Art of the Holocaust*, p. 148.
42 Ibid., p. 35.
43 *The Book of Alfred Kantor*, New York: McGraw Hill, 1971, forms an entire diary of images in watercolour and ink from his captivity in Theresienstadt and Auschwitz.
44 "Artists' responses to the Holocaust," *Imperial War Museum*, London, available online at https://www.iwm.org.uk/history/artists-responses-to-the-holocaust.

Part IV
Epilogue

18 Thinking About and Using Documents From the Perpetrators

Beth Griech-Polelle

For most people, thinking about the Holocaust means realising that terrible, unimaginable suffering took place at the hands of the Nazis and their collaborators. But generally knowing that tragic atrocities took place is somewhat different from reading about these crimes on a regular basis. Delving into primary source accounts for research or for teaching students means confronting the shocking reality of the everyday occurrences of sheer inhumanity and brutality that make up the reality of genocide. As scholars–teachers–students, how do we make sense of what we are reading? How do we transmit our responses to such violent descriptions so that students can somehow process the material we wish them to learn? There are no simple answers to such questions and most individuals will have to wrestle with these questions when teaching or learning about the Holocaust (or any genocide).

For many historians in the immediate post-war era, reading documents of violent actions taken by perpetrators, as shocking and horrible as they were, could serve a much larger purpose: that of bringing perpetrators' names and actions to light so that an investigation might be opened to bestow some sense of justice and closure to survivors. Now, nearly eight decades on, historians must recognise that locating perpetrators who are still alive is, at best, a long shot. That means that reading through eyewitness accounts of the crimes perpetrated leaves one often with the unsettling feeling that many perpetrators escaped any reckoning, except perhaps, with their own consciences. So, if reading primary source documents will not lead to a sense of legal closure or at least reach the end goal of bringing a perpetrator to account for his or her crimes, what are we left with as researchers and teachers?

In some instances, one could at least achieve a sense of historical justice when looking at primary source documents. For example, one could read Wendy Lower's 2021 publication, *The Ravine: A Family, A Photograph, A Holocaust Massacre Revealed*. In this case, Lower came across a rare photograph depicting smoke still coming from the barrels of guns being fired at victims in front of a pit in Ukraine. The faces of many of the killers were visible—some were Germans, and some were Ukrainians—and Lower began her search to uncover the identities of the perpetrators as well as the identities of the woman and two children being executed in the picture. Her work takes the readers on an odyssey stretching over several continents, utilising various search techniques to locate the execution site. She also brought in other experts such as forensic archaeologists and specialists in photographic analysis, to attempt to uncover the identities and fates of those in the photograph. Lower's passion, in the end, allows the historian to resolve some of the questions she had regarding the photograph, and it leads to the official documentation of the site of execution.[1]

DOI: 10.4324/9781003248620-23

Ultimately Lower's work allows the reader to experience the sense of some justice being meted out to the perpetrators, and it also gives names to some of the other victims of that specific killing action. Carrying out this type of dedicated research with just a photograph to reference takes years of commitment, energy, and resources to which most scholars will simply not have access in their careers, but the feeling of exposing criminal behaviour provides a true sense of historical justice taking place before our very eyes.

As a teacher–scholar with limited time and resources, one might never have the opportunity to pursue such an endeavour like Lower has done; but using published works of primary source documents can be energising even if one is not able to have that sense of historical justice. In fact, using some documents can allow one to harness the utter outrage one feels upon reading such inhumanity and transforming that outrage into energy for teaching. Years ago, as a relatively new teacher, I assigned the document collection edited by Ernst Klee, Willi Dressen, and Volker Riess, *"'The Good Old Days': The Holocaust as Seen by Its Perpetrators and Bystanders*, for an undergraduate class I was teaching in Ohio. To this day, I can still remember the powerful reaction my students had to one particular set of documents and the supercharged discussion that followed.

In this account, the scene is set in a Ukrainian village, Byelaya Tserkov (Bialacerkiew) and it is August 1941. We are told by the editors that the German military leader in the area requested that the *Sonderkommando* come to carry out an *Aktion* against the Jewish inhabitants of the village. As historians, we are unfortunately accustomed to encountering these types of atrocities. However, the documents took an unexpected turn in the minds of many of the students. The account continues with information on the units of *Waffen-SS* and local Ukrainian militia murdering hundreds of Jewish men and women and then taking approximately 90 of the youngest children, ranging in age from a few months old to 5–6 years of age, to be housed in a local building. The youngsters were left almost completely unattended with only a Ukrainian guard stationed at the door. The conditions inside were unimaginable with the young children crying from neglect and hunger.

Eventually a Catholic military chaplain, Ernst Tewes, and a Protestant colleague, Gerhard Wilczek, were approached by a German soldier, asking them to investigate the condition of the children. At this point, most students immediately assumed that the military chaplains, out of a basic sense of Christian charity, would intervene to save the lives of the 90 or so defenceless children. The two military chaplains visited the building and then reported to their local superior, Dr. Reuss, who subsequently went to personally investigate the scene. Dr. Reuss's report describes the wretched conditions of the rooms, the suffering and whimpering of the children, and then Reuss, also a chaplain, submitted his report to military officials. In his report, Reuss affirms the inhuman conditions, the total lack of sanitation or availability of water, and then points out that German soldiers were able to enter and exit the house to see for themselves what the crying was all about. Reuss recommends that something be done immediately to "remedy the situation" as the lack of hygiene could result in the outbreak of an epidemic that might spread to the German troops. He adds for good measure the reminder that anyone from the German army could enter and observe what was happening, implying that seeing defenseless children in such a state might offend the morale of the Wehrmacht soldiers.

Several documents then follow, as the complaints and questions regarding the status of the young children go up the chain of command. Ultimately the decision is made by

Paul Blobel, a German *Sicherheitsdienst* (SD) commander, best remembered as the man who planned and carried out the horrendous Babi Yar executions in September 1941. Blobel orders August Häfner to organise the *Waffen-SS* to transport the children to a nearby pit to be executed. Häfner suggests using local Ukrainian militia to carry out the shooting since his German men have children (!), and Häfner's account of 22 August 1941 states, "I went out to the woods alone. The *Wehrmacht* had already dug a grave. The children were brought along in a tractor ... The Ukrainians were standing round trembling. The children were taken down from the tractor. They were lined up along the top of the grave and shot so that they fell into it."[2] Häfner also recalled the crying of the victims, stating, "I find it very hard to bear. I particularly remember a small fair-haired girl who took me by the hand. She too was shot later."[3]

As one can imagine, the images of such young children, close enough to hold perpetrators' hands before being taken to the edge of a pit to be shot, almost makes one lose all faith in human goodness. For students reading such a series of horrendous accounts, they simply could not get over the role of military chaplains in the unfolding tragedy. Although the chaplains were not part of the shooting party, they certainly played a pivotal role in setting off the chain of events that led to the murder of the children. Particularly disheartening for the students was the information provided by the editors that both Chaplain Tewes and Dr. Reuss were ordained as bishops in the Catholic Church after the war had ended.[4]

As difficult as reading these accounts is, students had quite a lengthy discussion about Nazi ideology and propaganda and how it might have impacted the views of the German soldiers, the military chaplains, officers in the Wehrmacht, and so on. They also recognised the subservient position of the Ukrainian militia to the Nazi occupiers, and students frequently noted how the Germans were more than eager to let the Ukrainians get their hands dirty with such a despicable action against children. The series of documents allowed us to discuss the issues of post-war justice (or the lack thereof) particularly in the case of the Catholic chaplain and his superior. These types of document collections which provide the reader with a multitude of perspectives evoke anger, frustration, and disappointment in the students, but they also allow all of us to see the complex nature of what exactly was taking place in this case on Germany's eastern front. I often found it useful to repeat Christopher R. Browning's maxim, "Understanding is not forgiving."[5]

Browning's *Ordinary Men: Reserve Police Battalion 101 and the Final Solution in Poland*, while not a collection of primary source documents, still provides readers with the eyewitness reports of atrocities being carried out by the Reserve Police Battalion 101 and local collaborators. What shocks the conscience is the repeated lists of numbers of Jewish victims and the "game" that existed among competing *Einsatz* units to see which unit could kill more Jews. As one reads Browning's work, the psychological and physical issues that the Reserve Police officers often experience pales in comparison to the fate of their victims, yet even the perpetrators must be examined as complex human beings who are performing hideous work in the name of a perceived "greater cause." This is particularly jarring to have to consider: that the men performing the murders were not simply machines set in motion to fulfil a task. Instead, one must consider their own sense of agency (of lack thereof), their personal fears of punishment for disobeying orders, and the toll that many did experience owing to their participation in genocide. As distasteful as this as, since most of us would prefer to think that had we been placed in such extreme situations, we would have protested, evaded orders, and resisted, but the evidence simply does not support this.

Most of those who Browning studies in *Ordinary Men* are, just as the title states, "ordinary" in that they were not young men who had been heavily indoctrinated with Nazi ideology from an early age. Moreover, none volunteered to kill Jews, and none sought out the assignment to murder. To quote Browning's own explanation of why he wanted to study and understand the motivations of the killers, "What I do not accept, however, are the old cliches that to explain is to excuse, to understand is to forgive. Explaining is not excusing, understanding is not forgiving. Not trying to understand the perpetrators in human terms would make impossible not only this study but any history of Holocaust perpetrators that sought to go beyond one-dimensional caricature."[6] In order to truly capture and re-create some of the historical lived experience, one must be able to think of the perpetrators as more than cartoonish characters. This makes them truly even more frightening because then one must grapple with the dark realisation that anyone of us could, at any time, become a perpetrator given the right circumstances.

What can also be extremely challenging is trying to balance the numerous surviving *Einsatzgruppen* reports, some of which blandly list numbers of Jewish men, women and children killed with no further details provided. These lists come with the knowledge that we, as historians, will never have the full account of the events from the perspectives of the much more numerous victim group. To take a typical, early report from *Einsatzgruppe A*, located in Riga during August 1941 (just two months into the invasion of Soviet territory), one can read the following in the operational situation report transmitted to Berlin: "Special actions (*Sonderaktionen*) were carried out as follows: July 22, 1941: Pagirai: 1 Jew liquidated; July 23, 1941: Kedainiai: 125 persons (83 Communist Jews, 12 Communist Jewesses, 14 Russian and 15 Lithuanian Communist officials, 1 Politruk liquidated); 25 July 1941: Mariampol: 103 Jews (90 men, 13 women) liquidated." The list continues through killings on August 2, 1941. The report notes that between 22 July and 3 August, 1,592 people had been "liquidated."[7] Here one is simply left with the demoralising thought: what were the names and ages of the victims and what might their last thoughts have been, what were their lives like before this tragedy, and so on. Although there are some survivor accounts from *Einsatzgruppen* actions, they are simply outnumbered by the number of victims who did not survive and who died nameless in an unmarked pit. As historians, we must always remind our students that we will never have the entire picture of these killings, because the perpetrators gave their victims no opportunities to record final thoughts. This means we are forced to recognise the incompleteness of the historical record and that the Nazi attempt to erase their victims' voices from history were in some ways successful.

From the language used in these types of situational reports, one can also see Nazi ideology at work as the authors of the reports attempted to obfuscate the crimes being committed by the *Einsatzgruppen*. Time and time again, the word "liquidated" rather than "murdered" appears, while words such as "partisans" and "Communists" are also employed. The need to find justification for the murders is also present. In one document, from the early days of the invasion of Poland, one report claims to speak for the non-Jewish population of Warsaw, stating: "Almost everywhere there is agreement on the arrest of the Jews. Leading figures in Warsaw, too, are heard to ask again and again, 'When will the Jew disappear completely from Poland'?"[8]

One must imagine that writing such reports allowed the authors to find ways to justify what they had been doing and rationalise what they would continue to do to the Jewish population and to those Catholic Poles who were also believed to be non-compliant. In reality, one does not need to read many *Einsatzgruppen* reports to pick up on Nazi authors' attempts to blame the victims for their demise. One could go back in time to the much earlier years of the Nazi regime and read an account of the events of *Kristallnacht* and see the use of the passive voice whenever Jews suddenly had "accidents." If one reads the Gestapo report from Bielefeld about the destruction committed during *Kristallnacht,* written on 26 November 1938, one will see that the memo line "Regarding: *Protest action* against Jews on 10 November 1938"[9] frames the entire report from its outset as a defensive action taken by Aryan Germans against the local Jewish population. The report, after listing synagogues destroyed by fire, implying that synagogues spontaneously burst into flames (not lit by people), states, "During the action two people lost their lives, highlighting the fate of "the Jewess Miss Julie Hirschfeld, born on 29 September 1856 ... Hirschfeld is near-sighted and for this reason fell down the stairs. As a result, she died in the hospital in Detmold."[10] Clearly, Miss Hirschfeld, who was 82 years old in 1938, certainly might have stumbled on the stairs—but the report does not provide any details of who was forcing her out of her home and the passive voice allows one to gloss over who might have had a direct role in the death of this elderly woman. In some respects, reading documents such as the one mentioned above are maddening in their attempt to divert the truth from seeping into the report. When reading such documents, it is always necessary to stop and re-read each sentence so that one does not miss the attempts to excuse the inexcusable.

Almost as insidious are accounts in documents not left to us by the perpetrators. These types of documents provide valuable insight into how perpetrators were perceived by either their victims or from bystanders. The accounts that survive written by Jews who were on the receiving end of persecutory and discriminatory acts and who recorded their thoughts in their diaries are particularly insightful. In many cases, average Aryan Germans or local indigenous collaborators appear in the documents and, while many of the individuals being written about might not consider themselves to be perpetrators, we can see how their behaviours allowed further escalation of Nazi actions. These documents can be the most frightening for us, as we are reminded that not all perpetrators carried out shootings or gassings, yet their witnessing and at times active participation in attacks against Jews share a degree of the guilt of Nazi crimes. These might be ordinary people much like us who, when faced with a choice of action, selected the path of least resistance for themselves, ignoring the suffering they were inflicting on Jewish victims.[11]

In Marion Kaplan's *Between Dignity and Despair: Jewish Life in Nazi Germany*, one encounters innumerable instances of ordinary Aryan Germans ostracising their former Jewish friends and neighbours. Marta Appel, a young German Jewish woman living in Dortmund, had often, prior to Hitler's ascent to power, regularly met with her gentile friends at a local café. Marta decided after the Nazi seizure of power that she should stay away from the gatherings, thinking that that would keep her non-Jewish friends safe from the guilt-by-association reasoning of the Nazi regime. One day Marta encountered one of her gentile friends who urged her to return to their group's regular meetings at the café. Marta spent a restless night, worrying if she should truly go to the meeting or not, but the next day she worked up her courage and went to meet her friends. "It was not necessary for me to read their eyes or listen to the change in their

250   *Beth Griech-Polelle*

voices. The empty table in the little alcove which had always been reserved for us spoke the clearest language ... I could not blame them. Why should they have risked losing a position only to prove to me that we still had friends in Germany?"[12]

Looking at these early accounts of Jewish life in Nazi Germany, long before mass shootings, ghettos, or gas chambers had begun to appear, one can see the beginning of the end of the assimilation of Jews in German society. Their increased social isolation, with each new Nazi decree and edict redefining the Jewish position in German society, was leading Jews into "social death" and for many Aryan Germans it was preferable to simply ignore the plight of Jews around them. For Marta Appel's family, they noted that dear friends no longer spoke to them and when they went out in public the Appels purposefully avoided looking at their gentile friends for fear of bringing an accusation upon them for being "friendly to Jews." Marta noted: "But after some months of a regime of terror, fidelity and friendship had lost their meaning, and fear and treachery had replaced them ... With each day of the Nazi regime, the abyss between us and our fellow citizens grew larger."[13] From this account, one can see how quickly the relationships between Jews and gentiles were unravelling, ultimately leading to the public acquiescing to increasingly more violent moves against the Jewish population. Here again, I would remind my students that categories of perpetrator and bystander can be very fluid, with Aryan Germans often choosing when to actively involve themselves in a situation regarding the position of Jews in the Nazi state.

In the history of the Holocaust, one must examine the role of the murderous *Einsatzgruppen* and their auxiliary units to reveal the Nazi leadership's level of commitment to eradicate all Jews, of all ages, wherever they were encountered. Yet one can see the "social death" of the Jewish community in Nazi Germany long before the mass shootings began on the Eastern Front. Time and again, one encounters in recollections of survivors, in fragments in diaries, or in official reports, that many Aryan Germans had begun to accept the Nazi premise that all Jews everywhere represented a powerful threat to continued Aryan existence. It is in many of these documents that the sheer frustration with human nature is driven home to the reader. It is in the everyday slights, the seemingly "small" acts of inhumanity, that allowed the larger scale inhumanity to follow. On 1 April 1933, the Nazis decreed a nationwide boycott of all Jewish-owned and Jewish-operated stores. Hitler had only been in power since 30 January 1933. While many Aryan Germans rejected the boycott as senseless and economically wasteful, some still felt compelled to comply, at least outwardly. One woman, Dr. Paula Tobias (also married to a doctor), recounted how two younger men from their small community appeared in front of the doctors' property on the morning of the boycott. Although Dr. Tobias noted the young men's discomfort with having to act as sentries, barring potential patients from seeking treatment, it is worth noting that the young men still stayed posted there. Dr. Tobias perhaps hopefully noted how one farmer stated that his son could be doing something truly useful for Germany by cleaning out the stables rather than post sentry at the Tobias's gate. In her recollection, Dr. Tobias noted, "With the exception of one notorious rowdy none of the younger fellows—they were relieved every two hours—said an indecent word or did anything objectionable, everyone was glad, when his time was up."[14] When my students read this document, they are also hopeful, much like Dr. Tobias was in April 1933. Surely, they reason, this proves that Germans were not truly antisemitic and that they had no interest in harming Jews. They are partially correct, but then I ask them to consider this: why did the young men appear at the gate at all? Why did farmers simply walk away after complaining about the uselessness of the boycott? What I am hoping is that the students begin to see that even simply by watching, outwardly complying, and choosing to do nothing helpful, adds a level of complicity to the actions (or inactions). Each one of those sentries, the local farmers, and so on, accepted that they had a duty to comply with government orders. While it is certainly not the same thing as pulling the trigger of a gun placed at the back of someone's head, it does begin to reveal what people will tolerate in their everyday lives.

As one reads through primary documents between the 1933 boycott and the events of *Kristallnacht* in 1938, it is striking how so many people had come to accept the notion over the course of five years that there was, indeed, a "Jewish problem" in Germany. In a massive volume edited by Otto Dov Kulka and Eberhard Jäckel entitled *The Jews in the Secret Nazi Reports on Popular Opinion in Germany, 1933–1945*, one can track the acceptance, at least as it is presented in official reports to higher authorities within the regime, that increasing numbers of Aryan Germans had come to believe that "something" had to be done regarding the position of Jews. They might differ as to what form the "something" should take, but many seem to have accepted that action was required to stem the perceived power of the Jews.

In a report from Kassel in October 1934, one author wrote that the Nazi Party propaganda message was being embraced by the rural population, noting, "In the rural communities, hatred against the Jews has strengthened. In some localities, signs proclaiming 'Jews not wanted here' and 'Jews—entry prohibited' have been placed at the entrance to the locality and mounted on houses. ... There have also been attacks on Jews."[15] Even if one accounts for exaggeration on the part of the reporting official, some people were willingly putting up signs on their own homes, setting the tone that Jews were not to be welcomed in that locale. In documents such as these, one can see the decline of human interaction that would have normally taken place between Aryan Germans and Jews. Once lines of demarcation had begun to be established, the historian must confront the reality that long before bullets came into play, Jews and their increasingly dire plight in Nazi Germany were being either ignored by many people or at the very least, tolerated. This can be so disheartening to see the ugliest side of human nature when behaviour might have gone in a different direction with a much different outcome.

Documents in the Kulka and Jäckel collection take the reader down a dark and depressing path. One encounters in each report an assessment by the local officials of the "Jewish mood" and how Aryan Germans are responding to Nazi propaganda. The accounts range from accusations that Jews are attempting to "fit in" as Aryans by flying Nazi swastika flags, while still other accounts include denunciations that Jewish men are approaching Aryan young women in an inappropriate manner, and some detail how German policemen are registering complaints that they are considered "Friends of Jews" if they intervene to stop public acts of violence or humiliation perpetrated against local Jewish individuals. The chief of police in Berlin submitted a report for November and December 1934 where he concluded that "very large segments of the population do not comprehend why the authorities are exercising such restraint in dealing with this aggressive behavior"[16] of the Jews. As public behaviour allowing the humiliation of Jews continued, one sees in the documents how shaming and maltreatment, although officially reported, seemed to carry no punishment for the perpetrators. So, in the chief of police's report in Dresden, submitted in December 1944, he notes that "A Jew was forced to eat a roll that had been coated with shoe polish, toothpaste, and castor oil. An elderly man, after his hair had been shorn in the form of a wreath, was then chased down the street."[17] These types of reports force us to confront the growing, open hostility to the sheer presence of Jews in Germany and we must take note that no arrests were made of the harassers. Hopefully, we are also thinking about the role of average citizens and how they are allowing themselves to become complicit in Nazi crimes. By opting to do nothing to stop harassment and humiliation of Jews, those who remained silent allowed the true fanatics to go further and further in their attacks.

In the case of a state police report from Berlin in June 1935, the author of the report notes that several "outrageous incidents" have recently occurred against Jews but then continues by stating, "The *positive aspec*t of those events, however, is that the population is clearly having its eyes opened ever wider, and that opposition to the Jews is on the constant rise. Under these circumstances, it is not surprising that the population should on occasion express its indignation and take the law into its own hands."[18] This type of document astonishingly reveals that not only are the local police not interested in arresting Aryan Germans for crimes committed against the Jewish population, but they are also actually in support of vigilantism. For a country with a reputation for enormous respect for law and order, it is shocking to read that the police "understand" why crimes are being committed against the Jewish population and then excuse them. In this type of lawless atmosphere, it is no wonder that so many individuals had no sense of trepidation when attacking Jews.

Lest students begin to surmise that "only Aryan men" participated in attacking or isolating Jews, I often ask students to think about daily life for Jews in Nazi Germany and occupied Europe. In particular, one can assign students accounts of how some Aryan women went out of their way to make life as miserable for Jews as they could, including some of their former neighbours. One can discuss the ever-increasing list of prohibitions levied against the German Jewish population, including the onerous task of navigating the daily shopping. Jews were required to obtain special ration cards, on which were stamped the word "Jew." With the invasion of Poland in 1939, the daily caloric intake for most full Jews (so defined) was depleted. Jews were prohibited from shopping in certain stores, and in other cases, they were assigned one hour per day when they were allowed to shop, typically late in the afternoon when Aryan shoppers had already cleared the shelves of most products. In Nazi Germany, most shopping was done by women, and therefore Aryans and their encounters with Jews are relevant here. Again, one might hope for uplifting stories of women bonding over the shared experiences of motherhood, both Aryan and Jew attempting to find adequate food for their loved ones. Yet, time and again, one encounters in diaries and memoirs, what Erna Becker-Kohen (who was a devout Catholic convert married to a Catholic Aryan man) noted, after attempting to send her young son, Silvan, to the local store to purchase milk, "I go with him as far as I can but I cannot go inside the shop so I have to send him in alone. The other women have started to mercilessly gossip that the Jewish woman sends her child shopping at a time when it is forbidden to her. Now they do not want to serve the little one anymore. How cruel people are. Even mothers refuse to share my distress."[19] She notes time and again the daily slights, the petty insults, and the utter lack of empathy many Aryan women have for her and her young child.

For so many students, genocide is considered to be a "male" crime but exposing them to the various ways in which women could support, collaborate, and actively participate in the genocide is important. Using document collections, such as Alison

Owings's *Frauen: German Women Recall the Third Reich*, opens a window for students to understand that many women were complicit in committing Nazi crimes. Again, the "ordinariness" of their roles can often be overlooked in Holocaust classes—maybe they weren't pulling triggers, but their decisions to a certain extent enabled the killings. We could look at an interview, conducted by Owings, with Frau Ursula Meyer-Semlies, who was about 17 years old in 1932 and very interested in the Nazi Party and fighting communists. She regularly attended Nazi Party rallies, wore a swastika pin secretly attached to her lapel to school even though it violated the school's ban on wearing political symbols, and, by 1934, was a leader in the local *Bund deutscher Mädel* (League of German Girls, or BdM). She participated in "work duty" (farm work for the nation), began training to become a grade schoolteacher, and noted that she decided to officially join the Nazi Party in 1938. Why? Frau Meyer-Semlies answered there "wasn't war yet" and the Nazis "were not doing bad things to Jews," or, she corrected herself, "that she knew about."[20]

Frau Meyer-Semlies's interview continued, detailing her assignment to teach in occupied Poland. She noted that in the summer, she needed a new coat. Due to rationing, she had to turn her old coat in, then take a receipt that gave her permission to purchase a replacement. She heard that she could enter the Lodz ghetto where coats would be less expensive. As she rode through the ghetto on a streetcar, she said, "And I saw the Jews going around and they had the Star of David on their sleeves. I didn't see many, going around, but they looked horribly miserable. I thought, man, they ... are not getting enough to eat."[21] She also "sort of looked in" at empty Jewish houses[22] after an entire community of Jews had been removed from their village to a concentration camp. Here, our readers must confront her knowledge about what was happening to Jews in Poland, but when her interviewer asked her about feeling guilty, she avoided a direct answer and instead pointed out that other unoccupied countries could have taken in Jews, stating, "If they had taken in the Jews, ... maybe the National Socialists would not have killed them."[23] While Frau Meyer-Semlies might not be categorised as a "perpetrator" she certainly would not win any humanitarian awards. Her inability, years later, to even admit any degree of complicity is shocking and deeply disturbing, yet it was an all-too-common reaction by many Aryan Germans after the war.

Frau Meyer-Semlies might have claimed to know very little about crimes committed against Jews at home and in occupied territories, despite the fact she had observed first-hand the Lodz ghetto and an empty Jewish village. One can read in Security Service (SD) reports over and over again that knowledge about crimes and atrocities was circulating on the home front. In one SD report for December 1942 to January 1943, the local district office of Schwabach wrote an assessment of the rural population's reaction to stories coming from German soldiers who were serving on the Eastern Front. These stories provided locals with information regarding the shooting and extermination of the Jews. The author of the document then dryly notes, "This news leaves a sense of great anxiety, emotional distress, and worry among many in the circles of the population mentioned."[24] Are the locals filled with anxiety and distress regarding the fate of the dead Jews? Let's read on: "As broad circles of the rural population see the situation, it is not as yet certain that we will win the war, and if we do not, when the Jews return some day, they will take a horrible revenge."[25] This type of reasoning, that Jews represent a true problem for the Aryan Germans, and that if something drastic is not done, there will be hell to pay, permeates these official reports.

The SD Office in Minden in November 1943 mentions anonymous phone calls to the local authorities who have a Jewish woman in their custody. Over the phone, the caller demands "action" be taken against this still-living Jewish woman, threatening, "Don't be so soft. If we don't get tough, in the end the Jews will devour us."[26]

The fears of Jewish retribution reappear in even more grotesque form in an NSDAP District monthly report from August 1944, "The Volk say that as a consequence of a victory that is not ours, Jewry will pounce on the German Volk body and realize all its devilish and bestial plans, as described in our press. Which is why we have the slogan: Death and destruction to the Jews—the future and life are ours!"[27] Here one can highlight to students the black and white binary presented by the Nazi propaganda machine: either Jews die and Germans live, or Jews live and Germans die. It is important to note, too, the lateness of these declarations calling for the total destruction of the Jews. Many on the German home front had seemingly bought into Nazi propaganda which played on themes of Jewish Old Testament retribution, and the propaganda machine bound many Germans to this simplistic way of thinking. It was all or nothing, either Germans would be totally victorious, or they would be totally destroyed, and Jews would take over. There could be no compromise.

In this way, once again, we can see how average Germans were brought into the role of collaborators, and in some respects, perpetrators. As so many desperately wanted their country to win the war, they seemingly had the fear of a vengeful Jew returning from the East convinced many that extreme measures were needed to fully eradicate the remaining Jewish population. Other Germans voiced their concerns about their own fate at the war's end, recognising that they had been complicit in the crimes committed against the Jews. In an astonishingly cynical move, some Aryan Germans began searching for surviving Jews—not to murder them, but to co-opt them, "People don't believe in the final victory. Today they would really prefer to take precautionary measures and get on good terms with the Jews, if only that were possible."[28]

As a historian, one must confront the reality of evil when studying documents from the Nazi era. The more one reads the source material, the more one comes to realise that categories of perpetrator, collaborator, accomplice, and bystander are convenient when trying to capture some of the complexities of the time and conveying them to our readers. Yet, I would suggest that we also emphasise to our students that these categories are fluid and should not come with hard and fast definitions. In this chapter, I have tried to expand the idea of perpetrators as widely as possible, with the understanding that there are degrees of guilt involved in assessing documents of atrocities and persecution. Therefore, when thinking about who the perpetrators were, one might consider the role of average German citizens on the home front who participated in and accepted the notion that while there was a "Jewish Problem" that needed to be solved, yet they might not ever have imagined genocide as the answer. There were women and men who allowed discrimination and persecution to take place every day in their towns and villages. There were men and women who functioned in more active roles as more overt perpetrators as well: men and women who, after the war had ended, might have said to themselves and to others that they had no direct knowledge of gas chambers, execution pits, or starvation in ghettos, implying that they were not guilty of enabling the Holocaust. The role of daily slights, seemingly "minor" insults, shaming and harassment should not be allowed to escape our consideration of how genocide becomes possible.[29] In the words of Catholic theologian Harry James Cargas, "One day it became apparent to me, in a way it had not earlier, that every killer of Jews, of Gypsies, of Jehovah's Witnesses, of homosexuals was a baptized Christian. It takes a lot of people to kill a lot of people—and the murderers, the traitors, the profiteers, the onlookers all had Christian backgrounds."[30] Just as Harry James Cargas struggled to reconcile the professed Christianity of perpetrators of the Holocaust, so too must we as researchers, as teachers and as students of the Holocaust stop and contemplate how everyday actions and decisions made by individuals contributed to the decline in human feelings of compassion and empathy for those less fortunate than themselves and spiralled out of control into one of the world's most notorious genocides. With each document, we should realise that it took a lot of people to kill a lot of people.

Notes

1 W. Lower, *The Ravine: A Family, A Photograph, A Holocaust Massacre Revealed*, New York: HarperCollins, 2021.
2 E. Klee, W. Dressen, and V. Riess (ed.), *"The Good Old Days: The Holocaust as Seen by Its Perpetrators and Bystanders,"* Old Saybrook (CT): Konecky and Konecky, 1991, p. 154.
3 For the complete set of documents for this account, see ibid., pp. 138–54.
4 Ibid., p. 138.
5 C.R. Browning, *Ordinary Men: Reserve Police Battalion 101 and the Final Solution in Poland*, New York: HarperCollins, 1998, p. x.
6 Ibid.
7 Y. Arad, S. Krakowski, and S. Spector, *The Einsatzgruppen Reports: Selections from the Dispatches of the Nazi Death Squads' Campaign Against the Jews in Occupied Territories of the Soviet Union, July 1941-January 1943*, New York: Holocaust Library, 1989, pp. 90–1.
8 J. Matthäus, J. Böhler, and K.-M. Mallmann (ed.), *War, Pacification, and Mass Murder, 1939: The Einsatzgruppen in Poland*, Lanham (MD): Rowman and Littlefield, 2014, p. 75.
9 Steve Hochstadt, *Sources of the Holocaust*, New York: Palgrave Macmillan, p. 75 (emphasis mine).
10 Ibid., pp. 75–6.
11 See especially M. Wildt, *Hitler's Volksgemeinschaft and the Dynamics of Racial Exclusion: Violence Against Jews in Provincial Germany, 1919–1939*, New York: Berghahn, 2012, where he discusses the interplay between perpetrators, bystanders, and victims.
12 M. Kaplan, *Between Dignity and Despair: Jewish Life in Nazi Germany, 1933–1938*, New York: Oxford University Press, 1998, p. 41.
13 Ibid.
14 Hochstadt, *Sources*, pp. 39–40.
15 O.D. Kulka and E. Jäckel (ed.), *The Jews in the Secret Nazi Reports on Popular Opinion in Germany, 1933–1945*, New Haven: Yale University Press, 2010, pp. 61–2.
16 Ibid., p. 73.
17 Ibid., pp. 74–5.
18 Ibid., p. 130 (emphasis mine).
19 K.P. Spicer and M. Cucchiara (ed.), *The Evil that Surrounds Us: The WWII Memoir of Erna Becker-Kohen*, Bloomington: Indiana University Press, 2017, p. 52.
20 A. Owings, *Frauen: German Women Recall the Third Reich*, New Brunswick (NJ): Rutgers University Press, 2017, pp. 54–9.
21 Ibid. p. 64.
22 Ibid.
23 Ibid., p. 67.
24 Kulka and Jäckel, *The Jews in the Secret Nazi Reports*, pp. 607–8.
25 Ibid., p. 608.
26 Ibid., pp. 638–9.
27 Ibid., pp. 651–2.
28 Ibid., p. 636.

29 See J. Waller, *Becoming Evil: How Ordinary People Commit Genocide and Mass Murder*, New York: Oxford University Press, 2007; and T. Kühne, *Belonging and Genocide: Hitler's Community, 1918–1945*, New Haven: Yale University Press, 2010.
30 H.J. Cargas, *Voices from the Holocaust*, Lexington: University Press of Kentucky, 1993, p. x. See also his definitive statement on this topic: H.J. Cargas, *Reflections of a Post-Auschwitz Christian*, Detroit: Wayne State University Press, 1989.

Chronology of the Holocaust

Paul R. Bartrop

1919

January 5: The German Workers' Party (DAP) is founded by Anton Drexler and Karl Harrer
September 12: Adolf Hitler joins the DAP

1920

February 24: Nazi Party established when the DAP is renamed; it becomes the National Socialist German Workers' Party (NSDAP); Hitler presents a 25-point Programme, the Nazi Party Platform

1923

November 9: Hitler leads an attempt to overthrow the government of Bavaria; he fails

1924

February 24: Trial of Adolf Hitler for treason begins; he is found guilty and sentenced to five years in prison
December 19: Hitler released from Landsberg having served just eight months of his five-year sentence

1925

February 27: Hitler declares the Nazi Party (NSDAP) to be re-established, with himself as leader (Führer)

1933

January 30: Adolf Hitler is appointed Chancellor of Germany by President Paul von Hindenburg
February 27–28: Reichstag fire; arrests of political opponents of the Nazis begin almost immediately
March 5: Reichstag elections: Nazis gain 44 percent of vote in manipulated elections
March 20: Dachau concentration camp is established

March 27: The Enabling Act is passed
April 1: Jewish businesses are boycotted across Germany
April 26: Hermann Göring establishes the Gestapo
May 10: Books written by Jews and "undesirables" are publicly burned
July 14: The Law for the Prevention of Offspring with Hereditary Defects is passed, forcing many Germans with "undesirable genes" to be sterilised

1934

June 30: *Sturmabteilung* (SA) leadership is purged during what becomes known as the "Night of the Long Knives"
August 2: President Paul von Hindenburg dies; Hitler declares the office of president abolished, and names himself Führer of Germany

1935

September 15: The Nuremberg Laws are announced at the annual Party Rally

1936

July 1: Hitler Youth membership becomes compulsory for all Aryan boys
August 1: Summer Olympic Games begin in Berlin

1937

March 21: Papal encyclical *Mit Brennender Sorge* issued by Pope Pius XI
July 19: Buchenwald concentration camp is established

1938

March 12: The *Anschluss* (union) of Austria with Germany; all German antisemitic decrees are applied immediately to Austria
July 6–14: International conference on refugees held at Evian, France
August 1: Nazi Office of Jewish Emigration established to speed up the pace of Jewish emigration from Germany
August 8: Mauthausen concentration camp established in Austria
August 17: Nazis require Jewish women to add "Sarah" and men to add "Israel" to their names on all legal documents
August 19: Swiss government refuses entry to Austrian Jews seeking sanctuary
September 27: German Jews banned from practicing law
September 29–30: Munich Conference: Britain and France surrender the Sudetenland regions of Czechoslovakia to Germany by negotiation
October 5: Passports belonging to German Jews are marked with the letter "J" to indicate their identity
November 7: Ernst vom Rath, third secretary in the German Embassy in Paris, is shot and mortally wounded by Herschel Grynszpan; vom Rath dies on November 9, precipitating *Kristallnacht*

Chronology of the Holocaust 259

November 9–10: *Kristallnacht* pogrom occurs in Germany and Austria. Nazi figures give 91 Jews killed, and up to 10,000 are arrested; 267 synagogues are destroyed; figures are likely much higher

1939

March 15: Germany invades Czechoslovakia
May 15: The first prisoners arrive at Ravensbrück
June 17: The *S.S. St. Louis*, a ship carrying 936 Jewish passengers, returns to Europe after being denied entry into the United States and Cuba
August 23: The Nazi-Soviet Non-Aggression Pact is signed
September 1: Germany invades Poland; a curfew is imposed on German Jews
September 3: France and Britain declare war against Germany
September 17: Soviet Union invades Poland
September 21: Reinhard Heydrich orders *Einsatzgruppen* commanders to establish ghettos in German-occupied Poland
September 27: Warsaw surrenders; Jewish Councils (*Judenräte*) are established in Poland
November 23: Yellow stars required to be worn by Polish Jews over the age of 10

1940

February 8: Łódź ghetto is established
April 1: Thousands of refugees are permitted into Shanghai, China
April 9: Denmark and southern Norway are invaded and occupied by Germany; Heinrich Himmler issues a directive to establish a concentration camp at Auschwitz
April 30: The Łódź ghetto is sealed off from the outside world
May 7: Nearly 165,000 inhabitants are sealed in the Łódź ghetto.
May 10: France, the Netherlands, Belgium, and Luxembourg are invaded by Germany
May 20: Auschwitz concentration camp established for Polish political prisoners
June 4: Neuengamme concentration camp opens
June 22: France surrenders to Germany; Marshal Philippe Pétain leads the pro-Nazi government established in Vichy
July 17: The first anti-Jewish measures are taken in Vichy France
September 7: German forces begin aerial bombings of Britain
October 3: Vichy France passes its own version of the Nuremberg Laws
October 16: Germans officially establish the Warsaw Ghetto
November 4: Jewish civil servants in the Netherlands are dismissed
November 16: The Warsaw Ghetto, containing nearly 500,000 Jews, is sealed

1941

January 21–26: Romanian Iron Guard annihilates hundreds of Jews
February 9: Dutch Nazis riot against Amsterdam Jews
March 1: Construction of Birkenau begins
April 21: Natzweiler-Struthof concentration camp opens in France
May 14: Thousands of Jews are rounded up in Paris at the Vel' d'Hiv

260 Paul R. Bartrop

June 22: Germany violates its non-aggression pact with the Soviet Union and invades (Operation BARBAROSSA)
June 27: Białystok occupied by Nazis; Białystok ghetto established
July 2: Ukrainian nationalists murder thousands in Lvov
July 17: *Einsatzgruppen* ordered to execute captured communists and Jews during the Soviet campaign
July 20: Minsk ghetto established
July 31: Adolf Eichmann appointed to prepare the "Final Solution"
September 1: The German "Euthanasia" programme formally ended, following the deaths of some 100,000 people
September 6: The Vilna ghetto is established
September 19: Jews in Germany are ordered to wear yellow armbands bearing the Star of David
September 29: The *Einsatzgruppen* murders some 34,000 Jews at Babi Yar ravine, outside Kiev
October 7: Birkenau is established as the primary mass murder site of Auschwitz
October 22–24: Romanian and German forces massacre an estimated 50,000 Jews in Odessa
October 28: Approximately 9,000 Jews are killed outside of Kovno (Kaunas)
November 8: Plans are made for the creation of a ghetto in Lvov (Lwów, Lviv).
November 24: Terezín (Theresienstadt) ghetto/concentration camp established
December 7: Japan attacks Pearl Harbor, drawing the United States into World War II
December 8: Chełmno extermination camp becomes fully operational; some 320,000 Jews will be murdered here
December 11: Germany and Italy declare war on the United States

1942

January 10: *Armée Juive* (Jewish Army) created in France
January 20: The Wannsee Conference takes place in Berlin
January 16: Deportations from Łódź begin
February 23: Some 768 Jewish passengers, after being refused entry into Palestine, drown when the *S.S. Struma* sinks off of the Turkish coast.
March 1: Extermination by gas begins at Sobibór
March 17: Killings begin at Bełżec extermination camp
June: First anti-Nazi resistance pamphlet published by the White Rose group of Hans and Sophie Scholl
June 1: Jews in France, Holland, Belgium, Croatia, Slovakia, and Romania ordered to wear yellow stars
June 1: Treblinka extermination camp begins operation
July 13: Eighteen hundred Jews are massacred in Jozefów, Poland, by German Reserve Police Battalion 101
July 14: Mass deportation of Dutch and Belgian Jews to Auschwitz begins
July 16: Over 4,000 children are taken from Paris and sent to Auschwitz; overall, some 12,887 Jews in Paris are sent through Drancy
July 22: Mass deportation of Jews from the Warsaw Ghetto to Treblinka begins.
July 23: Adam Czerniaków commits suicide in Warsaw

July 28: The Jewish Combat Organisation is formed in the Warsaw Ghetto
August 7: Dr. Janusz Korczak and 200 orphans under his care are gassed in Treblinka
August 17: Kurt Gerstein visits Bełżec death camp and witnesses the gassing of up to 3,000 Jews
August 29: The Reigner Telegram is sent
September 2–3: Revolt of the Łachwa ghetto, arguably the first ghetto revolt of the Holocaust
October 15: The SS slaughters 25,000 Jews near Brest-Litovsk
October 25: The deportation of Norwegian Jews begins
October 28: First transport of Jews sent from Terezín (Theresienstadt) to Auschwitz
December 24: Armed operations by the Jewish Combat Organisation against German troops in Kraków

1943

January 18–21: Renewed deportations of Jews from the Warsaw Ghetto begin following a visit from Himmler; Jewish resistance begins in the ghetto
February 22: Christoph Probst, Hans Scholl, and Sophie Scholl are executed after admitting to distributing White Rose pamphlets
February 26: The first Roma arrive at Auschwitz
March 13–14: Liquidation of the Kraków ghetto
March 23: Nazi deportation of Greek Jews begins
April 5: Approximately 4,000 Jews are massacred in the Ponary Forest, outside Vilna
April 19: New deportations from the Warsaw Ghetto; first day of Warsaw Ghetto Uprising; Britain and the United States begin the Bermuda Conference
May 1: Bermuda Conference ends
May 8: Nazi forces capture the Jewish Combat Organisation's command bunker at Miła 18; Mordecai Anielewicz is among the dead found there
May 16: SS General Jürgen Stroop reports that the "Jewish quarter of Warsaw is no more."
May 19: Nazis declare Berlin to be *Judenfrei* ("cleansed of Jews")
June 2: 3,000 Jews killed following resistance in Lvov (Lwów, Lviv); another 7,000 are sent to the concentration camp at Janowska
June 11: Himmler orders liquidation of all ghettos in occupied Poland
August 2: Treblinka uprising
August 15–16: Uprising of the Białystok ghetto
October 1–2: German police begin deportations of Danish Jews; Danes respond with a rescue effort that saves the lives of 90 percent of the Jewish population.
October 14: Sobibór uprising
October 16: Major Nazi raid and *razzia* (roundup) against the Jews of Rome, who are sent to Auschwitz
October 21: Minsk ghetto liquidated

1944

January 22: US President Franklin D. Roosevelt creates the War Refugee Board
March 19: Germany begins its occupation of Hungary; Adolf Eichmann sent from Berlin to oversee the deportation of the Hungarian Jews

May 15: Beginning of the deportation of Jews from Hungary to Auschwitz; Jews from Ruthenia and Transylvania are deported
May 16: Germans offer to free one million Jews in exchange for 10,000 trucks
July 9: Raoul Wallenberg arrives in Hungary, where he distributes Swedish passports and sets up safe houses for Jews
July 11: Deportations from Hungary are halted by order of Regent Miklós Horthy
July 24: Majdanek extermination camp is liberated by the Russians
August 1–October 4: Warsaw Revolt
August 2: Germany destroys the so-called "Gypsy camp" at Auschwitz, gassing some 3,000 in the process
August 6: Łódź, the last Jewish ghetto in Poland, is liquidated with 60,000 Jews sent to Auschwitz
October 7: *Sonderkommando* revolt at Auschwitz; one of the gas chambers is destroyed, 15 SS guards and 400 members of the *Sonderkommando* are killed
November 8: Deportations resume in Budapest
November 19: The Vatican and four other neutral powers in Budapest issue a collective protest to the Hungarian government calling for the suspension of Jewish deportations
November 28: Himmler orders the gas chambers at Auschwitz destroyed
December 24–29: Hungarian Arrow Cross fascists attack Jews in Budapest

1945

January 5: Roza Robota, Estusia Wajcblum, Ala Gertner, and Regina Safirsztajn, accused of supplying gunpowder to the Auschwitz *Sonderkommando*, are executed
January 18: The evacuation of Auschwitz begins
January 19: The Soviet Army liberates Łódź
January 28: Soviet forces liberate Auschwitz
April 9: Evacuation of Mauthausen begins
April 11: American forces liberate Buchenwald
April 15: British forces liberate Bergen-Belsen
April 27: Soviet forces liberate Sachsenhausen
April 29: American forces liberate Dachau; Soviet forces liberate Ravensbrück
April 30: Hitler commits suicide
May 1: Joseph Goebbels kills his wife and children before shooting himself as Berlin is surrounded by the Soviet Army
May 2: Soviet forces capture Berlin
May 3: Theresienstadt is surrendered to the International Committee of the Red Cross
May 5: American forces liberate Mauthausen
May 7: Germany surrenders to the Allies in Reims
May 9: Wilhelm Keitel signs surrender documents in Berlin
May 23: Heinrich Himmler commits suicide
September 1: Japan surrenders to the Allies after the United States detonates atomic bombs at Hiroshima and Nagasaki, ending World War II
October 18: The International Military Tribunal of major war criminals begins at Nuremberg

1946

July 4: Forty-two Jews are killed in a pogrom in Kielce, Poland
October 1: The International Military Tribunal ends
October 15: Hermann Göring commits suicide in his cell at Nuremberg
October 16: Death sentences carried out at Nuremberg, as those condemned are hanged

Index

Aarons, Victoria 108
Academy of the Hebrew Language 157
Adler, Hans-Günther 158
The Advertiser (Adelaide) 137, 138
The Age (Melbourne) 137, 138
Aleichem, Sholem 144
Allman, Tony 52–53
Amen (film) 191
American Jewish Historical Society 156
amidah 38
Anis, Manci 236
Antze, Paul 51
Appel, Marta 249, 250
Aquinas, St. Thomas 157
archaeology/ists 173–174
The Argus (Melbourne) 137
Arieti, Silvano 1, 2
art 222–241
artefacts 166–177
Artificial Intelligence (AI) 161
Aryan Paragraph 117–118
Ashkenazi Jews 142
Association of Jewish Refugees 111, 113, 161
Auerbach, Rachel 38, 145
Auschwitz 16, 46, 58, 62, 63, 64, 108, 138, 149, 170, 172, 187, 188, 195, 210, 217, 222, 223, 228, 235
Australian Associated Press 137
"Axis Sally"; *see* Gillars, Mildred

Babbit, Dinah Gottliebova 235
Babi Yar 247
Bacharach, Walter Zvi 30
Baer, Richard 63
Ball-Kaduri, Kurt 11, 12, 13, 15
Bar-Hillel, Yehoshua 156
Bar-On, Zvi 11, 12, 15
Barsam, Richard Meram 204
Barton, Keith C. 27
Bartrop, Paul R. 132, 137–138, 147
Bayzler, Michael 95
Becker-Kohen, Erna 252

Behncke, Hugo 23
Bekennende Kirche; *see* Confessing Church
Bell, James 29, 30
Ben-Amos, Batsheva 35
Ben-Hayyim, Ze'ev 157
Ben Menachem, Arie 65
Bennett, June Mary 29, 30
Bergen-Belsen 63, 138, 195, 197, 238
Berger, Alan L. 108
Berlin Wall 154
Betar 144
Birken, Edith 238
Birkett, Sir Norman 98, 99
Björkdahl, Annika 160
Black, Edwin 155
Black-and-white films 188
Blatt, Thomas ("Toivi") 187
Blatter, Sylvia 237
Bletchley Park 155
Blobel, Paul 247
Bloch, Josef 68
Bloch, Marc 87, 192
Bloxham, Donald 24
Blumenthal, Nachman 38
Blutinger, Jeffrey 23–24
Board of Deputies of British Jews 109
Boder, David 9–10, 11, 15, 147
Boll, Uwe 188
Bonhoeffer, Dietrich 121
Book burning 79, 171
Bosch, Hieronymus 223
Boston Globe 130
Bowles, Brett 199
The Boy in the Striped Pyjamas (book) 209, 215, 217–218
Boyne, John 217–218
Brasse, Wilhelm 64
Brenner, Michael 151
British Library 161
Brizitz, Zlata 26–30
Browning, Christopher R. 167, 247–248
Buchenwald 93, 138, 226, 236

Buergenthal, Thomas 48
Bulgin, James 105–106
Bund 144
Busa, Fr. Roberto 157
Bush, Vannevar 156

Canadian Museum of Human Rights 171
Cargas, Harry James 15, 254–255
Cayrol, Jean 198
Cegesoma 158
censorship 131, 135
Central Committee of Liberated Jews in Germany 37
Central Jewish Committee 148
Central Jewish Historical Commission 37, 38
Chadwick, William R. 112
Chaplin, Charlie 190
Chevalier, Maurice 199
Chicago Tribune 131
children 184
Chirac, Jacques 215
Choueka, Yaakov 157
Church Documents 117–129
Churchill, Winston 90
Cochrane, Arthur C. 121
Colossus 155
Concordat 119, 124, 125
Confessing Church 118, 125
Conway, John S. 120–122
Coronavirus pandemic 5, 123, 160
Corsini, Adam 107
Costa-Gavras 191
Courier-Mail (Brisbane) 137
crimes against humanity 96
crimes against peace 95
Critical Race Theory 53
Cubitt, Geoffrey 97
"cultural genocide" 168

Dachau 93, 138, 222
Dachau Trials 92–93
Daily Mail (London) 137
Daniel, Jane 50
Dannenmann, Arnold 125
Dawidowicz, Lucy S. 97
de Rosnay, Tatiana 215–216
Defonseca, Misha 50, 51, 52
Delabre, Léon 172
The Deputy (play) 117, 124, 191
Der Angriff 83
Der Ewige Jude (film) 81
Der Giftpilz; see *The Poisonous Mushroom*
Der Stürmer 70, 83–84, 86
Des Pres, Terrence 14, 147
The Devil's Arithmetic (book) 209, 216–217
Diamant, Vera 112

diaries 33–44
Dicker-Brandeis, Friedl 230–231
Dierking, Lynn 104
Dietrich, Otto 79–80, 82
digital natives 154–155
"digital historiography" 162
digital immigrants 154–155
Digital Sources 154–165
Displaced Persons' Camps 10, 38, 149, 150, 151
Dix, Otto 223
documentaries 194–207
Dössekker, Bruno 52
Drancy internment camp 234
Dressen, Willi 246
Dror-Hechalutz 144

EBSCO Jewish Studies Source 160
Eichengreen, Lucille 47
Eichmann, Adolf 49, 144, 191, 230
Einsatzgruppen 58, 248, 249, 250
Eisenbach, Artur 38
Eisner, Pinchas 21, 28, 30, 31
Ekstein, Henry C. 157
Emory University 52
Engländerova, Raja 230
Escape from Sobibor (film) 187–188
The Eternal Jew; see *Der Ewige Jude*
European Holocaust Research Infrastructure (EHRI) 158, 161
European Union 169
Evans, Richard 26

"faith-chaos" 126
Falck-Ettlinger, Emmy 234
Falk, John H. 105
false memory 15–16
fantasy 185
Favier, August 226
Feldhandler, Leon 187
Felman, Shoshana 14, 46
Ferguson, Leland 167–168
Ferro, Marc 200
Feuchtwanger, Lion 80–81
Florida Gulf Coast University 4
Flossenbürg 93
The Forward (New York) 143
Fothergill, Robert A. 35
Fraenkel, Aviezri 157
Francis, Pope 123
Frankel, Viktor E. 54
Frank, Anne 33, 34, 36, 41, 53, 231
Free Polish Army 64
Friedman, Philip 38, 148, 150
Fritta, Bedrich 223
Frydman, Szmul 28

Gabanyi, Ewa 226, 235
Gale Archives Unbound 160
Gallo, Max
Ganzfried, Daniel 51
Garbarini, Alexandra 36, 38
German Christian Faith Movement 118, 125
German Student Association 171
Gazeta de Amsterdam 143
Gentry, Remee 170
Gerstein, Kurt 191
Ghetto Fighters' House 41
Gillars, Mildred 82
Godard, Jean-Luc 202
Goebbels, Joseph 79–80, 83, 86
Goldberg, Amos 36, 37
Goldfinger, Matylda Lamet 68
Goldhagen, Daniel 167
Good (film) 191
Goodin, Julie 53
Google Books 158
Gray, Martin 51
Greenman, Leon 107
The Grey Zone (film) 187–188
Grierson, John 194
Grimm, Eve 4
Grinberg, Zalman 106
Grosman, Mendel 65
Grzywaczewski, Leszek 65
Grzywacz, Nachum 105
Gunther, John 134
Gurs internment camp 222, 234

Haas, Leo 230
Häfner, August 247
Harlan, Veit 80
Hashomer Hatzair 144
Hebrew University 156, 157
Heimer, Ernst 84
Hermann, Vivette 4
Herzog, Chaim 29, 30
Heydecker, Joe 61
"hidden encyclical" 120
Hilberg, Raul 3, 38, 167, 201
Hillesum, Etty 35, 36, 41
Himmler, Heinrich 81, 83
Hippler, Fritz 81
Hirschfeld, Julie 249
Historical Commissions 149–150
historical memory 48
Hitler, Adolf 78, 79, 80, 83, 117, 125, 133, 149
Hitler Youth 79, 80
Hochhuth, Rolf 124, 191
Höcker, Karl-Friedrich 58, 62, 63
Hofmann, Ernst 63
Hollerith Machine 155
Holocaust Centre North, Huddersfield 106–107

Holocaust denial 186
Holocaust Memorial Day 113
Holocaust Memorial, Hyde Park 109
Höss, Rudolf 49, 62, 212, 235
Hössler, Franz 63
"hot button issues" 135
Howard, Tom 107
Howe, Irving 223
Humani Generis Unitas 120
humour 185
Hurricane Ian 5

Imperial War Museum 105–106
International Business Machines (IBM) 155
International Committee of the Red Cross (ICRC) 27–28, 31
International Data Corporation (IDC) 157
International Military Tribunal 58, 84, 90–91
Internet Archive 158
Isaacson, Judith 50
Ishon, Moshe 147
Ivanhorod, Ukraine 58
IWitness 161

Jäckel, Eberhard 251
Jackson, Peter 58
Jackson, Robert H. 91, 195
Jacobs, Robert A. 154
Jeff and Toby Herr Oral History Archive 15
Jensen, Olaf 109
Jewish Family and Children's Services Holocaust Center 161
JewishGen 159
Jewish Historical Institute; *see* Zydowski Instytut Historyczny
Jewish Museum London 107–108
Jewish National Fund 157
John XXIII, Pope 125
John Paul II, Pope 125
Joint Distribution Committee 38, 65
Jöst, Heinrich 60–61
Joyce, William 82
JSTOR 155, 160
Jud Süss (film) 80–81

Kalb, Marvin 133
Kantor, Alfred 223, 237
Kaplan, Israel 38, 149
Kaplan, Marion 249
Kappler, Stefanie 160
Karpinski, Lydia 111
Karski, Jan 202
Kassow, Samuel D. 145
Katz, Steven T. 97
Keneally, Thomas 211–212
Kent, Flor 110
Kermisz, Joseph 151

Kertzer, David I. 124
Kindertransport 103, 104, 106
Kinderstansport Monument 110–111
Kipp, Michaela 26
Kishinev Pogrom 34
Kitson Clark, George 4
Klee, Ernst 246
Klein, Fritz 46
Klemperer, Victor 34
Klinger, Jane E. 159, 173
Klüger, Ruth 47, 50
Knickerbocker, H.R. 134
Konrad, Franz 68
Kovno Ghetto 148, 230, 232
Krakow Ghetto 81, 189
Kramer, Josef 63
Kristallnacht 79, 104, 132, 171, 249, 251
Kruk, Hermann 35–36, 40
Kube, Wilhelm 22–23, 31–32n. 3
Kulka, Otto Dov 251
Kushner, Harold 54
Kusters, Anton 59

Ladino 142, 143, 150
LaFarge, John 120
Lambek, Michael 131
Lamet, Hania 68
Landsberg, Alison 104
Langer, Lawrence L. 37, 147
Lansky, Aaron 151
Lanzmann, Claude 197–198, 200–202, 202–203, 204
The Last of the Unjust (film) 201, 202–203, 204
Laub, Dori 12, 46
Law for the Restoration of the Professional Civil Service 117
Lawson, Murray G. 156
League of German Girls 253
Lee, Vera 50
Leff, Laurel 131
Lejeune, Philippe 41
Lemkin, Raphael 168
Lengyel, Olga 46–47
letters 21–32
Levi, Primo 40, 47, 54, 201
Levin, David Michael 189
Levin, Dov 11, 12, 15
Levine, Thomas H. 192
Lévy, Jeanne 234
Library of Congress (LOC) 93–94
Lipstadt, Deborah E. 52, 131
literature 208–221
Lodz Ghetto 40, 47, 65, 81, 230, 233, 238, 253
Loewinsohn, W.M. 112
London Agreement 90
long term memory 17

"Lord Haw-Haw"; *see* Joyce, William
Lower, Wendy 71, 245
Lurie, Esther 225, 232–233

Mächler, Stefan 48
Majdanek 68
Mändlová, Helena 230
Manhattan Project 156
Marcus, Alan S. 192
Margolis, Rebecca 131
Marian, Ferdinand 81
Mark, Bernard 38
Marker, Chris 203
Marks-Woldman, Olivia 113
Martin, Sally 51
Massachusetts Institute of Technology (MIT) 156
material culture 167–168
Maurel, Micheline 19
Mauriac, François 48
Maus (book) 52–53
Mauthausen 93, 198
Maws, Alex 113
Maxwell, Elizabeth and Robert 112
McMinn School Board 53
Mein Kampf 83–86
Meir, Golda 124
Meisler, Frank 110–111
memoirs 45–57
Mengele, Josef 63, 64, 187
Mercury (Hobart) 137
metadata 158, 160
Meyer-Semlies, Ursula 253
Michigan State University 52
microhistorical writing 25
Mielnicki, Michel 47
Ministry of Public Enlightenment and Propaganda 79, 86
Mit Brennender Sorge 119–120
Moll, Otto 62
Moscow Declaration 90
movies 179–193
Munich Crisis 137
Murmelstein, Benjamin 202–203
Murrow, Edward R. 134
Museums and Memorials 103–116
music 185
Music, Zoran 222, 235, 238–239
Musser, Charles 194
Mussolini, Benito 1

National Holocaust Centre and Museum, Newark 104, 109
National Science Foundation (NSF) 156
Nazi Concentration Camps (film) 194–195
Nelson Tim Blake 187

Index

Neuengamme 23
neural network 17
newspapers 130–141
New York Public Library 159
New York Times 130–131
Nietzsche, Friedrich 25
Night and Fog (film) 197–198, 204
Niewyk, Donald L. 10
Night (book) 48–49, 53, 54, 150, 209–210, 217
Niney, François 199
Nordhausen 93
Nostra Aetate 125
Nuremberg Charter 90
Nuremberg Military Tribunals (NMT) 91–92
Nuremberg Principles 91
Nussbaum, Felix 228–230
Nyiszli, Miklos 187

Oatley, Keith 45
Ofer, Dalia 27, 28
Olère, David 223
Olomucki, Halina 222, 223, 233, 235–236
Olympia (film) 82
Olympic Games, Berlin 185
Oneg Shabbat Archive 145
Ophuls, Marcel 197–198, 199–200
Oppenheim, Samuel 156
optical character recognition (OCR) 159
oral history 9–20
Owings, Alison 252–253
Oyneg Shabes; *see* Oneg Shabbat Archive

Pacelli, Eugenio 119
Pastors' Emergency League 118
Paul VI, Pope 123, 125
Pearce, Andy 111
Pechersky, Alexander (Sasha) 187
"People's Receiver" 79
Pepys, Samuel 33, 34
Peretz, J.L. 155
perpetrators, documents from 245–256
Pétain, Marshal Philippe 199
Philadelphia Inquirer 130
photographs 58–74
Pius XI, Pope 119
Pius XII, Pope 117, 123, 124, 125, 192
Pleasantville (film) 189
The Poisonous Mushroom (book) 84–85
Polish Historical Commission 38
Polish-Ukrainian Commonwealth 142
Pollinger, Andrew 50
Porat, Dan 71
Priemel, Kim Christian 96
propaganda 77–89
Propaganda Kompanie nr. 689 68, 69

ProQuest Historical American Jewish Newspaper 160
prosthetic memory 104, 195
provenance (artefacts) 169

Randall, Hannah 106
Rantzen, Esther 112
Rashke, Richard 187
Ravensbrück 19, 173
The Reader (book) 208, 213–215
real memory 48
Reich, Howard 208–209
Reich Press Chamber 79
Reserve Police Battalion 101, 247–248
Responsa Project 157
Resnais, Alain 197–198, 199
Reuss, Dr. 246–247
Riefenstahl, Leni 82
Riess, Volker 246
Ringel, Sharon 154
Ringelblum, Emanuel 145
Ringelheim, Joan 9
Robinson, Jacob 1, 183
Roosevelt, Franklin D. 90
Roques, Guiseppe Pardo 1
Rosen, Alan 208
Rosenbach, Abraham 156
Rosenberg, Pnina 111, 225, 234
Rosenblat, Herman 51, 52
Rosenstone, Robert A. 179–180
Roskies, David 34, 39
Rothermere, Lord 137
Royal Air Force 29
Royal Holloway, University of London 105
Rupprecht, Philipp 84
Russell, William Howard 133
Russian Revolution 78

Sarah's Key (book) 208, 209, 215–216
Scharf, Andrew 131
Schaumann, Caroline 50
Schindler, Oskar 188, 211, 212
Schindler's Ark (book) 209, 211–212
Schindler's List (film) 161, 188–190
Schlereth, Thomas J. 167–168
Schlink, Bernhard 213–215
Scholl, Hans and Sophie 121
Schulman, Faigel (Faye) 66
Schwarberg, Günther 60
Schwartz, Leo W. 147
Schwartz-Bart, André 202
Scott, Walter 34
Seforim, Mendele Mocher 144
Semprún, Jorge 47
sensory memory 17

Sephardic Jews 142
Sereny, Gitta 51
Setch, Eve 4
The Seventh Cross (film) 190–191
sexual abuse 50
Shaleck, Malva 223
Sharples, Caroline 109
Sheehan, Vincent 134
She'erit Hapletah 146, 151
Shindler, Colin 131
Shirer, William L. 133–134
Shoah (film) 200–202, 204
short term memory 17
Shwesig, Karl 222, 234
Sir Nicholas Winton Statue 111–113
Sirlin, Rhonda 213
Smith, Howard K. 134
Smith, Mark M. 189
Sobibor 169, 187
Solahütte 62–63
Solberg, Mary M. 125
Sonderkommando 66, 187, 201, 223, 246
Sontag, Susan 197, 203
Sophie's Choice (book) 208, 209, 212–213, 215
The Sorrow and the Pity (film) 199–200, 204
Speer, Albert 49
Spiegelman, Art 52
Spielberg, Steven 18, 161, 189
sport 185
"stab-in-the-back" legend 78
Stalin, Joseph 90
Stauffenberg, Klaus von 188
Stephieň-Bator, Zofia 225
Sternfeld, Joshua 154
Stevens, George 195
Streicher, Julius 83–84, 86, 96
Stroop, Jürgen 58, 61, 69
Stroop Report 61–62, 63, 65, 67–68, 70
Styron, William 212–213
"survivor scarcity" 18
Survivors of the Shoah Visual History Foundation 18
Swain, Donald C. 2, 15
Sydney Morning Herald 137, 138
Szajna, Josef 236
Szmajner, Stanislaw (Shlomo) 187
Szpilman, Wladyslaw 47
Szylgold-Szpiro, Hasia 62
Szylis, Hirsh 223

Tait, Rachel 4
Targosz, Franciszek 235
Taylor, Telford 95, 96
telegraph 130
Tewes, Ernst 246, 247

Theresienstadt (Terezín) 158, 203, 223, 230, 231
Thirty Years' War 9
Thompson, Dorothy 133, 134
Thylstrup, Nanna Bonde 162
The Times (London) 130, 131, 133
Tobias, Paula 250
Toubiana, Serge 202
Treblinka 51
trial documents 90–102
Trinity College, Cambridge 4
Triumph of the Will (film) 82
Trunk, Isaiah 38
Tserkov, Byelaya 246

UK Holocaust Map 113
United Nations War Crimes Commission 95
United States Holocaust Memorial Museum 14, 18, 41, 51, 53, 110, 158, 159, 161, 169–173
United States Library of Congress (LOC) 66–70
United States Office of Scientific Research and Development (OSRD) 156
Universal News Service 133
University College London 107
University of Huddersfield 106
University of Southern California 18
University of Toronto 45
USC Shoah Foundation 18, 146, 161
US National Archives 68, 69

Valensi, Lucette 201
Van Dam, Else 107
Vatican Archives 117, 123–124
Vatican II 117, 123, 124–125
Vel' d'Hiv Roundup 215
Versailles, Treaty of 78
Vice, Sue 208
Vichy France 65, 199, 215–216
Vilna Ghetto 35, 232
Vishniac, Roman 65
Völkischer Beobachter 83
Volksempfänger; see "People's Receiver"

Waffen-SS 246, 247
Walter, Bernhard 63
Waltzer, Kenneth 52
war correspondents 133
Warsaw Criminal District Court 62
Warsaw Ghetto 28, 52, 58, 60, 61, 65, 81, 145, 230
Warsaw Ghetto Uprising 68, 69, 145
Weiss, Susan 236
Weissova, Helga 231
West Australian (Perth)

270 *Index*

Westerbork transit camp 35, 108
Wiernik, Yankel 150
Wiesel, Elie 48–49, 53, 150, 208–209, 209–210, 217
Wilczek, Gerhard 246
Wilkomirski, Benjamin 51–52
Williams, Amy 110
Winfrey, Oprah 52, 53
Winton, Sir Nicholas 111–112
Wöhler, Otto 69
World Wide Web 157
Wright, Lord 95
Wyman, David S. 131

Yad Vashem 10, 18, 29, 41, 60, 67, 68, 110, 146, 155, 157, 158, 227
Yad Vashem Studies 11

Yerusha database 161
Yiddish Book Center 151
Yiddish press 143–144
Yiddish Sources 142–153
YIVO Institute for Jewish Research 18, 41, 146, 151
Yizkor 30
Yizkor books 159
Yolen, Jane 216–217
Young, James E. 37, 39, 103–104

Zekelman Holocaust Center 161
Zelkowicz, Josef 40
Zinnemann, Fred 190
Zydowski Instytut Historyczny 18, 41

Printed in the United States
by Baker & Taylor Publisher Services